The Kiss of
LAMOURETTE

W · W · NORTON & COMPANY · NEW YORK · LONDON

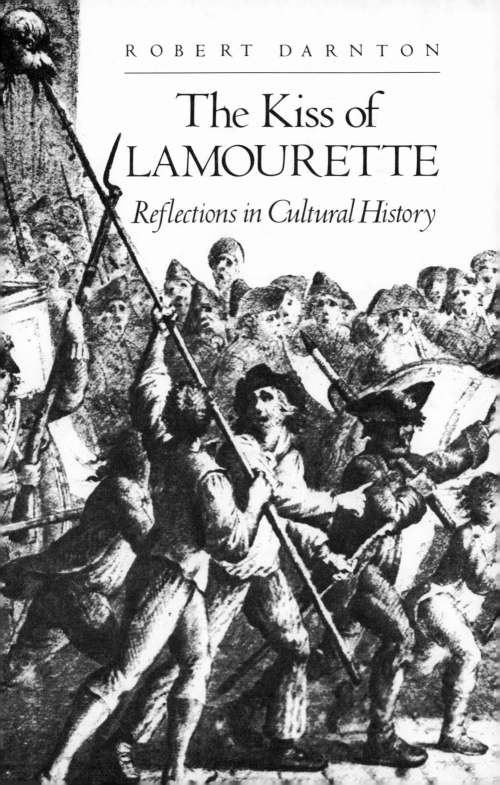

ROBERT DARNTON

The Kiss of
LAMOURETTE

Reflections in Cultural History

TITLE PAGE ILLUSTRATION: The crowd chants "Kiss papa! Kiss papa!" as it confronts the intendant of Paris, Bertier de Sauvigny, with the head of his father-in-law, Foullon, July 23, 1789.

ILLUSTRATION CREDITS: Title page, Bulloz; page xxii Bettmann Archive; page 34 Musée Carnavalet, photo Bulloz; pages 104 and 188 Bibliothèque Nationale; page 294 Musée Carnavalet, photo Bulloz.

FIRST EDITION

The text of this book is composed in Bembo, with display type set in Centaur. Composition and manufacturing by the Maple-Vail Book Manufacturing Group. Book design by Marjorie J. Flock.

Library of Congress Cataloging in Publication Data

Darnton, Robert.
    The kiss of Lamourette: reflections in cultural history / Robert
        Darnton.—1st ed.
        p.   cm.
    Includes index.
    1. France—History—Revolution, 1789–1799—Influence.
    2. Civilization, Modern—20th century.   3. Books and reading.
    I. Title.
    DC158.8.D37   1990
    944.04—dc20   89-9431
                                                     CIP

ISBN 0-393-02753-8

W. W. Norton & Company, Inc., 500 Fifth Avenue, New York, N. Y. 10110
W. W. Norton & Company Ltd., 37 Great Russell Street, London WC1B 3NU

1 2 3 4 5 6 7 8 9 0

For Kate

Contents

FIVE
Good Neighbors

Introduction

EVERYONE HAS FANTASIES. Mine are historical daydreams, a way of playing Rip van Winkle in reverse. I slide deep into my armchair, a heavy tome growing heavier in my hands, and let myself nod off. Then I wake up in Paris, at the height of the Revolution, aroused by a kiss. At times it is the kiss of death, at times the kiss of love, a little love, love lost amid the passions of the past: *le baiser de Lamourette*.

The first kind of kiss comes out of a nightmare. Foullon de Doué, an official in the War Ministry, has been seized by the crowd. The Bastille has just fallen, and rumors fly through the streets about conspiracies to starve the common people and to suppress their insurrection. Foullon is said to be involved in one of the plots. The rioters fell him, drag him to a lantern by the Hôtel de Ville, and string him up on the improvised gallows. He dangles for a moment in the air, until the rope breaks. Up he goes again. Again it breaks. On the third attempt, at last, the life is choked out of him. A heavy hand grapples with the body, slices off its head, pries apart the jaws, and stuffs the mouth with straw. "Let them eat hay," Foullon is supposed to have said, echoing the famous "Let them eat cake" attributed to the queen. Did he really say it? No matter. His head proclaims the message now, paraded through the streets at the end of a pike.

Soon afterward another crowd, as furious as the first, captures Foullon's son-in-law, Bertier de Sauvigny, the intendant of Paris, while he is riding in an open carriage on the outskirts of the city. They haul him toward the Place de Grève, the great open space before the Hôtel de Ville marked off in everyone's imagination as a place of struggle and of death; for it is there that workers gather to be hired and to strike *("faire la grève"),* and it is there that Sanson, the public hangman, admired and feared as a *maître des hautes oeuvres,* exercises his art, wrenching limbs from sockets, smashing bones, and snapping necks on the official gallows of the Old Regime, a theater of violence that will be abolished when the Revolution ordains death by the guillotine. But the machine promoted by Dr. Guillotin, who is now sitting in the National Assembly contemplating constitutions and other such projects, will not begin to function until August 21, 1792. On July 23, 1789, justice is in the hands of the crowd.

The rioters drag Bertier in his carriage toward execution and dismemberment at the place of death. As they roar through the streets, they meet the first group of rioters, who are parading with the head of Foullon. The two crowds merge in a single wave of violence, carrying Bertier on its crest. He stares in horror through the pikes and sees the head of his father-in-law, coming closer and closer, until it is thrust into his face: "Kiss papa! Kiss papa!" chants the crowd.

Antoine Adrien Lamourette occupies history for only a moment, the time it took for another kind of kiss. The kiss of Lamourette was as improbable as his name, one of those wonderful, rococo names like Papillon de La Ferté and Fabre d'Eglantine that make the eighteenth century seem like a dream. More improbably still, Lamourette was a bishop, a "constitutional" bishop, for he had sworn the oath of loyalty to the constitution of 1791 and sat in the Legislative Assembly in 1792 as a deputy from Rhône-et-Loire. In the first stages of the Revolution he had worked as a ghost writer for Mirabeau, turning out speeches in favor of a new organization for the Church (its land was to be confiscated, its priests elected) and a new apprenticeship for the heir to the throne (he would be schooled in civics in a national *lycée*.) Lamourette was full of ideas, many of them picked up from the enlightened reading and elevated conversation of the Lazarite order, which he had joined before the Revolution. But he was more a man of generous impulses than of deep thought, more a rhetorician than a politician in the Legislative Assembly.

When this *abbé*-turned-*philosophe*-turned-revolutionary-turned-bishop flutters, cupidlike, into my dreams, the politics of the Assembly have developed into a life-and-death struggle over the destiny of France. It is July 7, 1792, a terrible moment. The front is collapsing before the invading armies. Lafayette has already abandoned his troops in an attempt to overthrow the Assembly, and soon he will defect to the enemy. The king and queen are secretly plotting to promote an Austrian victory; and if the Austrians take Paris, they will wreak a terrible vengeance on everyone who supports the Revolution—the Brunswick Manifesto will soon make that clear. Yet the revolutionaries who led France into war, the party of the Brissotins, are doing nothing to win it. Instead of organizing the military campaign, they have become embroiled in a quarrel with their enemies in the Jacobin Club. Even worse, they are about to enter into secret negotiations with the king in the hopes of taking over some ministries. In fact, France has no government. The last of the moderate, Feuillant ministers will resign on July 10, leaving no one in charge of affairs. The price of bread is rising. The Parisian sections are arming. The batallions of National Guards pouring into Paris from the provinces are preparing to storm the Tuileries Palace in order to overthrow the monarchy. Everything is ready to explode in the great insurrection of August 10 and the September Massacres.

On July 7 the deputies in the Assembly seem bent on massacring one another. Their quarrels have become so bitter that no consensus can hold them together and no opposition can exist without the taint of treason. The experiment with constitutional monarchy seems doomed, condemned to self-destruction, and parliamentary debating only makes things worse. At this moment, in the thick of the debate, Lamourette rises. He has a solution to propose: love. Fraternal love. Love can heal anything, overcome any division. His name alone proclaims the message, and the deputies respond. They hug, they kiss, they swear fraternity. They even invite in the king, who swears it back at them. The Revolution is saved! *Vive la nation! Vive le roi!*

What was the kiss of Lamourette? A reenactment of the medieval kiss of love, meant as a ritual to put an end to civil war? Or an outburst of preromantic sentiment derived from the plays of Sedaine and the paintings of Greuze? Or a momentary victory of eros over thanatos, a brief battle won in some hidden sector of the soul?

I do not know. Exposure to the past unsettles the sense of the knowable. One is always running up against mysteries—not simply ignorance (a familiar phenomenon) but the unfathomable strangeness of life among the dead. Historians return from that world like missionaries who once set out to conquer foreign cultures and then come back converted, won over to the otherness of others. When we resume our daily rounds we sometimes harangue the public with our tales. But few stop to listen. Like the ancient mariner, we have talked with the dead, but we find it hard to make ourselves heard among the living. To the quick we are a bore.

I decided to attempt this book after being struck by a swarm of such dizzy thoughts at Forty-third and Broadway. I had just met with the editor of *The New York Times Magazine*. The bicentenary of the French Revolution was approaching, and he wanted me to do a piece on it—something short and snappy about the inability of the French to agree on what to celebrate about the events that had torn them apart two hundred years earlier. It was an opportunity to explore the undercurrents of events, the way history refuses to confine itself to the past and flows into the present, pushing and moving things that seem to be fixed in a narrow frame of time.

But I didn't want to rewrite history as present politics. On the contrary, having lectured on the French Revolution to bewildered undergraduates for twenty years, I wanted to try to make sense of it to the general educated reader. Americans know next to nothing about what went on in Europe two centuries ago, yet the French Revolution is one of those rare events that redefined the human condition and redirected the course of history. For my part, I am one of the few Americans who specialize in the study of the French Revolution. So I thought I ought to try to explain what was so revolutionary about it, writing as a fellow citizen for the general citizenry (see Chapter 1).

After some arm twisting, the editor agreed. I could write a history essay. Real history, not current events. Nothing esoteric, of course: I should know what to expect of the readers of *The New York Times*. He would give me six thousand words, but not very big words, please.

I thought I understood. Twenty-five years earlier I had covered police headquarters for *The Times,* and I knew that I was supposed to aim every story at an imaginary twelve-year-old girl (see Chapter 5). That was when the dizziness struck. I crossed Times Square, my head swimming with memories of all the stories I had written about riots and murders, and I laughed. The French Revolution as an "assignment"? Could I "cover" it? Could I get the "story"?

The answer arrived in the mail a few weeks later. No. My six thousand words hadn't done the job. Too complicated, too demanding of the reader. The joke was on me. And as the echo of the laughter faded, my disappointment gave way to sadness. Is there nothing we can do, we professionals of history, to make contact with the general reader? Have we walled ourselves up behind a barrier of monographs and cut ourselves off from a dialogue with ordinary citizens who are curious about the past?

The fault is certainly ours, at least in part. Monographism has taken over academic history and confined it to a corner of our culture, where professors write books for other professors and review them in journals restricted to members of the profession (see Chapter 6). We write in a way that will legitimize ourselves in the eyes of the professionals and that will make our work inaccessible to anyone else. The disease must have infected me, for there I was, a former police reporter, incapable of putting the Revolution into words that would pass with an editor of *The New York Times*.

But what passwords are required to gain access to the general public? I thought of my favorite slogan scribbled among the graffiti on the walls of the reporters' "shack" opposite police headquarters in Manhattan in 1964: "All the news that fits we print." Reducing events to stories and getting stories into print is a matter of cultural fit—of narrative conventions and newsroom traditions that work as a way of imposing form on the booming, buzzing confusion of the day's events. When I gave up news for history, I found myself fascinated by the general process of cultural fitting and misfitting. I studied publishing and journalism—or, as the current passwords of the profession would have it, "communication" and "the media."

Evidently, however, I had failed to learn my own lesson. I should have realized that my history lecture was not fit to print in *The New York Times*. Or should I share some of the blame with the editor—not personally, of course (he probably is as highminded and highbrow in his tastes as the rest of us), but as part of a communication system, what we call "the news"? Do editors, film directors, television producers, and book publishers collaborate unwittingly in a general effort to make culture palatable by making it into pulp? Are the culture industries themselves organized in such a way as to make their products easy to consume?

This book is an attempt to explore those questions. It is not meant as an indictment of anyone, because the problem is systemic, not a matter of conspiracy among the masters of the media. I admit that I sometimes feel tempted to think of them as a new breed of unacknowledged legislators of the world, the wizards who pull the strings in an era when communication itself—the selling of messages, the packaging of presidents—appears as the main ingredient of public life. But then I remind myself that communication systems have a history, although historians have rarely studied it. The power of the media to shape events by covering them was a crucial factor in the French Revolution, when journalism first emerged as a force in the affairs of state. The revolutionaries knew what they were doing when they carried printing presses in their civic processions and when they set aside one day in the revolutionary calendar for the celebration of public opinion.

So, in short, this is a book about history, the media, and the history of the media. It has four purposes: first, to show how the past operates as an undercurrent in the present (Part I); second, to analyze the operation of the media by specific case studies (Part II); third, to outline a particular discipline, the history of the book, which provides a historical dimension to media studies (Part III); and fourth, to move outward from those considerations to a broad discussion of history itself and of history's neighbors within the human sciences (Parts IV and V).

Put so schematically, the plan of the book may produce a specious air of coherence. In fact, the individual essays were written for different purposes on different occasions, and I have not tried to reshape them so that they would fit together smoothly as a whole. The first half dozen were not written for scholarly journals or for scholars. They are aimed at the General Educated Reader—not the twelve-year-old girl but someone who exists somewhere out there, on the far side of the editors, producers, and other cultural mediators who separate the author from the audience. These essays concern the process of mediation itself, as I have encountered it, willy-nilly, in my own stumbling through the culture industries. More often than not, I have stubbed my toe. But the experience has been enlightening and may at least provide some amusement for anyone who wants to know what it is like to extract news from a homicide squad or to confront a TV script in the raw or to wade through the agenda of an editorial board.

The last nine essays are more scholarly; but I hope that they, too, will interest the General Educated Reader, because I have a high opinion of him or her, even if I cannot see his/her face any better than I can see the far side of the moon. This reader deserves a richer diet than the fast food dispensed by the media. So I have dared to offer some unmitigated, unmediated scholarship.

Call it history. History without footnotes, or without very many of them, because only a few of these essays provide reports on findings in the archives. Most report on the state of play in various sectors of social, cultural, and intellectual history. So they are review articles, or historiography, or history as reportage—and why not? Why shouldn't history be as interesting as homicide? I hope to inform the reader of what is going on in my beat and of what is at stake in the debates about subjects that might seem arcane but that really represent an attempt to make contact with most of humanity—that is, the great majority of the human race who have vanished into the past as opposed to the tiny number of their descendants walking the earth today. The most exciting and innovative varieties of history are those that try to dig beneath events in order to uncover the human condition as it was experienced by our predecessors. These varieties go under many names: the history of mentalities, the social history of ideas, ethnographic history, or just cultural history (my own preference). But whatever the label, the ambition is the same: to understand the meaning of life, not by a vain attempt to provide ultimate answers to the great philosophical conundrums but by providing access to answers that others have made, in the daily rounds of their existence as well as in the formal organization of their ideas, centuries ago.

The century that keeps reappearing in these pages is the eighteenth. Perhaps it doesn't deserve more space than the seventeenth or nineteenth, and we should not slice time into arbitrary hundred-year units in the first place. But the eighteenth century and the twentieth happen to be the ones in which I live, the centuries that I play off against one another in order to study the interpenetration of the present and the past.

And finally, the eighteenth century is a source of fantasy. It provides an inexhaustible supply of material for dreams: love, laughter, faith, horror, sex, death, hope, fear—all of it dressed in unfamiliar colors and textures, from Pompadour pink to the coarse canvas of the sans-culottes' culottes. Who can resist the kiss of Lamourette? It invites us to attend the play of passion across the whole range of the human comedy in a world that is no more.

But how can fantasy be history? This book provides no brief for romantic *Einfühlung,* nor does it philosophize over the metaphysics of narratology and fact. Instead, it registers two shocks to the system—my own unsystematic system of bouncing from subject to subject, which may be symptomatic of procedures in history as a whole.

The first shock occurred in Newark, New Jersey, when I learned that news is not what happened in the immediate past but rather someone's story about what happened. That lesson seemed convincing to me, but every day I meet professional historians, grown men and women in full possession of their wits, who treat newspapers as repositories of hard facts instead of as collections of stories.

My own experience with news pointed me down the slippery slope of narratology. With help from literary theorists, I began seeing stories everywhere, from the Nicene Creed to the gestures of traffic cops. But try behaving as if all behavior is a text and all texts can deconstruct themselves: soon you will be trapped in a maze of mirrors, lost in a semiotic wonderland, overwhelmed with epistemological jitters.

I was approaching such a state in May 1981, when I wandered into Poland and received a second shock (see Chapter 2). Try telling a dockworker from Solidarity that dates don't matter and that events are trivial. He will reply that a world of difference separates May 1, the official Labor Day, from May 3, the popular celebration of constitutional liberty and the attempt to save Poland from partition in 1791. A plaque commemorating a dead soldier in a Warsaw church contains nothing more in the way of commentary than a place and a date: "Katyn, 1940." According to official Polish history,* the Pol-

---

*In February 1989, while opening a new round of negotiations with Solidarity, the government reversed its position and accused the Soviets of perpetrating the massacre.

ish officer corps—the flower of an entire generation—was destroyed in a gigantic massacre by the Germans when the German army reached the forest of Katyn during its invasion of Soviet territory in 1941. According to the Germans, the massacre happened at least a year earlier and they found nothing but a mass grave at Katyn. If the event took place in 1940, it was the work of the Soviets—and it did. It did. It did.

To Poles, the difference between 1940 and 1941 is a matter of life and death. Before their understanding of the past, the historian can only fall to his knees, like Willy Brandt before the memorial in Warsaw to the victims of the holocaust. What is our science in the face of great events like wars and revolutions? What is our sophistication in the light of the lives that never made the news, that never had obituaries?

To visit the dead, the historian needs something more than methodology, something like a leap of faith or a suspension of disbelief. No matter how skeptical we may be about the life to come, we cannot but feel humbled before all the lives that have gone. Not that I am arguing for mysticism, or ancestor worship. Nor am I disputing the validity of semiotics and narratology. I am convinced that we must think hard about what we do when we try to make sense of life and death in the past. But how can we do justice to the dead? If ever I repose in the satisfaction of having got it right, I hope to be shocked back to my senses by something unexpected, like the kiss of Lamourette.

Princeton, New Jersey
May 1989

DÉCLARATION
DES DROITS
DE L'HOMME
ET DU
CITOYEN

L'EGALITE

A ORLEANS. CHEZ
LE TOURMY

PART ONE

Currents in Events

L'EGALITÉ *holds the* Declaration of the Rights of Man *in this enduring symbol of the revolutionary period.*

The Kiss of Lamourette

W HAT WAS SO REVOLUTIONARY about the French Revolution? The question might seem impertinent at a
time like this, when all the world is congratulating
France on the two hundredth anniversary of the storming of
the Bastille, the destruction of feudalism, and the Declaration
of the Rights of Man and of the Citizen. But the bicentennial
fuss has little to do with what actually happened two centuries
ago.

Historians have long pointed out that the Bastille was almost empty on July 14, 1789. Many of them argue that feudalism had already ceased to exist by the time it was abolished,
and few would deny that the rights of man were swallowed
up in the Terror only five years after they were first proclaimed. Does a sober view of the Revolution reveal nothing
but misplaced violence and hollow proclamations—nothing
more than a "myth," to use a term favored by the late Alfred
Cobban, a skeptical English historian who had no use for
guillotines and slogans?

One might reply that myths can move mountains. They
can acquire a rocklike reality as solid as the Eiffel Tower,
which the French built to celebrate the one hundredth anniversary of the Revolution in 1889. France will spend millions
in 1989, erecting buildings, creating centers, producing concrete contemporary expressions of the force that burst loose
on the world two hundred years ago. But what was it?

Although the spirit of '89 is no easier to fix in words than

in mortar and brick, it could be characterized as energy—a
will to build a new world from the ruins of the regime that fell
apart in the summer of 1789. That energy permeated everything during the French Revolution. It transformed life, not
only for the activists trying to channel it in directions of their
own choosing but for ordinary persons going about their daily
business.

The idea of a fundamental change in the tenor of everyday
life may seem easy enough to accept in the abstract, but few
of us can really assimilate it. We take the world as it comes and
cannot imagine it organized differently, unless we have experienced moments when things fall apart—a death perhaps, or
a divorce, or the sudden obliteration of something that seemed
immutable, like the roof over our heads or the ground under
our feet.

Such shocks often dislodge individual lives, but they rarely
traumatize societies. In 1789 the French had to confront the
collapse of a whole social order—the world that they defined
retrospectively as the Ancien Régime—and to find some new
order in the chaos surrounding them. They experienced reality as something that could be destroyed and reconstructed,
and they faced seemingly limitless possibilities, both for good
and for evil, for raising a utopia and for falling back into
tyranny.

To be sure, a few seismic upheavals had convulsed French
society in earlier ages—the bubonic plague in the fourteenth
century, for example, and the religious wars in the sixteenth
century. But no one was ready for a revolution in 1789. The
idea itself did not exist. If you look up "revolution" in standard
dictionaries from the eighteenth century, you find definitions
that derive from the verb to revolve, such as "the return of a
planet or a star to the same point from which it parted."

The French did not have much of a political vocabulary

before 1789, because politics took place at Versailles, in the remote world of the king's court. Once ordinary people began to participate in politics—in the elections to the Estates General, which were based on something approximating universal male suffrage, and in the insurrections of the streets—they needed to find words for what they had seen and done. They developed fundamental new categories, such as "left" and "right," which derive from the seating plan of the National Assembly, and "revolution" itself. The experience came first, the concept afterward. But what was that experience?

Only a small minority of activists joined the Jacobin clubs, but everyone was touched by the Revolution because the Revolution reached into everything. For example, it recreated time and space. According to the revolutionary calendar adopted in 1793 and used until 1805, time began when the old monarchy ended, on September 22, 1792—the first of Vendémiaire, Year I.

By formal vote of the Convention, the revolutionaries divided time into units that they took to be rational and natural. There were ten days to a week, three weeks to a month, and twelve months to a year. The five days left over at the end became patriotic holidays, *jours sans-culottides,* given over to civic qualities: Virtue, Genius, Labor, Opinion, and Rewards.

Ordinary days received new names, which suggested mathematical regularity: *primidi, duodi, tridi,* and so on up to *décadi.* Each day was dedicated to some aspect of rural life so that agronomy would displace the saints' days of the Christian calendar. Thus November 22, formerly devoted to Saint Cecilia, became the day of the turnip; November 25, formerly Saint Catherine's day, became the day of the pig; and November 30, once the day of Saint Andrew, became the day of the pick. The names of the new months also made time seem to conform to the natural rhythm of the seasons. January 1, 1989,

for example, would be the twelfth of Nivôse, Year 197, Ni-
vôse being the month of snow, located after the months of fog
(Brumaire) and cold (Frimaire) and before the months of rain
(Pluviôse) and wind (Ventôse).

The adoption of the metric system represented a similar
attempt to impose a rational and natural organization on space.
According to a decree of 1795, the meter was to be "the unit
of length equal to one ten-millionth part of the arc of the
terrestrial meridian between the North Pole and the Equator."
Of course, ordinary citizens could not make much of such a
definition. They were slow to adopt the meter and the gram,
the corresponding new unit of weight, and few of them favored the new week, which gave them one day of rest in ten
instead of one in seven. But even where old habits remained,
the revolutionaries stamped their ideas on contemporary consciousness by changing everything's name.

Fourteen hundred streets in Paris received new names, because the old ones contained some reference to a king, a queen,
or a saint. The Place Louis XV, where the most spectacular
guillotining took place, became the Place de la Révolution;
and later, in an attempt to bury the hatchet, it acquired its
present name, Place de la Concorde. The Church of Saint-
Laurent became the Temple of Marriage and Fidelity; Notre
Dame became the Temple of Reason; Montmartre became
Mont Marat. Thirty towns took Marat's name—thirty of six
thousand that tried to expunge their past by name changes.
Montmorency became Emile, Saint-Malo became Victoire
Montagnarde, and Coulanges became Cou Sans-Culottes (*anges*
or angels being a sign of superstition).

The revolutionaries even renamed themselves. It wouldn't
do, of course, to be called Louis in 1793 and 1794. The Louis
called themselves Brutus or Spartacus. Last names like Le Roy
or Lévêque, very common in France, became La Loi or Lib-

erté. Children got all kinds of names foisted on them—some from nature (Pissenlit or Dandelion did nicely for girls, Rhubarb for boys) and some from current events (Fructidor, Constitution, The Tenth of August, Marat-Couthon-Pique). The foreign minister Pierre-Henri Lebrun named his daughter Civilisation-Jémappes-République.

Meanwhile, the queen bee became a "laying bee" *(abeille pondeuse);* chess pieces were renamed, because a good revolutionary would not play with kings, queens, knights, and bishops; and the kings, queens, and jacks of playing cards became liberties, equalities, and fraternities. The revolutionaries set out to change everything: crockery, furniture, law codes, religion, the map of France itself, which was divided into departments—that is, symmetrical units of equal size with names taken from rivers and mountains—in place of the irregular old provinces.

Before 1789, France was a crazy-quilt of overlapping and incompatible units, some fiscal, some judicial, some administrative, some economic, and some religious. After 1789, those segments were melted down into a single substance: the French nation. With its patriotic festivals, its tricolor flag, its hymns, its martyrs, its army, and its wars, the Revolution accomplished what had been impossible for Louis XIV and his successors: it united the disparate elements of the kingdom into a nation and conquered the rest of Europe. In doing so, the Revolution unleashed a new force, nationalism, which would mobilize millions and topple governments for the next two hundred years.

Of course, the nation-state did not sweep everything before it. It failed to impose the French language on the majority of the French people, who continued to speak all sorts of mutually incomprehensible dialects, despite a vigorous propaganda drive by the revolutionary Committee on Public Instruction. But in wiping out the intermediary bodies that separated the citizen from the state, the Revolution transformed the basic character of public life.

It went further: it extended the public into the private sphere, inserting itself into the most intimate relationships. Intimacy in French is conveyed by the pronoun *tu* as distinct from the *vous* employed in formal address. Although the French sometimes use *tu* quite casually today, under the Old Regime they reserved it for asymmetrical or intensely personal relations. Parents said *tu* to children, who replied with *vous*. The *tu* was used by superiors addressing inferiors, by humans commanding animals, and by lovers—after the first kiss, or exclusively between the sheets. When French mountain climbers reach a certain altitude, they still switch from the *vous* to the *tu,* as if all men become equal in the face of the enormousness of nature.

The French Revolution wanted to make everybody *tu.* Here is a resolution passed on 24 Brumaire, Year II (November 14, 1793), by the department of the Tarn, a poor, mountainous area in southern France:

Considering that the eternal principles of equality forbid that a citizen say "vous" to another citizen, who replies by calling him "toi" . . . decrees that the word "vous," when it is a question of the singular [rather than the plural, which takes *vous*], is from this moment banished from the language of the free French and will on all occasions be replaced by the word "tu" or "toi."

A delegation of sans-culottes petitioned the National Convention in 1794 to abolish the *vous,* ". . . as a result of which there will be less pride, less discrimination, less social reserve, more open familiarity, a stronger leaning toward fraternity, and therefore more equality." That may sound laughable today, but it was deadly serious to the revolutionaries: they wanted to build a new society based on new principles of social relations.

So they redesigned everything that smacked of the inequality built into the conventions of the Old Regime. They ended letters with a vigorous "farewell and fraternity" *("salut et fraternité")* in place of the deferential "your most obedient and humble servant." They substituted Citizen and Citizeness for Monsieur and Madame. And they changed their dress.

Dress often serves as a thermometer for measuring the political temperature. To designate a militant from the radical sections of Paris, the revolutionaries adopted a term from clothing: *sans-culotte,* one who wears trousers rather than breeches. In fact, workers did not generally take up trousers, which were mostly favored by seamen, until the nineteenth century. Robespierre himself always dressed in the uniform of the Old Regime: culottes, waistcoat, and a powdered wig. But the model revolutionary, who appears on broadsides, posters, and crockery from 1793 to the present, wore trousers, an open shirt, a short jacket (the carmagnole), boots, and a liberty cap (Phrygian bonnet) over a "natural" (that is, uncombed) crop of hair, which dropped down to his shoulders.

Women's dress on the eve of the Revolution had featured low necklines, basket-skirts, and exotic hair styles, at least among the aristocracy. Hair dressed in the "hedgehog" style *("en hérisson")* rose two or more feet above the head and was decorated with elaborate props—as a fruit bowl or a flotilla or a zoo. One court coiffure was arranged as a pastoral scene with a pond, a duck hunter, a windmill (which turned), and a miller riding off to market on a mule while a monk seduced his wife.

After 1789, fashion came from below. Hair was flattened, skirts were deflated, necklines raised, and heels lowered. Still later, after the end of the Terror, when the Thermidorian Reaction extinguished the Republic of Virtue, fast-moving society women like Mme. Tallien exposed their breasts, danced about in diaphanous gowns, and revived the wig. A true *merveilleuse,* or fashionable lady, would have a wig for every day of the *décade;* Mme. Tallien had thirty.

At the height of the Revolution, however, from mid-1792 to mid-1794, virtue was not merely a fashion but the central ingredient of a new political culture. It had a puritanical side, but it should not be confused with the Sunday school variety preached in nineteenth-century America. To the revolutionaries, virtue was virile. It meant a willingness to fight for the fatherland and for the revolutionary trinity of liberty, equality, and fraternity.

At the same time, the cult of virtue produced a revalorization of family life. Taking their text from Rousseau, the revolutionaries sermonized on the sanctity of motherhood and the importance of breastfeeding. They treated reproduction as a civic duty and excoriated bachelors as unpatriotic. "Citizenesses! Give the Fatherland Children!" proclaimed a banner in a patriotic parade. "Now is the time to make a baby," admonished a slogan painted on revolutionary pottery.

Saint-Just, the most extreme ideologist on the Committee of Public Safety, wrote in his notebook: "The child, the citizen, belong to the fatherland. Common instruction is necessary. Children belong to their mother until the age of five, if she has [breast-]fed them, and to the Republic afterwards . . . until death."

It would be anachronistic to read Hitlerism into such statements. With the collapse of the authority of the Church, the revolutionaries sought a new moral basis for family life. They turned to the state and passed laws that would have been unthinkable under the Old Regime. They made divorce possible; they accorded full legal status to illegitimate children; they abolished primogeniture. If, as the Declaration of the Rights

of Man and of the Citizen proclaimed, all men are created free
and equal in rights, shouldn't all men begin with an equal start
in life? The Revolution tried to limit "paternal despotism" by
giving all children an equal share in inheritances. It abolished
slavery and gave full civic rights to Protestants and Jews.

To be sure, one can spot loopholes and contradictions in
the revolutionary legislation. Despite some heady phrasing in
the so-called Ventôse Decrees about the appropriation of
counterrevolutionaries' property, the legislators never envisaged anything like socialism. And Napoleon reversed the most
democratic provisions of the laws on family life. Nevertheless, the main direction of revolutionary legislation is clear: it
substituted the state for the Church as the ultimate authority
in the conduct of private life, and it grounded the legitimacy
of the state in the sovereignty of the people.

Popular sovereignty, civil liberty, equality before the law—
the words fall so easily off the tongue today that we cannot
begin to imagine their explosiveness in 1789. We cannot think
ourselves back into a mental world like that of the Old Regime, where most people assumed that men were unequal,
that inequality was a good thing, and that it conformed to the
hierarchical order built into nature by God himself. To the
French of the Old Regime, liberty meant privilege—that is,
literally, "private law" or a special prerogative to do something denied to other persons. The king, as the source of all
law, dispensed privileges, and rightly so, for he had been
anointed as the agent of God on earth. His power was spiritual
as well as secular, so by his royal touch he could cure scrofula,
the king's disease.

Throughout the eighteenth century, the philosophers of
the Enlightenment challenged those assumptions, and pam-
phleteers in Grub Street succeeded in tarnishing the sacred

aura of the crown. But it took violence to smash the mental frame of the Old Regime, and violence itself, the iconoclastic, world-destroying, revolutionary sort of violence, is also hard for us to conceive.

True, we treat traffic accidents and muggings as everyday occurrences. But compared with our ancestors, we live in a world where violence has been drained out of our daily experience. In the eighteenth century, Parisians commonly passed by corpses that had been fished out of the Seine and hung by their feet along the riverbank. They knew a *"mine patibulaire"* was a face that looked like one of the dismembered heads exposed on a fork by the public executioner. They had witnessed dismemberments of criminals at public executions. And they could not walk through the center of the city without covering their shoes in blood.

Here is a description of the Paris butcheries, written by Louis-Sébastien Mercier a few years before the outbreak of the Revolution:

They are in the middle of the city. Blood courses through the streets; it coagulates under your feet, and your shoes are red with it. In passing, you are suddenly struck with an agonized cry. A young steer is thrown to the ground, its horns tied down; a heavy mallet breaks its skull; a huge knife strikes deep into its throat; its steaming blood flows away with its life in a thick current. . . . Then blood-stained arms plunge into its smoking entrails; its members are hacked apart and hung up for sale. Sometimes the steer, dazed but not downed by the first blow, breaks its ropes and flees furiously from the scene, mowing down everyone in its paths. . . . And the butchers who run after their escaped victim are as dangerous as it is. . . . These butchers have a fierce and bloody appearance: naked arms, swollen necks, their eyes red, their legs filthy, their aprons covered with blood, they carry their massive clubs around with them always spoiling for a fight. The blood they spread seems to inflame their faces and their temperaments. . . . In streets near the butcheries, a cadaverous odor hangs heavy in the air; and vile prostitutes—huge, fat, monstrous objects sitting in the streets—display their debauchery in public. These are the beauties that those men of blood find alluring.

A serious riot broke out in 1750 because a rumor spread through the working-class sections of Paris that the police were kidnapping children to provide a blood-bath for a prince of the royal blood. Such riots were known as "popular emotions"—eruptions of visceral passion touched off by some spark that burned within the collective imagination.

It would be nice if we could associate the Revolution exclusively with the Declaration of the Rights of Man and of the Citizen, but it was born in violence and it stamped its principles on a violent world. The conquerors of the Bastille did not merely destroy a symbol of royal despotism. One hundred and fifty of them were killed or injured in the assault on the prison; and when the survivors got hold of its governor, they cut off his head and paraded it through Paris on the end of a pike.

A week later, in a paroxysm of fury over high bread prices and rumors about plots to starve the poor, a crowd lynched an official in the war ministry named Foullon de Doué, severed his head, and paraded it on a pike with hay stuffed in its mouth as a sign of complicity in the plotting. A band of rioters then seized Foullon's son-in-law, the intendant of Paris, Bertier de Sauvigny, and marched him through the streets with the head in front of him, chanting, "Kiss papa, kiss papa." They murdered Bertier in front of the Hôtel de Ville, tore the heart out of his body, and threw it in the direction of the municipal government. Then they resumed their parade with his head beside Foullon's. "That is how traitors are punished," said an engraving of the scene.

Gracchus Babeuf, the future leftist conspirator, described the general delirium in a letter to his wife. Crowds applauded at the sight of the heads on the pikes, he wrote:

Oh! That joy made me sick. I felt satisfied and displeased at the same time. I said, so much the better and so much the worse. I understood that the common people were taking justice into their own hands. I approve that justice . . . but could it not be cruel? Punishments of all kinds, drawing and quartering, torture, the wheel, the rack, the whip, the stake, hangmen proliferating everywhere have done such damage to our morals! Our masters . . . will sow what they have reaped.

It also would be nice if we could stop the story of the Revolution at the end of 1789, where the current French government wants to draw the line in its celebrating. But the whole story extends through the rest of the century—and of the following century, according to some historians. Whatever its stopping point, it certainly continued through 1794; so we must come to terms with the Terror.

We can find plenty of explanations for the official Terror, the Terror directed by the Committee of Public Safety and the Revolutionary Tribunal. By twentieth-century standards, it was not very devastating, if you make a body count of its victims and if you believe in measuring such things statistically. It took about seventeen thousand lives. There were fewer than twenty-five executions in half the departments of France, none at all in six of them. Seventy-one percent of the executions took place in regions where civil war was raging; three quarters of the guillotined were rebels captured with arms in their hands; and 85 percent were commoners—a statistic that is hard to digest for those who interpret the Revolution as a class war directed by bourgeois against aristocrats. Under the Terror the word "aristocrat" could be applied to almost anyone deemed to be an enemy of the people.

But all such statistics stick in the throat. Any attempt to condemn a person by suppressing his individuality and by slotting him into abstract, ideological categories such as "aristocrat" or "bourgeois" is inherently inhuman. The Terror *was* terrible. It pointed the way toward totalitarianism. It was the trauma that scarred modern history at its birth.

Historians have succeeded in explaining much of it (not all, not the hideous last month of the "Great Terror" when the killing increased while the threat of invasion receded) as a response to the extraordinary circumstances of 1793 and 1794: the invading armies about to overwhelm Paris; the counter-revolutionaries, some imaginary, many real, plotting to overthrow the government from within; the price of bread soaring out of control and driving the Parisian populace wild with hunger and despair; the civil war in the Vendée; the municipal rebellions in Lyons, Marseilles, and Bordeaux; and the factionalism within the National Convention, which threatened to paralyze every attempt to master the situation.

It would be the height of presumption for an American historian sitting in the comfort of his study to condemn the French for violence and to congratulate his countrymen for the relative bloodlessness of their own revolution, which took place in totally different conditions. Yet what is he to make of the September Massacres of 1792, an orgy of killing that took the lives of more than one thousand persons, many of them prostitutes and common criminals trapped in prisons like the Abbaye?

We don't know exactly what happened, because the documents were destroyed in the bombardment of the Paris Commune in 1871. But the sober assessment of the surviving evidence by Pierre Caron suggests that the massacres took on the character of a ritualistic, apocalyptic mass murder. Crowds of sans-culottes, including men from the butcheries described by Mercier, stormed the prisons in order to extinguish what they believed to be a counterrevolutionary plot. They improvised a popular court in the prison of the Abbaye. One by one the prisoners were led out, accused, and summarily judged according to their demeanor. Fortitude was taken to be a sign of innocence, faltering as guilt. Stanislas Maillard, a conqueror of the Bastille, assumed the role of prosecutor; and the crowd, transported from the street to rows of benches, ratified his judgment with nods and acclamations. If declared innocent, the prisoner would be hugged, wept over, and carried triumphantly through the city. If guilty, he would be hacked to death in a gauntlet of pikes, clubs, and sabers. Then his body would be stripped and thrown on a heap of corpses or dismembered and paraded about on the end of a pike.

Throughout their bloody business, the people who committed the massacres talked about purging the earth of counterrevolution. They seemed to play parts in a secular version of the Last Judgment, as if the Revolution had released an undercurrent of popular millenarianism. But it is difficult to know what script was being performed in September 1792. We may never be able to fathom such violence or to get to the bottom of the other "popular emotions" that determined the course of the Revolution: the Great Fear of the peasants in the early summer of 1789; the uprisings of July 14 and October 5–6, 1789; and the revolutionary "days" of August 10, 1792, May 31, 1793, 9 Thermidor, Year II (July 27, 1794), 12 Germinal, Year III (April 1, 1795). In all of them the crowds cried for bread and blood, and the bloodshed passes the historian's understanding.

It is there, nonetheless. It will not go away, and it must be incorporated in any attempt to make sense of the Revolution. One could argue that violence was a necessary evil, because the Old Regime would not die peacefully and the new order could not survive without destroying the counterrevolution. Nearly all the violent "days" were defensive—desperate attempts to stave off counterrevolutionary coups, which threatened to annihilate the Revolution from June 1789 until November 1799, when Bonaparte seized power. After the religious schism of 1791 and the war of 1792, any opposition could be made to look like treason, and no consensus could be reached on the principles of politics.

In short, circumstances account for most of the violent swings from extreme to extreme during the revolutionary decade. Most, but not all—certainly not the Slaughter of the Innocents in September 1792. The violence itself remains a mystery, the kind of phenomenon that may force one back into metahistorical explanations: original sin, unleashed libido, or the cunning of a dialectic. For my part, I confess myself incapable of explaining the ultimate cause of revolutionary violence, but I think I can make out some of its consequences. It cleared the way for the redesigning and rebuilding that I mentioned above. It struck down institutions from the Old Regime so suddenly and with such force that it made anything seem possible. It released utopian energy.

The sense of boundless possibility—"possibilism" one could call it—was the bright side of popular emotion, and it was not restricted to millenarian outbursts in the streets. It could seize lawyers and men of letters sitting in the Legislative Assembly. On July 7, 1792, A.-A. Lamourette, a deputy from Rhône-et-Loire, told the Assembly's members that their troubles all arose from a single source: factionalism. They needed more fraternity. Whereupon the deputies, who had been at each other's throats a moment earlier, rose to their feet and started hugging and kissing each other as if their political divisions could be swept away in a wave of brotherly love.

The "kiss of Lamourette" has been passed over with a few

indulgent smiles by historians who know that a month later the Assembly would fall apart before the bloody uprising of August 10. What children they were, those men of 1792, with their overblown oratory, their naive cult of virtue, their simple-minded sloganeering about liberty, equality, and fraternity!

But we may miss something if we condescend to people in the past. The popular emotion of fraternity, the strangest in the trinity of revolutionary values, swept through Paris with the force of a hurricane in 1792. We can barely imagine its power, because we inhabit a world organized according to other principles, such as tenure, take-home pay, bottom lines, and who reports to whom. We define ourselves as employers or employees, as teachers or students, as someone located somewhere in a web of intersecting roles. The Revolution at its most revolutionary tried to wipe out such distinctions. It really meant to legislate the brotherhood of man. It may not have succeeded any better than Christianity christianized, but it remodeled enough of the social landscape to alter the course of history.

How can we grasp those moments of madness, of suspended disbelief, when anything looked possible and the world appeared as a tabula rasa, wiped clean by a surge of popular emotion and ready to be redesigned? Such moments pass quickly. People cannot live for long in a state of epistemological exhilaration. Anxiety sets in—the need to fix things, to enforce borders, to sort out "aristocrats" and patriots. Boundaries soon harden, and the landscape assumes once more the aspect of immutability.

Today most of us inhabit a world that we take to be not the best but the only world possible. The French Revolution has faded into an almost imperceptible past, its bright light obscured by a distance of two hundred years, so far away that we may barely believe in it. For the Revolution defies belief. It seems incredible that an entire people could rise up and transform the conditions of everyday existence. To do so is to contradict the common working assumption that life must be fixed in the patterns of the common workaday world.

Have we never experienced anything that could shake that conviction? Consider the assassinations of John F. Kennedy, Robert Kennedy, and Martin Luther King, Jr. All of us who lived through those moments remember precisely where we were and what we were doing. We suddenly stopped in our tracks, and in the face of the enormity of the event we felt bound to everyone around us. For a few instants we ceased to see one another through our roles and perceived ourselves as equals, stripped down to the core of our common humanity. Like mountaineers high above the daily business of the world, we moved from *vous* to *tu*.

I think the French Revolution was a succession of such events, events so terrible that they shook mankind to its core. Out of the destruction, they created a new sense of possibility—not just of writing constitutions or of legislating liberty and equality, but of living by the most difficult of revolutionary values, the brotherhood of man.

Of course, the notion of fraternity comes from the Revolution itself rather than from any higher wisdom among historians, and few historians, however wise, would assert that great events expose some bedrock reality underlying history. I would argue the opposite: great events make possible the social reconstruction of reality, the reordering of things-as-they-are so they are no longer experienced as given but rather as willed, in accordance with convictions about how things ought to be.

Possibilism against the givenness of things—those were the forces pitted against one another in France from 1789 to

1799. Not that other forces were absent, including something that might be called a "bourgeoisie" battling something known as "feudalism," while a good deal of property changed hands and the poor extracted some bread from the rich. But all those conflicts were predicated on something greater than the sum of their parts—a conviction that the human condition is malleable, not fixed, and that ordinary people can make history instead of suffering it.

Two hundred years of experimentation with brave new worlds have made us skeptical about social engineering. In retrospect, the Wordsworthian moment can be made to look like a prelude to totalitarianism. The poet bayed at a blood moon. He barked, and the caravan passed, a line of generations linked together like a chain gang destined for the gulag.

Maybe. But too much hindsight can distort the view of 1789 and of 1793–1794. The French revolutionaries were not Stalinists. They were an assortment of unexceptional persons in exceptional circumstances. When things fell apart, they responded to an overwhelming need to make sense of things by ordering society according to new principles. Those principles still stand as an indictment of tyranny and injustice. What was the French Revolution all about? Liberty, equality, fraternity.

Let Poland Be Poland

W_{HEN THE STRIKERS} in Gdańsk met to assess their victory over the government in August 1980, they discussed not only practical questions about how to organize their new union but also the need for a "new history."* "They wanted to know how Poland got to be the way it is. They wanted hard fact, the whole truth," explained Bronislaw Geremek, a medievalist, who has been a key adviser to Solidarity from the time it came into being in the shipyard of Gdańsk.

The hunger for history, "true history" as opposed to the official version, stands out as clearly as the bread lines in Poland today. The Party newspaper in Krakow, which took up muckraking after the Gdańsk strike, is now running a series, "Blank Spaces in the History of Poland." Everywhere streets are being renamed "May Third" in honor of the constitution of 1791. The official celebration of May 1 paled into insignificance beside the festivities on May 3, Poland's prewar national holiday, which was revived this year and produced an outpouring of speeches about constitutions, democracy, and national sovereignty. As a Russian invasion put an end to the constitution and precipitated the second of the three

---

*This essay was written just after a visit to Poland in May 1981, when Solidarity seemed to have gained the upper hand in its struggle with the government. At that time, many Poles feared that the Soviet Union would intervene to suppress their newly won liberties, but the suppression that took place in December 1981 was already being prepared by the Polish authorities under General Wojciech Jaruzelski.

eighteenth-century partitions of Poland, the speeches seemed to concern the present as much as the past.

"No more Targowicas," read a banner carried in Warsaw on the new May Day. *Targowica,* a common pejorative in Poland, derives from the name of a group of renegade noblemen who invited in the Russians in 1792. A banner in a recent demonstration for rural Solidarity celebrated Tadeusz Kosciuszko, the Polish hero of the American Revolution, who led an uprising against the partition in 1794. The peasant carrying the banner seemed to have a firm grip on eighteenth-century history. When asked about the events of 1794, he said that a few weeks ago the men of his village had gone to a demonstration with their scythes fixed as bayonets, exactly as their ancestors had done when they rallied to Kosciuszko.

The eighteenth century also seemed to hover over the strike last August. At the height of the crisis, a Party official warned the country on television to step back from "the brink of a catastrophe that recalls the events of the eighteenth century," while Stefan Cardinal Wyszynski stood before the Black Madonna in the holy shrine of Jasna Gora and instructed the faithful to "remember with what difficulty it was that we regained our freedom after one hundred twenty-five years."

Such remarks carry a great deal of weight in a country that seemed, during a two-week visit in May 1981, to be as obsessed with its past as it is worried about its present. The Poles cannot separate the past from the present and consign it to history books, because the regime has ruled so much of it out of bounds. It returns to haunt them, nonetheless, and it will not be laid to rest until the government permits an open confrontation with the past along with openness in every other sphere of public life.

The partitions of the eighteenth century illustrate the tendency to telescope the past and present. They belong to current events in Poland, because the Poles see their history as a constant struggle against partition, partition from the East as well as the West, right up to the present.

A weak state with no natural boundaries, Poland was carved up by Russia, Prussia, and Austria in 1772, 1793, and 1795. It survived only as a culture in the nineteenth century, thanks to its poets and its church. After being recreated as a national state by the Treaty of Versailles, Poland barely escaped destruction in the war defending itself against the forces of Bolshevik Russia in 1920. In 1939, a secret protocol of the Ribbentrop–Molotov Pact divided Poland between Germany and the Soviet Union, so the Poles were partitioned once again soon after World War II exploded from the post office of Gdańsk. They still feel divided today, because their culture and religion attach them to the West, while the Soviet empire binds them to the East. They inhabit the most explosive point in a partitioned Europe.

But they seem determined not to take history lying down. The most common joke now going around Warsaw could have been told at almost any point during the last two hundred years. "Question: If the Russians attack from the east and the Germans attack from the west, who do we fight first? Answer: the Germans. Business before pleasure." The most common question asked of an American is: "Why did you sell us at Yalta?" To the Poles, Yalta represents the culmination of a whole history of partitions.

History obsesses the Poles not merely because it seems to repeat itself but because it, too, is divided. Officially, history conforms to the Party line. Unofficially, it clings to the taboo. A film shown every day in the Warsaw Historical Museum shows German troops leveling the city after the uprising of 1944. Finally the Soviet troops liberate the rubble, having been detained on the east bank of the Vistula, as official history would have it, by overextended lines of communication. According to the accounts that circulate by word of mouth, the "liberators" let the Germans do their dirty work for them, in order to encounter no opposition when they extended their empire to the west. That version is generally accepted in the West, but nothing could be more heretical in Communist Poland—except perhaps talk of the Ribbentrop-Molotov Pact, which often accompanies it in the historical discussions that have sprung up everywhere since the Gdańsk strike.

The heresies accumulate as the talk turns toward the present. A few blocks away from the Historical Museum, the Solidarity branch of the photographers' union mounted an exhibition entitled simply "1956, 1968, 1970, 1976, 1980." It showed shots of the riots that have punctuated postwar Polish history, marking shifts in power from Gomulka to Gierek to Kania. To American eyes, accustomed to seeing street violence on television, the photographs looked mild. Blurred figures threw stones and ran from the police in vaguely urban settings. The Poles drank it in. They crammed into the exhibit and stared and stared. Having come face to face with the blank spaces of their history, they could not get enough.

Someone had written "Bandits" under a photograph of Gierek and other members of the Politburo. A visitors' book contained a host of similar comments. One read, "Next time Katyn." For the regime, the massacre of at least four thousand Polish troops, mainly officers, in the forest of Katyn is the greatest taboo subject in Poland today. According to official history, the Germans killed the troops after capturing them in 1941. According to discussions held in hushed tones with glances over the shoulder, the Russians did the killing while grabbing their share of the Hitler-Stalin partition in 1940.

Which version to believe? The Poles debate the evidence.

How many of the names on the list of victims published by the Nazis can be verified? How sound is the American monograph *Death in the Forest* by J. K. Zawodny, which circulates underground? Is it not significant that the families of the prisoners stopped receiving mail in 1940, not 1941? Most Poles seem to have drawn their own conclusions. An official guide showing an American around a church pointed to a series of memorial plaques on the wall. "Katyn," he said. The visitor did not get it. "The date, the date," he repeated and then lapsed into a prudent silence. The plaques read "Katyn 1940."

The emotive power of a date may be hard to understand for someone who has not experienced the disparity between official and underground history. May 3 can bring moisture to the eyes, 1940 can produce a firm set in the jaw, because those dates are not supposed to exist historically. The regime has also tried to keep its repression of the Gdańsk strike in 1970 a nonevent. But the strikers of 1980 forced it to let them build a huge monument to the dead of 1970 at the main entrance to the shipyards. It towers over the workplace, a pillar of steel twisted into three crosses at the top, its base covered every day with fresh bouquets of flowers.

Flowers mark the scars left by history everywhere in Poland. Six million Poles died in World War II, almost 20 percent of the population. Hardly a family escaped untouched, and many of the survivors know where and how their loved ones died. They leave flowers on the spot. They hang red and white ribbons on plaques to the Resistance. They burn candles in streets and churches, where memories are sharpest. How could the Poles forget the past? They walk around in it every day.

Official history has an explanation for the devastation. The war and its aftermath are to be attributed to oppression and revanchism from Germany. But there are limits to the hatred

of Germans, even in Poland. The Poles know that Willy Brandt
sank to his knees on the site of the Warsaw ghetto, weeping,
and that they cannot talk openly about Katyn.

The contradictions between official and repressed history
can be played out in gestures. Flowers commemorate the Poles
who fought partition as well as the dead from World War II.
They lie by the plaque to Kosciuszko and the statue to Adam
Mickiewicz, the nationalist poet, in the market square of Krakow. They are thickest at the crypt of Josef Pilsudski, in Krakow's Wawel Cathedral. The crypt is lit by candles from the
faithful and adorned with school badges deposited by children. Yet Pilsudski remains something of a nonperson in official history. After taking command of the newly reborn Poland
in 1919, he led the war against Russia in 1920.

The most sacred site in Warsaw is probably the tomb of
the unknown soldier. It is where Solidarity demonstrations
usually end and where visits from foreign dignitaries usually
begin. But laying a wreath on the tomb does not express
sympathy for the USSR, because the soldier was killed while
fighting the Bolsheviks under Pilsudski; so the Poles take special pleasure in watching Soviet ambassadors execute that gesture.

They also enjoy the ironies and ambiguities that make their
history deviate from the Party line. The official version has
militants rising in Warsaw to support the Russian revolution
of 1905. But students in the university will tell you that their
predecessors rose against Russification, because lectures could
not be given in Polish during the occupation of the nineteenth
century. When the members of Solidarity march through the
streets, they change the words of a traditional hymn from
"God keep Poland free" to "God make Poland free." They do
not need to tamper with the national anthem, because its refrain, "March Dabrowski," is a call for liberation which echoes

from 1797, when Polish patriots hoped that the Polish legion under General Henryk Dabrowski would leave Napoleon's forces in Italy in order to free them from the partitioning powers.

The regime seems to be giving some ground to the advance of figures such as Kosciuszko, Dabrowski, and Pilsudski in the popular vision of history. It has permitted an impressive, walrus-mustached Pilsudski to play a major part in a new film, *Polona Restitua,* which celebrates the regaining of independence after World War I. It also has made concessions to the cult of Wladyslaw Sikorski, the anticommunist leader of the Resistance in World War II, whose remains are to be transferred to the Wawel Cathedral from England.

This preoccupation with songs, banners, and tombs might indicate that a new nationalism is welling up against the Soviet empire just as Polish nationalists tried to overthrow the rule of tsarist, Prussian, and Austro-Hungarian empires in the nineteenth century. The obsession with history certainly suggests the reawakening of a national consciousness, which finds expression in the current popular slogan, "Let Poland be Poland." But Solidarity's orators do not thunder in the manner of the nineteenth-century poets and generals. Instead of ranting against the government, Lech Walesa jokes about how he will make Gierek work a full forty-hour week and stand in line for bread at the end of each shift. The Poles seem fed up with the grand abstractions of official history. They want to trim away the rhetoric to get the story straight. They prefer irony to oratory. "We gave America two generals for its revolution, Kosciuszko and Pulaski," runs a current quip. "Now America should give us two: General Motors and General Electric."

Where does this popular history, a history expressed by joke and gesture, leave the professionals? Poland certainly has an adequate supply of excellent historians, even though it now lacks the paper to print their work, and it would be wrong to dismiss what they wrote before last August as propaganda. An elderly historian in Krakow said that his generation looked more to Paris than to Moscow, but they used ruses and *double entendre* where their successors now speak openly. For example, articles in the dictionary of national biography on officers killed at Katyn cannot give the date of death as 1940 without offending the Soviets or as 1941 without offending the truth. So they read, "Died after 1939," and everyone catches their meaning.

The older generation lived too close to Stalinism to take chances. They learned to censor themselves before submitting their texts to the official censorship and to watch what they said in lectures. Although virtually all of them, like everyone else in the universities, have joined Solidarity, they sometimes feel that they represent official history in the eyes of the public. They were glad to be able to lecture on liberty and constitutionalism on May 3rd.

The younger historians seem more outspoken. But they, too, worry that the walls have ears, and they will request an interviewer not to use their names. A young professor in Torun turned on the radio to scramble the sound before talking shop. After dishing out generous portions of spring vegetables, about the only food available on the market today, he began dinner with an old joke, "We Poles are like radishes, red on the outside, white within." Then he ripped through the Party-line version of the past as if it were a tissue of lies, and he explained how his students experienced the contradictions between official and popular history.

As children they hear one thing at school and another at home. They often discount their parents' version. But sooner or later it is confirmed by something that reaches them from the underground press. They may take courses in the quasi-underground "flying university." And now they can read through whole shelves of uncensored books in libraries set up by Solidarity. Thus their historical education goes through three stages: exposure to oral tradition, absorption of the printed word through clandestine mimeographing and photocopying, and formal study. In the end, they develop a Rankean rage to know history "as it actually happened."

Meanwhile, several of their professors are participating in history by advising Solidarity. When Walesa made his fateful decision to call off the general strike last April, he consulted Bronislaw Geremek, on the right wing of the movement, and another medievalist, Karol Modzelewski, on the left. Although the union's governing council resisted, Walesa forced it to adopt the more moderate strategy. Solidarity retreated for the first time, and Modzelewski went back to his students in Wroclaw. They questioned him for hours about democracy and decision making in political institutions. When he left the lecture hall, he noticed that someone had printed the opening words of the American Declaration of Independence on a sign in the back of the room.

Although a large number of historians serve as advisers to Solidarity, they do not consider themselves tutors to the movement. It took them by surprise. They were astonished at the force of the discontent that welled up from the working classes; and like everyone else, they were swept off their feet by it. They also were surprised to learn that the workers had absorbed a great deal of history through the popular tradition. When one professor was explaining the secret protocol of the Hitler-Stalin Pact to a Solidarity discussion group, he was upbraided by a worker, who insisted that it be called by its right name, since it was formed by Ribbentrop and Molotov. The Poles want to get history right this time, to know how it "actually happened."

If you ask Polish historians to explain what has happened

in Poland since August 1980, they will confess that it caught them professionally unprepared. Many describe it as a revolution. "It was bloodless, a glorious revolution, our 1688," said one professor. "It was greater than Kosciuszko," said another. "His was just an uprising. This is a revolution, a movement from the depths of the people against the whole regime."

If the movement qualifies as a revolution, it does not fit any common model. Marxism has no room for an uprising of the working class against an allegedly proletarian regime. And American-style political sociology seems too sophisticated to account for the antigovernment passions of the Poles. One cannot find the "J" curve in the current economic crisis, even though it followed a factitious boom under Gierek. The same goes for the other formulas: relative deprivation, blocked mobility, status crystallization, rising expectations, failed reform, even class struggle. Some Poles argue that the apparatchiks constitute a class, which has monopolized the means of production, but they do so with a twinkle in their eye, for the sheer pleasure of turning a Marxist cliché against itself. They see some force in another cliché, the alienation of the intellectuals. But they all agree that the movement began with ordinary workers and that the intelligentsia had to run fast to catch up with it.

According to most accounts, the movement has passed through three phases. From the shipyard in Gdańsk it spread to the entire industrial working class; then it swept through the peasantry, which comprises 30 percent of the population and tills 80 percent of the land in small, independent farms. Now it is rising through the lower ranks of the Communist Party, which is electing its leaders by secret ballot and relatively open nominations—an astonishing break with Communist Party practice. The third phase could be the most dangerous of all, especially if it leads to a revolt against the leadership at the Party congress in July. If the Party structure crumbles while the economy collapses, the Soviets may intervene, and the events from August to July will have been a prerevolution or a prelude to a bloody war.

Few Poles I met expect such a tragedy to take place. To them, talk of intervention is a form of hysteria that arrives in reports from Washington, and it is a bad thing. It can be used to force moderation on Solidarity, or it might turn into a self-fulfilling prophecy. A writer in Warsaw said it made her break out in what she has diagnosed as a "Weinberger rash," referring to the American secretary of defense. But there have been no outbreaks of panic. Despite the history of their relations with Russia, or perhaps because of it, the Poles go about their business without searching the sky for MIGs.

If asked to name the most dramatic event during the last few months, most Poles would cite the attempted assassination of the pope on May 14, 1981. John Paul II towers over every public figure in Poland. After the shooting, the entire country seemed to flood into the churches. At the one o'clock mass on May 14 in the Cathedral of St. John in Warsaw, the crowd covered every inch of floor space. It spilled out on the street and extended, shoulder to shoulder, for a block in either direction, beyond the range of the public-address system broadcasting the service outdoors. At the elevation of the host, the crowd in the cathedral knelt, and the kneeling passed in waves down the nave and into the street, as far as the eye could see. The death of Cardinal Wyszynski produced an equal outpouring of devotion—more than a quarter of a million mourners attended a religious mass for him in Victory Square, Warsaw, on May 31.

The fervor of Catholicism in Poland serves as a rebuke to the regime. As during the nineteenth century, when the Church represented almost all that remained of the national culture, Polish Catholicism expresses a partition mentality, a shift of loyalties from state to church. This internal migration of the spirit burst into the open during the pope's visit of 1979, which Poles often describe as the starting point of their "revolution." Now it has become institutionalized in Solidarity.

Solidarity is inseparable from the Church. Its banners were unfurled at the masses for the pope, just as crosses have been carried in all of the rallies for the union. When rural Solidarity was declared legal by the courts, the first act of its leaders was to drop to their knees and kiss a cross. When the Gdańsk strikers defied the government, priests took confession and said mass in the shipyard. The Church, led by Wyszynski, generally counseled moderation, but it legitimated the movement at the very moment when the government had lost its legitimacy in the eyes of the people.

Solidarity and the Church now seem to be the only institutions that command the loyalties of the entire nation. Ninety-five percent of Poland's 35 million people are practicing Catholics. Ten million of them had joined Solidarity at last count, when rural Solidarity was just beginning to get organized. By the end of the summer, when it will hold its first general congress, the union will include virtually the entire work force of the country, including many members of the Communist Party.

This wholesale withdrawal of allegiance from the state and its reinvestment in a movement that began illegally is what the Poles have in mind when they refer to the "revolution." But they do not have a clear concept of Solidarity itself. Despite the influence of KOR and other dissident groups, it has no coherent ideology, no clear vision of an alternative social order, not even a general program for reform. The only thing holding it together is a deep, pervasive hatred of the regime.

No one can predict how long it can continue in such a fashion. At the moment, however, it represents an extraordinary situation: the complete alienation of society from the state.

Perhaps that is why history matters so much to the movement. Omaciej Szamowski, editor of the *Gazeta Krakowska*, said that his journal was running its series on "Blank Spaces in the History of Poland" for "the good of national cohesion." "We are saving history from political manipulation," he explained. The Poles need to repossess their past in order for Poland to be Poland. So they want to throw out official history and discover what "actually happened."

The Rankean formula seems apt and urgent in Poland today. It sounds archaic in Western Europe, where avant-garde historians abandoned it long ago in order to study the play of "structure" and "conjuncture" over the *longue durée*. These formulas come from the *Annales* school, which has pronounced "event history," *histoire événementielle,* dead—"a corpse that we must still kill," in the words of Jacques Le Goff, a former president of the VIe Section of the Ecole Pratique des Hautes Etudes in Paris.

Try telling a Pole that events don't matter, that diplomacy and politics are epiphenomena, that one can neglect dates in order to study structures. He will reply that the difference between 1940 and 1941 is a matter of life and death; that nothing could be more important than the secret provisions of the Ribbentrop-Molotov pact; that the whole meaning of Poland can be strung out on dates: 1772, 1793, 1795, 1830, 1863, 1919–1920, 1939, 1944–1945, 1956, 1968, 1970, and 1980. The events of August transformed the world for him. For the rest of us they suggest that history can play tricks on itself, and that it can go back to work at its old task, teaching lessons and shaping a national consciousness. In Poland that consciousness will determine the future as well as the past.

Dessiné de souvenir
le 5 avril 1796

PART TWO

Media

J-B Wille's drawing of Danton—hands tied—on the way to the guillotine.

THREE

Film: Danton and Double Entendre

A T THE BEGINNING of the political year in September 1983, when Frenchmen returned from their vacations to face a declining franc, an escalating arms race, a crisis in the Middle East, and trouble everywhere on the home front, François Mitterand summoned his ministers to the Elysée Palace and lectured them on the sorry state of history—not the current turn of events but the history that French children were failing to learn in school. No doubt the president had other worries. But the crisis that he placed at the top of his agenda was the inability of the electorate to sort out the themes of its past. What would become of a citizenry that could no longer distinguish between Louis XIII and Louis XIV, between the Second Republic and the Third, or (and this seems to have been what really hurt) between Robespierre and Danton?

Mitterand may not have mentioned the controversy aroused by Andrzej Wajda's film, but he probably had *Danton* on his mind. He had disapproved of it when he saw it at a private screening before its release in January 1983. It had outraged his supporters on the Socialist-Communist left when it was shown at the Assemblée Nationale. And for the next half year it provided left-wing intellectuals with an opportunity to score points in the popular press by demonstrating their ability to set the historical record straight and their determination to overhaul the curriculum of secondary schools.

While the opposition gloated—"Thank you, Monsieur Wajda," crowed Michel Poniatowski of the Gaullists—the left thundered with indignation. "What history!" exclaimed Pierre Joxe, the leader of the Socialist deputies in the Assemblée Nationale. And the worst thing was that it could be taken as truth by French schoolchildren. Victims of curricular reforms that had "cut them off from history," they "will not be able to know who Danton was after having seen him portrayed like that." Louis Mermaz, the Socialist president of the assembly, issued the same warning:

The teaching of history has become so bad . . . that the young people of today lack the knowledge of chronology that the men of my generation were fortunate enough to acquire from primary school onward. The film is misleading. . . . It makes me want to make a plea for the revival of the teaching of history, something essential for a nation, for a civilization.

Such vehemence may seem puzzling to the American viewers of *Danton*. We know that the French take their history seriously and that it doesn't do to tamper with their Revolution. But why should the Socialists disavow a version of the feud between Danton and Robespierre that puts Danton in a favorable light? Could not Danton's attempts to stop the Terror be seen as a heroic foreshadowing of the resistance to Stalinism? Is not Wajda a hero of Solidarity? And shouldn't Wajda's *Danton* be expected to appeal to the moderate left in France, the champions of socialism with a human face, the party that covered billboards during Mitterand's campaign with pictures of a rose extending from a fist?

Now that *Danton* has crossed the ocean, it seems appropriate to pursue those questions, for they take us into the strange symbolic world of the European left, a world in which

intellectuals become entangled in the myths they have created
and where lines easily cross, even when they are strung out
with the best of intentions between the *bien pensants* of Paris
and Warsaw.

Danton grew out of both capitals, like a contemporary tale
of two cities. Having survived the repression of Solidarity,
Wajda devoted his next film to a historical theme, one located
safely back in Paris, two centuries before the *zomos* stamped
out the last remnants of free speech in the streets of Warsaw.
The film opens with some grim scenes in the streets of Paris at
the end of 1793. Danton arrives from his country estate in
order to turn back the Terror that he himself had helped to
create after the overthrow of the monarchy in August 1792.
Soon he is engaged in a desperate struggle over the course of
the Revolution, which pits the moderates or "Indulgents"
against the hard-liners around Robespierre in the Committee
of Public Safety. The film dramatizes Danton's inability to
stop the guillotining and ends with his own execution on April
5, 1794.

In order to compress such a complex story into a movie,
Wajda had to trim the historical record and to cut his text. He
worked from a Polish play by Stanislawa Przybyszewska, which
celebrated Robespierre as a champion of the people and which
had served as a rallying point for the Polish left in the 1930s.
In adapting the play for the screen, Wajda used a French
screenwriter, Jean-Clause Carrière, and the French Ministry
of Culture contributed three million of the twenty-four million francs in his budget. The actors, evenly divided between
Poles and Frenchmen, spoke their native languages, leaving it
to the dubbers to create an illusion of a mutually comprehensible dialogue. (In the version shown in the United States the
sound is in French and the subtitles in English, while the lips
of the Polish actors follow the rhythm of their own tongue.)

As a result, *Danton* became intensely Polish and intensely French. It also appeared as a quasi-official production of the Mitterand government, as if the Socialists wanted to align the French revolutionary tradition with the quasi-revolution of Solidarity. The mixture of ingredients was perfectly suited for scrambling meanings and confounding critics.

Wajda quickly disposes of the simplest version of what the film might mean to the Poles. It was not an allegory, he stated over and over again to interviewers from the French press. "Let one thing be clear," he told *Le Monde*. "Danton is not Lech Walesa and Robespierre is not Jaruzelski!" "If you must find historical analogies, you should look for them in a completely different period," he said to *Le Matin*. "Those two years of Solidarity were not a revolution, or in any case not of the same nature as the French Revolution."

True, one could construct parallels between the two pairs of political rivals. Robespierre's personal fastidiousness and unbending dogmatism evoke the ramrod stiffness of the Polish general, and Danton's earthy conviviality suggests the popular manner of the hero from the Gdańsk dockyards. But Wajda refuses to let his story fall into a simple formula—the apparatchik versus the man of the people—and produces plenty of incriminating evidence against Danton. If Gérard Depardieu were acting out an apology for Walesa, it would be foolish to insist on Danton's corruption at the very time when the Polish government was attempting to blacken Walesa's reputation by accusing him of pocketing funds from Solidarity.

The fact remains, however, that Danton and Robespierre personify two kinds of revolution and that the film tilts the balance in favor of Danton. "Robespierre is the world of the East; Danton is the Western world," Wajda told *Le Matin*. "The attitude and arguments of [Danton] are very close to us. The clash between these two men is exactly the moment we are living through today." Depardieu's powerful acting makes Danton the dominant and the more sympathetic figure, but his insistence on Danton's self-indulgence could be taken as bourgeois decadence. When he meets Robespierre for dinner to discuss their differences he gets sloppily drunk. His inability to take decisive action against the Reign of Terror in the crisis of March and April 1794 might even suggest the failure of the West to rescue Solidarity in 1981.

But the film is too ambiguous to provide a precise moral for the present. One cannot even gauge how much Wajda cast his weight on the side of Dantonism, because the texts of the original Polish drama and the screenplay are not available for comparison. Nonetheless, one can spot the points at which the film deviated from the historical record. Three of them would probably stand out clearly to a Polish audience.

Near the beginning of the film, a small boy, the picture of innocence, stands naked in a tub, trying to recite the Declaration of the Rights of Man and Citizen while his older sister bathes him. Whenever the words fail to come, he holds out a hand and she slaps him over the knuckles. She is not so much washing him as brainwashing him in order to ingratiate herself with her father's distinguished boarder, Citizen Robespierre. Soon afterward, Robespierre orders some thugs from the secret police to destroy the shop in which Camille Desmoulins has been printing *Le Vieux Cordelier,* the journal that popularized the Dantonists' attempts to turn back the Terror. Having dwelled on the pain etched on the face of the boy, the camera picks up every detail in the smashing of the presses. Neither episode took place—and, as far as one can tell, did not occur in the Przybyszewska play. But the Polish viewer would not have to know that Wajda invented them in order to see them as a comment on thought control at home.

The third episode provides an even clearer indictment of

Stalinist indoctrination. Robespierre, wrapped in the robes of a Caesar, is posing for his portrait in David's studio. He stops to berate the prosecutor of the Revolutionary Tribunal, who is having difficulty rigging Danton's trial. Then he notices a gigantic canvas, where David has begun to paint his famous version of the Tennis Court Oath of June 20, 1789. In the crowd of patriots, Robespierre spies the freshly painted head of Fabre d'Eglantine, who is then being tried along with Danton. "Wipe it out," he orders. "But he was there," David objects. Nonetheless, Robespierre insists and so Fabre disappears like all the victims of Stalinist historiography. Yet this scene never happened. Fabre did not participate in the Tennis Court Oath, because he was not a deputy to the Estates General in 1789. Wajda seems to have been so intent on exposing the falsification of history by the Stalinists that he was willing to falsify it himself.

Wajda's Polish viewers could not be expected to know a great deal about the biography of an obscure character like Fabre d'Eglantine; but they would be certain to have strong views about history, because national consciousness is passionately historical in Poland. From the first moments of its existence, Solidarity tried to free the past as well as the present. Having been educated in the historical ideology that the regime used to legitimate itself—above all the line that leads from Robespierrism to Bolshevism—the shipyard workers of Gdańsk demanded the right to strip their history of dogma and to confront facts, especially the awkward facts that extend from the Soviet massacre of Polish officers at Katyn in 1940 to the partitions of Poland in the eighteenth century.

Wajda staged a production of *Danton* in the shipyards in 1981. His early films showed that he shared his countrymen's passion for the past. *Landscape after Battle* (1970) linked a popular uprising to a play-within-a-play, one that commemorated the Polish victory over the Teutonic knights at the Battle of Tannenberg in 1410, and *Man of Marble* (1977) recounted the attempt of a filmmaker to recover the true story of a proletarian hero from the rubbish of Stalinist propaganda. An audience familiar with that theme might see a similar message in Wajda's dissection of Robespierrist mythology.

Of course, no one can know what the Poles see in *Danton* without interviewing large numbers of them at a safe distance from the police. But it seems likely that many episodes of the film would take on special meaning in the conditions after the suppression of Solidarity. The bread lines of Parisians muttering against the Committee of Public Safety could be cursing the military dictatorship in Warsaw, Danton hurling defiance at the Revolutionary Tribunal could be Walesa in the shipyards of Gdańsk: "The people has but one enemy: the government." Robespierre's justification of the Terror—the need for tyranny in the service of democracy—could be Jaruzelski's. As Bernard Guetta, the former Warsaw correspondent of *Le Monde,* reported after seeing the film, "A hundred things in it have a resonance that Poles, or anyone who has lived among them for the last few years, could not fail to pick up."

Picking up that resonance is not a matter of spotting allegories or detecting a secret code. The Poles have learned to live with veiled meanings and ambiguous protests. Their muchhated six o'clock news has taught them to be sophisticated in reacting to images on screens, and they can be expected to note the way the imagery is weighted in *Danton*. It adds up to an overwhelming indictment of government oppression.

Although the film allows Robespierre a few moments of triumph from the rostrum, its camera work undoes the effect of his words. While he cows the deputies of the Convention with the official line on Terror and Virtue, the screen fills with a closeup of his dainty shoes. He rises to the climactic movements of his speech on tiptoe, more like a dancing master than a champion of the people, in contrast to Danton, who roars to the crowd in the courtroom like a caged lion.

If Robespierre scores any points in the debates, they are wiped away in the end by the guillotining. The blade comes down on Danton's neck with sickening inexorability. Blood gushes into the hay below the scaffold. The executioner holds the severed head before the crowd, and the camera dwells on it in a sequence of overexposed shots, taken from below and into the sun, that leave the viewer feeling dizzy and nauseated. Then the scene shifts to Robespierre, sweating like a madman in his bed, while the young boy, who at last has learned his catechism recites the Declaration of the Rights of Man and Citizen. As he parrots the words, the boy's voice is drowned out by dissonant background music; and on that harsh note the movie ends.

Despite little publicity and few reviews, *Danton* has been showing to packed houses everywhere in Poland. One can only guess as its reception, but it is difficult to imagine an audience leaving the theater without a revived sense of loathing for the Polish government. In France, everything seemed disposed to make *Danton* a hit. Wajda was lionized; Solidarity had captured the heart of the public; and the newly elected Socialist government was eager to present the film as its overture to the bicentennial of the French Revolution in 1989.

Yet *Danton* created a scandal, especially on the left, where the uneasy alliance between the Socialists and Communists leaves some uncertainty about who may represent the Revolutionary tradition. The Communists tried to mount the strongest condemnation of the film: "It is counterrevolutionary," wrote a critic in *L'Humanité*. Not to be outdone, the Socialists replied in kind. "It disfigures everything most beautiful [in the Revolution]," Philippe Boucher declared in *Le*

Monde. And Pierre Joxe added: "[Wajda's] history is not ours."

"Our" history was that of the left, a great tradition developed by a succession of great historians—Michelet, Jaurès, Mathiez, Lefebvre—and taught to many generations of schoolchildren since the triumph of the *école laïque* in the nineteenth century. In order to make their pupils into citizens, the teachers of the old school drilled a great many facts into their heads. The children gave the chronology a preliminary going-over in elementary school, often using the little textbooks of the "Petit Lavisse" series, which served up the work of the great historians in easily digestible portions. Then they settled down to systematic study in the *lycée*.

By the end of their *cinquième,* a class composed mainly of thirteen year olds, they had got through the barbarian invasions. They entered the "modern" era, the sixteenth through the eighteenth centuries, in *troisième.* Then in *seconde,* at age sixteen, they spent a full year studying the Revolution and the Empire—and they frequently returned to it in *terminale* (age eighteen). The Revolution served as the keystone to the whole sequence. When the students left to face the *baccalauréat* or the *boches,* they knew what had happened between 1789 and 1799, and especially in the supreme crisis of 1793–1794. Although the textbooks varied, the message remained the same: in the year of the Terror, a republican France had stood up against the combined forces of a feudal Europe and had defeated them.

Danton occupied an important place in this vision—not the Danton of the September Massacres but the Danton of *"Il nous faut de l'audace"* (We must have daring), who still defies the foreign forces invading France from a pedestal off the Boulevard Saint-Germain. He had been put on a pedestal by Alphonse Aulard, the first historian to occupy the chair of the French Revolution created in the University of Paris in 1891.

Aulard's student and successor, Albert Mathiez, turned against his master and tried to knock Danton off his perch by proving that he had sold himself to the counterrevolution. In his place, Mathiez erected Robespierre, the ideological strategist who formed an alliance with the common people in order, Mathiez maintained, to force France down the road to social revolution.

Mathiez's Robespierre fit nicely into Leninism and the notion of the dictatorship of the proletariat, and Mathiez's successors, Georges Lefebvre and Albert Soboul, a Marxist and a Marxist-Communist, made sure that Robespierre maintained his place in what soon hardened into an orthodox version of the French Revolution and of revolutions in general, which henceforth were supposed to follow a course leading from class war to Terror and socialism, unless diverted by a Thermidorean reaction of the kind that followed the overthrow of Robespierre in July 1794.

This orthodoxy still shapes the history taught in Eastern Europe; hence the audacity of Wajda's rehabilitation of Danton. But it never swept aside rival interpretations in France. Most French historians today probably would concede that Danton's finances do not stand up to close scrutiny. In 1789 he was a not especially successful lawyer loaded down with at least forty-three thousand livres in debts. In 1791 he paid off his creditors and bought an estate worth eighty thousand livres without an ostensible improvement in his practice or the acquisition of another legitimate source of income. He probably took money from the court. But a politician may fatten his purse without betraying his country, and Danton certainly led the resistance to the invading armies after the overthrow of the monarchy on August 10, 1792. His statue still stands in the Place Danton as the embodiment of patriotism. It could be Wajda's Man of Iron.

Robespierre does not occupy a comparable place in his countrymen's imagination, although he still dominates their historiography. "Despite the considerable historical role played by Robespierre, he has not won much acceptance as a personage in France," Louis Mermaz explained in *Le Monde*. "It should be noted that there is no rue Robespierre in Paris." As if to answer, Jean Marcenac put the Communist case before the readers of *L'Humanité:*

I live in Saint-Denis, the only city in France where there is a statue of Robespierre. . . . I shall buy three red roses and place them at the foot of his bust in the Square Robespierre. It's on my path. That has always been my path. Wajda has lost his way.

The heavy symbolism of such statements shows how much the Revolution retains its mythical force in France. To control the myth is to exert political power, to stake out a position as the authentic representative of the left. The Revolution established the basic categories of French politics, beginning with the distinction of left and right, which derives from the seating pattern of the Constituent Assembly. The politicians sitting in the Assemblée Nationale today understand that they can head off challenges by manipulating the categories. Like Robespierre, they try to speak in the name of the sovereign people and to outflank their enemies on the left.

The left flank of the Socialists looked vulnerable when *Danton* opened in January 1983. The government had changed course and had adopted economic policies closer to those of Raymond Barre or Margaret Thatcher than to the radical program on which Mitterand had been elected. Its temporizing smacked of Dantonism, and the Communists began to snipe at it from the left, just as Robespierre had done when he attacked the moderates in the Convention, aligning himself with the popular demands of the sans-culottes. The Socialists needed to prove their ideological purity. So they rushed to the defense of the orthodox view of the French Revolution. They fell over themselves in the scramble to denounce the heresies in *Danton*. It was an extraordinary spectacle, party stalwarts haranguing one another about history as if they were schoolmasters lecturing to a class. Every point scored against Wajda could be counted toward a victory over the opposition and a demonstration of one's superior faithfulness to the true revolutionary tradition.

Everyone could play at this game—everyone, that is, with a good old-fashioned education. Wajda, it was charged, had made the Terror seem gratuitous by eliminating all references to its context: the civil war in the Vendée, the federalist revolts in the provinces, the counterrevolutionary intrigues in Paris, and the invasion about to burst across the border. Wajda had ignored Robespierre's campaign against the left-wing extremists led by Jacques René Hébert, thereby making nonsense of the leftist opposition to Robespierre in the Committee of Public Safety and obscuring the political rationale for Robespierre's stroke against the Dantonists: a need to preserve the allegiance of the sans-culottes and to prevent the Revolution from veering to the right after the purge of the Hébertist left. Wajda had even cut out the sans-culottes themselves. The common people hardly appear in the film, yet the French Revolution was an uprising of the masses, not a parliamentary duel between a few bourgeois orators. (In fact, Wadja had planned to film some crowd scenes in Krakow, but the Polish government, which had its own crowds to worry about, refused to let him do so.)

Finally, the critics raked over the film in search of anachronisms. Wajda's Saint-Just wore an earring and cavorted about like a modern hippie instead of the grim "Angel of Death" in the orthodox history. He threw his hat into the fire in Robespierre's room, whereas that fit of rage actually took place during a dramatic debate in the Committee of Public Safety. In the film Robespierre and Danton were called "Maxime" and "Georges" by their followers, but the revolutionaries rarely used first names even after adopting the democratic *tu*.

These details offended the critics not because of their inaccuracy but because they made the leaders of the Revolution look more familiar and less heroic than the figures in the history books. Billaud-Varenne was too unshaven, Desmoulins too weak, Danton too drunk. Wojciech Pszoniak's portrayal of an icy, neurotic, inhuman Robespierre seemed especially offensive, because Robespierre was the touchstone of orthodoxy in interpretations of the Revolution. Equally important, he was the model of the modern intellectual. He personified *engagement*. A theorist turned man of action, he laid out party lines and devised strategy in the interest of the masses.

The Socialist leaders think of themselves as intellectuals of that kind. Mitterrand likes to be considered a man of letters and lets it be known that he keeps a copy of Michelet's history of the Revolution at his bedside. In one of his first key appointments, he named Claude Manceron, the historian of the Revolution, to be his *attaché culturel* charged with a special mission to prepare a spectacular celebration of the bicentennial, one that could also serve to celebrate the Socialists' victory in the presidential election of 1988. Max Gallo, the government spokesman, is a former history professor who wrote a biography of Robespierre that reads like Mathiez spiced up with Freud.

These men and many others at the top of the Socialist party find it natural for intellectuals to exercise power. Indeed, they assume that power is intellectual, at least in part, as Michel Foucault has argued in a series of influential books. Thus Jack Lang, a former theater director now minister of culture and the man behind the French sponsorship of *Danton,* decided that one way to cope with the recession was to convoke a gigantic jamboree of intellectuals in Paris. They made speeches at one another for two days last winter and disbanded with the hope that they had raised the country's morale if not its GNP. But spirits flagged, so in the summer the government issued another general appeal for support from the intellectual left. Even then things failed to improve; and at the last party congress a delegate rose to his feet, pointed a finger at the leaders, and quoted Robespierre on the need for heads to roll.

Such talk makes sense in a political culture that still bears the imprint of 1794. Thus the debate about Danton really concerned symbolic power, even though it seemed to turn on questions of fact that could be settled from the primers of the Third Republic. In appealing to the facts, however, the politicians exposed themselves to some difficulties raised by their fellow travelers from the intelligentsia. The primers were out of date. Worse, factuality itself had been consigned by the avant-garde to the scrapheap of outmoded notions like liberalism and positivism. Foucault and a host of literary critics had dissolved facts into "discourse," and the most fashionable historians, those identified with the *Annales* school and based in the Ecole des Hautes Etudes en Sciences Sociales, had turned their backs on politics and events in order, to study structures and *mentalités*.

Long before the opening of *Danton,* the split between the new and the old history had been dramatized by a feud between two of the leading historians of the Revolution, Albert Soboul and François Furet. Soboul, a Communist and professor at the Sorbonne, stood in the direct line of descendance from Mathiez. Furet, a former Communist and eminent Annalist from the Ecole des Hautes Etudes, attacked the entire tradition from Mathiez to Lefebvre as a myth perpetrated in the cause of Stalinism.

The polemics shook the Left Bank for several years in the 1970s. But they had subsided by the time the Socialists and Communists cooperated to elect Mitterrand. In the autumn of 1982 Soboul died. His funeral was a sad affair, a high Communist mass with red roses and black suits at the Mur des Fédérés, the most sacred territory of the left in the Cimetière du Père-Lachaise. It seemed to mark the end of a vision of the Revolution that had inspired Frenchmen for more than a century.

Insofar as any other vision now prevails, it derives from the Ecole des Hautes Etudes. Furet, now president of the Ecole, has attempted to rethink the Revolution as a struggle for the control of political discourse. In one of the few favorable articles on *Danton,* he praised Wajda for puncturing the myth of Robespierrism and exposing its ties to Stalinism.

Meanwhile, as the professionals were settling scores, the schoolchildren had to get their homework done and make it through the *baccalauréat* examination. They could not do so by poring over the texts that had tortured the memories of their parents, because history had disappeared from the curriculum. After a devastating series of reforms, it had been swallowed up in the *sciences humaines,* modernized out of existence. French children no longer work their way chronologically through the entire past of their country. They study themes like urban society, comparative peasantries, and ecological systems. Strong on discourse and weak on events, they cannot tell the difference between Robespierre and Danton.

So in debating *Danton,* the politicians were caught in a double bind. They appealed to an old-fashioned kind of history that no longer seemed tenable to their intellectual avantgarde and no longer existed for their children or grandchildren. They had brought that trouble on themselves, for they had commissioned a hero of the left, an intellectual of the

purest anti-Stalinism, to celebrate their Revolution, and he
had denigrated it. What was the world coming to? The Socialists could only shake their heads and lecture one another about
Wajda's heresies, unaware that their indignation demonstrated how much they remained prisoners of their own mythology.

In search of a way out of this dilemma, they took the
predictable course: another school reform. An "Estates General" of historians has already met and has proposed new changes
in the curriculum. Refreshed by his reading of Michelet, the
president of the republic wants history to be placed at the core
of the new system—a rigorous history with the facts set straight
and the heroes slotted into the correct categories.

However, there remains a problem about how to straighten
facts. Having adhered so convincingly in the old orthodoxy
and suffered so much from the last rounds of revisionism, they
may resist further modernization. But one thing seems clear
from the debate on *Danton:* Facts do not speak for themselves.
The film could be seen in completely different ways. It was
not the same in Warsaw and in Paris. Its ability to generate
double entendre suggests that meaning itself is shaped by context and that the significance of the French Revolution will
never be exhausted. The debate may look like harmless shad-
owboxing, but there is life in the shadows yet. The ghosts of
Robespierre and Danton still haunt the European left, and we
all may have to come to terms with terror between those
symbolic dates, 1984 and 1989.

Television: An Open Letter to a TV Producer

Dear sir:

I admit I'm an Ivy League professor, but I don't think I'm a snob. When you asked me to review the television script about Napoleon and Josephine, I gladly agreed. I thought it would be fascinating to see a Hollywood version of the period I study. My studies also concern the history of popular culture, and so you offered me an opportunity to shape the culture being broadcast to millions of Americans. Your phone call sounded like a summons to put my monographs aside: here was a chance to do something, from my small corner of the profession, about the quality of the history that reaches the general public. And professors being as greedy as everyone else, I thought I might make some money.

Since you warned me that the script was for a "docudrama," I expected to find some fictitious dialogue, and I made an effort to be as unpedantic as a professor possibly could be. I was prepared for the worst. And on the very first page I found it:

CLOSE SHOT—SEVERED HEAD
Slack-mouthed in surprise. Neatly slashed veins and tendons trail bloodily from the head. The eyelids twitch.
MOB ROAR HEIGHTENED OFF STAGE.

Now, I would not deny that the French Revolution was a bloody affair. People really were guillotined, although most

of them were counterrevolutionaries captured with weapons
in hand behind the French lines during a desperate war that
pitted the new republic against the combined forces of the old
regimes of Europe. But your scriptwriter smears the screen
with blood. When he can't find enough of it in standard histories, if he read any, he manufactures it.

Take, for example, Josephine's famous escape in a carriage
from Austrian fire along Lake Garda during her visit to Bonaparte in the midst of the first Italian campaign. It was a near
miss, and I imagined the scriptwriter would make the most of
it. But he made most of it up. Instead of settling for Austrian
shots falling so close that they kill a horse and one of Josephine's guards, he has the Austrians storm the carriage:

Josephine is petrified as the Austrian throws open the carriage door.
He stops, surprised at the sight of a woman. Marchand (Josephine's
guard) skewers him through the throat with his bayonet. Turn.
Twist. And the Austrian falls forward into the carriage. Blood pumps
from his jugular onto Josephine's clothes.

Confident, it seems, that he has tickled the appetite of a
public that might otherwise be dozing in front of some his-
tory-as-it-actually-happened, your writer rips Josephine from
the carriage and throws her onto a battlefield strewn with
corpses. Night falls. She huddles beside Marchand, a fictitious
substitute for General Junot, who actually rescued Josephine
in a dashing manner but unfortunately without any shedding
of blood. They hear some ruffians who are robbing corpses
and killing the wounded, apparently for amusement. The
camera dwells on one ruffian smashing a head and another
plunging a knife into a helpless soldier. Josephine is about to
scream; then she sinks to the ground:

JOSEPHINE'S POINT OF VIEW—ANGLE ON CORPSE
A disintegrating body. Her hand is on the torn face.

At this point, presumably, moms and dads all over the country wake up, and the kids are glued to the screen. History wasn't like this in the classroom.

I shouldn't imply that the script has nothing but violence. It also contains a good deal of sex. I had expected that, too, because the Thermidorean period, when Josephine became Bonaparte's mistress, was a time of reaction against republican puritanism. Women really did swirl through balls in diaphanous gowns, picking up lovers and fortunes—women in high society, that is: the poor suffered horribly from inflation and starvation, though the script does not bother with them, except in the early scenes when they provide "orgasmic" cheers for the guillotine. But I was amazed at your writer's ability to invent pretexts for undressing Josephine or presenting her to us "in a rumpled, postcoital state more lively than *triste*." (He seems to feel a need for French when he gets to sex, and spells it right. Nonlibidinal words like "victoire" and "Tuileries" are beyond the range of his spelling, but of course television needn't concern itself with such pedantic details.)

The rawest sex is reserved for the supporting roles, perhaps because your writer's flair for dialogue falters when he takes the principal characters between the sheets:

BONAPARTE:
I love you.   I love you.   I love you.   Do you love me?

When words fail, we get images, though sometimes only a glimpse, as in this clever camera shot:

The maid is in an open doorway. In her underclothes, and very little of those.

Best of all are the antics of Napoleon's sister Pauline, age sixteen. She takes a fancy to one of his generals, Charles-Victor Leclerc, during the Italian campaign. First we see her

. . . all but raping him publicly. Unbuttoning his uniform shirt, running her hand up and down his sheathed sword as her eyes roll in her head, biting his ear lobe.

Then she drags him behind a screen that is unaccountably standing in front of a vast throng of diners in a banqueting hall in Milan. In their passion, they knock the screen over, and the camera tells all:

ANGLE ON PAULINE AND LE CLERC
They are *in flagrante delicto*. Pauline's breasts are exposed. Le Clerc's pants are down to his knees. They are obviously rutting.

Why shouldn't history steal a page from *Penthouse?* It might brighten up the living room and give the kids a new taste for their studies. Why worry about factual details? Does it matter that your writer makes Robespierre tall (better for contrast with the stumpy Bonaparte, who is always striking his hand-in-the-tunic pose as in the brandy ads), when we know he was short? Is it important that we are told Bonaparte was a captain when he was actually a brigadier general; or that Robespierre has him arrested for refusing a command in the Vendée when he actually was imprisoned after the fall of Robespierre and declined the Vendée assignment later; or that Robespierre himself is presented as a kind of Hitler, the source of all evil and all the guillotining, when in fact he was only one of twelve members of the Committee of Public Safety, a body that handled questions of war and politics, leaving the guillotine for the most part to the Committee of General Security and the Revolutionary Tribunal?

Avant-garde historians have derided the superficiality of "event history" for the last forty years. Having turned their backs on "facticity," how can they complain if television gets things wrong? I twinge, nonetheless, when I see the Bonapartes, who were fairly prosperous members of the Corsican nobility, presented as filthy, foul-mouthed peasants. By way of a glimpse at their home life, the camera shows Louis Bonaparte lugging a sack of turnips and Jerome chasing a rooster around their hovel. Their mother, the formidable Madame Mère, then seizes the fowl and snaps its neck, exclaiming:

This is how the mother of the great General Nabouglione Buonaparte, the pride of the blood, wrings a neck.

It's a vivid scene. Why worry if it never took place any more than the confrontation scenes between Bonaparte and Robespierre, Bonaparte and Talleyrand, and Talleyrand and Mme. de Stael? What does it matter, considering that we are in the never-never land of docudrama?

Yet somehow as the unfacts and nonevents spin around me, I find I do begin to worry. A voice inside, some residue of professional conscience and pre-TV culture or a distant whisper from Leopold von Ranke, says that the French Revolution "as it actually happened" does matter, that the American public deserves an accurate view of the Napoleonic era, that history should be saved from docudrama.

Without some concern for accuracy, history drifts loose from its moorings and, as your script demonstrates, anything goes. Consider your writer's treatment of revolutionary politics. He does not want to entangle the viewer in a complicated account of parties and coups, so he relegates politics to the background. I can understand that. He is writing a love story, not giving a lecture. But why can't the background be correct? I don't wince, not very much at least, when the script has Bonaparte utter the famous phrase, "whiff of grapeshot," during the attempted coup of 13 Vendémiaire (October 5, 1795)—and then repeats it, in case we missed it the first time round. It's an English expression, invented at the high tide of Victorianism by Thomas Carlyle. But no matter. What *does* matter is that the grapeshot of the script destroys a mob of "unregenerate worshippers of Robespierre." In fact, Bonaparte directed his cannon fire against insurrectionaries coming from the very opposite end of the political spectrum: they were royalists, and he was protecting a still largely Jacobin Convention against an uprising of the right, not the left, as the Revolution moved out of the phase known as the Thermidorean Reaction and into a period of republican rule under the Directory. The script suggests the Directory followed immediately on the heels of Robespierre's overthrow on 9 Thermidor (July 27, 1794). It gives a wildly inaccurate account of Thermidor: Barras simply pulls a gun on Robespierre, smilingly wickedly, and Robespierre realizes the jig is up. Then it empties the prisons and presents Barras as the strong man of the Directory, as if the Thermidorean interlude had never occurred. Once the guillotine has dispatched Robespierre, Jacobinism ceases to exist and we can frolic with the upper classes in their skintight trousers and see-through gowns.

I hope I don't sound demagogic if I suggest that the Revolution involved the entire French nation. It was an uprising of the common people against an exploitative aristocracy, an absolute monarchy, and an obscurantist church. It pitted poor against rich, peasant against lord, burgher against nobleman. Divisions and contradictions ran through those lines of opposition. But the revolutionaries were united by a common commitment to the rights of man and the ideal of liberty, equality, fraternity. For my part, I find those aspirations valid and moving, a crucial part of history "as it actually was."

Your writer never mentions them. Instead of worrying about distinctions between left and right, revolution and counterrevolution—questions of life and death for the revolutionaries—he blurs everything into the background. The Revolution appears as nothing more than an "establishing shot, tilted angle" and a "mob roar, off stage." It is the revolution he might have read about in *A Tale of Two Cities* and thought he could translate into the idiom of *Dallas* and *Animal House*. It is a soap opera revolution, full of sex and violence, signifying nothing.

Despite every effort to discard my tweed, I see that I am sounding professorial after all. As a historian, I hold with those who see history as an imaginative construct, something that needs to be thought through and reworked endlessly. But I don't think it can be made into anything that strikes our fancy. We cannot ignore the facts or spare ourselves the trouble of digging them up, simply because we hear that everything is "discourse." History can be done worse rather than better, and the worst version of all, at least for a nation of television watchers, may be history as docudrama.

Yours sincerely,
Robert Darnton

Journalism: All the News That Fits We Print

ANYONE STRUGGLING with the social history of ideas is bound to look to the social sciences for inspiration, or at least shortcuts. For my part, when I get mired in research on the ideological origins of the French Revolution, I often lift up my eyes to sociology, anthropology, and political science and strain for a glimpse of something like a Northwest Passage to the past. But I have never broken through.

The fault, I know, lies with my own feebleness of wit, yet sometimes I suspect that social scientists live in a world beyond the reach of ordinary mortals, a world organized in perfect patterns of behavior, peopled by ideal types, and governed by correlation coefficients that exclude everything but the most standard of deviations. Such a world can never be joined with the messiness of history. It cannot even find anchorage in the present—or so it seemed to me after an attempt to circumnavigate the literature in one of the most vital social sciences, communication theory. I ran aground while reading "Newsmen's Fantasies, Audiences, and Newswriting" by Ithiel de Sola Pool and Irwin Shulman in *Public Opinion Quarterly* (Summer 1959). It touched off some reflections on my earlier experience as a newspaper reporter, which I offer in the hope of providing some perspective on what is now hardening into a distinct discipline, the sociology of the media.

Pool and Shulman set out to understand the communication process as it occurs in newswriting. They supplied four groups of journalism students with facts culled from newspaper stories, some of which conveyed good news; others, bad. Each student assembled the facts into his own version of the stories and then listed people who came to mind when he thought back over the writing. The result was a list of "image persons," who could be taken to represent the student writers' internal sense of their readership. The experimenters then interviewed the students in order to classify these imaginary readers into two groups, the "critical" and the "supportive." Finally, they checked the stories for accuracy; and, sure enough, a correlation emerged: the students with supportive "image persons" reported good news more accurately than they reported bad news, while those with critical "image persons" reported bad news with more accuracy.

Pool and Shulman had come up with a formula for measuring the distortion factor in newswriting. They seemed to have uncovered governing laws, which could be expressed with mathematical precision, behind the mysterious process of reducing the day's events to stories. And their work fit nicely into the growing debate about "feedback" and "noise" and other variables that are central to communication theory, now that a new generation has abandoned the model that prevailed in the innocent days when communication was understood as a one-way process of implanting messages in receivers. We have now graduated to "images."

The logic seemed unassailable. Yet when I thought back to my own work on *The New York Times,* I remembered that the only "image person" I had encountered was a twelve-year-old girl. The reporters in the newsroom believed that the editors expected them to aim their stories at this imaginary creature. Some thought that she appeared in *The Style Book of The New York Times,* although she only existed in our minds.

"Why twelve years old?" I used to ask myself. "Why a girl?" "What are her views on slum clearance in the South Bronx?" But I knew that she was nothing more than a figure in the folklore of 43rd Street and that she merely functioned as a reminder for us to keep our copy clear and clean.

We never wrote for the "image persons" conjured up by social science. We wrote for one another. Our primary "reference group," as it might be known in communication theory, was spread around us in the newsroom, or the "snake pit," as we called it. We knew that no one would jump on our stories as quickly as our colleagues, for reporters make the most voracious readers, and they have to win their status anew each day as they expose themselves before their peers in print.

The Structure of the Newsroom

There are structural elements to the status system of the newsroom, as its layout indicates. The managing editor rules from within an office; and lesser editors command clusters of "desks" (foreign desk, national desk, city or "metropolitan" desk) at one end of the room, an end that stands out by the different orientation of the furniture and that is enclosed behind a low fence. At the other end, row upon row of reporters' desks face the editors across the fence. They fall into four sections. First, a few rows of star reporters led by luminaries like Homer Bigart, Peter Kihss, and McCandlish Phillips. Then three rows of rewrite men, who sit to the side of the stars at the front of the room so that they can be near the command posts during deadline periods. Next, a spread of middle-aged veterans, who have made their names and can be trusted with any story. And finally, a herd of young reporters on the make in the back of the room, the youngest generally occupying the remotest positions. Function determines some locations: sports, shipping, "culture," and "society" have their own corners; and copy readers sit accessibly to the side. But to the eye of the initiate, the general lines of the statue system stand out as clearly as a banner headline.[1]

The most expert eye in the city room belongs to the city editor. From his point of maximal visibility, he can survey his entire staff and can put each man in his place, for he alone knows the exact standing of everyone. The "staffer" is only aware of occupying an indeterminate position in one of the four sections. He therefore tries to trace the trajectory of his career by watching the key variable in the functioning of the city room: the assignment. A reporter who keeps a string of good assignments going for several weeks is destined to move up to a desk nearer the editor's end of the room, while a man who constantly bungles stories will stagnate in his present position or will be exiled to Brooklyn or "society" or "the West Side shack" (a police beat now extinct and replaced, functionally, by New Jersey). The daily paper shows who has received the best assignments. It is a map, which reporters learn to read and to compare with their mental map of the city room in an attempt to know where they stand and where they are headed.

But once you have learned to read the status system, you must learn to write. How do you know when you have done a good job on a story? When I was a greenhorn on *The Times,* I began one week with a "profile" or man-in-the-news, which won a compliment from the assistant city editor and a coveted out-of-town assignment for the next day. Half the police force of a small town had been arrested for stealing stolen goods, and I found a cop who was willing to talk, so the story made the "second front," the front page of the second section, which attracts a good deal of attention. On the third day, I covered the centenary celebrations at Cornell. They satisfied my ego

(I rode back to New York in the private plane that normally served the president of the university) but not my editor: I filed seven hundred and fifty words, which were cut down to five hundred. Next, I went to a two-day convention of city planners at West Point. Once again my ego swelled as the planners scrambled to get their names in *The Times,* but for the life of me I could not find anything interesting to say about them. I filed five hundred words, which did not even make the paper. For the next week I wrote nothing but obituaries.

Assignments, cuts, and the situating or "play" of stories therefore belong to a system of positive and negative reinforcements. By-lines come easily on *The Times,* unlike many papers, so reporters find gratification in getting their stories past the copy desk unchanged and into a desirable location in the paper, that is, close to the front and above the fold. Every day every foreign correspondent gets his reinforcement in the form of "frontings," a cable telling him which stories have made the front page and which have been "insided." Compliments also carry weight, especially if they come from persons with prestige, like the night city editor, the stars, or the most talented reporters in one's own territory. The city editor and managing editor dispense pats on the back, occasional congratulatory notes, and lunches; and every month the publisher awards cash prizes for the best stories. As the reinforcements accrue, one's status evolves. A greenhorn may eventually become a veteran or embark on more exotic channels of upward mobility by winning a national or foreign assignment. The veterans also include a sad collection of men on the decline, foreign correspondents who have been sent home to pasture, or bitter, ambitious men who have failed to get editorships. I often heard it said that reporting was a young man's game, that you passed your prime by forty, and that as you got older all stories began to seem the same.

Reporters naturally write to please the editors manipulating the reward system from the other end of the room, but there is no straightforward way of winning reinforcement by writing the best possible story. In run-of-the-mill assignments, a voice over the public address system—"Jones, city desk"—summons the reporter to the assignment editor, who explains the assignment: "The Kiwanis Club of Brooklyn is holding its annual luncheon, where it will announce the results of this year's charity drive and the winner of its Man of the Year Award. It's probably worth a good half-column, because we haven't done anything on Brooklyn recently, and the drive is a big deal over there." The editor tries to get the best effort from Jones by playing up the importance of the assignment, and he plants a few clues as to what he thinks "the story" is. A potential lead sentence may actually rattle around in Jones's head as he takes the subway to Brooklyn: "This year's charity drive in Brooklyn produced a record-breaking $. . . . . , the Kiwanis Club announced at its annual luncheon meeting yesterday." Jones arrives, interviews the president of the club, sits through a chicken dinner and several speeches, and learns that the drive produced a disappointing $300,000 and that the club named a civic-minded florist as its man of the year. "So what's the story?" the night city editor asks him upon his return. Jones knows better than to play up this nonevent to the night city editor, but he wants something to show for his day's work; so he explains the unspectacular character of the drive, adding that the florist seemed to be an interesting character. "You'd better lead with the florist, then. Two hundred words," says the night city editor. Jones walks off to the back of the room and begins the story: "Anthony Izzo, a florist who has made trees grow in Brooklyn for a decade, received the annual Man of the Year Award from the Brooklyn Kiwanis Club yesterday for his efforts to beautify the city's streets. The club also announced that its annual charity drive netted $300,000, a slight drip from last year's total, which the Club's president, Michael Calise, attributed to the high rate of unemployment in the area." The story occupies a mere fourth of a column well back in the second section of the paper. No one mentions it to Jones on the following day. No letters arrive for him from Brooklyn. And he feels rather dissatisfied about the whole experience, especially as Smith, who sits next to him in the remote centerfield section of the city room, made the second front with a colorful story about garbage dumping. But Jones consoles himself with the hope that he might get a better assignment today and with the reflection that the allusion to the tree growing in Brooklyn was a nice touch, which might have been noticed by the city editor and certainly had been appreciated by Smith. But Jones also knows that the story did not make his stock rise with the assignment editor, who had had a different conception of it, or with the night city editor, who had not had time to devote more than two or three minutes' thought to it, nor to the other editors, who must have perceived it as the hack job that it was.

In the case of an important assignment, like a multi-column "take out," the city editor might walk over to Jones' desk and discuss the story with him in a kind of conspiratorial huddle before a sea of eyes. Jones contacts a dozen different sources and writes a story that differs considerably from what the editor had in mind. The editor, who gets a carbon copy of everything submitted to the copy desk, disapproves of the text and has Jones summoned to him by the public address system. After huddling in alien territory, Jones negotiates his way back to his desk through the sea of eyes and tries again. Eventually he reaches a version that represents a compromise between the editor's preconceptions and his own impressions—but he knows that he would have won more points if his impressions had come closer to the mark imagined by the editor in the first place. And he did not enjoy walking the tightrope between his desk and the city editor before the crowd of reporters waiting for his status to drop.

Like everyone else, reporters vary in their sensitivity to pressure from their peer group, but I doubt that many of them—especially from the ranks of the greenhorns—enjoy being summoned to the city desk. They learn to escape to the bathroom or to crouch behind drinking fountains when the hungry eye of the editor surveys the field. When the fatal call comes over the public address system—"Jones, city desk"— Jones can feel his colleagues thinking as he walks past them, "I hope he gets a lousy assignment or that he gets a good one and blows it." The result will be there for everyone to see in to-morrow's paper. Editors sometimes try to get the best effort out of their men by playing them off against one another and by advocating values like competitiveness and "hustling." "Did you see how Smith handled that garbage story?" the city editor will say to Jones. "That's the kind of work we need from the man who is going to fill the next opening in the Chicago bureau. You should hustle more." Two days later, Jones may have outdone Smith. The immediacy and the irregularity of reinforcement in the assignment-publication process mean that no one, except a few stars, can be sure of his status in the newsroom.

Chronic insecurity breeds resentment. While scrambling over one another for the approval of the editors, the reporters develop great hostility to the men at the other end of the room, and some peer-group solidarity develops as a counter-force to the competitiveness. The reporters feel united by a sentiment of "them" against "us," which they express in horseplay and house jokes. (I remember a clandestine meeting in the men's room where one reporter gave a parody of urinating techniques among "them.") Many reporters, especially among the embittered veterans, deride the editors, who are mostly former reporters, for selling out to the management and for losing contact with the down-to-earth reality that can only be appreciated by honest "shoe-leather men." This antimanagement ideology creates a barrier to the open courting of editors and makes some reporters think that they write only to please themselves and their peers.

The feeling of solidarity against "them" expresses itself most strongly in the reporters' taboo against "piping" or distorting a story so that it fits an editor's preconceptions. Editors apparently think of themselves as "idea men," who put a reporter on the scent of a story and expect him to track it down and bring it back in publishable form. Reporters think of editors as manipulators of both reality and men. To them, an editor is a person who cares mainly about improving his position in his own, separate hierarchy by coming up with bright ideas and getting his staff to write in conformity to them. The power of editor over reporter, like that of publisher over editor, does indeed produce bias in newswriting, as has been emphasized in studies of "social control in the newsroom." But the reporters' horror of "piping" acts as a countervailing influence. For example, an assistant city editor on *The Times* once got an inspiration for a pollution story from his son, who complained that an ice-cream cone had become so filthy as he walked down the street that he had had to throw it into a trash can. The reporter dutifully built the story around the anecdote, adding as an embellishment that the unnamed little boy missed the trash can and walked away. The editor did not delete this last touch. He was delighted with the story, which presumably improved his standing with the other editors and the reporter's standing with him. But it made the reporter's reputation plummet among her peers and served as a deterrent against further "piping" on the other side of the fence.

The peer group's own standards of craftsmanship also pit reporters against copyeditors. Copyeditors tend to be a separate breed among newspapermen. Quiet, intense, perhaps more eccentric and more learned than most reporters, they are cast in the role of being sticklers for language. They go by the book—*The Style Book of The New York Times* on *The Times*—and they have their own hierarchy, which leads from the lowly members of their desk to the "slot man," who apportions the copy among them, to the "bull pen," where the final tailoring of each edition takes place, and ultimately to an assistant managing editor, who in my day was Theodore Bernstein, a man of great power and prestige. Copyeditors apparently think of themselves as second-class citizens in the newsroom: every day, as they see it, they save the reporters from dozens of errors of fact and grammar; yet the reporters revile them. "The game is to sneak some color or interpretation past that line of humorless zombies," one reporter explained to me. Copyeditors seem to view stories as segments in an unremitting flow of "copy," which cries out for standardization, while reporters regard each piece as their own. Personal touches—bright quotations or observations—satisfy the reporter's sense of craftsmanship and provoke the blue-penciling instinct of the copyeditor. Lead sentences produce the worst injuries in the reporter's unending battle with his editors and copyeditors; he may attribute cuts and poor play of his stories to the pressure of circumstances, but a change in his lead is a challenge to his news judgment, the ineffable quality that marks him as a "pro." To reverse the order of a reporter's first two paragraphs is to wound his professional identity. He will even take offense at slight changes of phrasing in his first sentence that he would hardly notice further down in the story. And a really bad lead can damage a man's career. A friend of mine once led a story with a remark about a baby who had been burned "to an almost unrecognizable crisp." It was the "almost" that especially outraged the editors. That lead cost him ten years in the lowliest position of the newsroom, or so we believed.

Reporters are held together by subgroups, which also mitigate competitiveness and insecurity and influence ways of writing. Clusters of reporters form according to age, lifestyle, or cultural background (City College vs. Harvard in the early 1960s at *The Times*). Some have lunch together, buy each other drinks in certain bars, or exchange family visits. A reporter develops trust in his subgroup. He consults it while working on stories and pays attention to its shop talk. A reporter in my group once had to do a rushed story about a confusing change in the city's incomprehensible welfare programs. Four or five of us went over his material, trying to extract some meaning from it, until one person finally pronounced, "It's a holding operation." That became the lead of the story and the idea around which the entire article was organized. Almost every article develops around a core conception of what constitutes "the story," which may emerge from the reporter's contacts with allies in the city room as well as from his dialogue with the editors. Just as messages pass through a "two step" or multistep communication process on the receiving end, they pass through several stages in their formation. If the communicator is a city reporter, he filters his ideas through reference groups and role sets in the city room before turning them loose on "the public."

The adjustment of writer to milieu is complicated by a final factor: institutional history. Long-term shifts in the power structure of a newspaper affect the way reporters write, even though the rank and file does not know exactly what goes on among editors and executives. Many papers are divided into semi-autonomous dukedoms ruled by the city editors, the foreign editor, and the national editor. Each of these men commands clusters of assistant editors and owes fealty to the managing editor, who in turn shares power with other executives, such as the business manager, and submits to the supreme sovereign of all, the publisher. At *The Times,* each editor dominates a certain proportion of the paper, so that in an issue of *n* columns, the city editor can expect to command *x* columns, the foreign editor *y* columns, and so forth. Of course, the proportions vary every day according to the importance of events, but in the long run they are determined by the ability of each potentate to defend and extend his domain. Changes in territoriality often take place at the "four o'clock conference" in the managing editor's office, where the day's paper takes shape. Here each editor summarizes the output of his staff and, day after day, builds up a case for the coverage of his area. A forceful city editor can get more space for city-room reporters and can inspire them with a fresh sense of the newsworthiness of their subjects.

City news underwent such a revival during my period at *The Times,* owing to the influence of a new city editor, A. M. Rosenthal. Before Rosenthal's editorship, New York stories tended to be thorough, reliable, conventional, and dull. Rosenthal wanted snappier, more original copy, and he wanted his men to "hustle." He therefore gave the best assignments to the reporters who conformed most closely to his standards, regardless of their position in the city room. This policy infuriated the veterans, who had learned to write according to the old rules and who believed in the established principle that one earned the right to the best assignments by years of solid service. They complained about trendiness, jazziness, superficiality, and sophomorism. Some of them resigned, some succeeded in brightening up their copy, and many withdrew into a world of private or peer-group bitterness. Most of the greenhorns responded by exuberant hustling. An alliance grew up between them and Rosenthal, a poor boy from the Bronx and City College who had hustled his way to the top of *The Times*. The qualities that had made him succeed—talent, drive, enthusiasm—now made for success in the city room. Of course those qualities were recognized under the old seniority system (otherwise Rosenthal himself would never have had such a spectacular career), but the new editor shifted the balance among the norms: the emphasis on hustling at the expense of seniority meant that achievement outweighed ascription in the determination of status.

The institutionalization of this new value system created more confusion and pain than can be conveyed by sociological terminology. In disturbing the established routes of mobility, Rosenthal did not completely cut himself off from the veterans. He did not interfere with the stars, and he did not win over all the greenhorns. Instead, he produced status anxiety everywhere, perhaps even for himself; for he seemed to have been surprised at the hostility he evoked from men who had been his friends, and he probably had worries about his own standing among the other editors and executives. The first months of his editorship constituted a difficult, transitional period in the city room. While the rules of the game were changing, no one knew where he stood; for standing seemed to fluctuate as erratically as the apportionment of assignments. A reporter might keep a string of good assignments going for a week, while a deadly rain of obituaries fell all around him, but he could also be banished overnight to the obit page or the "caboose" (the last news section of the Sunday paper). Hence the dread character of the summons over the public address system. Eventually, however, a new status system became established according to the new norms. Bolstered by raises and promotions, the bright, aggressive young men set the tone in the newsroom and moved on to more prestigious posts. By now several of them have become stars. Changes also occurred throughout the executive ranks. The paper acquired a new foreign editor, city editor, national editor, Washington bureau chief, and, ultimately, a new managing editor—A. M. Rosenthal. Gossips attributed these changes to personal machinations, but in its brutal, awkward way *The Times* was really rejuvenating itself by putting power into the hands of the generation that was ready and eager to succeed those who had reached their prime during World War II. Institutional evolution—the redistribution of power, the disturbance of role-sets, and the modification of norms—had an important influence on the way we wrote news, even though we were only half aware of the forces at work.

Secondary Reference Groups and the Public

Whatever their subliminal "images" and "fantasies," newspapermen have little contact with the general public and receive almost no feedback from it. Communication through newspapers is far less intimate than through specialized journals, whose writers and readers belong to the same professional group. I have received many more responses from articles in scholarly journals with tiny readerships than from front-page stories in *The Times* that must have been read by half a million persons. Even well-known reporters do not receive more than one or two letters a week from their readers, and very few reporters are really well known. The public rarely reads by-lines and is not apt to know that Smith has taken over the city hall beat from Jones.

It may be misleading to talk of "the public" as if it were a meaningful entity, just as it is inadequate, according to diffusion studies, to conceive of a "mass" audience of undifferentiated, atomistic individuals. The management of *The Times* assumes that its readers consist of heterogeneous groups: housewives, lawyers, educators, Jews, suburbanites, and so on. It calculates that certain groups will read certain parts of the paper, and not that a hypothetical general reader will read everything. It therefore encourages specialization among reporters. It hires a physician to cover medical news; it sends a future Supreme Court reporter to law school for a year; and it constantly opens up new beats such as advertising, architecture, and folk music. A serious sociology of newswriting ought to trace the evolution of beats and the branching out of specializations. It might also profit from the market research done by newspapers themselves, which hire specialists to devise sophisticated strategies for increasing their circulation.

The tendency toward specialization within newspapers encourages reporters to write for particular publics. City hall took notice when Smith replaced Jones, and Smith expected city hall to give his stories a careful reading. When Tom Wicker was covering the Kennedy White House, he not only knew that Kennedy read his stories attentively, he also knew exactly when and where Kennedy read them. The Pentagon correspondent, I was told, knew that MacNamara read defense stories between 7 and 8 A.M. every day while being driven to the office. Those reporters must have had vivid images of Kennedy and MacNamara scowling or smiling at their prose at certain times in certain places, and those images probably had more effect on their writing than any fuzzy view of the general public. For a reporter with a beat, "the morning after" begins to exist, psychologically, in the early afternoon, when he turns in a summary of the story he is about to write; for he knows that he must confront his news sources on the next day and that they can hurt his attempt to cover subsequent stories if he wounds them in writing this one. A reporter on general assignment suffers less from anticipatory retaliation, because he develops fewer stable relationships with the subjects of his stories.

I got the impression that newspapermen were very sensitive to the danger of becoming captives of their informants and of slipping into self-censorship. Conventional news sources, especially in government, struck me as being sophisticated about the give-and-take with reporters. Press spokesmen and public relations men are often former reporters, who adopt a tone of "we are all in this together" and try to seem frank or even irreverent in their off-the-record comments. In this way they can influence the "angle" or the "slant" of a story—the way it is handled and the general impression it creates—rather than its substance, which is often beyond their control. They attempt to influence the reporter during the stage before "the story" has congealed in his mind, when he is casting about for a central, organizing conception. If his lead sentence begins "The decline in unemployment . . ." instead of "The rise in inflation. . . ," they have succeeded in their task. Some press spokesmen hoard big stories and dispense them to reporters who write favorably; but that strategy can backfire, because reporters are sensitive to favoritism and, in my experience, tend to be cliquish rather than competitive. Outright manipulation may be less effective than the establishment of a certain amicable familiarity over a long period of daily contact. After a year or so on a single beat, reporters tend insensibly to adopt the viewpoint of the people about whom they write. They develop sympathy for the complexities of the mayor's job, the pressures on the police commissioners, and the lack of room for maneuver in the welfare department. The head of the London bureau of *The Times* when I worked there was vehemently pro-British, while the head of the Paris bureau was pro-French. They wrote against each other, while reporting Britain's negotiations to enter the Common Market. *The Times*

is so wary of the tendency among its foreign correspondents
to develop a bias in favor of the countries they inhabit that it
shifts them around every three years. On a humbler level, the
veteran crime reporters who dominate the press rooms in most
police headquarters develop a symbiotic relationship with the
police. In Newark there were four tough old reporters who
had done more time in headquarters than most of the cops.
They knew everyone of importance on the force: they drank
with cops, played poker with cops, and adopted the cops'
view of crime. They never wrote about police brutality.

A sociology of newswriting ought to analyze the symbiosis as well as the antagonisms that grow up between a
reporter and his sources, and it ought to take account of the
fact that those sources constitute an important element of his
"public." The reporting of news runs in closed circuits: it is
written for and about the same people, and it sometimes is
written in a private code. After finishing a story by James
Reston, which mentions "concern" about the Middle East
situation among "the highest sources," the initiate knows that
the President has confided his worries to "Scotty" in an inter-
view. It used to be said that the defense correspondent of the
Manchester Guardian wrote in a code that could be understood
only by the defense minister and his entourage, while the
ostensible message of the articles was intended for the general
public. The sense of belonging to a common in-group with
the persons who figure in their stories—the tendency toward
sympathy and symbiosis—creates a kind of conservatism among
reporters. You often hear that newsmen tend to be liberals or
Democrats, and as voters they may indeed belong to the left.
But as reporters, they generally struck me as hostile to ideology, suspicious of abstractions, cynical about principles, sensitive to the concrete and the complex, and therefore apt to
understand, if not condone, the status quo. They seemed

scornful of preachers and professors and quick with pejoratives like "do-gooder" and "egghead." Until some social psychologist devises a way to make an inventory of their value system, I am inclined to disagree with the common contention that journalism suffers from a liberal or left-wing bias. It does not follow, however, that the press consciously favors "the establishment." The "shoe-leather man" and the "flatfoot," the diplomatic correspondent and the foreign minister, are bound together by the nature of their jobs and inevitably develop some common points of view.

The producer-consumers of news who make up the inner circle of a reporter's public also include reporters from other papers who constitute his wider, occupational reference group. He knows that the competition will give his stories a careful going over, although, paradoxically, nothing could be less competitive than a group of reporters on the same story. The greenhorn may arrive on the scene with his editor's injunction to hustle ringing in his ears, but he soon will learn that the greatest of all sins is to scoop the other side, and that the penalty can be ostracism on the next assignment. If he works from a pressroom outside his paper, he may become totally absorbed in a group of interpaper peers. "Them" then becomes the city desks of all the papers and news services in town, who invade the repose and security of the men on the beat. Under those conditions, the failure to share information is such a crime that some reporters leak "exclusives" to colleagues on their own paper, so that the story will seem to come from "them" and will not disturb relations in the pressroom. In some pressrooms, one man does all the "leg work," or research, while the others play poker. Once he has collected the facts, he dictates them to the group, and each man writes his own version of the story or phones it in to a rewrite man in his city room. If a man is being pushed by his desk, he may by tacit agreement make extra phone calls to dig up exclusive quotes, "color," and "angles," but he would be condemned for doing this digging on his own initiative. An independent hustler can force hustling upon everyone else and will certainly break up the poker game, which is an important institution in many pressrooms. In the old press shack (now destroyed) behind police headquarters in Manhattan, the pot often came to fifty dollars, and the gamblers gathered around it included an assortment of cops and robbers. At critical moments, a cop who had dropped out of a hand would take calls from city desks. Reporters would suppress stories in order to avoid interrupting the game. The group was cohesive enough to keep "them" from discovering the news, except in the case of big stories, which threatened every reporter's security by arousing the appetite for "angles" and "exclusives" among his editors. To protect themselves, the reporters shared leads as well as details of their stories. After a news conference, they would mingle, filtering impressions and sounding one another out as to what the "story" was, until they reached a consensus and were able to file variants on the same lead: "Well, what d'ya think?" "Don't know." "Not much new, was there?" "Naw, that bit about weeding out corruption, he's said that before." "Maybe the part about civilianizing the force. . . ." "Yeah, civilianizing. . . ."

Competitiveness has also declined as a result of the attrition rate among newspapers. Reporters in one-newspaper cities only need to keep ahead of the wire services and television, which represent different genres of reporting and do not provide real competition. But if they work out of an important bureau, they are bound to be read by reporters who cover the same stories for papers in other towns. They know that the way those colleagues judge their work will determine their position in the status hierarchy of the local press corps. Professional reputation is an end in itself for many reporters, but it also leads to job offers. Recruiting often takes place through reporters who learn to respect one another by working together, just as promotions result from impressions created within a reporter's paper. *The Times* has a tenure system: once one has "made staff," he can remain there for life, but many lifers never make it out of the veterans' ranks in the city room. Professionalism is therefore an important ingredient in reportage: stories establish status, and reporters write to impress their peers.

They also get some feedback from friends and family, who look out for their by-lines and who provide such comments as: "That was a nice piece on Kew Gardens. I was down there last week, and the place really is going to hell"; or "Is Joe Namath really as obnoxious as he sounds?" Such remarks carry less weight than the reaction of fellow professionals, but they give reporters a reassuring sense that the message got through. "Mom" may not be a critical reader, but she is comforting. Without her, publishing a story can be like dropping a stone in a bottomless pit: you wait and wait, but you never hear the splash. Reporters also can expect some reaction from special segments of the public—from some readers in Kew Gardens or from some football players. Much of this kind of feedback tends to be negative, but reporters learn to discount for discontent among special interest groups. What they have difficulty in imagining is the effect of their stories upon the "mass" public, which probably is no mass at all but a heterogeneous collection of groups and individuals.

In short, I think Pool and Shulman err in assuming that newswriting is determined by a reporter's image of the general public. Newspapermen may have some such image, though I doubt it, but they write with a whole series of reference groups in mind: their copyreaders, their various editors, their different sets of colleagues in the city room, the sources and subjects of their articles, reporters on other papers, their friends and family, and special interest groups. Which of these readers takes precedence may vary from writer to writer and from story to story. They can make competing and contradictory demands upon a reporter. He may even find it impossible to reconcile the conception of "the story" that he gets from the assignment editor, the city editor, the night city editor, the copy reader, and his colleagues. Most of the time he tries to minimize "noise" and muddle through.

Occupational Socialization

Although some reporters may learn to write in journalism schools, where Pool and Shulman selected the subjects for the student group in their experiment, most of them (including many journalism school graduates) pick up newswriting in the course of an apprenticeship. They acquire attitudes, values, and a professional ethos while serving as copy boys in the city room; and they learn to perceive news and to communicate it while being "broken in" as rookie reporters.

By watching the smoke rise from Homer Bigart's typewriter near deadline time, by carrying his hot copy to the editors, and by reading it in cold print on the next day, the copy boy internalizes the norms of the craft. He acquires the tone of the newsroom by listening. Slowly he learns to sound more like a New Yorker, to speak more loudly, to use reporter's slang, and to increase the proportion of swear words in his speech. These techniques ease communication with colleagues and with news sources. It is difficult, for example, to get much out of a telephone conversation with a police lieutenant unless you know how to place your mouth close to the receiver and shout obscenities. While mastering these manner-isms, the copy boy insensibly stocks his mind with values. I remember vividly the disgust on a copy reader's face when he read a dispatch from a correspondent in the Congo that contained some hysterical phrases about bullets whizzing through the hotel room. It did not do to lose one's cool. Another correspondent, who had seen some rough fighting during the Algerian revolution, impressed me with a story about a lizard that got caught in the fan of his cooling unit in the Algiers bureau. He did not mention the slaughter of Algerians, but he had a great deal to say about the difficulty of writing while being sprayed with chopped lizard. One does not have to eavesdrop very had to get the gist of reporters' talk. They talk about themselves, not the personages of their stories—just as history professors talk about history professors, not Frederick II. It takes only a few weeks of carrying copy to learn how Mike Berger interviewed Clare Booth Luce, how Abe Rosenthal anatomized Poland, and how Dave Halberstam scored against the Diems in South Vietnam. In fact, the talk of *The Times* is institutionalized and appears as *Times Talk,* a house publication in which reporters describe their work. So even if you feel timid about approaching Tom Wicker, you may still read his own version of how he covered the assassination of President Kennedy.

Like other crafts, newspapering has its own mythology. Many times have I heard the tale of how Jamie MacDonald covered a raid over Germany from the turret of an RAF Bomber and how his wife Kitty, the greatest telephone operator of all time, put Mike Berger, the greatest city reporter, in touch with the governor of New York by establishing a radio link-up to a yacht in the middle of the Atlantic, where the governor was trying to remain incommunicado. The newsroom will not soon forget the day that Edwin L. James took up his duties as managing editor. He arrived in his fabled fur coat, sat down at the poker game that was always under way behind the rewrite desks, cleaned everybody out, and then joined "them" at the other end of the room, where he reigned thenceforth with supreme authority. Reporters sense an obligation to measure up to standards set in the past, though they know that they must look small in comparison with their mythical titans. It does not matter that Gay Talese can never write about New York as well as Mike Berger or that Abe Rosenthal can never command the managing editorship with the intelligence and flaire of Edwin L. James. The cult of the dead gives life to the quick. We wrote for Berger and James as well as for the living members of the city room.

Reporters' talk also concerns the conditions of their work: the problems of telephone and telegraph communication in underdeveloped countries, the censorship in Israel and the USSR, expense accounts. (I was so obtuse about filing for expenses in London that I did not even get the point of the classic stories about the Canadian correspondent who put in for a dogsled, or the African correspondent who invited reporters to spend weekends in his villa and then presented them with fake hotel bills to be filed with their expense accounts. I had to be told that my paltry expenses were lowering the living standard of the whole bureau.) One city room reporter told me that his proudest moment came when he was sent to cover a fire, discovered it was a false alarm, and returned with a story about false alarms. He felt he had transforms the humdrum into "news" by finding a new "angle." Another reporter said that he felt he had crossed the line dividing greenhorns and veterans one day when he was covering the civil war in the Congo. He got an open line to London at an unexpectedly early moment, when he had hardly finished reading over his notes. Knowing that he could not postpone communication and that every minute was terribly expensive, he wrote the story at great speed directly on the teletype machine. Some reporters remarked that they did not feel fully professional until they had completed a year on night rewrite, an assignment that requires great speed and clarity in writing. Others said that they gained complete confidence after successfully covering a big story that broke right on deadline.

Reporters gradually develop a sense of mastery over their craft—of being able to write a column in an hour on anything, no matter how difficult the conditions. The staff in London had great respect for Drew Middleton's ability to dictate a new lead to a story immediately after being awakened in the middle of the night and informed of a major new development. Failure to make a deadline is considered unspeakably unprofessional. One man near me in the city room had missed several deadlines. At about 4 P.M. when he had a big story, he would furtively gulp down a dixie cup full of bourbon from a bottle that he hid in the bottom drawer of his desk The copy boys knew all about him. In one sweep of the eye, they could take in the deadline agonies of dozens of men. Their job virtually forces anticipatory socialization upon them, for they have no fixed position but rove all over the city room, working with editors and copyreaders as well as reporters. They quickly learn to read the status system and have no difficulty in choosing positive and negative identity models. By listening to shop talk and observing behavior patterns, they assimilate an ethos: unflappability, accuracy, speed, shrewdness, toughness, earthiness, and hustle. Reporters seem somewhat cynical about the subjects of their stories and sentimental about themselves. They speak of the "shoe-leather man" as if he were the only honest and intelligent person in a world of rogues and fools. While everyone about him manipulates and falsifies reality, he stands aside and records it. I remember how one reporter introduced the figure of the newspaperman into an anecdote about politicians, ad men, and p.r. men: ". . . and then there was this guy in a trenchcoat." I never saw a trenchcoat anywhere in *The Times*. The reporters tended to outfit themselves at Brooks Brothers, which may have been a sign of ambivalence about an "establishment" that they pretended to despise. But they had a trenchcoat image of themselves. In fact, they had whole repertory of stylized images, which shaped the way they reported the news, and they acquired this peculiar mental set through their on-the-job training.

Standardizing and Stereotyping

Although the copy boy may become a reporter through different rites of passage, he normally undergoes a training period at police headquarters. After the "probation," as it is known at *The Times,* he is supposed to be able to handle anything; for the police story passes as an archetypical form of "news," and he is ready for the White House if he has survived headquarters—a parallel, incidentally, that suggests something of the spirit in which reporters approach their material.

I was inducted at the police headquarters of Newark, New Jersey, in the summer of 1959, when I worked for the *Newark Star Ledger*. On my first day of work, a veteran reporter gave me a tour of the place, which came to a climax in the photographic section. Since a police photographer takes a picture of every corpse that is found in Newark, the police have developed a remarkable collection of pictures of ripped-open and decomposed cadavers (the corpses of drowned persons are the most impressive), and they enjoy showing it off to greenhorns from the press. Press photographers build up their own collections, sometimes with help from the police, who get arrested prostitutes to pose for them. When I returned to the pressroom, a photographer from the *Mirror* gave me one of his obscene mug shots and showed me his homemade pinup collection, which featured his fiancée. A woman reporter than asked me whether I was a virgin, which produced a round of laughs from the men at the poker game. She was leaning back in her chair with her feet on the desk and her skirt around her hips, and my face changed instantly from green to red. Once the initiation was over, the poker game resumed, and I was left to do the "leg work" for everyone. That meant collecting the "squeal sheets," or summary reports of every action by the police, from an office upstairs. The reporters depended on the police radio and on tips from friends on the force to inform them of big stories, but they used the squeal sheets to check out the odd, man-bites-dog occurrence that has potential news value. Every hour or so I would bring a batch of squeal sheets down to the pressroom and would read them aloud to the poker game, announcing anything that struck me as a potential story. I soon discovered that I was not born with a nose for news; for when I smelled something newsworthy, the veterans usually told me that it was not a story, while they frequently picked up items that seemed unimportant to me. I knew, of course, that no news is good news and that only something awful could make a really "good" story. But it took some time before I learned not to get excited at a "d.o.a." (dead on arrival—a notation that often refers to heart attacks) or a "cutting" (a stabbing, usually connected with minor thefts or family quabbles that were too numerous to be newsworthy). Once I thought I had found such a spectacular squeal sheet—I think it included murder, rape, and incest—that I went directly to the homicide squad to check it out. After reading the sheet, the detective looked up at me in disgust. "Can't you see that it's 'black,' kid? That's no story." A capital "B" followed the names of the victim and the suspect. I had not known that atrocities among black persons did not constitute "news."

The higher the victim's status, the bigger the story: that

principle became clear when Newark was lucky enough to get the biggest crime story of the summer. A beautiful, wealthy debutante disappeared mysteriously from the Newark airport, and immediately the pressroom filled with hot-shot reporters from all over the East, who filed such stories as NEWARK HUNTS THE MISSING DEB, FIANCEE DISAPPEARS IN BROAD DAYLIGHT, and FATHER GRIEVES KIDNAPPED HEIRESS. We had not been able to get our desks to take more than a paragraph on the best muggings and rapes, but they would accept anything about the missing deb. A colleague and I filed a long report on HER LAST STEPS, which was nothing more than a description of the airport's floor plan with some speculation as to where the girl could have gone, but it turned out that "side bars" (stories devoted to secondary aspects of an event) about last steps often accompany stories about kidnappings and vanishings. We simply drew on the traditional repertory of genres. It was like making cookies from an antique cookie cutter.

Big stories develop in special patterns and have an archaic flavor, as if they were metamorphoses of Ur-stories that have been lost in the depths of time. The first thing a city-room reporter does after receiving an assignment is to search for relevant material among earlier stories filed in the "morgue." The dead hand of the past therefore shapes his perception of the present. Once he has been through the morgue, he will make a few phone calls and perhaps do some interviewing or observing outside the office. (I found that reporters consumed little shoe leather and ran up enormous telephone bills.) But the new information he acquires must fit into categories that he has inherited from his predecessors. Thus many stories are remarkably similar in form, whether they concern "hard news" or more stylized "features." Historians of American journalism—with the exception of Helen MacGill Hughes, a sociologist—seem to have overlooked the long-term cultural determinants of "news." French historians, however, have observed some remarkable cases of continuity in their own journalistic tradition. One story concerns a case of mistaken identity in which a father and mother murder their own son. It first was published in a primitive Parisian news-sheet of 1618. Then it went through a series of reincarnations, appearing in Toulouse in 1848, in Angoulême in 1881, and finally in a modern Algerian newspaper, where Albert Camus picked it up and reworked it in existentialist style for *L'Etranger* and *Malentendu*.[2] Although the names, dates, and places vary, the form of the story is unmistakably the same throughout those three centuries.

Of course, it would be absurd to suggest that newsmen's fantasies are haunted by primitive myths of the sort imagined by Jung and Lévi-Strauss, but newswriting is heavily influenced by stereotypes and by preconceptions of what "the story" should be. Without preestablished categories of what constitutes "news," it is impossible to sort out experience. There is an epistemology of the *fait divers*. To turn a squeal sheet into an article requires training in perception and in the manipulation of standardized images, clichés, "angles," "slants," and scenarios, which will call forth a conventional response in the minds of editors and readers. A clever writer imposes an old form on new matter in a way that creates some tension—will the subject fit the predicate?—and then resolves it by falling back on the familiar. Hence Jones's satisfaction with his lead sentence. Jones began by summoning up a standard image, the tree growing in Brooklyn, and just when the reader began to feel uneasy about where it might be going, Jones snapped it on the "peg" or the event of the day: the man-of-the-year award. "A florist gets a prize for making trees grow in Brooklyn," the reader thinks. "That's neat." It is the neatness of the

fit that produces the sense of satisfaction, like the comfort that
follows the struggle to force one's foot into a tight boot. The
trick will not work if the writer deviates too far from the
conceptual repertory that he shares with his public and from
the techniques of tapping it that he has learned from his predecessors.

The tendency toward stereotyping did not mean that the
half-dozen reporters in Newark police headquarters wrote exactly the same thing, though our copy was very similar and
we shared all our information. Some reporters favored certain
slants. One of the two women regulars in the pressroom frequently phoned around district police stations asking, "Any
teen-age sex parties lately?" As the acknowledged expert in
her field, she filed stories on teen-age sex that the rest of us
would not touch. Similarly, a fire buff among the Manhattan
reporters—a strange man with a wooden leg, who wore a
revolver around his chest—reported more fires than anyone
else. To remain as a "regular" in a police pressroom probably
calls for some congruity in temperament and subject matter,
and also for a certain callousness. I learned to be fairly casual
about "cuttings" and even "jumpers" (suicides who leap off
buildings), but I never got over my amazement at the reporters' ability to get "reaction" stories by informing parents of
their childrens' death: " 'He was always such a good boy.'
exclaimed Mrs. MacNaughton, her body heaving with sobs."
When I needed such quotes, I used to make them up, as did
some of the others—a tendency that also contributed toward
standardization, for we knew what "the bereaved mother"
and "the mourning father" should have said and possibly even
heard them speak what was in our minds rather than what was
on theirs. "Color" or feature stories left more room for im-
provization, but they, too, fell into conventional patterns.
Animal stories, for example, went over very well with the city

desk. I did one on policeman's horses and learned after its publication that my paper had carried the same story, more or less, at least twice during the previous ten years.

By the end of my summer in Newark, I had written a great many stories but had not received a by-line. One day, when I had nothing better to do, I checked out a squeal sheet about a boy who had been robbed of his bicycle in a park. I knew that my desk would not take it, but I produced four paragraphs on it anyway, in order to practice writing, and I showed it to one of the regulars during a lull in the poker game. You can't write that kind of a story straight as if it were a press release, he explained. And in a minute or so he typed out an entirely different version, making up details as he needed them. It went something like this:

Every week Billy put his twenty-five-cent allowance in his piggy bank. He wanted to buy a bike. Finally, the big day came. He chose a shiny red Schwinn, and took it out for a spin in the park. Every day for a week he rode proudly around the same route. But yesterday three toughs jumped him in the middle of the park. They knocked him from the bike and ran off with it. Battered and bleeding, Billy trudged home to his father, George F. Wagner of 43 Elm Street. "Never mind son," his dad said. "I'll buy you a new bike, and you can use it on a paper route to earn the money to pay me back." Billy hopes to begin work soon. But he'll never ride through the park again.

I got back on the phone to Mr. Wagner with a new set of questions: Did Billy get an allowance? Did he save it in a piggy bank? What was the color of the bicycle? What did Mr. Wagner say to him after the robbery? Soon I had enough details to fit the new pattern of the story. I rewrote it in the new style, and it appeared the next day in a special box, above the fold, on the front page, and with a by-line. The story produced quite a response, especially on Elm Street, where the Wagners' neighbors took up a collection for a new bicycle, as Mr. Wagner told me later. The commissioner of parks was upset and telephoned to explain how well the parks were patrolled and how new measures were being taken to protect citizens in the Elm Street area. I was astonished to discover that I had struck several chords by manipulating stock sentiments and figures: the boy and his bike, piggy-bank saving, heartless bullies, the comforting father. The story sounded strangely old-fashioned. Except for the bicycle, it might have come out of the mid-nineteenth century.

Several years later, when I did some research on popular culture in early modern France and England, I came across tales that bore a striking resemblance to the stories that we had written from the pressroom of police headquarters in Newark. English chapbooks, broadside ballads, and penny dreadfuls, French *canards, images d'Epinal.* and the *bibliothèque bleue* all purvey the same motifs, which also appear in children's literature and probably derive from ancient oral traditions. A nursery rhyme or an illustration from Mother Goose may have hovered in some semi-conscious corner of my mind while I wrote the tale of Billy and the bullies.

> I had a little moppet [a doll]
> I kept it in my pocket
> And fed it on corn and hay;
> Then came a proud beggar
> And said he would have her,
> And stole my little moppet away.

In their original version, nursery rhymes were often intended for adults. When journalists began to address their stories to a "popular" audience, they wrote as if they were communicating with children, or *"le peuple, ce grand enfant,"* as the French say. Thus the condescending, sentimental, and moralistic character of popular journalism. It would be misleading, however, to conceive of cultural diffusion exclusively as a "trickle-down" process, for currents move up from the common people as well as down from the élite. The *Tales* of Perrault, *The Magic Flute* by Mozart, and Courbet's *Burial at Ornans* illustrate the dialectical play between "high" and "low" culture in three genres during three centuries. Of course, we did not suspect that cultural determinants were shaping the way we wrote about crimes in Newark, but we did not sit down at our typewriters with our minds a *tabula rasa*. Because of our tendency to see immediate events rather than long-term processes, we were blind to the archaic element in journalism. But our very conception of "news" resulted from ancient ways of telling "stories."

Tabloid stories and crime reporting may be more stylized than the writing that goes into *The New York Times*, but I found a great deal of standardization and stereotyping in the stories of *The Times'* London bureau, when I worked there in 1963–64. Having spent more time in England than the other correspondents in the bureau, I thought I could give a truer picture of the country; but my copy was as stylized as theirs. We had to work within the conventions of the craft. When we covered diplomatic stories, the press spokesman for the Foreign Office would provide an official statement, an off-the-record explanation, and a background analysis for anything we needed to know. The information came so carefully packaged that it was difficult to unwrap it and to put it together in another way; as a result, diplomatic stories all sounded very much alike. In writing "color" stories, it was almost impossible to escape American clichés about England. The foreign desk devoured everything about the royal family, Sir Winston Churchill, cockneys, pubs, Ascots, and Oxford. When Churchill was ailing, I wrote a story about the crowds that gathered outside his window and quoted one man who had caught a glimpse of him as saying, "Blimey he's beautiful."

The cockney-Churchill combination could not be resisted. *The Times* put it on the front page, and it was picked up by dozens of other papers, wire services, and news magazines. Few foreign correspondents speak the language of the country they cover. But that handicap does not hurt them because, if they have a nose for news, they do not need a tongue or ears; they bring more to the events they cover than they take away from them. Consequently, we wrote about the England of Dickens, and our colleagues in Paris portrayed the France of Victor Hugo, with some Maurice Chevalier thrown in.

After leaving London, I returned to the newsroom of *The Times*. One of my first stories concerned a "homicidal maniac" who had scattered his victims' limbs under various doorsteps of the West Side. I wrote it up as if I were composing an ancient *canard: "Un homme de 60 ans coupé en morceaux. . . . Détails horribles!!!"*[3] When I had finished the story, I noticed one of the graffiti scribbled on the walls of the pressroom in the headquarters of the Manhattan police: "All the news that fits we print." The writer meant that one can only get articles into the paper if there is enough space for them, but he might have been expressing a deeper truth: newspaper stories must fit cultural preconceptions of news. Yet 8 million people live out their lives every day in New York City, and I felt overwhelmed by the disparity between their experience, whatever it was, and the tales that they read in *The Times*.

One man's encounter with two newspapers hardly provides enough material to construct a sociology of newswriting. I would not presume to pronounce on the meaning of other reporters' experience, because I never got beyond the greenhorn stage and because I did not work on papers that typify either "yellow" or "quality" journalism. Styles of reporting vary according to time, place, and the character of each newspaper. The American way of writing news differs from the European and has differed throughout American history. Benjamin Franklin probably did not worry about an occupational ethos when he wrote the copy, set the type, pulled the sheets, distributed the issues, and collected the revenue of *The Pennsylvania Gazette*. But since Franklin's time, newspapermen have become increasingly enmeshed in complex professional relationships, in the newsroom, in the bureau, and on the beat. With specialization and professionalization, they have responded increasingly to the influence of their professional peer group, which far exceeds that of any images they may have of a general public.

In emphasizing this influence, I do not mean to discount others. Sociologists, political scientists, and experts on communication have produced a large literature on the effects of economic interests and political biases on journalism. It seems to me, however, that they have failed to understand the way reporters work. The context of work shapes the content of news, and stories also take form under the influence of inherited techniques of storytelling. Those two elements of news-writing may seem to be contradictory, but they come together during a reporter's "breaking in," when he is most vulnerable and most malleable. As he passes through this formative phase, he familiarizes himself with news, both as a commodity that is manufactured in the newsroom and as a way of seeing the world that somehow reached *The New York Times* from *Mother Goose*.

Publishing: A Survival Strategy for Academic Authors

Y OU ARE UNPUBLISHED, unknown, and have just finished a dissertation on urban politics in the Midwest. Or you made tenure in the 1960s but haven't yet made it into print, although your friends assure you that your manuscript on the structure of metaphor in Jane Austen will be gobbled up by a university press. Or you are a veteran of the lecture hall and want to recast your course on "Byzantium Between East and West" as a book. What do you do? You certainly face difficulties, because hard times in higher education and in publishing have made it harder than ever for academic authors to get their work accepted by university presses.

I can appreciate the degree of difficulty, because I recently completed a four-year term on the editorial board of the Princeton University Press. Having cleaned out my files—not "files" actually, but seven cardboard cartons crammed with readers' reports and minutes of board meetings—I can offer an account of the publishing process to the person it affects most deeply but who knows least about it—namely, the academic author. Princeton follows some procedures that do not exist in other houses, but its experience is fairly typical of the better university presses. So a report on how manuscripts are

accepted at Princeton should be of some help to authors dealing with presses everywhere in the world of scholarly publishing.

First, dear author, you should know that the odds are stacked
against you. I figure them at nine to one or ten to one, calculating the number of manuscripts submitted against the number accepted. Despite the hard times that have hit academic
life—or because of them—the submissions increase almost every
year. In fiscal 1972, the first year for which we have figures,
the Princeton University Press received 740 manuscripts. In
1981, it received 1,129—an increase of 52 percent. In 1971 it
accepted 83 manuscripts. In 1981 it accepted 118—an increase
of 42 percent. In retrospect, the pattern seems clear: the pressure from submissions rose steadily throughout the 1970s,
shot up in 1976 and 1977, and broke the 1,000 mark in 1980.
The press responded to the flood of manuscripts by increasing
the flow of books, so that it now plans to accept about 120
manuscripts a year, financial conditions permitting.

That is a huge job both for the editorial board, which faces
tougher decisions at every meeting, and for the editors, who
must cope with wave after wave of manuscripts and pass on
an increasing number of "nos" to an increasing population of
disappointed authors. Seen from the author's point of view,
the process looks still tougher. In a given year, your manuscript will be one of about 1,100 considered by the press, and
you hope that it will be one of 120 accepted for publication.
To do so, it must clear a series of hurdles. It must catch the eye
of an editor, win the favor of two or sometimes three readers,
make a preliminary cut at a pre-editorial board meeting, and
survive the final selection at a monthly meeting of the editorial
board, when four professors will choose a dozen manuscripts
from a field of fifteen to nineteen. There is no ironclad quota,
but there are always losers—and more of them each year as

the competition gets stiffer. So how to win? After going through my cardboard cartons, I have come up with the answer: a surefire survival strategy for authors, using six easy stratagems.

I. Don't submit a book. Submit a series. We at Princeton turn down books by the hundreds, but as far as I know we have never turned down a series, and we took on a half dozen during my four years on the board. Other presses do the same, especially in the natural sciences, where the craze for series is strongest. If you are merely a humanist, you could propose a series on the human condition and then slip in as its first volume your monograph on Jane Austen or urban politics in the Midwest.

II. If you must propose a book, make it a book about birds. We never turn down field guides, and we have accepted books about birds from every corner of the earth—Colombia, West Africa, Russia, China, Australia. . . . You can't lose, at least not with Princeton. Other presses find other subjects irresistible. You might try country houses with Yale and cookery with Harvard.

III. If you can't come up with a field guide to birds, choose one of the following subjects: William Blake; Samuel Beckett; the nobility of almost any French province between the sixteenth and eighteenth centuries; a new theory of justice; a translation of anything Japanese, but preferably poetry, which should be "linked" and located at some point in the period between 2000 B.C. and 1960, although any other period will do.

IV. Tactics. It is not enough to select the right subject. You have to tackle it in the right manner, and the tactics vary according to field. For example:

Politics. The press reader must be able to say in his report, "This study combines hard digging in empirical data with a significant contribution to theory." I especially recommend the mining industry in Peru and dependency theory, or Bolivian copper and modernization, in a suitably revisionist version.

English. You must prove that you know all about the latest lit-crit theory from Paris and New Haven and that you don't believe in it.

Art History. Keep it esoteric. Thirteenth-century stained glass will do, but it must be from Burgundy, not Paris or Chartres. You can always turn in a *catalogue raisonné* of some collection, although we have about exhausted the Metropolitan Museum of Art.

History. Say it's anthropology.

Anthropology. Say it's history.

History and Anthropology. Use the microcosm-macrocosm device. In history you must be able to see the universe in a grain of sand—say, Springfield, Massachusetts, in the eighteenth century. In anthropology you should be able to construct a symbolic universe from a rite of passage—say, a Javanese funeral.

V. Here are some tactical principles to follow, irrespective of field:

Be interdisciplinary. Mix fields; it makes you seem more innovative. You can even mix metaphors to show that you are at the cutting edge of the frontiers of knowledge. Emulate the Princeton faculty wife who remarked to a visiting dignitary at a university reception for members of the Institute for Advanced Study, "It's so nice of you people from the institute to come here and cross-fertilize us."

Be risky or, rather, appear to be. Say, in effect, "This is a far-out book. I dare you to publish it." And then write something ordinary. When I was on the editorial board, I felt oppressed by creeping monographism, the tendency to write more and more about less and less, to smother subjects in erudition, and to reduce the idea-to-footnote ratio to the vanishing point. So I proposed a risk quota. We were to build risk taking into our regular publishing program by setting aside a half-dozen slots for unorthodox books. I thought we might even allot a risk book or two to each editor, with a minimum of vetoing by the editorial board, so that the editors could enjoy some free rein. As a result, the same kind of monographs continued to come in, but a new argument accompanied them: "It's a risky book; it will draw some criticism, but it will stir things up." This made us all feel better.

Be revisionist. It is always good to overturn some "classic" thesis. But be careful to catch the cycle at the right moment, because a revision of a revision has a way of making you seem to be back at square one.

Be naughty, just a little bit. A manuscript that is not merely risky but also risqué stands a chance of standing out from the other 1,119. This stratagem is especially recommended for tables of contents, which in any case are all that most board members will be able to read. A recent example: "Sequential Sex Reversal," "Conflict Situations for the Sex Ratio," "Outcrossed Hermaphrodites." We accepted this manuscript for our series on population biology without a blush. It is all about birds and bees, although it contains a section on barnacles too. Before joining the board, I had never considered the sex life of barnacles.

VI. Choose the right title. Two principles prevail here: alliteration and the colon. The alliteration usually occurs in the main title. It should be short, suggestive, poetic if possible, and so literary that the reader can form only the foggiest idea of the book's contents. Then comes the colon followed by a subtitle telling what the book is about. Some examples, chosen from the lists of "Manuscripts Submitted," which the press receives almost every week (I must admit that we chose very few of these for publication):

The Pause of the Pendulum: Portugal Between Revolution and Counter-Revolution

Notice the prevalence of p's and the carryover of the alliteration from the main title to the subtitle. It's what I call the Peter Piper Principle. Thus:

Peril, Pestilence, and Perfidy: The Making of Colonial Lucknow, 1856–1877

Pashas, Pilgrims, and Provincial Groups: Ottoman Rule in Damascus, 1807–1858

The Promise of Punishment: Prisons in Nineteenth-Century France

Pictures and Punishment: Art in the Service of Criminal Prosecution During the Florentine Renaissance

Why this domination of the letter p? I don't know, unless Peter Piper invaded the collective subconscious from the nursery. But variations are permitted. You may alliterate in the subtitle:

Women in Agriculture: Peasant Production and Proletarianization in Three Andean Regions

And you may use other letters. M is very good; it warms up the reader:

The Mediated Muse: English Translations of Ovid, 1560–1700

Measures and Men: Visual and Verbal Political Satire in Early Georgian England, from Pope to Churchill

Metaphors of Masculinity: Sex and Status in Andalusian Folklore

L can have a lilting, lyrical effect:

Lives, Lovers, and Lyrics: The Biographies of the Troubadours

R is also recommended. It revs up the reader:

Rhetoric, Royce, and Romanticism: The Impact of Idealism on Nineteenth-Century Theories of Discourse

This last title illustrates another imperative: go from the big to the small. A title should operate like a funnel. Suck the reader in by announcing something grand in the main title, then squeeze him through the subtitle into a monograph:

Reform, Repression, and Revolution: Radicalism and Loyalism in the North-West of England, 1789–1803

Class, Conflict, and Control: Culture and Ideology in Two Neighborhoods of Kingston, Jamaica

Personality and Politics: Hidden Patterns in Late Medici Art Patronage

Drink and Disorder: Temperance Reform in Cincinnati from the Washingtonian Revival to the WCTU

Land and Labor: Economic Dependency and Social Order in Springfield, Massachusetts, 1636–1703

The Irish Inner Circle: Slatemaking in Daley's Illinois

Neither Sleet, nor Snow, nor Sabbath: The Sunday Mail Controversy, 1810–1830

Fashion and Fetishism: A History of Tight-Lacing and Other Forms of Body Sculpture in the West

By way of refinement, you can add a "from . . . to" construction. It conveys a sense of direction and seems to be especially effective when alliterated with the letter *c*:

From Concessions to Confrontation: The Politics of the Mahar Community in Maharashtra

*From Custom to Capital: The English Novel and the Industrial
   Revolution*
*From Clan to Class: The Relationship of Social Structure to Eco-
   nomic and Demographic Chance in São Paulo, Brazil, 1554–
   1850*

Occasionally, but only with the greatest caution, it is permitted to stray from alliteration. But you must have very
strong reasons, such as the need to overwhelm the reader by a
blast of poetry:

Forked Branches: Unpublished Medieval Translations of Ezra Pound
*The Windless Perpetual Morning: Archetypal Primitive Symbolism
   in the Poetry of Theodore Roethke*

The poetic touch naturally goes best with literary subjects:

*Strange Chords, Lucent Verdure: Mastery and Madness in John
   Ruskin*

But it may be used in art history:

The Armor of Light: Stained Glass in Western France, 1250–1325

And it will do nicely for any subject that is sufficiently deep:

*The Secret of the Black Chrysanthemum: Charles Olson's Use of
   the Writings of C. G. Jung*

Poetic effect also can be achieved by evocative use of the
indefinite article:

*A Complex Weave: The Writing of Thoreau's "A Week on the
   Concord and Merrimack Rivers" with the Text of the First
   Draft*
A Playful Judgment: Satire and Society in Wilhelmine Germany

If you favor the definite article, you had better stick with
alliteration:

The Sultan's Servants: The Transformation of Ottoman Provincial Administration, 1550–1650

The Wanton Warrior: A Study of Elizabethan Dramatic Convention and the Decline of Figural Representation

But a sufficiently vivid image can free you from the need to alliterate. Indeed, it can conjure up an entire civilization, especially if it evokes territory in the eastern hemisphere:

Mandarin Ducks and Butterflies: Popular Fiction in Early Twentieth-Century Chinese Cities

Bear in the Land of Morning Calm: Soviet Policy Toward Korea, 1964–1968

The Pagoda, the Skull, and the Samurai

The last title provides a rare example of poetry triumphing over the colon. But you should never do without a subtitle unless you are absolutely certain of the power of your poetry; thus:

Trumpets Blown in the Empty Night

I still don't know what that book was about, nor what the subject is of another manuscript without a subtitle that we received recently: *Mostly Chaos*. It seems to have something to do with physics.

A last class of exceptions concerns unorthodox moves, in which you take the reader by surprise instead of captivating him by sounds and images. With the strategem of the all-embracing title, you are bound to get him somewhere and so may drop the alliteration:

Marxism and Domination: A Neo-Hegelian, Feminist, Psychoanalytic Theory of Sexual, Political, and Technological Liberations

Psychoaesthetics, Psychologism, Psychology: A Phenomenological Inquiry into Their Relations

You may even try to tickle the reader's funny bone:

On the Rocks: A Geology of Britain
Loom with a View: Vincent van Gogh "A Son Métier"
La Vie en Prose: Readings of Early French Novels

And finally, you can try to hit him between the eyes:

The Phallic Imperative: An Analysis and Critique of Masculine Sexual Priorities
Certainly: A Refutation of Skepticism

I should end on that positive note. But in reviewing the strategies available to academic authors, I must confess to some skepticism about certainty of any sort in the publishing business—and to a secret admiration for two professors: the first is a physicist who called his books *Lecture Notes for Astrophysical Sciences 522,* the second a biologist who called his *The Nesting Behavior of Dung Beetles.* Neither, I'm sorry to say, made it into print.

PART THREE

The Printed Word

REPUBLICAN SCHOOLTEACHER, *1793*.

SEVEN

What Is the History
of Books?

"*Histoire du livre*" in France, *"Geschichte des Buchwesens"* in Germany, "history of books" or "of the book" in English-speaking countries—its name varies from place to place, but everywhere it is being recognized as an important new discipline. It might even be called the social and cultural history of communication by print, if that were not such a mouthful, because its purpose is to understand how ideas were transmitted through print and how exposure to the printed word affected the thought and behavior of mankind during the last five hundred years. Some book historians pursue their subject deep into the period before the invention of movable type. Some students of printing concentrate on newspapers, broadsides, and other forms besides the book. The field can be extended and expanded in many ways; but for the most part, it concerns books since the time of Gutenberg, an area of research that has developed so rapidly during the last few years that it seems likely to win a place alongside fields like the history of science and the history of art in the canon of scholarly disciplines.

Whatever the history of books may become in the future, its past shows how a field of knowledge can take on a distinct scholarly identity. It arose from the convergence of several disciplines on a common set of problems, all of them having to do with the process of communication. Initially, the prob-

lems took the form of concrete questions in unrelated branches
of scholarship: What were Shakespeare's original texts? What
caused the French Revolution? What is the connection between culture and social stratification? In pursuing those questions, scholars found themselves crossing paths in a no-man's
land located at the intersection of a half-dozen fields of study.
They decided to constitute a field of their own and to invite in
historians, literary scholars, sociologists, librarians, and anyone else who wanted to understand the book as a force in
history. The history of books began to acquire its own journals, research centers, conferences, and lecture circuits. It accumulated tribal elders as well as Young Turks. And although
it has not yet developed passwords or secret handshakes or its
own population of Ph.D.'s, its adherents can recognize one
another by the glint in their eyes. They belong to a common
cause, one of the few sectors in the human sciences where there
is a mood of expansion and a flurry of fresh ideas.

To be sure, the history of the history of books did not
begin yesterday. It stretches back to the scholarship of the
Renaissance, if not beyond; and it began in earnest during the
nineteenth century when the study of books as material objects led to the rise of analytical bibliography in England. But
the current work represents a departure from the established
strains of scholarship, which may be traced to their nineteenth-century origins through back issues of *The Library* and
Börsenblatt für den Deutschen Buchhandel or theses in the Ecole
des Chartes. The new strain developed during the 1960s in
France, where it took root in institutions like the Ecole Pratique des Hautes Etudes and spread through publications like
L'Apparition du livre (1958), by Lucien Febvre and Henri-Jean
Martin, and *Livre et société dans la France du XVIIIᵉ siècle* (two
volumes 1965 and 1970) by a group connected with the VIᵉ
section of the Ecole Pratique des Hautes Etudes.

The new book historians brought the subject within the range of themes studied by the "*Annales* school" of socioeconomic history. Instead of dwelling on fine points of bibliography, they tried to uncover the general pattern of book production and consumption over long stretches of time. They compiled statistics from requests for *privilèges* (a kind of copyright), analyzed the contents of private libraries, and traced ideological currents through neglected genres like the *bibliothèque bleue* (primitive paperbacks). Rare books and fine editions had no interest for them; they concentrated instead on the most ordinary sort of books because they wanted to discover the literary experience of ordinary readers. They put familiar phenomena like the Counter Reformation and the Enlightenment in an unfamiliar light by showing how much traditional culture outweighed the avant-garde in the literary fare of the entire society. Although they did not come up with a firm set of conclusions, they demonstrated the importance of asking new questions, using new methods, and tapping new sources.[1]

Their example spread throughout Europe and the United States, reinforcing indigenous traditions, such as reception studies in Germany and printing history in Britain. Drawn together by their commitment to a common enterprise, and animated by enthusiasm for new ideas, book historians began to meet, first in cafés, then in conferences. They created new journals—*Publishing History, Bibliography Newsletter, Nouvelles du livre ancien, Revue française d'histoire du livre* (new series), *Buchhandelsgeschichte,* and *Wolfenbütteler Notizen zur Buchgeschichte.* They founded new centers—the Institut d'Etude du Livre in Paris, the Arbeitskreis für Geschichte des Buchwesens in Wolfenbüttel, the Center for the Book in the Library of Congress. Special colloquia—in Geneva, Paris, Boston, Worcester, Wolfenbüttel, and Athens, to name only a few that

took place in the late 1970s—disseminated their research on an
international scale. In the brief span of two decades, the history of books had become a rich and varied field of study.

So rich did it prove, in fact, that it now looks less like a
field than a tropical rain forest. The explorer can hardly make
his way across it. At every step he becomes entangled in a
luxuriant undergrowth of journal articles and disoriented by
the crisscrossing of disciplines—analytical bibliography pointing
in this direction, the sociology of knowledge in that, while
history, English, and comparative literature stake out overlapping territories. He is beset by claims to newness—*"la nouvelle
bibliographie matérielle,"* "the new literary history"—and bewildered by competing methodologies, which would have
him collating editions, compiling statistics, decoding copyright law, wading through reams of manuscript, heaving at
the bar of a reconstructed common press, and psychoanalyz-
ing the mental processes of readers. The history of books has
become so crowded with ancillary disciplines that one can no
longer see its general contours. How can the book historian
neglect the history of libraries, of publishing, of paper, type,
and reading? But how can he master their technologies, especially when they appear in imposing foreign formulations, like
Geschichte der Appellstruktur and *Bibliométrie bibliologique?* It is
enough to make one want to retire to a rare book room and
count watermarks.

To get some distance from interdisciplinarity run riot, and
to see the subject as a whole, it might be useful to propose a
general model for analyzing the way books come into being
and spread through society. To be sure, conditions have varied so much from place to place and from time to time since
the invention of movable type that it would be vain to expect
the biography of every book to conform to the same pattern.
But printed books generally pass through roughly the same

life cycle. It could be described as a communications circuit that runs from the author to the publisher (if the bookseller does not assume that role), the printer, the shipper, the bookseller, and the reader. The reader completes the circuit because he influences the author both before and after the act of composition. Authors are readers themselves. By reading and associating with other readers and writers, they form notions of genre and style and a general sense of the literary enterprise, which affects their texts, whether they are composing Shakespearean sonnets or directions for assembling radio kits. A writer may respond in his writing to criticisms of his previous work or anticipate reactions that his text will elicit. He addresses implicit readers and hears from explicit reviewers. So the circuit runs full cycle. It transmits messages, transforming them en route, as they pass from thought to writing to printed characters and back to thought again. Book history concerns each phase of this process and the process as a whole, in all its variations over space and time and in all its relations with other systems, economic, social, political, and cultural, in the surrounding environment.

That is a large undertaking. To keep their task within manageable proportions, book historians generally cut into one segment of the communications circuit and analyze it according to the procedures of a single discipline—printing, for example, which they study by means of analytical bibliography. But the parts do not take on their full significance unless they are related to the whole, and some holistic view of the book as a means of communication seems necessary if book history is to avoid being fragmented into esoteric specializations cut off from each other by arcane techniques and mutual misunderstanding. The model shown in Figure 7.1 provides a way of envisaging the entire communication process. With minor adjustments, it should apply to all periods in the history of the

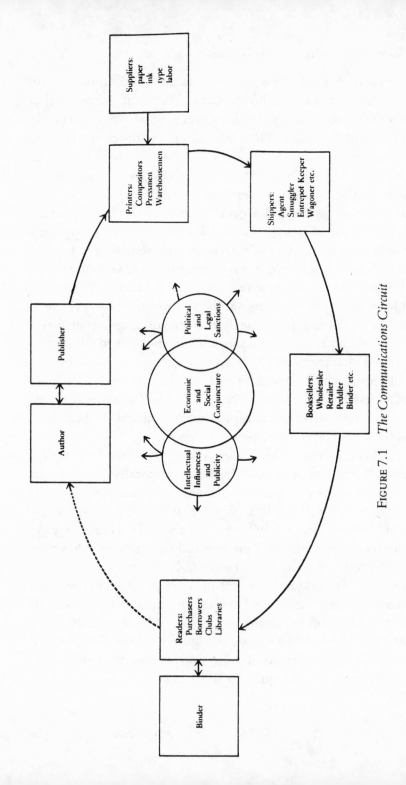

FIGURE 7.1   *The Communications Circuit*

printed book (manuscript books and book illustrations will have to be considered elsewhere), but I would like to discuss it in connection with the period I know best, the eighteenth century, and to take it up phase by phase, showing how each phase is related to (1) other activities that a given person has underway at a given point in the circuit, (2) other persons at the time point in other circuits, (3) other persons at other points in the same circuit, and (4) other elements in society. The first three considerations bear directly on the transmission of a text, while the last concerns outside influences, which could vary endlessly. For the sake of simplicity, I have reduced the later to the three general categories in the center of the diagram.

Models have a way of freezing human beings out of history. To put some flesh and blood on this one, and to show how it can make sense of an actual case, I will apply it to the publishing history of Voltaire's *Questions sur l'Encyclopédie,* an important work of the Enlightenment, and one that touched the lives of a great many eighteenth-century bookmen. One could study the circuit of its transmission at any point—at the stage of its composition, for example, when Voltaire shaped its text and orchestrated its diffusion in order to promote his campaign against religious intolerance, as his biographers have shown; or at its printing, a stage in which bibliographical analysis helps to establish the multiplication of editions; or at the point of its assimilation in libraries, where, according to statistical studies by literary historians, Voltaire's works occupied an impressive share of shelf space.[2] But I would like to consider the least familiar link in the diffusion process, the role of the bookseller, taking Isaac-Pierre Rigaud of Montpellier as an example, and working through the four considerations mentioned above.[3]

I

On August 16, 1770, Rigaud ordered thirty copies of the nine-volume octavo edition of the *Questions,* which the Société typographique de Neuchâtel (STN) had recently begun to print in the Prussian principality of Neuchâtel on the Swiss side of the French-Swiss border. Rigaud generally preferred to read at least a few pages of a new book before stocking it, but he considered the *Questions* such a good bet that he risked making a fairly large order for it, sight unseen. He did not have any personal sympathy for Voltaire. On the contrary, he deplored the philosophe's tendency to tinker with his books, adding and amending passages while cooperating with pirated editions behind the backs of the original publishers. Such practices produced complaints from customers, who objected to receiving inferior (or insufficiently audacious) texts. "It is astonishing that at the end of his career M. de Voltaire cannot refrain from duping booksellers," Rigaud complained to the STN. "It would not matter if all these little ruses, frauds, and deceits were blamed on the author. But unfortunately the printers and still more the retail booksellers are usually held responsible."[4] Voltaire made life hard for booksellers, but he sold well.

There was nothing Voltairean about most of the other books in Rigaud's shop. His sales catalogues show that he specialized somewhat in medical books, which were always in demand in Montpellier, thanks to the university's famous faculty of medicine. Rigaud also kept a discreet line of Protestant works, because Montpellier lay in Huguenot territory. And when the authorities looked the other way, he brought in a few shipments of forbidden books.[5] But he generally supplied his customers with books of all kinds, which he drew from an inventory worth at least forty-five thousand livres, the largest in Montpellier and probably in all Languedoc, according to a report from the intendant's *subdélégué*.[6]

Rigaud's way of ordering from the STN illustrates the character of his business. Unlike other large provincial dealers, who speculated on a hundred or more copies of a book when they smelled a best seller, he rarely ordered more than a half dozen copies of a single work. He read widely, consulted his customers, took soundings by means of his commercial correspondence, and studied the catalogues that the STN and his other suppliers sent to him (by 1785 the STN's catalogue included seven hundred and fifty titles). Then he chose about ten titles and ordered just enough copies of them to make up a crate of fifty pounds, the minimum weight for shipment at the cheaper rate charged by the wagoners. If the books sold well, he reordered them; but he usually kept his orders rather small, and made four or five of them a year. In this way, he conserved capital, minimized risks, and built up such a large and varied stock that his shop became a clearinghouse for literary demand of every kind in the region.

The pattern of Rigaud's orders, which stands out clearly from the STN's account books, shows that he offered his customers a little of everything—travel books, histories, novels, religious works, and the occasional scientific or philosophical treatise. Instead of following his own preferences, he seemed to transmit demand fairly accurately and to live according to the accepted wisdom of the book trade, which one of the STN's other customers summarized as follows: "The best book for a bookseller is a book that sells."[7] Given his cautious style of business, Rigaud's decision to place an advance order for thirty nine-volume sets of the *Questions sur l'Encyclopédie* seems especially significant. He would not have put so much money on a single work if he had not felt certain of the demand—and his later orders show that he had calculated correctly. On June 19, 1772, soon after receiving the last shipment of the last volume, Rigaud ordered another dozen sets; and he ordered two more two years later, although by then the STN had exhausted its stock. It had printed a huge edition, twenty-five hundred copies, approximately twice its usual press run, and the booksellers had fallen all over themselves in the rush to purchase it. So Rigaud's purchase was no aberration. It expressed a current of Voltaireanism that had spread far and wide among the reading public of the Old Regime.

II

How does the purchase of the *Questions* look when examined from the perspective of Rigaud's relations with the other booksellers of Montpellier? A book-trade almanac listed nine of them in 1777:[8]

Printer-Booksellers:	Aug. Franç. Rochard
	Jean Martel
Booksellers:	Isaac-Pierre Rigaud
	J. B. Faure
	Albert Pons
	Tournel
	Bascon
	Cézary
	Fontanel

But according to a report from a traveling salesman of the STN, there were only seven.[9] Rigaud and Pons had merged and completely dominated the local trade; Cézary and Faure scraped along in the middle ranks; and the rest teetered on the brink of bankruptcy in precarious boutiques. The occasional binder and under-the-cloak peddler also provided a few books, most of them illegal, to the more adventuresome readers of the city. For example, the demoiselle Bringand, known as "the students' mother," stocked some forbidden fruit "under the bed on the room to the right on the second floor," according to the report of a raid that was engineered by the established booksellers.[10] The trade in most provincial cities fell into the same pattern, which can be envisaged as a series of concentric circles: at the center, one or two firms tried to monopolize the market; around the margin, a few small dealers survived by specializing in chapbooks and old volumes, by setting up reading clubs *(cabinets littéraires)* and binderies, or by peddling their wares in the back country; and beyond the fringe of legality, adventurers moved in and out of the market, selling forbidden literature.

When he ordered his shipment of the *Questions,* Rigaud was consolidating his position at the center of the local trade. His merger with Pons in 1770 provided him with enough capital and assets to ride out the mishaps—delayed shipments, defaulting debtors, liquidity crises—that often upset smaller businesses. Also, he played rough. When Cézary, one of the middling dealers, failed to meet some of his payments in 1781, Rigaud drove him out of business by organizing a cabal of his creditors. They refused to let him reschedule the payments, had him thrown in prison for debt, and forced him to sell off his stock at an auction, where they kept down the prices and gobbled up the books. By dispensing patronage, Rigaud controlled most of Montpellier's binderies; and by exerting pressure on the binders, he produced delays and snags in the affairs of the other booksellers. In 1789 only one of them remained, Abraham Fontanel, and he stayed solvent only by maintaining a *cabinet littéraire,* "which provokes terrible fits of jealousy by the sieur Rigaud, who wants to be the only one left and who shows his hatred of me every day,"[11] as Fontanel confided to the STN.

Rigaud did not eliminate his competitors simply by out-doing them in the dog-eat-dog style of commercial capitalism of early modern France. His letters, theirs, and the correspon-dence of many other booksellers show that the book trade contracted during the late 1770s and 1780s. In hard times, the big booksellers squeezed out the small, and the tough out-lasted the tender. Rigaud had been a tough customer from the very beginning of his relations with the STN. He had ordered his copies of the *Questions* from Neuchâtel, where the STN was printing a pirated edition, rather than from Geneva, where Voltaire's regular printer, Gabriel Cramer, was producing the original, because he had extracted better terms. He also de-manded better service, especially when the other booksellers in Montpellier, who had dealt with Cramer, received their copies first. The delay produced a volley of letters from Ri-gaud to the STN. Why couldn't the STN work faster? Didn't it know that it was making him lose customers to his compet-itors? He would have to order from Cramer in the future if it could not provide quicker shipments at a lower price. When volumes one through three finally arrived from Neuchâtel, volumes four through six from Geneva were already on sale in the other shops. Rigaud compared the texts, word for word, and found that the STN's edition contained none of the addi-tional material that it had claimed to receive on the sly from Voltaire. So how could he push the theme of "additions and corrections" in his sales talk? The recriminations flew thick and fast in the mail between Montpellier and Neuchâtel, and they showed that Rigaud meant to exploit every inch of every advantage that he could gain on his competitors. More impor-tant, they also revealed that the *Questions* were being sold all over Montpellier, even though in principle they could not circulate legally in France. Far from being confined to the under-the-cloak trade of marginal characters like "the students' mother," Voltaire's work turned out to be a prize item in the scramble for profits at the very heart of the established book trade. When dealers like Rigaud scratched and clawed for their shipments of it, Voltaire could be sure that he was succeeding in his attempt to propel his ideas through the main lines of France's communications system.

III

The role of Voltaire and Cramer in the diffusion process raises the problem of how Rigaud's operation fit into the other stages in the life cycle of the *Questions*. Rigaud knew that he was not getting a first edition; the STN had sent a circular letter to him and its other main customers explaining that it would reproduce Cramer's text, but with corrections and additions provided by the author himself, so that its version would be superior to the original. One of the STN's directors had visited Voltaire at Ferney in April 1770 and had returned with a promise that Voltaire would touch up the printed sheets he was to receive from Cramer and then would forward them to Neuchâtel for a pirated edition.[12] Voltaire often played such tricks. They provided a way to improve the quality and increase the quantity of his books, and therefore served his main purpose—which was not to make money, for he did not sell his prose to the printers, but to spread Enlightenment. The profit motive kept the rest of the system going, however. So when Cramer got wind of the STN's attempt to raid his market, he protested to Voltaire, Voltaire retracted his promise to the STN, and the STN had to settle for a delayed version of the text, which it received from Ferney, but with only minimal additions and corrections.[13] In fact, this setback did not hurt its sales, because the market had plenty of room to absorb editions, not only the STN's but also one that Marc Michel

Rey produced in Amsterdam, and probably others as well. The booksellers had their choice of suppliers, and they chose according to whatever marginal advantage they could obtain on matters of price, quality, speed, and reliability in delivery. Rigaud dealt regularly with publishers in Paris, Lyon, Rouen, Avignon, and Geneva. He played them off against each other and sometimes ordered the same book from two or three of them so as to be certain of getting it before his competitors did. By working several circuits at the same time, he increased his room for maneuver. But in the case of the *Questions,* he was outmaneuvered and had to receive his goods from the circuitous Voltaire-Cramer-Voltaire-STN route.

That route merely took the copy from the author to the printer. For the printed sheets to reach Rigaud in Montpellier from the STN's shop in Neuchâtel, they had to wind their way through one of the most complex stages in the book's circuit. They could follow two main routes. One led from Neuchâtel to Geneva, Turin, Nice (which was not yet French), and Marseilles. It had the advantage of skirting French territory—and therefore the danger of confiscation—but it involved huge detours and expenses. The books had to be lugged over the Alps and pass through a whole army of middlemen—shipping agents, bargemen, wagoners, entrepôt keepers, ship captains, and dockers—before they arrived in Rigaud's storeroom. The best Swiss shippers claimed they could get a crate to Nice in a month for thirteen livres, eight sous per hundredweight; but their estimates proved to be far too low. The direct route from Neuchâtel to Lyon and down the Rhône was fast, cheap, and easy—but dangerous. The crates had to be sealed at their point of entry into France and inspected by the booksellers' guild and the royal book inspector in Lyon, then reshipped and inspected once more in Montpellier.[14]

Always cautious, Rigaud asked the STN to ship the first

volumes of the *Questions* by the roundabout route, because he knew he could rely on his agent in Marseilles, Joseph Coulomb, to get the books into France without mishap. They left on December 9, 1771, but did not arrive until after March, when the first three volumes of Cramer's edition were already being sold by Rigaud's competitors. The second and third volumes arrived in July, but loaded down with shipping charges and damaged by rough handling. "It seems that we are five or six thousand leagues apart," Rigaud complained, adding that he regretted he had not given his business to Cramer, whose shipments had already reached volume six.[15] By this time, the STN was worried enough about losing customers throughout southern France to set up a smuggling operation in Lyon. Their man, a marginal bookdealer named Joseph-Louis Berthoud, got volumes four and five past the guild inspectors, but then his business collapsed in bankruptcy; and to make matters worse, the French government imposed a tax of sixty livres per hundredweight on all book imports. The STN fell back on the Alpine route, offering to get its shipments as far as Nice for fifteen livres per hundredweight if Rigaud would pay the rest of the expenses, including the import duty. But Rigaud considered the duty such a heavy blow to the international trade that he suspended all his orders with foreign suppliers. The new tariff policy had made it prohibitively expensive to disguise illegal books as legal ones and to pass them through normal commercial channels.

In December, the STN's agent in Nice, Jacques Deandreis, somehow got a shipment of volume six of the *Questions* to Rigaud through the port of Sète, which was supposed to be closed to book imports. Then the French government, realizing that it had nearly destroyed the foreign book trade, lowered the tariff to twenty-six livres per hundredweight. Rigaud proposed sharing the cost with his suppliers: he would pay one third if they would pay two thirds. This proposal suited the STN, but in the spring of 1772 Rigaud decided that the Nice route was too expensive to be used under any conditions. Having heard enough complaints from its other customers to reach the same conclusion, the STN dispatched one of its directors to Lyon, and he persuaded a more dependable Lyonnais dealer, J.-M. Barret, to clear its shipments through the local guild and forward them to its provincial clients. Thanks to this arrangement, the last three volumes of Rigaud's *Questions* arrived safely in the summer.

It had required continuous effort and considerable expense to get the entire order to Montpellier, and Rigaud and the STN did not stop realigning their supply routes once they had completed this transaction. Because economic and political pressures kept shifting, they had constantly to readjust their arrangements within the complex world of middlemen, who linked printing houses with bookshops and often determined, in the last analysis, what literature reached French readers.

How the readers assimilated their books cannot be determined. Bibliographical analysis of all the copies that can be located would show what varieties of the text were available. A study of notarial archives in Montpellier might indicate how many copies turned up in inheritances, and statistics drawn from auction catalogues might make it possible to estimate the number in substantial private libraries. But given the present state of documentation, one cannot know who Voltaire's readers were or how they responded to his text. Reading remains the most difficult stage to study in the circuit that books follow.

IV

All stages were affected by the social, economic, political, and intellectual conditions of the time; but for Rigaud, these general influences made themselves felt within a local context. He sold books in a city of thirty-one thousand inhabitants. Despite an important textile industry, Montpellier was essentially an old-fashioned administrative and religious center, richly endowed with cultural institutions, including a university, an academy of sciences, twelve Masonic lodges, and sixteen monastic communities. And because it was a seat of the provincial estates of Languedoc and an intendancy, and had as well an array of courts, the city had a large population of lawyers and royal officials. If they resembled their counterparts in other provincial centers,[16] they probably provided Rigaud with a good many of his customers and probably had a taste for Enlightenment literature. He did not discuss their social background in his correspondence, but he noted that they clamored for the works of Voltaire, Rousseau, and Raynal. They subscribed heavily to the *Encyclopédie,* and even asked for atheistic treatises like *Système de la nature* and *Philosophie de la nature.* Montpellier was no intellectual backwater, and it was good book territory. "The book trade is quite extensive in this town," an observer remarked in 1768. "The booksellers have kept their shops well stocked ever since the inhabitants developed a taste for having libraries."[17]

These favorable conditions prevailed when Rigaud ordered his *Questions.* But hard times set in during the early 1770s; and in the 1780s Rigaud, like most booksellers, complained of a severe decline in his trade. The whole French economy contracted during those years, according to the standard account of C. E. Labrousse.[18] Certainly, the state's finances went into a tailspin: hence the disastrous book tariff of 1771, which belonged to Terray's unsuccessful attempt to reduce the deficit accumulated during the Seven Years' War. The government also tried to stamp out pirated and forbidden books, first by more severe police work in 1771–74, then by a general reform of the book trade in 1777. These measures eventually ruined Rigaud's commerce with the STN and with the other publishing houses that had grown up around France's borders during the prosperous mid-century years. Foreign publishers produced both original editions of books that could not pass the censorship in Paris and pirated editions of books put out by the Parisian publishers. Because the Parisians had acquired a virtual monopoly over the legal publishing industry, their rivals in the provinces formed alliances with the foreign houses and looked the other way when shipments from abroad arrived for inspection in the provincial guild halls *(chambres syndicales)*. Under Louis XIV, the government had used the Parisian guild as an instrument to suppress the illegal trade: but under Louis XV it became increasingly lax, until a new era of severity began with the fall of Choiseul's ministry (December 1770). Thus Rigaud's relations with the STN fit perfectly into an economic and political pattern that had prevailed in the book trade since the early eighteenth century and that began to fall apart just as the first crates of the *Questions* were making their way between Neuchâtel and Montpellier.

Other patterns might show up in other research, for the model need not be applied in this manner, nor need it be applied at all. I am not arguing that book history should be written according to a standard formula but trying to show how its disparate segments can be brought together within a single conceptual scheme. Different book historians might prefer different schemata. They might concentrate on the book trade of all Languedoc, as Madeleine Ventre has done; or on the general bibliography of Voltaire, as Giles Barber, Jeroom Vercruysse, and others are doing; or on the overall pattern of book production in eighteenth-century France, in the manner of François Furet and Robert Estivals.[19] But however they define their subject, they will not draw out its full significance unless they relate it to all the elements that worked together as a circuit for transmitting texts. To make the point clearer, I will go over the model circuit once more, noting questions that have been investigated successfully or that seem ripe for further research.

I *Authors*

Despite the proliferation of biographies of great writers, the basic conditions of authorship remain obscure for most periods of history. At what point did writers free themselves from the patronage of wealthy noblemen and the state in order to live by their pens? What was the nature of a literary career, and how was it pursued? How did writers deal with publishers, printers, booksellers, reviewers, and one another? Until those questions are answered, we will not have a full understanding of the transmission of texts. Voltaire was able to manipulate secret alliances with pirate publishers because he did not depend on writing for a living. A century later, Zola proclaimed that a writer's independence came from selling his prose to the highest bidder.[20] How did this transformation take place? The work of John Lough begins to provide an answer, but more systematic research on the evolution of the republic of letters in France could be done from police records, literary almanacs, and bibliographies *(La France littéraire* gives the names and publications of 1,187 writers in 1757 and 3,089 in 1784). The situation in Germany is more obscure, owing to the fragmentation of the German states before 1871. But German scholars are beginning to tap sources like *Das gelehrte Teutschland,* which lists four thousand writers in 1779, and to trace the links between authors, publishers, and readers in regional and monographic studies.[21] Marino Berengo has shown how much can be discovered about author-publisher relations in Italy.[22] And the work of A. S. Collins still provides an excellent account of authorship in England, although it needs to be brought up to date and extended beyond the eighteenth century.[23]

II Publishers

The key role of publishers is now becoming clearer, thanks to articles appearing in the *Journal of Publishing History* and monographs like Martin Lowry's *The World of Aldus Manutius*, Robert Patten's *Charles Dickens and His Publishers*, and Gary Stark's *Entrepreneurs of Ideology: Neoconservative Publishers in Germany, 1890–1933*. But the evolution of the publisher as a distinct figure in contrast to the master bookseller and the printer still needs systematic study. Historians have barely begun to tap the papers of publishers, although they are the richest of all sources for the history of books. The archives of the Cotta Verlag in Marbach, for example, contain at least one hundred fifty thousand documents, yet they have only been skimmed for references to Goethe, Schiller, and other famous writers. Further investigation almost certainly would turn up a great deal of information about the book as a force in nineteenth-century Germany. How did publishers draw up contracts with authors, build alliances with booksellers, negotiate with political authorities, and handle finances, supplies, shipments, and publicity? The answers to those questions would carry the history of books deep into the territory of social, economic, and political history, to their mutual benefit.

The Project for Historical Biobibliography at Newcastle upon Tyne and the Institut de Littérature et de Techniques Artistiques de Masse at Bordeaux illustrate the directions that such interdisciplinary work has already taken. The Bordeaux group has tried to trace books through different distribution systems in order to uncover the literary experience of different groups in contemporary France.[24] The researchers in Newcastle have studied the diffusion process through quantitative analysis of subscription lists, which were widely used in the sales campaigns of British publishers from the early seventeenth to the early nineteenth centuries.[25] Similar work could be done on publishers' catalogues and prospectuses, which have been collected in research centers like the Newberry Library. The whole subject of book advertising needs investigation. One could learn a great deal about attitudes toward books and the context of their use by studying the way they were presented—the strategy of the appeal, the values invoked by the phrasing—in all kinds of publicity, from journal notices to wall posters. American historians have used newspaper advertisements to map the spread of the printed word into the back reaches of colonial society.[26] By consulting the papers of publishers, they could make deeper inroads in the nineteenth and twentieth centuries.[27] Unfortunately, however, publishers usually treat their archives as garbage. Although they save the occasional letter from a famous author, they throw away account books and commercial correspondence, which usually are the most important sources of information for the book historian. The Center for the Book in the Library of Congress is now compiling a guide to publishers' archives. If they can be preserved and studied, they might provide a different perspective on the whole course of American history.

III *Printers*

The printing shop is far better known than the other stages in the production and diffusion of books because it has been a favorite subject of study in the field of analytical bibliography, whose purpose, as defined by R. B. McKerrow and Philip Gaskell, is "to elucidate the transmission of texts by explaining the processes of book production."[28] Bibliographers have made important contributions to textual criticism, especially in Shakespearean scholarship, by building inferences backward from the structure of a book to the process of its printing and hence to an original text, such as the missing Shakespeare manuscripts. That line of reasoning has been undercut recently by D. F. McKenzie.[29] But even if they can never reconstruct an Ur-Shakespeare, bibliographers can demonstrate the existence of different editions of a text and of different states of an edition, a necessary skill in diffusion studies. Their techniques also make it possible to decipher the records of printers and so have opened up a new, archival phase in the history of printing. Thanks to the work of McKenzie, Leon Voet, Raymond de Roover, and Jacques Rychner, we now have a clear picture of how printing shops operated throughout the handpress period (roughly 1500–1800).[30] More work needs to be done on later periods, and new questions could be asked: How did printers calculate costs and organize production, especially after the spread of job printing and journalism? How did book budgets change after the introduction of machine-made paper in the first decade of the nineteenth century and Linotype in the 1880s? How did the technological changes affect the management of labor? And what part did journeymen printers, an unusually articulate and militant sector of the working class, play in labor history? Analytical bibliography may seem arcane to the outsider, but it could make a great contribution to social as well as literary history, especially if it were seasoned with a reading of printers' manuals and autobiographies, beginning with those of Thomas Platter, Thomas Gent, N. E. Restif de la Bretonne, Benjamin Franklin, and Charles Manby Smith.

IV *Shippers*

Little is known about the way books reached bookstores from printing shops. The wagon, the canal barge, the merchant vessel, the post office, and the railroad may have influenced the history of literature more than one would suspect. Although transport facilities probably had little effect on the trade in great publishing centers like London and Paris, they sometimes determined the ebb and flow of business in remote areas. Before the nineteenth century, books were usually sent in sheets, so that the customer could have them bound according to his taste and his ability to pay. They traveled in large bales wrapped in heavy paper and were easily damaged by rain and the friction of ropes. Compared with commodities like textiles, their intrinsic value was slight, yet their shipping costs were high, owing to the size and weight of the sheets. So shipping often took up a large proportion of a book's total cost and a large place in the marketing strategy of publishers. In many parts of Europe, printers could not count on getting shipments to booksellers in August and September because wagoners abandoned their routes to work the harvest. The Baltic trade frequently ground to a halt after October, because ice closed the ports. Routes opened and shut everywhere in response to the pressures of war, politics, and even insurance rates. Unorthodox literature has traveled underground in huge quantities from the sixteenth century to the present, so its influence has varied according to the effectiveness of the smuggling industry. And other genres, like chapbooks and penny dreadfuls, circulated through special distribution systems, which need much more study, although book historians are now beginning to clear some of the ground.[31]

V *Booksellers*

Thanks to some classic studies—H. W. Bennett on early modern England, L. C. Wroth on colonial America, H.-J. Martin on seventeenth-century France, and Johann Goldfriedrich on Germany—it is possible to piece together a general picture of the evolution of the book trade.[32] But more work needs to be done on the bookseller as a cultural agent, the middleman who mediated between supply and demand at their key point of contact. We still do not know enough about the social and intellectual world of men like Rigaud, about their values and tastes and the way they fit into their communities. They also operated within commercial networks, which expanded and collapsed like alliances in the diplomatic world. What laws governed the rise and fall of trade empires in publishing? A comparison of national histories could reveal some general tendencies, such as the centripetal force of great centers like London, Paris, Frankfurt, and Leipzig, which drew provincial houses into their orbits, and the countervailing trend toward alignments between provincial dealers and suppliers in independent enclaves like Liège, Bouillon, Neuchâtel, Geneva, and Avignon. But comparisons are difficult because the trade operated through different institutions in different countries, which generated different kinds of archives. The records of the London Stationers' company, the Communauté des Libraires et Imprimeurs de Paris, and the Leipzig and Frankfurt book fairs have had a great deal to do with the different courses that book history has taken in England, France, and Germany.[33]

Nevertheless, books were sold as commodities everywhere. A more unabashedly economic study of them would provide a new perspective to the history of literature. James Barnes, John Tebbel, and Frédéric Barbier have demonstrated the importance of the economic element in the book trades of nineteenth-century England, America, and France.[34] But more work could be done—on credit mechanisms, for example, and the techniques of negotiating bills of exchange, of defense against suspensions of payment, and of exchanging printed sheets in lieu of payment in specie. The book trade, like other businesses during the Renaissance and early modern periods, was largely a confidence game, but we still do not know how it was played.

VI *Readers*

Despite a considerable literature on its psychology, phenomenology, textology, and sociology, reading remains mysterious. How do readers make sense of the signs on the printed page? What are the social effects of that experience? And how has it varied? Literary scholars like Wayne Booth, Stanley Fish, Wolfgang Iser, Walter Ong, and Jonathan Culler have made reading a central concern of textual criticism because they understand literature as an activity, the construal of meaning within a system of communication, rather than a canon of texts.[35] The book historian could make use of their notions of fictitious audiences, implicit readers, and interpretive communities. But he may find their observations somewhat time-bound. Although the critics know their way around literary history (they are especially strong on seventeenth-century England), they seem to assume that texts have always worked on the sensibilities of readers in the same way. But a seventeenth-century London burgher inhabited a different mental universe from that of a twentieth-century American professor. Reading itself has changed over time. It was often done aloud and in groups, or in secret and with an intensity we may not be able to imagine today. Carlo Ginsburg has shown how much meaning a sixteenth-century miller could infuse into a text, and Margaret Spufford has demonstrated that still humbler workmen fought their way to mastery over the printed word in the era of *Areopagitica*.[36] Everywhere in early modern Europe, from the ranks of Montaigne to those of Menocchio, readers wrung significance from books; they did not merely decipher them. Reading was a passion long before the *"Lesewut"* and the *"Wertherfieber"* of the romantic era; and there is *Strum und Drang* in it yet, despite the vogue for speed-reading and the mechanistic view of literature as the encoding and decoding of messages.

But texts shape the response of readers, however active they may be. As Walter Ong has observed, the opening pages of *The Canterbury Tales* and *A Farewell to Arms* create a frame and cast the reader in a role, which he cannot avoid no matter what he thinks of pilgrimages and civil wars.[37] In fact, typography as well as style and syntax determine the ways in which texts convey meanings. McKenzie has shown that the bawdy, unruly Congreve of the early quarto editions settled down into the decorous neoclassicist of the *Works* of 1709 as a consequence of book design rather than bowdlerization.[38] The history of reading will have to take account of the ways that texts constrain readers as well as the ways that readers take liberties with texts. The tension between those tendencies has existed wherever men confronted books, and it has produced some extraordinary results, as in Luther's reading of the Psalms, Rousseau's reading of *Le Misanthrope,* and Kierkegaard's reading of the sacrifice of Isaac.

If it is possible to recapture the great rereadings of the past, the inner experience of ordinary readers may always elude us. But we should at least be able to reconstruct a good deal of the social context of reading. The debate about silent reading during the Middle Ages has produced some impressive evidence about reading habits,[39] and studies of reading societies in Germany, where they proliferated to an extraordinary degree in the eighteenth and nineteenth centuries, have shown the importance of reading in the development of a distinct bourgeois cultural style.[40] German scholars have also done a great deal in the history of libraries and in reception studies of all kinds.[41] Following a notion of Rolf Engelsing, they often maintain that reading habits became transformed at the end of the eighteenth century. Before this *"Leserevolution,"* readers tended to work laboriously through a small number of texts, especially the Bible, over and over a gain. Afterwards, they raced through all kinds of material, seeking amusement rather than edification. The shift from intensive to extensive reading coincided with a desacralization of the printed word. The world began to be cluttered with reading matter, and texts began to be treated as commodities that could be discarded as casually as yesterday's newspaper. This interpretation has recently been disputed by Reinhart Siegert, Martin Welke, and other young scholars, who have discovered "intensive" reading in the reception of fugitive works like almanacs and newspapers, notably the *Noth- und Hülfsbüchlein* of Rudolph Zacharias Becker, an extraordinary best seller of the *Goethezeit*.[42] But whether or not the concept of a reading revolution will hold up, it has helped to align research on reading with general questions of social and cultural history.[43] The same can be said of research on literacy,[44] which has made it possible for scholars to detect the vague outline of diverse reading publics two and three centuries ago and to trace books to readers at several levels of society. The lower the level, the more intense the study. Popular literature has been a favorite topic of research during the last decade,[45] despite a growing tendency to question the notion that cheap booklets like the *bibliothèque bleue* represented an autonomous culture of the common people or that one can distinguish clearly between strains of "elite" and "popular" culture. It now seems inadequate to view cultural change as a linear, or trickle-down, movement of influences. Currents flowed up as well as down, merging and blending as they went. Characters like

Gargantua, Cinderella, and Buscon moved back and forth through oral traditions, chapbooks, and sophisticated literature, changing in nationality as well as genre.[46] One could even trace the metamorphoses of stock figures in almanacs. What does Poor Richard's reincarnation as *le Bonhomme Richard* reveal about literary culture in America and France? And what can be learned about German-French relations by following the Lame Messenger *(der hinkende Bote, le messager boiteux)* through the traffic of almanacs across the Rhine?

Questions about who reads what, in what conditions, at what time, and with what effect, link reading studies with sociology. The book historian could learn how to pursue such questions from the work of Douglas Waples, Bernard Berelson, Paul Lazarsfeld, and Pierre Bourdieu. He could draw on the reading research that flourished in the Graduate Library School of the University of Chicago from 1930 to 1950, and that still turns up in the occasional Gallup report.[47] And as an example of the sociological strain in historical writing, he could consult the studies of reading (and nonreading) in the English working class during the last two centuries by Richard Altick, Robert Webb, and Richard Hoggart.[48] All this work opens onto the larger problem of how exposure to the printed word affects the way men think. Did the invention of movable type transform man's mental universe? There may be no single satisfactory answer to that question because it bears on so many different aspects of life in early modern Europe, as Elizabeth Eisenstein has shown.[49] But it should be possible to arrive at a firmer understanding of what books meant to people. Their use in the taking of oaths, the exchanging of gifts, the awarding of prizes, and the bestowing of legacies would provide clues to their significance within different societies. The iconography of books could indicate the weight of their authority, even for illiterate laborers who sat in church before pictures of the tablets of Moses. The place of books in folklore, and of folk motifs in books, shows that influences ran both ways when oral traditions came into contact with printed texts, and that books need to be studied in relation to other media.[50] The lines of research could lead in many directions, but they all should issue ultimately in a larger understanding of how printing has shaped man's attempts to make sense of the human condition.

One can easily lose sight of the larger dimensions of the enterprise because book historians often stray into esoteric byways and unconnected specializations. Their work can be so fragmented, even within the limits of the literature on a single country, that it may seem hopeless to conceive of book history as a single subject, to be studied from a comparative perspective across the whole range of historical disciplines. But books themselves do not respect limits either linguistic or national. They have often been written by authors who belonged to an international republic of letters, composed by printers who did not work in their native tongue, sold by booksellers who operated across national boundaries, and read in one language by readers who spoke another. Books also refuse to be contained within the confines of a single discipline when treated as objects of study. Neither history nor literature nor economics nor sociology nor bibliography can do justice to all the aspects of the life of a book. By its very nature, therefore, the history of books must be international in scale and interdisciplinary in method. But it need not lack conceptual coherence, because books belong to circuits of communication that operate in consistent patterns, however complex they may be. By unearthing those circuits, historians can show that books do not merely recount history; they make it.

The Forgotten Middlemen of Literature

H AVING SURFEITED themselves with theory, literary scholars are now turning to history. "The new historicism" and "the new literary history" announced in a recent spate of books and articles represents an attempt to halt the work of deconstruction and to ground the study of literature in a reappraisal of the past. But which past? The old literary history sliced time into segments marked off by the appearance of great writers and great books—*l'homme et l'oeuvre,* according to the classic French formula. Today's historian needs to work with a broader conception of literature, one that will take account of men and women in every walk of life who had a way with words.

The folkways of the word include mothers who sing nursery rhymes, children who chant jump-rope verse, teen-agers who tell dirty jokes, and blacks who trade ritual insults ("playing the dozens"). Historians might prefer to leave such people to the anthropologists. But even if they restrict literature to communication through the printed word, their conception of it could be expanded to include some unfamiliar figures—ragpickers, papermakers, typesetters, wagon drivers, booksellers, and even readers. Bookish literature belongs to a system for producing and distributing books. Yet most of the people who made that system work have disappeared from literary history. The great men have squeezed out the middlemen. If seen from the perspective of the transmitters of the work, literary history could appear in a new light.

I would like to present this point of view by discussing some of the characters I have encountered in the papers of the Société typographique de Neuchâtel (STN), a major publisher and wholesaler of French books during the last two decades of the Old Regime. Neuchâtel, a tiny Swiss principality on the eastern border of France, was an ideal site for producing the kind of books that could not pass censorship in France—that is, anything that might offend the Catholic Church, the state, or conventional morality. Some of the STN's books—*The Private Life of Louis XV*, for example, or *The Black Gazette by a Man Who Isn't White*—managed to offend all three and became best sellers, although they, too, have dropped out of literary history. Others were classics of the Enlightenment or inoffensive works, such as travel books and sentimental novels, which the STN pirated. To the Swiss publishers and their clients in the French book trade, literature was a business. As one customer put it, "The best book for a bookseller is a book that sells."[1]

How did the business look to the people involved in it? Consider the publisher and his attempts to extract copy from authors. The two main partners of the STN, Frédéric-Samuel Ostervald and Abraham Bosset de Luze, took business trips to Paris at the height of the Enlightenment. One can follow them from their reports to the home office as they crossed France by coach, found a suitable hotel, had their wigs freshened, hired a lackey, and made the rounds of the literary world.

French by culture but provincial and Protestant in temperament, they felt a little overwhelmed at first by "this immense and noisy city." They needed a guide to find their way around. When they called on booksellers, they discovered that the Parisians did business only until two in the afternoon—and were never at home if a bill was to be collected. But the evenings compensated for the frustrations of the day. "To tell you the truth," Ostervald wrote home after one dinner party, "I drank some graves, some champagne, some hermitage, some malaga; and seated as I was between two amiable ladies, my ideas got a little scrambled."[2]

The publishers picked up literary gossip. D'Alembert told them that he had asked Frederick the Great to hold a service for the repose of the soul of Voltaire soon after Voltaire's death. "I consent," Frederick had replied, "although I don't much believe in eternity."[3]

But mainly they talked business. They calculated how they could undercut the Parisian publishers by shaving costs and profits and then set out to steal the best authors. Soon they were deluged with proposals from obscure hacks. "An author poor as Job came by again yesterday, offering to sell me a manuscript about the Jesuits," Bosset wrote. But he and Ostervald preferred to publish the biggest names. Having dealt with Voltaire and Rousseau in Switzerland, they knew how to beard a philosophe. They entered into pourparlers with d'Alembert, Raynal, Beaumarchais, Mably, Marmontel, and Morellet. They even approached Benjamin Franklin with a scheme to peddle French books in the New World.[4]

All this parleying did not result in many contracts, but it illustrates the character of publishing as an activity. The publishers were always in negotiation. A dozen plots were always brewing, and the ones that succeeded were the exception—the transactions that brought into being a small amount of literature from the nebulous vastness of the literature-that-might-have-been.

One work that congealed out of the shoptalk in Paris was *Du gouvernement et des loix de la Pologne* (On the Government and Laws of Poland, 1781) by Gabriel Bonnot de Mably. Like many authors, Mably knew his book would be a best seller; and he asked for only one hundred free copies in exchange for his manuscript. But it flopped. The STN was to blame, Mably complained in a post-mortem discussion conducted through the mail. Instead of capitalizing on the public's interest in the partition of Poland (1772), the Swiss had become bogged down in their production schedule.

Ostervald defended the STN with a brief account of its market research:

Having printed up a great number of title pages and sample tables of contents, which we sent to several good booksellers in Paris, Versailles, Lyon, and Rouen, I did not find a single one who would place an advance order. They all said that although they were persuaded of the merit of the work, the public was no longer interested in its subject. I had to fall back on Germany and northern Europe; and as soon as I was sure of a hundred orders, I started the presses rolling . . . Voilà, Monsieur, a disagreeable subject of contention.[5]

Authors were a difficult species. Ostervald found them "vain." "They are puffed up with real or supposed knowledge." However witty they might be at the dinner table, they seemed to be governed by greed when it came to signing contracts. Even d'Alembert, a charming conversationalist, struck Bosset as someone who "is greatly concerned with the lucrative side of his writing."[6]

Not that the publishers suffered from an underdeveloped profit motive. They made a business of Enlightenment. "We must stress once again," Ostervald and Bosset wrote from Paris, "that it is not difficult to find good, admirable, marvelous things to print; the crucial thing, the supreme object to which we must apply ourselves, is to be sure before printing that we can turn the copy into cash." When profits dropped, the Swiss shut down presses, fired workers, and lived off their stock. They had no illusions about the nobility of literature as a calling. "This job produces more bile than any other," they concluded. After years of bargaining with authors and battling with competitors, Ostervald summarized his views of his profession as follows: "You should not promise more butter than bread, nor believe anything that you can't see with your own eyes, nor count on anything that you can't hold in your hand with all four fingers and the thumb."[7]

Those remarks suggest the perspective from one position on the circuit of communications. There were many others. The dossier of Jean-Nicolas Morel, a paper miller from the tiny village of Meslières in the Jura Mountains of the Franche-Comté, shows how the book business appeared to someone who supplied its raw material. Morel filled his letters with palaver, scribbling away with superb indifference to spelling and grammar. He was especially eloquent on two subjects: the excellence of his paper and his own virtue. He assured the STN that he bought nothing but the best rags for his stuff (the watery pulp from which paper was made). He patronized ragpickers who knew how to get the cream of the crop by wooing servant girls with sweet talk and gifts of pins and needles. Morel's water was the purest in the whole mountain range. He was the king of the trade in the Franche-Comté. And unlike his competitors, he never cheated by mixing inferior rags in his vat or by slipping defective sheets into underweight reams. No, he assured the Neuchâtelois, whom he took to be pious Calvinists, he ran his business according to the precepts of Saint Paul and the Sermon on the Mount.

Still, if they wanted to knock a few sous off the price, he could add some quicklime to his stuff. That would make the sheets look as white as superior grade paper, but it did have an unfortunate side effect: after a while the ink would turn yellow on the pages. For this reason, the French government had forbidden the use of quicklime in papermaking and penalized offenders with a fine of three hundred livres. Morel did not expect to get caught, however, because he hadn't put his name and watermark on the molds that he had had woven—which was also a violation of the law.

The Swiss did not give in to this temptation, but they let Morel get away with supplying reams that were slightly underweight (quality in paper was determined mainly by weight and whiteness)—and then they retaliated by paying him with bills of exchange drawn on relatively weak companies with unusually long dates of maturity.

Morel countered with an appeal to the sentimental side of the publishers. His son had been laid low by a strange disease. The doctors insisted that there was only one cure: Neuchâtel wine. Morel had tried all kinds of medicaments and all kinds of drink: "burgundies, malaga, côte roti, hermitage, muscadet, tinto, Alsatian . . . even the good wines of the Comté." Nothing but the very best Neuchâtel, white or red, would do the job. Morel would accept two barrels in place of the bills of exchange and would collect them when he delivered the next batch of paper.[8]

And so it went in letter after letter, each side bargaining for every advantage it could extract from the other. Haggling like this, vast amounts of it, conducted with passion and humor, went into every book in the era of the common press. But it has remained hidden from our view because we have not had access to publishers' archives. Bartering over paper was especially important, because paper represented from 50 to 75 percent of the production costs of early modern books. And early modern readers had an eye for paper. They usually bought books unbound and inspected the sheets carefully, rubbing them between their fingers, holding them up to the light, testing for texture, color, and blemishes.

The readers also paid close attention to the printing. After producing volume 15 of the quarto edition of Diderot's *Ency-*

clopédie, the STN received complaints from customers who had received copies disfigured by fingerprints from the pressmen. While examining a copy in the municipal library of Neuchâtel, I found a vivid thumbprint on page 635. The foreman's wage book showed that that page (sheet 4L) had been printed by a certain "Bonnemain." He also turned up in the STN's correspondence with the recruiting agents who supplied it with workers who tramped from shop to shop on the typographical tour de France. So I could learn a little bit about his life.

Bonnemain—like many printers he traveled under a nickname—was dark haired and Norman. He had learned the tricks of the trade in the printing shops of Paris and then took to tramping. In Lyon he fell in with the Kindelem family—a father, mother, and son—who also lived on the road between irregular stints of employment. Together they hiked northward through Bresse and the Franche-Comté to the town of Dôle, where they found work with a master printer named Tonnet. The younger Kindelem seduced the salesgirl of the shop, while the others became embroiled in quarrels with Tonnet. One day after collecting their week's wages, they dumped some half-printed sheets on the shop floor and ran for Switzerland, taking the girl with them.

They turned up in Neuchâtel a few days later. All of them worked on the *Encyclopédie,* but the Kindelems got in trouble with the STN foreman and took to the road again. Bonnemain remained in the shop for twenty months, one of the longest stints put in by any of the STN pressmen. He did not overexert himself, however. The STN discovered that he spread an excessive amount of ink on the type so that he would not have to pull hard on the bar of the press in order to get an impression: hence the origin of the thumbprint.

By tracing the fingerprint to its origins, one can see into

the lives behind the greatest book of the Enlightenment. The *Encyclopédie* was an intensely human work, produced by craftsmen like Bonnemain as well as by philosophers like Diderot. It deserves to be studied not merely as a text but also as a physical object, warts and all.[9]

One can also study the campaign to sell the book. The STN promoted the *Encyclopédie* through advertisements and prospectuses; but it relied primarily on its commercial correspondence, because retailers paid special attention to information that arrived through the grapevine of their trade. They also listened to the pitches of sales representatives. So in 1778 the STN sent one of its employees, Jean-François Favarger, on a sales trip.

He traveled by horse, flogging encyclopedias and everything else in the publisher's stock for six months along an itinerary that led through nearly all the major towns of southern and central France. It was hard going. Favarger carried a brace of pistols in case he should encounter any of the highwaymen who preyed on traffic in the Rhône Valley. Reports of ambushes by unemployed workers from the silk industry reached him in Aix-en-Provence; so he changed his route and made it safely to Toulon. But by Nîmes he had to cope with another problem: saddle sores. They caused him so much pain that he was afraid he would have to take to bed, despite the best help that contemporary medicine could provide: "I must have myself bled one day and purged the other."[10]

At Montpellier the horse began to limp. It took to vomiting and falling to the ground on the way to Toulouse. Bad weather set in at the beginning of October, and by La Rochelle man and beast were soaked to the bones from two weeks of steady rain: "The paths were so bad that I could hardly do seven leagues a day, especially as the poor animal was so weak that it was ready to collapse at any moment." Favarger finally got rid of the horse in Loudun. Having developed swellings and fissures all along its legs, it fetched only four louis, and he had to pay twice as much for a sturdier animal, which appears in his expense account along with the treatments for the saddle sores and occasional splurges in cabarets. Once mounted on a horse that could stand up to the weather and bear his load of catalogues, prospectuses, and sample copies of books, Favarger wound his way up the Loire Valley and across the Jura Mountains without further mishap. He made it back to the home office in early December, covered with mud and dropping with fatigue.[11]

It was a difficult journey but a great education, for Favarger returned with an intimate knowledge of the provincial world of books. He had learned to steer clear of the inspector of the book trade in Marseille, "a very bad man, one of those who would eat his brother in order to fill his plate." In Lyon, by contrast, he found out how to ship huge crates of forbidden books right through the offices of the authorities. Dijon was another great capital of the clandestine trade, but Toulouse, "a center of bigotry," was to be avoided. Only one of its booksellers, La Porte, would carry Protestant works. "They even go through all the binderies in order to confiscate anything that isn't perfectly orthodox. They have the strictest guild imaginable, and the booksellers themselves made it that way by denouncing one another with a vindictiveness that can hardly be believed." Toulon and Bordeaux were also disappointments, but for economic rather than political reasons, because their commerce had suffered terribly from the American war. The fair of Beaucaire had gone into decline as a center of exchange, and the smaller cities turned out to be surprisingly underequipped with bookstores. Carpentras, Viviers, and Montélimar did not have a single dealer. "Orange has only one, a wigmaker named Touït, who merely sells a few devotional works as a sideline. Calamel, who is listed in the book-sellers' almanach, is a draper who used to sell books but doesn't deal in them anymore." Thus, city by city, Favarger noted the kind of books that circulated and the cast of characters who handled them.[12]

In order to get a clearer idea of the demand, he had to confront the dealers in their dens. But he found them difficult to corner:

> When you have made your offer, they say to you that they will examine your catalogue etc. and that you should come back. You return three or four times, and each time the boss is out. If you find him in, he has not had time to consider your propositions. So you must come back once again, and for what? For nothing most of the time. Almost all of them are like that. They make a stranger run from one end of town to the other and conduct all his business in the morning, for it is rare to find any of these gentlemen in their shops after dinner. I wish I could proceed faster, but the people I have to deal with are too fond of taking it easy, even though their business hardly amounts to anything. They can never find time to make things easier for a foreigner.[13]

Cultural middlemen operated everywhere in scenes such as this, sorting out supply and demand, filtering the flow of literature before it took the form of books loaded on wagons traveling toward readers at the final stop of a distribution system. The traveling salesmen kept the system going, but the going got harder as they pushed further into it. Favarger found that Swiss efficiency made little headway against the bazaar style of barter in the Mediterranean. But even when he failed to sell his wares to Buchet in Nîmes and Mossy in Marseille, he left their shops with a richer knowledge of the marketplace. He often picked up tips about what would be best to pirate. In Bourg-en-Bresse, for example, Vernarel urged him to recommend a reprint of *"Lois et constitutions de Pensilvanie, traduit de l'anglais, dédié au docteur Franklin, chez Jombert et*

Cellot" (*The Laws and Constitutions of Pennsylvania,* translated from The English and dedicated to Dr. Franklin, sold by Jombert and Cellot.) Vernarel promised to take fifty copies if the STN produced an edition. When he arrived at his next stop, Lyon, Favarger dangled the proposition alongside a project for a new edition of the works of Condillac. But no bookseller would bite: "No one here thinks that the Condillac would be a good work to reprint. They say that Barret still has copies of his edition. Instead they favor the works of Riccoboni. A new edition would surely sell, if copied from the edition of Paris. The demand for that item has never let up. As to the book proposed by Vernarel, no one has heard of it here and no one is interested in it." Favarger received the same response farther down the road, in the bookshop of Brette in Grenoble: "I saw the *Laws of Pennsylvania* in his shop; he says that no one cares for it here. It is just a compilation of regulations and such, . . . the kind of thing that only sells when it first appears. What he thinks we should reprint is the *Dictionary of Chemistry.*"[14]

Opinions varied, and the demand looked different in different places. But a few works seemed destined to be best sellers everywhere—above all, the *Confessions* of Rousseau. They had not yet been published, but all the booksellers were convinced quite rightly that publishers were secretly bidding for the manuscript, and all were clamoring for copies. Having consulted the grapevine in Lyon, Valence, Orange, Avignon, Nîmes, and Marseille, Favarger reported, "Everyone asks me for the memoirs of J. J. Rousseau, and everyone firmly believes that they exist, if not in Paris, most likely in Holland. It would be a book to print at three thousand, if we could get it early enough." The dialogue continued in this fashion over a vast stretch of the kingdom. When he returned to Neuchâtel, Favarger had learned more about the social conditions of eighteenth-century literature than any historian can ever hope to know.[15]

Once workers like Bonnemain had printed the books and agents like Favarger had sold them, the merchandise had to reach customers scattered throughout Europe. About half the clients of the STN were retail booksellers in France; and a large proportion of the books they ordered were illegal, either pirated editions of inoffensive works published in France or prohibited works that could not be sold openly and could not be shipped without precautionary measures—smuggling, we would call it; "insurance," as it was known in the underground book trade of the eighteenth century.

Entrepreneurs ("insurers") contracted with the STN to get the books across the French border. They hired teams of "porters," gave them a stiff drink at an inn on the Swiss side of the border, and sent them off through mountain paths with backpacks of books, which they delivered to secret entrepôts on the French side. A French agent then transferred the books to crates and sent them as domestic merchandise under false bills of lading to bookshops everywhere in the kingdom. Flying squadrons of the customs service patrolled the border. If they caught a porter, they confiscated the books, and the insurer had to pay compensation to the STN. The porter might be branded with the letters GAL for *galérien* and sent off in irons to row in the galleys, either for a few years or for the rest of his life if he had repeated his offense.

Insurance was therefore a tough business, and the businessmen who ran it drove hard bargains, calculating profit margins and risks with precision. Guillon *l'aîné,* an insurer from Clairvaux, charged 16 percent of the value of the merchandise for a border crossing. His men backpacked the books in loads of eighty pounds, seventy when the snow was deep. In March 1773 two of them, including their "chief," got caught. Guillon feared he could never pry them out of prison, because the bishop of Saint-Claude took a special interest in the case and the books included Mercier's utopian novel, *The Year*

2440, which did not make the Church look good. Guillon paid up, at a cost of two hundred and forty livres (roughly a half year's wages for one of the STN's workers), and lectured the STN on his good faith as a businessman: "I profess to be honest and upright. . . . I would be distraught if I caused you to lose as little as a farthing." He then raised his fee to 20 percent of value. What became of the porters cannot be determined.[16]

The difficulties did not end once the books arrived in the retail stores because the booksellers had to sell them and pay their bills to the STN, which in turn used the money to compensate the printers, papermakers, and authors of the next works on the production line. The bookseller might be considered the most important middleman of the entire system, for he operated in the crucial area where supply met demand.

Booksellers came in many varieties. Some were pillars of society, some lived by their wits on the far side of the law. I have a weak spot for the latter, whose ways of doing business can be appreciated from the case of Nicholas Gerlache.

Gerlache began life as a tanner. Tanning led to binding, binding to book peddling, peddling to smuggling, and smuggling to prison. In his police report, Gerlache appears as the leader of a smuggling ring that operated on the northeastern border of France: "He inhabits the sewer of Parnassus, lives off its muck, and animates the swarm of insects that cover the border area and threaten to spread throughout the kingdom." (The police of the Old Regime favored a more literary mode of expression than that of their successors in the twentieth century.)[17]

After his release in 1767, Gerlache promised to go straight. He took up tanning again in Metz, and reports of police spies indicated that he kept away from "bad books," as the police called them. (They were "philosophical books" to the professionals in the trade.) By 1770 things were looking up. Gerlache had wooed and won a young woman who provided him with a dowry of twenty-four hundred livres—a good sum for a bride in the upper ranks of the lower classes—and a sympathetic mother-in-law.[18]

The young couple decided to establish a small bookshop and bindery. The bride's mother advanced eight hundred livres for skins, and the dowry went for furniture, rent, and binding equipment. The stock came from J. L. Boubers, a publisher and wholesaler in Brussels who specialized in "philosophical books" and was then cooperating with the STN in an edition of d'Holbach's notorious *System of Nature*.

At this point Gerlache surfaced in the correspondence in Neuchâtel. He appears in his letters as a serious, hardworking young man intent on starting a business and on making something of his life.

I am from a family that has fallen on hard times and now has nothing. I was obliged to learn the craft of tanning; but being full of zeal for commerce, I gladly quit my profession to take up the offer M. Boubers made to me. . . . And now I have put into my business the hundred louis I received in marrying the person whom I am happy to possess and who seems to have been born for work and commerce.[19]

One should allow for the fact that Gerlache was trying to impress a supplier and win some credit. But the STN made inquiries with local businessmen, and they described him as "a young man who works hard and is very correct in his conduct." Gerlache purchased a *lettre de maîtrise* for eight hundred and three livres, which gave him the right to participate in the book trade under the supervision of the guild in nearby Nancy. He established supply lines with the STN and the Société typographique de Sarrebruck as well as with Boubers in Brussels. He bought a horse and cart and peddled books around the countryside while his wife minded the shop in Metz. And he founded a reading club *(cabinet littéraire)*, where the townspeople, especially the soldiers from the local garrison, could read anything in his shop for three livres a month—little more than a day's wages for a skilled carpenter.[20]

Gerlache carried a general assortment of books, but he seemed to specialize in the "bad" or "philosophical" variety that had got him into trouble with the police five years earlier. His letters indicate that his customers hungered for the most forbidden kind of fruit: atheism *(System of Nature, The Three Imposters)*, pornography *(Theresa the Philosopher)*, and political scandal *(The Gazeteer in Armor)*.

Gerlache's correspondence makes it possible to follow the fate of the little business month by month. The first year was especially hard because it took time to build up a clientele. But the reading club brought in a promising flow of customers in the second year, even though Gerlache had to be away from home on long and arduous peddling expeditions. He also did some smuggling for Boubers, who, it turned out, preferred to use him for running books rather than for retailing them. Relations with Brussels soured, and the supply from the northwest dried up. But Gerlache tightened his alliance with the Société typographique de Sarrebruck. By June 1772 his reading club had grown to one hundred fifty members, and he estimated that the shop was bringing in twenty-four hundred livres a year, enough to feed a family.

The Gerlaches prepared to fit a baby into the rooms above their shop. But as Mme. Gerlache neared the end of her pregnancy, her mother fell dangerously ill. "I am in a critical moment," Gerlache wrote to the STN. "My mother-in-law is about to die and my wife to give birth, and I'm afraid that the death of her mother will cause her grave harm." The wife and the baby pulled through, but the mother-in-law died. She left six thousand livres, and Gerlache began to order in larger quantities, paying by bills of exchange with twelve to eighteen months' maturation.[21]

Soon he had overextended himself. When a garrison of soldiers, who included some of his best customers, was transferred in 1773, he saw that he would not be able to pay off some of the notes. He begged for a reprieve, protesting that "I would rather die than let any note of mine go unpaid."[22]

But a few months later his back was to the wall and he was fighting for his life. The tone of the letters changed. If any creditor tried to crush him, he warned, "I will set fire to everything I have in order to keep the law from seizing it." He begged the STN to ship him more audacious works "in the genre of the *Social System*" (a radical tract by the Baron d'Holbach) so that he could capitalize on the demand for forbidden books. But when the STN saw him taking greater risks, it refused to extend any more credit. In October 1774 his supplier in Saarbrücken went bankrupt—a disaster, Gerlache reported, that "plunges me into a desperate situation." He arranged a legal separation from his wife so that her property could not be claimed by the creditors. And in November he disappeared, leaving wife and baby behind.[23]

No bookseller can be taken to typify the trade, but I have found a great many careers that ended as Gerlache's did: Pascot of Bordeaux, "decamped"; Brotes of Anduze, "fugitive"; Boyer of Marseille, "doesn't exist here anymore, ran off to America"; Planquais of Saint-Maixant, "it's said that he enrolled in the army"; Blondel of Bolbec, "ran away, was summoned to justice by the town crier beating a drum"; the widow Reguilliat of Lyon, bankrupt and in hiding in order to "keep my person in a safe place so I will avoid the horrors of prison"; Boisserand's clerk in Roanne, disappeared with the cash box, "in such a way that it's impossible for me to have him arrested"; then Boisserand himself: "left town, since he couldn't cope with his debts. . . . His poor wife asks me to solicit your pity . . . because he worked hard and lived miserably all his life and left several children unable to fend for themselves"; Jarfaut of Melun: "Three years ago this bookseller disappeared, signed up for the colonies, they say. His wife and children, who are living off charity here, haven't received any news at all from him. Perhaps he is dead. . . . The only thing certain is that Jarfaut's wife and her five children are living in the most horrible penury."[24]

Of course, many booksellers remained "solid," to use one of their favorite terms. But I am amazed at how many went under. Before limited liability and the industrial revolution, capitalism suffered from a heavy casualty rate among the entrepreneurs. Large businessmen and small tradesmen often gambled with everything they had; and when they lost, they lost everything. The last letter in many of the dossiers in Neuchâtel comes from an abandoned wife or a family friend, and it ends with a phrase that, in the eighteenth century, meant the abandonment of hope: "He left his keys under the door."[25]

Do these brief glimpses into the lives of literary middlemen change our picture of literature? I cannot claim that the works of Voltaire and Rousseau take on a new meaning if one knows who sold them. But by getting to know Ostervald, Bosset, Morel, Bonnemain, Favarger, Guillon, and Gerlache, one can get the feel of books as artifacts from the eighteenth century. It is crucial, of course, to study the original editions. By seizing them in all their physicality, one can grasp something of the experience of literature two centuries ago.

That may sound like mysticism, but it also may diffuse some of the mystification that set in with the great-man, great-book view of literary history. The great books belong to a canon of classics selected retrospectively over the years by the professionals who took charge of literature—that is, by the critics and college professors whose successors are now deconstructing it. This kind of literature may never have existed outside the imagination of the professionals and their students.

To eighteenth-century Frenchmen, literature—or the Republic of Letters, as they would have put it—certainly included Voltaire and Rousseau. But it also included Pidansat de Mairobert, Moufle d'Angerville, and a multitude of other writers who have disappeared from literary history. Their works sat on eighteenth-century shelves alongside *Candide* and *The Social Contract*. A best-seller list from the Old Regime would have to include *The Year 2440, Theresa the Philosopher,* and a great many other "bad books." How bad were they? They make very good reading today. More important, they open up the possibility of rereading literary history. And if studied in connection with the system for producing and diffusing the printed word, they could force us to rethink our notion of literature itself.

First Steps Toward a History of Reading

O VID OFFERS ADVICE on how to read a love letter: "If your lover should make overtures by means of some words inscribed on tablets delivered to you by a clever servant, meditate on them carefully, weigh his phrases, and try to divine whether his love is only feigned or whether his prayers really come from a heart sincerely in love." The Roman poet might be one of us. He speaks to a problem that could arise in any age, that appears to exist outside of time. In reading about reading in *The Art of Love,* we seem to hear a voice that speaks directly to us across a distance of two thousand years.

But as we listen further, the voice sounds stranger. Ovid goes on to prescribe techniques for communicating with a lover behind a husband's back:

It is consonant with morality and the law that an upright woman should fear her husband and be surrounded by a strict guard. . . . But should you have as many guardians as Argus has eyes, you can dupe them all if your will is firm enough. For example, can anyone stop your servant and accomplice from carrying your notes in her bodice or between her foot and the sole of her sandal? Let us suppose that your guardian can see through all these ruses. Then have your confidante offer her back in place of the tablets and let her body become a living letter.[1]

The lover is expected to strip the servant girl and read her body—not exactly the kind of communication that we associate with letter writing today. Despite its air of beguiling contemporaneity, *The Art of Love* catapults us into a world we can barely imagine. To get the message, we must know something about Roman mythology, writing techniques, and domestic life. We must be able to picture ourselves as the wife of a Roman patrician and to appreciate the contrast between formal morality and the ways of a world given over to sophistication and cynicism at a time when the Sermon on the Mount was being preached in a barbarian tongue far beyond the Romans' range of hearing.

To read Ovid is to confront the mystery of reading itself. Both familiar and foreign, it is an activity that we share with our ancestors yet can never be the same as what they experienced. We may enjoy the illusion of stepping outside of time in order to make contact with authors who lived centuries ago. But even if their texts have come down to us unchanged—a virtual impossibility, considering the evolution of layout and of books as physical objects—our relation to those texts cannot be the same as that of readers in the past. Reading has a history. But how can we recover it?

We could begin by searching the record for readers. Carlo Ginzburg found one, a humble miller from sixteenth-century Friulia, in the papers of the Inquisition. Probing for heresy, the inquisitor asked his victim about his reading. Menocchio replied with a string of titles and elaborate comments on each of them. By comparing the texts and the commentary, Ginzburg discovered that Menocchio had read a great deal of biblical stories, chronicles, and travel books of the kind that existed in many patrician libraries. Menocchio did not simply receive messages transmitted down through the social order. He read aggressively, transforming the contents of the material at his disposition into a radically non-Christian view of the world. Whether that view can be traced to an ancient popular tradition, as Ginzburg claims, is a matter of debate; but Ginzburg certainly demonstrated the possibility of studying reading as an activity among the common people four centuries ago.[2]

I ran across a solidly middle-class reader in my own research on eighteenth-century France. He was a merchant from La Rochelle named Jean Ranson and an impassioned Rousseauist. Ranson did not merely read Rousseau and weep: he incorporated Rousseau's ideas in the fabric of his life as he set up business, fell in love, married, and raised his children. Reading and living run parallel as leitmotifs in a rich series of letters that Ranson wrote between 1774 and 1785 and show how Rousseauism became absorbed in the way of life of the provincial bourgeoisie under the Old Regime. Rousseau had received a flood of letters from readers like Ranson after the publication of *La Nouvelle Héloïse*. It was, I believe, the first tidal wave of fan mail in the history of literature, although Richardson had already produced some impressive ripples in England. The mail reveals that readers everywhere in France responded as Ranson did and, furthermore, that their responses conformed to those Rousseau had called for in the two prefaces to his novel. He had instructed his readers how to read him. He had assigned them roles and provided them with a strategy for taking in his novel. The new way of reading worked so well that *La Nouvelle Héloïse* became the greatest best seller of the century, the most important single source of romantic sensibility. That sensibility is now extinct. No modern reader can weep his way through the six volumes of *La Nouvelle Héloïse* as his predecessors did two centuries ago. But in his day, Rousseau captivated an entire generation of readers by revolutionizing reading itself.[3]

The examples of Menocchio and Ranson suggest that reading and living, construing texts and making sense of life, were much more closely related in the early modern period than they are today. But before jumping to conclusions, we need to work through more archives, comparing readers' accounts of their experience with the protocols of reading in their books and, when possible, with their behaviour. It was believed that *The Sorrows of Young Werther* touched off a wave of suicides in Germany. Is not the *Wertherfieber* ripe for fresh examination? The pre-Raphaelites in England provide similar instances of life imitating art, a theme that can be traced from *Don Quixote* to *Madame Bovary* and *Miss Lonely Hearts*. In each case the fiction could be fleshed out and compared with documents— actual suicide notes, diaries, and letters to the editor. The correspondence of authors and the papers of publishers are ideal sources of information about real readers. There are dozens of letters from readers in the published correspondence of Voltaire and Rousseau and the unpublished papers of Balzac and Zola.[4]

In short, it should be possible to develop a history as well as a theory of reader response. Possible, but not easy; for the documents rarely show readers at work, fashioning meaning from texts, and the documents are texts themselves, which also require interpretation. Few of them are rich enough to provide even indirect access to the cognitive and affective elements of reading, and a few exceptional cases may not be enough for one to reconstruct the inner dimensions of that experience. But historians of the book have already turned up a great deal of information about the external history of reading. Having studied it as a social phenomenon, they can answer many of the "who," "what," "where," and "when" questions, which can be of great help in attacking the more difficult "whys" and "hows."

Studies of who read what at different times fall into two main types, the macro- and the microanalytical. Macroanalysis has flourished above all in France, where it feeds on a powerful tradition of quantitative social history. Henri-Jean Martin, François Furet, Robert Estivals, and Frédéric Barbier have traced the evolution of reading habits from the sixteenth century to the present, using long-term series constructed from the *dépôt légal,* registers of book privileges, and the annual *Bibliographie de la France.* One can see many intriguing phenomena in the undulations of their graphs: the decline of Latin, the rise of the novel, the general fascination with the immediate world of nature and the remote worlds of exotic countries that spread throughout the educated public between the time of Descartes and Bougainville. The Germans have constructed a still longer series of statistics, thanks to a peculiarly rich source: the catalogues of the Frankfurt and Leipzig book fairs, which extend from the mid-sixteenth to the mid-nineteenth century. (The Frankfurt catalogue was published without interruption from 1564 to 1749, and the Leipzig catalogue, which dates from 1594, can be replaced for the period after 1797 by the *Hinrichssche Verzeichnisse.*) Although the catalogues have their drawbacks, they provide a rough index to German reading since the Renaissance; and they have been mined by a succession of German book historians since Johann Goldfriedrich published his monumental *Geschichte des deutschen Buchhandels* in 1908–09. The English-reading world has no comparable source; but for the period after 1557, when London began to dominate the printing industry, the papers of the London Stationers' Company have provided H. S. Bennett, W. W. Greg, and others with plenty of material to trace the evolution of the English book trade. Although the British tradition of bibliography has not favored the compilation of statistics, there is a great deal of quantitative information in the short-title catalogues that run from 1475. Giles Barber has drawn some Frenchlike graphs from customs records. And Robert Winans and G. Thomas Tanselle have taken the measure of early American reading by reworking Charles Evans's enormous *American Bibliography* (eighteen thousand entries for the period 1638–1783, including, unfortunately, an undetermined population of "ghosts").[5]

All this compiling and computing has provided some guidelines to reading habits, but the generalizations sometimes seem too general to be satisfying. The novel, like the bourgeoisie, always seems to be rising; and the graphs drop at the expected points—most notably during the Thirty Years' War at the Leipzig fair, and during World War I in France. Most of the quantifiers sort their statistics into vague categories like "arts and sciences" and "belles-lettres," which are inadequate for identifying particular phenomena like the Succession Controversy, Jansenism, the Enlightenment, or the Gothic Revival—the very subjects that have attracted the most attention among literary scholars and cultural historians. The quantitative history of books will have to refine its categories and sharpen its focus before it can have a major impact on traditional strains of scholarship.

Yet the quantifiers have uncovered some significant statistical patterns, and their achievements would look even more impressive if there were more of an effort to make comparisons from one country to another. For example, the statistics suggest that the cultural revival of Germany in the late eighteenth century was connected with an epidemiclike fever for reading, the so-called *Lesewut* or *Lesesucht*. The Leipzig catalogue did not reach the level it had attained before the Thirty Years' War until 1764, when it included 1,200 titles of newly published books. With the onset of *Sturm und Drang*, it rose to 1,600 titles in 1770; then 2,600 in 1780 and 5,000 in 1800. The

French followed a different pattern. Book production grew steadily for a century after the Peace of Westphalia (1648)—a century of great literature, from Corneille to the *Encyclopédie*, which coincided with the decline in Germany. But in the next fifty years, when the German figures soared, the French increase looks relatively modest. According to Robert Estivals, requests for authorization to publish new books (*privilèges* and *permissions tacites*) came to 729 in 1764, 896 in 1770, and only 527 in 1780; and the new titles submitted to the *dépôt légal* in 1800 totaled 700. To be sure, different kinds of documents and standards of measurement could produce different results, and the official sources exclude the enormous production of illegal French books. But whatever their deficiencies, the figures indicate a great leap forward in German literary life after a century of French domination. Germany also had more writers, although the population of the French- and German-speaking areas was roughly the same. A German literary almanac, *Das gelehrte Teutschland,* listed 3,000 living authors in 1772 and 4,300 in 1776. A comparable French publication, *La France littéraire,* included 1,187 authors in 1757 and 2,367 in 1769. While Voltaire and Rousseau were sinking into old age, Goethe and Schiller were riding a wave of literary creativity that was far more powerful than one might think if one considered only the conventional histories of literature.[6]

Cross-statistical comparisons also provide help in charting cultural currents. After tabulating book privileges throughout the eighteenth century, François Furet found a marked decline in the older branches of learning, especially the humanist and classical Latin literature that had flourished a century earlier according to the statistics of Henri-Jean Martin. Newer genres such as the books classified under the rubric "arts and sciences" prevailed after 1750. Daniel Roche and Michel Marion noticed a similar tendency in surveying Parisian notarial archives.

Novels, travel books, and works on natural history tended to crowd out the classics in the libraries of noblemen and wealthy bourgeois. All the studies point to a significant drop in religious literature during the eighteenth century. They confirm the quantitative research in other areas of social history—Michel Vovelle's on funeral rituals, for example, and Dominique Julia's investigation of clerical ordinations and teaching practices.[7]

The thematic surveys of German reading complement those of the French. Rudolf Jentzsch and Albert Ward found a strong drop in Latin books and a corresponding increase in novels in the fair catalogues of Leipzig and Frankfurt. By the late nineteenth century, according to Eduard Reyer and Rudolf Schenda, borrowing patterns in German, English, and American libraries had fallen into a strikingly similar pattern: 70–80 percent of the books came from the category of light fiction (mostly novels); 10 percent came from history, biography, and travel; and less then 1 percent came from religion. In little more than two hundred years, the world of reading had been transformed. The rise of the novel had balanced a decline in religious literature, and in almost every case the turning point could be located in the second half of the eighteenth century, especially in the 1770s, the years of the *Wertherfieber*. *Die Leiden des jungen Werthers* produced an even more spectacular response in Germany than *La Nouvelle Héloïse* had in France or *Pamela* in England. All three novels marked the triumph of a new literary sensitivity, and the last sentences of *Werther* seemed to announce the advent of a new reading public along with the death of a traditional Christian culture: "Workmen carried [the body.] No priest accompanied it."[8]

Thus for all their variety and occasional contradictions, the macroanalytical studies suggest some general conclusions, something akin to Max Weber's "demystification of the world."

That, however, may seem too cosmic for comfort. Those who prefer precision may turn to microanalysis, although it usually goes to the opposite extreme—excessive detail. We have hundreds of lists of books in libraries from the Middle Ages to the present, more than anyone can bear to read. Yet most of us would agree that a catalogue of a private library can serve as a profile of a reader, even though we don't read all the books we own and we do read many books that we never purchase. To scan the catalogue of the library in Monticello is to inspect the furnishings of Jefferson's mind.[9] And the study of private libraries has the advantage of linking the "what" with the "who" of reading.

The French have taken the lead in this area, too. Daniel Mornet's essay of 1910, "Les Enseignements des bibliothèques privées," demonstrated that the study of library catalogues could produce conclusions that challenged some of the commonplaces of literary history. After tabulating titles from five hundred eighteenth-century catalogues, he found only one copy of the book that was to be the Bible of the French Revolution, Rousseau's *Social Contract*. The libraries bulged with the works of authors who had been completely forgotten, and they provided no basis for connecting certain kinds of literature (the work of the philosophes, for example) with certain classes of readers (the bourgeoisie). Seventy years and several refutations later, Mornet's work still looks impressive. But a vast literature has grown up around it. We now have statistics on the libraries of noblemen, magistrates, priests, academicians, burghers, artisans, and even some domestic servants. The French scholars have studied reading across the social strata of certain cities—the Caen of Jean-Claude Perrot, the Paris of Michel Marion—and throughout entire regions—the Normandy of Jean Quéniart, the Languedoc of Madeleine Ventre. For the most part, they rely on *inventaires après décès,* notarial records of books in the estates of the deceased. So they suffer from the bias built into the documents, which generally neglect books of little commercial value or limit themselves to vague statements like "a pile of books." But the notarial eye took in a great deal in France, far more than in Germany, where Rudolf Schenda considers inventories woefully inadequate as a guide to the reading habits of the common people. The most thorough German study is probably Walter Wittmann's survey of inventories from the late eighteenth century in Frankfurt am Main. It indicates that books were owned by 100 percent of the higher officials, 51 percent of the tradesmen, 35 percent of the master artisans, and 26 percent of the journeymen. Daniel Roche found a similar pattern among the common people of Paris: only 35 percent of the salaried workers and domestic servants who appear in the notarial archives around 1780 owned books. But Roche also discovered many indications of familiarity with the written word. By 1789 almost all the domestic servants could sign their names on the inventories. A great many owned desks, fully equipped with writing implements and packed with family papers. Most artisans and shopkeepers spent several years of their childhood in school. Before 1789 Paris had five hundred primary schools, one for every thousand inhabitants, most of them free. Parisians were readers, Roche concludes, but reading did not take the form of the books that show up in inventories. It involved chapbooks, broadsides, posters, personal letters, and even the signs on the streets. Parisians read their way through the city and through their lives, but their ways of reading did not leave enough evidence in the archives for the historian to follow closely on their heels.[10]

He must therefore search for other sources. Subscription lists have been a favorite, though they normally cover only rather wealthy readers. From the late seventeenth to the early nineteenth century, many books were published by subscription in Britain and contained lists of the subscribers. Researchers at the Project for Historical Biobibliography at Newcastle upon Tyne have used these lists to work toward a historical sociology of readership. Similar efforts are under way in Germany, especially among scholars of Klopstock and Wieland. Perhaps a sixth of new German books were published by subscription between 1770 and 1810, when the practice reached its peak. But even during their *Blütezeit,* the subscription lists do not provide an accurate view of readership. They left off the names of many subscribers, included others who functioned as patrons instead of as readers, and generally represented the salesmanship of a few entrepreneurs rather than the reading habits of the educated public, according to some devastating criticism that Reinhard Wittmann has directed against subscription-list research. The work of Wallace Kirsop suggests that such research may succeed better in France, where publishing by subscription also flourished in the late eighteenth century. But the French lists, like the others, generally favor the wealthiest readers and the fanciest books.[11]

The records of lending libraries offer a better opportunity to make connections between literary genres and social classes, but few of them survive. The most remarkable are the registers of borrowings from the ducal library of Wolfenbüttel, which extend from 1666 to 1928. According to Wolfgang Milde, Paul Raabe, and John McCarthy, they show a significant "democratization" of reading in the 1760s: the number of books borrowed doubled; the borrowers came from lower social strata (they included a few porters, lackeys, and lower officers in the army); and the reading matter became lighter, shifting from learned tomes to sentimental novels (imitations of *Robinson Crusoe* went over especially well). Curiously, the registers of the Bibliothèque du Roi in Paris show that it had the same number of users at this time—about fifty a year, including one Denis Diderot. The Parisians could not take the books home, but they enjoyed the hospitality of a more leisurely age. Although the librarian opened his doors to them only two mornings a week, he gave them a meal before he turned them out. Conditions are different in the Bibliothèque Nationale today. Librarians have had to accept a basic law of economics: there is no such thing as a free lunch.[12]

The microanalysts have come up with many other discoveries—so many, in fact, that they face the same problem as the macroquantifiers: how to put it all together? The disparity of the documentation—auction catalogues, notarial records, subscription lists, library registers—does not make the task easier. Differences in conclusions can be attributed to the peculiarities of the sources rather than to the behavior of the readers. And the monographs often cancel each other out: artisans look literate here and unlettered there; travel literature seems to be popular among some groups in some places and unpopular in others. A systematic comparison of genres, milieux, times, and places would look like a conspiracy of exceptions trying to disprove rules.

So far only one book historian has been hardy enough to propose a general model. Rolf Engelsing has argued that a "reading revolution" *(Leserevolution)* took place at the end of the eighteenth century. From the Middle Ages until sometime after 1750, according to Engelsing, men read "intensively." They had only a few books—the Bible, an almanac, a devotional work or two—and they read them over and over again, usually aloud and in groups, so that a narrow range of traditional literature became deeply impressed on their consciousness. By 1800 men were reading "extensively." They read all kinds of material, especially periodicals and newspapers, and read it only once, then raced on to the next item. Engelsing does not produce much evidence for his hypothesis. Indeed, most of his research concerns only a small sampling of burghers in Bremen. But it has an attractive before-and-after simplicity, and it provides a handy formula for contrasting modes of reading very early and very late in European history. Its main drawback, as I see it, is its unilinear character. Reading did not evolve in one direction, extensiveness. It assumed many different forms among different social groups in different eras. Men and women have read in order to save their souls, to improve their manners, to repair their machinery, to seduce their sweethearts, to learn about current events, and simply to have fun. In many cases, especially among the public of Richardson, Rousseau, and Goethe, the reading became more intensive, not less. But the late eighteenth century does seem to represent a turning point, a time when more reading matter became available to a wider public, when one can see the emergence of a mass readership that would grow to giant proportions in the nineteenth century with the development of machine-made paper, steam-powered presses, linotype, and nearly universal literacy. All these changes opened up new possibilities, not by decreasing intensity but by increasing variety.[13]

I must therefore confess to some skepticism about the "reading revolution." Yet an American historian of the book, David Hall, has described a transformation in the reading habits of New Englanders between 1600 and 1850 in almost exactly the same terms as those used by Engelsing. Before 1800, New Englanders read a small corpus of venerable "steady sellers"—the Bible, almanacs, the *New England Primer,* Philip Doddridge's *Rise and Progress of Religion,* Richard Baxter's *Call to the Unconverted*—and read them over and over again, aloud, in groups, and with exceptional intensity.' After 1800 they were swamped with new kinds of books—novels, newspapers, fresh and sunny varieties of children's literature—and they read through them ravenously, discarding one thing as soon as they could find another. Although Hall and Engelsing had never heard of one another, they discovered a similar pattern in two quite different areas of the Western world. Perhaps a fundamental shift in the nature of reading took place at the end of the eighteenth century. It may not have been a revolution, but it marked the end of an Old Regime—the reign of Thomas à Kempis, Johann Arndt, and John Bunyan.[14]

The "where" of reading is more important than one might think, because placing the reader in his setting can provide hints about the nature of his experience. In the University of Leyden there hangs a print of the university library, dated 1610. It shows the books, heavy folio volumes, chained on high shelves jutting out from the walls in a sequence determined by the rubrics of classical bibliography: *Jurisconsulti, Medici, Historici,* and so on. Students are scattered about the room, reading the books on counters built at shoulder level below the shelves. They read standing up, protected against the cold by thick cloaks and hats, one foot perched on a rail to ease the pressure on their bodies. Reading cannot have been comfortable in the age of classical humanism. In pictures done a century and a half later, "La Lecture" and "La Liseuse" by Fragonard, for example, readers recline in chaises longues or well-padded armchairs with their legs propped on footstools. They are often women, wearing loose-fitting gowns known at the time as *liseuses.* They usually hold a dainty duodecimo volume in their fingers and have a faraway look in their eye. From Fragonard to Monet, who also painted a "Liseuse," reading moves from the boudoir to the outdoors. The reader backpacks books to fields and mountaintops where, like Rousseau and Heine, he can commune with nature. Nature must have seemed out of joint a few generations later in the trenches of World War I, where the young lieutenants from Göttingen and Oxford somehow found room for a few slim volumes of poetry. One of the most precious books in my own small collection is an edition of Hölderlin's *Hymnen an die Ideale der Menschheit,* inscribed "Adolf Noelle, Januar 1916, nord-Frankreich"—a gift from a German friend who was trying to explain Germany. I'm still not sure I understand, but I think the general understanding of reading would be advanced if we thought harder about its iconography and accoutrements, including furniture and dress.[15]

Of course, one cannot take pictures literally, as a depiction of how people actually read. But they can reveal hidden assumptions about what people thought reading should be or the atmosphere in which it should take place. Greuze certainly sentimentalized the collective character of reading in his painting of "A Father Reading the Bible to His Children." Restif de la Bretonne probably did the same in the family Bible readings described in *La Vie de mon père:* "I cannot recall without tenderness the rapt attention with which that reading was heard and the way it spread a feeling of good-hearted brotherhood throughout the numerous family (and in the family I include the domestic servants). My father would begin with these words: 'Prepare your souls, my children; the Holy Spirit is about to speak.' "

But for all their sentimentality, such descriptions proceed from a common assumption: for the common people in early modern Europe, reading was a social activity. It took place in workshops, barns, and taverns. It was almost always oral but not necessarily edifying. Thus the peasant in the country inn described, with some rose tinting around the edges, by Christian Schubart in 1786:

> Und bricht die Abendzeit herein,
> So trink ich halt mein Schöpple Wein;
> Da liest der Herr Schulmeister mir
> Was Neues aus der Zeitung für.[16]

When the evening time comes round,
I always drink my glass of wine.
Then the schoolmaster reads to me
Something new out of the newspaper.

The most important institution of popular reading under the Old Regime was a fireside gathering known as the *veillée* in France and the *Spinnstube* in Germany. While children played, women sewed, and men repaired tools, one of the company who could decipher a text would regale them with the adventures of *Les quatre fils Aymon, Till Eulenspiegel,* or some other favorite from the standard repertory of the cheap, popular chapbooks. Some of these primitive paperbacks indicated that they were meant to be taken in through the ears by beginning with phrases such as, "What you are about to hear . . ." In the nineteenth century, groups of artisans, especially cigar makers and tailors, took turns reading or hired a reader to keep themselves entertained while they worked. Even today many people get their news by being read to by a telecaster. Television may be less of a break with the past than is generally assumed. In any case, for most people throughout most of history, books had audiences rather than readers. They were better heard than seen.[17]

Reading was a more private experience for the minority of educated persons who could afford to buy books. But many of them joined reading clubs, *cabinets littéraires,* or *Lesegesellschaften,* where they could read almost anything they wanted, in a social atmosphere, for a small monthly payment. Françoise Parent-Lardeur has traced the proliferation of these clubs in Paris under the Restoration, but they went back well into the eighteenth century. Provincial booksellers often turned their stock into a library and charged dues for the right to frequent it. Good light, some comfortable chairs, a few pictures on the wall, and subscriptions to a half-dozen newspapers were enough to make a club out of almost any bookshop. Thus the *cabinet littéraire* advertised by P. J. Bernard, a minor bookseller in Lunéville: "A large, comfortable, well-lit, and well-heated house, which will be open every day from nine in the morning until noon and from one o'clock until ten in the evening, will provide members with two thousand volumes; and the stock will be increased by four hundred each year. . . . A room on the ground floor and another on the second floor will be reserved for conversation; all the others will be placed at the disposition of readers of newspapers and books." By November 1779, the club had two hundred members, mostly officers from the local *gendarmerie*. For the modest sum of three livres a year, they had access to five thousand books, thirteen journals, and special rooms set aside for socializing.[18]

German reading clubs provided the social foundation for a distinct variety of bourgeois culture in the eighteenth century, according to Otto Dann. They sprang up at an astounding rate, especially in the northern cities. Martin Welke estimates that perhaps one of every five hundred adult Germans belonged to a *Lesegesellschaft* by 1800. Marlies Prüsener has been able to identify well over four hundred of the clubs and to form some idea of their reading matter. All of them had a basic supply of periodicals supplemented by uneven runs of books, usually on fairly weighty subjects like history and politics. They seem to have been a more serious version of the coffeehouse, itself an important institution for reading, which spread through Germany from the late seventeenth century. By 1760, Vienna had at least sixty coffeehouses. They provided newspapers, journals, and endless occasions for political discussions, just as they had in London and Amsterdam for more than a century.[19]

Thus we already know a good deal about the institutional bases of reading. We have some answers to the "who," "what," "where," and "when" questions. But the "why's" and "how's" elude us. We have not yet devised a strategy for understanding the inner process by which readers made sense of words. We do not even understand the way we read ourselves, despite the efforts of psychologists and neurologists to trace eye movements and to map the hemispheres of the brain. Is the cognitive process different for Chinese, who read pictographs, and for Westerners, who scan lines? For Israelis who read words without vowels moving from right to left and for blind people who transmit stimuli through their fingers? For Southeast Asians whose languages lack tenses and order reality spatially and for American Indians whose languages have been reduced to writing only recently by alien scholars? For the holy man in the presence of the Word and for the consumer studying labels in a supermarket? The differences seem endless, for reading is not simply a skill but a way of making meaning, which must vary from culture to culture. It would be extravagant to expect to find a formula that could account for all those variations. But it should be possible to develop a way to study the changes in reading within our own culture. I would like to suggest five approaches to the problem.

First, I think it should be possible to learn more about the ideals and assumptions underlying reading in the past. We could study contemporary depictions of reading in fiction, autobiographies, polemical writings, letters, paintings, and prints in order to uncover some basic notions of what people thought took place when they read. Consider, for example, the great debate about the craze for reading in late eighteenth-century Germany. Those who deplored the *Lesewut* did not simply condemn its effects on morals and politics. They feared it would damage public health. In a tract of 1795, J. G. Heinzmann listed the physical consequences of excessive reading: "susceptibility to colds, headaches, weakening of the eyes, heat rashes, gout, arthritis, hemorrhoids, asthma, apoplexy, pulmonary disease, indigestion, blocking of the bowels, nervous disorder, migraines, epilepsy, hypochondria, and melancholy." On the positive side of the debate, Johann Adam Bergk accepted the premises of his opponents but disagreed with their conclusions. He took it as established that one should never read immediately after eating or while standing up. But by correct disposition of the body, one could make reading a force for good. The "art of reading" involved washing the face with cold water and taking walks in fresh air as well as concentration and meditation.

No one challenged the notion that there was a physical element in reading, because no one drew a clear distinction between the physical and the moral world. In the eighteenth and nineteenth centuries, readers attempted to "digest" books, to absorb them in their whole being, body and soul. A few extremists took to reading-as-digestion literally: thus the case of a woman in Hampshire, England, who "ate a New Testament, day by day and leaf by leaf, between two sides of bread and butter, as a remedy for fits." More often the devouring of books took the form of a spiritual exercise, whose physicality still shows on the surviving pages. The volumes from Samuel Johnson's library, now owned by Mrs. Donald F. Hyde, are bent and battered, as if he had wrestled his way through them.[20]

Reading as a spiritual exercise predominated in the sixteenth and seventeenth centuries. But how was it performed? One could look for guidance in the manuals of Jesuits and the hermeneutical treatises of Protestants. Family Bible readings took place on both sides of the great religious divide. And as the example of Restif de la Bretonne indicates, the Bible was approached with awe, even among some Catholic peasants. Of course, Boccaccio, Castiglione, Cervantes, Erasmus, and Rabelais had developed other uses of literacy for the elite. But for most people, reading remained a sacred activity. It put you in the presence of the Word and unlocked holy mysteries. As a working hypothesis, it seems valid to assert that the farther back in time you go the farther away you move from instrumental reading. Not only does the "how-to" book become rarer and the religious book more common, reading itself is different. In the age of Luther and Loyola, it provided access to absolute truth.

On a more mundane level, assumptions about reading could be traced through advertisements and prospectuses for books. Thus some typical remarks from an eighteenth-century prospectus taken at random from the rich collection in the Newberry Library: a book seller is offering a quarto edition of the *Commentaires sur la coutume d'Angoumois,* an excellent work, he insists, for its typography as much as its content: "The text of the *Coutume* is printed in *gros-romain* type; the summaries that precede the commentaries are printed in *cicéro;* and the commentaries are printed in *Saint-Augustin.* The whole work is made from very beautiful paper manufactured in Angoulême."[21] No publisher would dream of mentioning paper and type in advertising a law book today. In the eighteenth century advertisers assumed that their clients cared about the physical quality of books. Buyers and sellers alike shared a typographical consciousness that is now nearly extinct.

The reports of censors also can be revealing, at least in the case of books from early modern France, where censorship was highly developed if not enormously effective. A typical travel book, *Nouveau voyage aux isles de l'Amérique* (Paris, 1722) by J.-B. Labat, contains four "approbations" printed out in full next to the *privilège.* One censor explains that the manuscript piqued his curiosity: "It is difficult to begin reading it without feeling that mild but avid curiosity that impels us to read further." Another recommends it for its "simple and concise style" and also for its utility: "Nothing in my opinion is so useful to travelers, to the inhabitants of that country, to tradesmen, and to those who study natural history." And a third simply found it a good read: "I had great pleasure in reading it. It contains a multitude of curious things." Censors did not simply hound out heretics and revolutionaries, as we tend to assume in looking back through time across the Inquisition and the Enlightenment. They gave the royal stamp of approval to a work, and in doing so they provided clues as to how it might be read. Their values constituted an official standard against which ordinary readings might be measured.

But how did ordinary readers read? My second suggestion for attacking that problem concerns the ways reading was learned. In studying literacy in seventeenth-century England, Margaret Spufford discovered that a great deal of learning went on outside the schoolroom, in workshops and fields, where laborers taught themselves and one another. Inside the school, English children learned to read before they learned to write instead of acquiring the two skills together at the beginning of their education as they do today. They often joined the work force before the age of seven, when instruction in writing began. So literacy estimates based on the ability to write may be much too low, and the reading public may have included a great many people who could not sign their names. The disparity between reading and writing stands out even more sharply in Sweden, where the archives are rich enough to provide reliable statistics. By 1770, according to Egil Johansson, Swedish society was almost fully literate. Church records show that 80–95 percent of the population could both read and respond satisfactorily when interrogated about the meaning of religious texts. Yet only 20 percent could write, and only a tiny fraction had ever gone to school. A vast literacy campaign had taken place in homes, without the aid of professional teachers, in response to a church law of 1686, which required that everyone, and especially children, farm hands, and domestic servants, should "learn to read and see with their own eyes [i.e., be able to understand] what God bids and commands in His Holy Word."[22]

Of course, "reading" for such people meant something quite different from what it means today, and it differed in the Protestant North from what it had become in the Catholic South. Children in early modern France learned their three R's in sequence: first reading, then writing, then arithmetic. Their primers—ABCs like the *Croix de Jésus* and the *Croix de par Dieu*—began as modern manuals do, with the alphabet. But the letters had different sounds. The pupil pronounced a flat vowel before each consonant, so that *p* came out as "eh-p" rather than "pé," as it is today. When said aloud, the letters did not link together phonetically in combinations that could be recognized by the ear as syllables of a word. Thus *p-a-t* in *pater* sounded like "ehp-ah-eht". But the phonetic fuzziness did not really matter, because the letters were meant as a visual stimulus to trigger the memory of a text that had already been learned by heart—and the text was always in Latin. The whole system was build on the premise that French children should not begin to read in French. They passed directly from the alphabet to simple syllables and then to the *Pater Noster, Ave Maria, Credo,* and *Benedicite.* Having learned to recognize these common prayers, they worked through liturgical responses printed in standard chapbooks. At this point many of them left school. They had acquired enough mastery of the printed word to fulfill the functions expected of them by the Church— that is, to participate in its rituals. But they had never read a text in a language they could understand.

Some children—we don't know how many, perhaps a minority in the seventeenth century and a majority in the eighteenth—remained in school long enough to learn to read in

French. Even then, however, reading was often a matter of recognizing something already known rather than a process of acquiring new knowledge. Nearly all of the schools were run by the Church, and nearly all of the schoolbooks were religious, usually catechisms and pious textbooks like the *Escole paroissiale* by Jacques de Batencour. In the early eighteenth century the Frères des Ecoles Chrétiennes began to provide the same text to several pupils and teach them as a group—a first step toward standardized instruction, which was to become the rule a hundred years later. At the same time, a few tutors in aristocratic households began to teach reading directly in French. They developed phonetic techniques and audio-visual aids like the pictorial flash cards of the abbé Berthaud and the *bureau typographique* of Louis Dumas. By 1789 their example had spread to some progressive primary schools. But most children still learned to read by standing before the master and reciting passages from whatever text they could get their hands on while their classmates struggled with a motley collection of booklets on the back benches. Some of these "schoolbooks" would reappear in the evening at the *veillée,* because they were popular best sellers from the *bibliothèque bleue.* So reading around the fireside had something in common with reading in the classroom: it was a recital of a text that everyone already knew. Instead of opening up limitless vistas of new ideas, it probably remained within a closed circuit, exactly where the post-Tridentine Church wanted to keep it. "Probably," however, is the governing word in that proposition. We can only guess at the nature of early modern pedagogy by reading the few primers and the still fewer memoirs that have survived from that era. We don't know what really happened in the classroom. And whatever happened, the peasant reader-listeners may have construed their catechism as well as their adventure stories in ways that completely escape us.[23]

If the experience of the great mass of readers lies beyond the range of historical research, historians should be able to capture something of what reading meant for the few persons who left a record of it. A third approach could begin with the best-known autobiographical accounts—those of Saint Augustine, Saint Theresa of Avila, Montaigne, Rousseau, and Stendhal, for example—and move on to less familiar sources. J.-M. Goulemot has used the autobiography of Jamerey-Duval to show how a peasant could read and write his way up through the ranks of the Old Regime, and Daniel Roche discovered an eighteenth-century glazier, Jacques-Louis Ménétra, who read his way around a typical tour de France. Although he did not carry many books in the sack slung over his back, Ménétra constantly exchanged letters with fellow travelers and sweethearts. He squandered a few sous on broadsides at public executions and even composed doggerel verse for the ceremonies and farces that he staged with the other workers. When he told the story of his life, he organized his narrative in picaresque fashion, combining oral tradition (folk tales and the stylized braggadocio of male bull sessions) with genres of popular literature (the novelettes of the *bibliothèque bleue*). Unlike other plebeian authors—Restif, Mercier, Rousseau, Diderot, and Marmontel—Ménétra never won a place in the Republic of Letters. He showed that letters had a place in the culture of the common man.[24]

That place may have been marginal, but margins themselves provide clues to the experience of ordinary readers. In the sixteenth century marginal notes appeared in print in the form of glosses, which steered the reader through humanist texts. In the eighteenth century the gloss gave way to the footnote. How did the reader follow the play between text and paratext at the bottom or side of the page? Gibbon created ironic distance by masterful deployment of footnotes. A careful study of annotated eighteenth-century copies of *The De-*

cline and Fall of the Roman Empire might reveal the way that distance was perceived by Gibbon's contemporaries. John Adams covered his books with scribbling. By following him through his copy of Rousseau's *Discourse on the Origin of Inequality,* one can see how radical Enlightenment philosophy looked to a retired revolutionary in the sober climate of Quincy, Massachusetts. Thus Rousseau, in the first English edition:

> There was no kind of moral relation between men in this state [the state of nature]; they could not be either good or bad, and had neither vices nor virtues. It is proper, therefore, to suspend judgment about their situation . . . until we have examined whether there are more virtues or vices among civilized men.

And Adams, in the margin:

> Wonders upon wonders. Paradox upon paradox. What astonishing sagacity had Mr. Rousseau! Yet this eloquent coxcomb has with his affectation of singularity made men discontented with superstition and tyranny.

Christiane Berkvens-Stevelinck has found an excellent site for mapping the Republic of Letters in the marginalia of Prosper Marchand, the bibliophile of eighteenth-century Leyden. Other scholars have charted the currents of literary history by trying to reread great books as great writers have read them, using the annotations in collectors' items such as Diderot's copy of the *Encyclopédie* and Melville's copy of Emerson's essays. But the inquiry needn't be limited to great books or to books at all. Peter Burke is currently studying the graffiti of Renaissance Italy. When scribbled on the door of an enemy, they often functioned as ritual insults, which defined the lines of social conflict dividing neighborhoods and clans. When attached to the famous statue of Pasquino in Rome, this public scribbling set the tone of a rich and intensely political street culture. A history of reading might be able to advance by great leaps from the Pasquinade and the Commedia dell'Arte to Molière, from Molière to Rousseau, and from Rousseau to Robespierre.[25]

My fourth suggestion concerns literary theory. It can, I agree, look daunting, especially to the outsider. It comes wrapped in imposing labels—structuralism, deconstruction, hermeneutics, semiotics, phenomenology—and it goes as rapidly as it comes, for the trends displace one another with bewildering speed. Through them all, however, runs a concern that could lead to some collaboration between literary critics and historians of the book—the concern for reading. Whether they unearth deep structures or tear down systems of signs, critics have increasingly treated literature as an activity rather than an established body of texts. They insist that a book's meaning is not fixed on its pages; it is construed by its readers. So reader response has become the key point around which literary analysis turns.

In Germany, this approach has led to a revival of literary history as *Rezeptionsästhetik* under the leadership of Hans Robert Jauss and Wolfgang Iser. In France, it has taken a philosophical turn in the work of Roland Barthes, Paul Ricœur, Tzvetan Todorov, and Georges Poulet. In the United States, it is still in the melting-pot stage. Wayne Booth, Paul de Man, Jonathan Culler, Geoffrey Hartman, J. Hillis Miller, and Stanley Fish have supplied ingredients for a general theory, but no consensus has emerged from their debates. Nonetheless, all this critical activity points toward a new textology, and all the critics share a way of working when they interpret specific texts.[26]

Consider, for example, Walter Ong's analysis of the first sentences of *A Farewell to Arms*:

In the late summer of that year we lived in a house in a village that looked across the river and the plain to the mountains. In the bed of the river there were pebbles and boulders, dry and white in the sun, and the water was clear and swiftly moving and blue in the channels.

What year? What river? Ong asks. Hemingway does not say. By unorthodox use of the definite article—"the river" instead of "a river"—and sparse deployment of adjectives, he implies that the reader does not need a detailed description of the scene. A reminder will be enough, because the reader is deemed to have been there already. He is addressed as if he were a confidant and fellow traveler who merely needs to be reminded in order to recollect the hard glint of the sun, the coarse taste of the wine, and the stench of the dead in World War I Italy. Should the reader object—and one can imagine many responses such as, "I am a sixty-year-old grandmother and I don't know anything about rivers in Italy"—he won't be able to "get" the book. But if he accepts the role imposed on him by the rhetoric, his fictionalized self can swell to the dimensions of the Hemingway hero; and he can go through the narrative as the author's companion in arms.[27]

Earlier rhetoric usually operated in the opposite manner. It assumed that the reader knew nothing about the story and needed to be oriented by rich descriptive passages or introductory observations. Thus the opening of *Pride and Prejudice:*

It is a truth universally acknowledged, that a single man in possession of a good fortune must be in want of a wife.

However little known the feelings or views of such a man may be on his first entering a neighbourhood, this truth is so well fixed in the minds of the surrounding families that he is considered as the rightful property of some one or other of their daughters.

"My dear Mr Bennet," said his lady to him one day, "have you heard that Netherfield Park is let at last?"

This kind of narrative moves from the general to the particular, like a lens zooming in from a wide-angle shot to a close-up. It places the indefinite article first and helps the reader get his bearing by degrees. But it always keeps him at a distance, because he is presumed to enter the story as an outsider and to be reading for instruction, amusement, or some high moral purpose. As in the case of the Hemingway novel, he must play his role for the rhetoric to work; but the role is completely different.

Writers have devised many other ways to initiate readers into stories. A vast distance separates Melville's "Call me Ishmael" from Milton's prayer for help to "justify the ways of God to men." But every narrative presupposes a reader, and every reading begins from a protocol inscribed within the text. The text may undercut itself, and the reader may work against the grain or wring new meaning from familiar words: hence the endless possibilities of interpretation proposed by the deconstructionists and the original readings that have shaped cultural history—Rousseau's reading of *Le Misanthrope,* for example, or Kierkegaard's reading of Genesis 22. But whatever one makes of it, reading has reemerged as the central fact of literature.

If so, the time is ripe for making a juncture between literary theory and the history of books. The theory can reveal the range in potential responses to a text—that is, to the rhetorical constraints that direct reading without determining it. The history can show what readings actually took place—that is, within the limits of an imperfect body of evidence. By paying heed to history, literary critics may avoid the danger of anachronism; for they sometimes seem to assume that seventeenth-century Englishmen read Milton and Bunyan as if they were twentieth-century college professors. By taking account of rhetoric, historians may find clues to behavior that would otherwise be baffling, such as the passions aroused from *Clarissa* to *La Nouvelle Héloïse* and from *Werther* to *René.* I would therefore argue for a dual strategy, which would combine textual analysis with empirical research. In this way it should

be possible to compare the implicit readers of the texts with
the actual readers of the past and, by building on such comparisons, to develop a history as well as a theory of reader
response.

Such a history could be reinforced by a fifth mode of analysis, one based on analytical bibliography. By studying books
as physical objects, bibliographers have demonstrated that the
typographical disposition of a text can to a considerable extent
determine the way it was read. The most striking instances of
linkage between typography and meaning occur in baroque
poems such as the following, from Gottfried Kleiner's *Garten-
Lust im Winter* (1732):

geh.
Früchte
und dort voll
hinnen geh,
Biß ich von
O mach mich grün,
O laß mich blühn,
Bewässert gutt
Dein mildes Blutt
Die deine Liebe sucht.
Und pflantz in mich die Frucht,
In meinem Hertzen selbst den Platz,
Bereite Dir, Du Seelen-Schatz!
Ich nihm mich mir, und gieb mich Dir!
Als Du, mein JESU, meine Zier!
Soll Niemand seyn, und Niemand werden,
Mein Alles, dort, und hier auf Erden,
Mein auserkohrnes GOTTES-Lamm,
Mein schönster Himmels-Bräutigam,
Mein Seelen-Ruhm,
Mein Eigenthum,
Mein Port,
Mein Hort,
Mein Theil,
Mein Heil,
Mein Steig,
Mein Zweig,
Mein Raum,
Mein Baum,

[Literal translation: "My tree, / My space, / My bough, / My path, / My salvation, / My share, / My refuge, / My port, / My property / My soul's fame / My most beautiful, celestial bridegroom / My elected lamb of GOD / My all, there and here on earth, / Let no one be and no one come into being / But thou, my JESUS, my adornment! / Oh! take me from me and give me to thee! / Thou treasure of the soul, prepare / A place for yourself in my heart, / And plant in me the fruit, / That seeks your love. / Your mild blood / Waters well. / Oh, let me blossom, / Oh, make me green, / Until I go / From hence, / And stand there / Full of / Fruit.]

Through its shape as a tree, the poem invites the reader to reverse his normal mode of scanning and to read from the bottom up, as if he were climbing toward heaven. At the heart of the tree, the reader encounters the word "Jesus." By then he has become so absorbed in the rhetoric that the poet's voice speaks for him and he can identify with the poet's ecstasy. He has read himself into a position where he imagines being penetrated by the love of Christ. It grows within him like a seed. It makes his life flower and bear fruit in good works, and in the end it helps him to ascend into paradise. Metaphors of climbing, growing, and sexual fecundation reinforce one another and are reinforced in turn through the combined effect of the meter, which rises to a crescendo at "Jesus" in line 15, and of the grammar, which sweeps the reader upward through a series of clauses culminating with the end of the sentence in that same critical line, where the reader is exposed to the Word and saved.[28]

Print does not often embody poetry so completely, but every text has typographical properties that guide the reader's response. The design of a book can be crucial to its meaning. In a remarkable study of Congreve, D. F. McKenzie has shown that the bawdy, neo-Elizabethan playwright known to us from the quarto editions of the late seventeenth century underwent a typographical rebirth in his old age and emerged as the stately, neoclassical author of the three-volume octavo *Works* published in 1710. Individual words rarely changed from one edition to another, but a transformation in the design of the books gave the plays an entirely new flavor. By adding scene divisions, grouping characters, relocating lines, and bringing out *liaisons des scènes,* Congreve fit his old texts into the new classical model derived from the French stage. To go from the quarto to the octavo volumes is to move from Elizabethan to Georgian England.[29]

Roger Chartier found similar but more sociological implications in the metamorphoses of a Spanish classic, *Historia de la vida del Buscón* by Francisco de Quevedo. The novel was originally intended for a sophisticated public, both in Spain where it was first published in 1626 and in France where it came out in an elegant translation in 1633. But in the midseventeenth century the Oudot and Garnier houses of Troyes began to publish a series of cheap paperback editions, which made it a staple of the popular literature known as the *bibliothèque bleue* for two hundred years. The popular publishers did not hesitate to tinker with the text, but they concentrated primarily on book design, what Chartier calls the *"mise en livre."* They broke the story into simple units, shortening sentences, subdividing paragraphs, and multiplying the number of chapters. The new typographical structure implied a new kind of reading and a new public: humble people who lacked the facility and the time to take in lengthy stretches of narrative. The short episodes were autonomous. They did not need to be linked by complex subthemes and character development because they provided just enough material to fill a *veillée.* So the book itself became a collection of fragments rather than a continuous story, and it could be put together by each reader-listener in his own way. Just how this "appropriation" took place remains a mystery, because Chartier limits his analysis to the book as a physical object. But he shows how typography opens onto sociology, how the implicit reader of the author became the implicit reader of the publisher, moving down the social ladder of the Old Regime and into the world that would be recognized in the nineteenth century as *"le grand public."*[30]

A few adventuresome bibliographers and book historians have begun to speculate about long-term trends in the evolution of the book. They argue that readers respond more directly to the physical organization of texts than to their surrounding social environment. So it may be possible to learn something about the remote history of reading by practicing a kind of textual archeology. If we cannot know precisely how the Romans read Ovid, we can assume that, like most Roman inscriptions, the verse contained no punctuation, paragraphing, or spaces between words. The units of sound and meaning probably were closer to the rhythms of speech than to the typographical units—the ens, words, and lines—of the printed page. The page itself as a unit of the book dates only from the third or fourth century A.D. Before then, one had to unroll a book to read it. Once gathered pages (the *codex*) replaced the scroll *(volumen)*, readers could easily move backward and forward through books, and texts became divided into segments that could be marked off and indexed. Yet long after books acquired their modern form, reading continued to be an oral experience, performed in public. At an indeterminate point, perhaps in some monasteries in the seventh century and certainly in the universities of the thirteenth century, men began to read silently and alone. The shift to silent reading might have involved a greater mental adjustment than the shift to the printed text, for it made reading an individual, interior experience.[31]

Printing made a difference, of course, but it probably was

less revolutionary than is commonly believed. Some books had title pages, tables of contents, indexes, pagination, and publishers who produced multiple copies from scriptoria for a large reading public before the invention of movable type. For the first half century of its existence, the printed book continued to be an imitation of the manuscript book. No doubt it was read by the same public in the same way. But after 1500 the printed book, pamphlet, broadside, map, and poster reached new kinds of readers and stimulated new kinds of reading. Increasingly standardized in its design, cheaper in its price, and widespread in its distribution, the new book transformed the world. It did not simply supply more information. It provided a mode of understanding, a basic metaphor of making sense of life.

So it was that in the sixteenth century men took possession of the Word; in the seventeenth century they began to decode the "book of nature"; and in the eighteenth century they learned to read themselves. With the help of books, Locke and Condillac studied the mind as a tabula rasa, and Franklin formulated an epitaph for himself:[32]

> The Body of
> B. Franklin, Printer,
> Like the cover of an old Book,
> Its Contents torn out,
> And stript of its Lettering & Gilding
> Lies here, Food for Worms.
> But the Work shall not be lost;
> For it will, as he believ'd,
> Appear once more
> In a new and more elegant Edition
> Corrected and improved
> By the Author.

I don't want to make too much of the metaphor, since Franklin has already flogged it to death, but rather to return to a point so simple that it may escape our notice. Reading has a history. It was not always and everywhere the same. We may think of it as a straightforward process of lifting information from a page; but if we considered it further, we would agree that information must be sifted, sorted, and interpreted. Interpretive schemes belong to cultural configurations, which have varied enormously over time. As our ancestors lived in different mental worlds, they must have read differently, and the history of reading could be as complex as the history of thinking. It could be so complex, in fact, that the five steps suggested here may lead in disparate directions or set us circling around the problem indefinitely without penetrating to its core. There are no direct routes or shortcuts because reading is not a distinct thing, like a constitution or a social order, that can be tracked through time. It is an activity involving a peculiar relation—on the one hand the reader, on the other the text. Although readers and texts have varied according to social and technological circumstances, the history of reading should not be reduced to a chronology of those variations. It should go beyond them to confront the relational element at the heart of the matter: how did changing readerships construe shifting texts?

The question sounds abstruse, but a great deal hangs on it. Think how often reading has changed the course of history— Luther's reading of Paul, Marx's reading of Hegel, Mao's reading of Marx. Those points stand out in a deeper, vaster process—man's unending effort to find meaning in the world around him and within himself. If we could understand how he has read, we could come closer to understanding how he made sense of life; and in that way, the historical way, we might even satisfy some of our own craving for meaning.

PART FOUR

The Lay of the Land

FREEDOM OF THE PRESS, *1797*.

Intellectual and
Cultural History

A MALAISE is spreading among intellectual historians in the United States. Twenty years ago, they saw their discipline as the queen of the historical sciences. Today she seems humbled. No dramatic dethronement has occurred; but after a realignment of research during the last two decades, she now sits below the salt, surrounded by rude new varieties of sociocultural history and bewildering language— *mentalité, episteme,* paradigm, hermeneutics, semiotics, hegemony, deconstruction, and thick description.

Evidently some historians continue to feel comfortable within the intellectual framework established by Arthur Lovejoy and Perry Miller, for one still finds "unit-ideas" and "mind" amid the overgrowth of trendier terms.[1] But the trend toward self-doubt and beleaguered self-assertion can be found wherever intellectual historians discuss the state of their craft—and the historiographical-methodological discussions have multiplied in the past few years. Murray Murphey began a recent article with a lament:

Thirty years ago intellectual history occupied an envied place in the American university; its courses were full to overflowing and its practitioners—men such as Merle Curti, Ralph Gabriel, and Perry Miller—were famous throughout the profession, and indeed beyond. But thirty years have brought a marked change. Students no longer see intellectual history as the place "where the action is," and the profession seems to concur that the "cutting edge" of historical scholarship lies elsewhere.[2]

At the same time, Dominick La Capra sounded the alarm in calling for a conference at Cornell on the future of intellectual history:

In the recent past intellectual history has been shaken by a number of important developments. Social historians have posed questions not answerable through traditional techniques of narrating or analyzing ideas. These questions bear upon the nature of collective "mentalities" and the genesis or impact of ideas. At times the impetus of social historians seems imperialistic: the reduction of intellectual history to a function of social history and the elevation of social problems to the status of the only truly significant historical problems.[3]

The same theme ran through a set of papers presented at a conference on American intellectual history at Racine, Wisconsin, in December 1977.[4] It had emerged seven years earlier in a conference on the state of historical studies held in Rome.[5] It has reappeared regularly at conventions of the American Historical Association.[6] And it can be detected everywhere in the reviews and articles through which intellectual historians try to take one another's pulse. To be sure, many of them claim that they never felt healthier, and they welcome the current crisis as an opportunity to reorient their discipline. But optimists and pessimists agree that a crisis exists and that its outcome hangs on the relations between intellectual and social history.[7]

That view derives in part from a sharpened sense of the history of intellectual history in the United States. John Higham and Robert Skotheim have shown that intellectual history and social history came of age together early in the twentieth century, as ingredients in the New History of James Harvey Robinson, Charles A. Beard, Frederick Jackson Turner, and Carl

Becker.[8] The two genres seemed new in that they challenged an older view of history as past politics. They worked their way into college curricula as allies, the "intellectual and social history" courses that proliferated in the 1920s and 1930s. The alliance fell apart during the next two decades, however, when Arthur Lovejoy and Perry Miller raised the level of intellectual history by stripping it of any concern for social context. Among Americanists, Miller's success stimulated his successors to chase after abstractions—myths, symbols, and images. They also drew on the attempts of Vernon Parrington, Ralph Gabriel, and Merle Curti to determine the distinctive character of American thought. By the 1960s the American Studies movement had cut American intellectual history free of its moorings in social history and had drifted off in pursuit of a disembodied national mind. At that point, the professors' universities exploded beneath them. Racial conflict, "countercultures," student radicalism, the war in Southeast Asia, the collapse of the presidency destroyed the vision of American history as a spiritual consensus. Social historians rushed in, not to fill the vacuum but to pick apart the ruins of the old New History, not to reconstruct a single past but to burrow in different directions. Black history, urban history, labor history, the history of women, of criminality, sexuality, the oppressed, the inarticulate, the marginal—so many lines of inquiry opened up that social history seemed to dominate research on all fronts. The abandoned ally had regained command of the profession.

Some American historians probably would consider this account of their professional past overdramatic or inaccurate. Some have always disparaged intellectual history as unworkable, if not quite un-American—"like trying to nail jelly to the wall," in the words of one old-time, hard-line political historian.[9] And indeed, the homegrown varieties of intellectual history seem stunted in comparison with those of Europe. Europeans do not speak of intellectual history in the American manner but rather to the history of ideas, *histoire des idées, Geistesgeschichte, storia della filosofia*—different names that denote different traditions. Those traditions have rubbed off on American students of European history, especially the students who did their graduate work after 1950, when fellowships, charter flights, and a strong dollar made study abroad more accessible than ever before. Those who remained at home often learned their European history from the European refugees who had flocked to American universities in the 1930s. And those who somehow escaped the immediate influence of Europe still dealt with European subjects, subjects often transmitted in foreign languages and located in a remote past, where there was no difficulty about defining American character or culture. Sources, teachers, and subjects made the intellectual history of Europe inherently cosmopolitan.

Yet the American version of that history has reached a critical point. It has converged with the crisis in American studies, although it has developed along a different course. The course was set between the world wars by Arthur Lovejoy and Carl Becker. Lovejoy traced the filiation of key ideas over vast stretches of time, while Becker sketched the intellectual climate of entire areas. But each man worked from classic texts, which he could locate easily in his own library. For the next generation of intellectual historians, Crane Brinton demonstrated the importance of following ideas beyond libraries and to "their ultimate refuge in the mind of the common man."[10] By 1950 this approach had crystallized as a course, Harvard's History 134a, "Intellectual History of Europe in the Eighteenth and Nineteenth Centuries," and a textbook, *Ideas and Men*.[11] During the next two decades, H. Stuart Hughes and Peter Gay extended the attempt to trace connections between ideas and men in several studies of the social dimensions of thought. They usually organized their books as Brinton had done, allotting chapters to thinkers and tying them together with dialectical formulas: consciousness and society, antiquity and modernity.[12] Similar concerns inspired a group of gifted biographers, Arthur Wilson, Frank Manuel, and Jacques Barzun.[13] But the emphasis on "the method of men," as Brinton called it, raised the danger that intellectual history would develop into the history of intellectuals and that it would lose touch with the "common man."

Meanwhile, social historians were rediscovering that rare species in Europe, or rather they were reconstructing the common ground of experience for different groups of men and women by using techniques borrowed from demography, economics, and sociology. Some of the impetus for this tendency did not come from social scientists but from a cosmopolitan group of scholars who gathered around Georges Lefebvre in Paris and, like him, reinterpreted the French Revolution from the perspective of peasants and sans-culottes.[14] "History from below" became a rallying cry for those who wanted to make contact with the submerged mass of humanity and to rescue the lives of ordinary men and women from oblivion in the past. It spread everywhere in Europe, especially to England, where it reinvigorated a strong tradition of labor history. George Rudé, E. J. Hobsbawm, and E. P. Thompson wrote masterful studies of popular protest and working-class movements, and the journal *Past and Present* championed a view of history as the development of society rather than the unfolding of events. At the same time, a sister journal in France, *Annales: Economies, sociétés, civilisations,* was waging a parallel campaign against *l'histoire événementielle* and in favor of a related version of social history—history as the long-term interplay of structure and conjuncture, inertia and innovation, *histoire totale*. The catchwords of the so-called *Annales* school sometimes sounded like slogans, but they were given force by a succession of stunning doctoral theses, notably those of C. E. Labrousse, Fernand Braudel, Pierre Goubert, and Emmanuel Le Roy Ladurie. By 1970, social history seemed to turn around the *Past and Present–Annales* axis and to be sweeping everything before it.

It certainly swept a great many American historians off their feet and reinforced the indigenous revival of social history. Radicals called for a fresh look at the American Revolution "from below." Labor historians developed a Thompsonesque view of the history of work. And representatives *en mission* from the *Annales* traveled to campuses throughout the country, after establishing strongholds at Princeton, Ann Arbor, and Binghamton. The vogue seemed to extend everywhere—except to the camp of the intellectual historians. When looked at from the bottom up, the myths and images of the Americanists nearly disappeared from sight, and the ideas and "isms" of the Europeanists could be seen as ideologies or *mentalités*—that is, collective attitudes, which needed to be studied by the methods of the social sciences. Insofar as this approach left any room for the intellectual historian, it threatened to make him over as a sociologist or anthropologist. Robinson, Brinton, and Hughes had hoped to make a juncture with social history. Their successors worried about being cannibalized by it. As Paul K. Conkin put it, they succumbed to the view that "intellectual history has had a brief but glorious past, suffers a beleaguered present, and has no future."[15]

Before attempting to assess the validity of that view, one might try to measure it against some indication of the way American historians have actually behaved, both as teachers and as scholars, since World War II. Of course it would be vain to search for a precise behavior pattern among professors, who reputedly give way to idiosyncrasy and absent-mindedness rather than the herd instinct. But it should be possible to locate areas of emphasis within the profession by taking soundings in three sources: course catalogues, dissertation abstracts, and scholarly journals.

If the catalogues fail to convey the flavor of the lecture hall, they describe the subject matter of courses fully enough to enable one to classify courses by genre. To be sure, most courses involve several genres. They cover periods rather than themes—American History, 1865–1945, rather than American Intellectual History since the Civil War—so they cannot be classified under a single rubric. But an important minority of courses, from 17.1 percent of the sample in 1948 to 24.6 percent in 1978, can be classified unambiguously in one of the seven categories in Tables 10.1 and 10.2. Those courses provide a reasonably accurate indication of shifting emphases in the types of history taught to American undergraduates. Table 10.1 shows their relative importance in eight major universities at ten-year intervals between 1948 and 1978. Table 10.2 gives their proportions in the curricula of the eight universities as a whole during the same years.

The picture varied somewhat from campus to campus. Wisconsin developed strength in economic history in the 1940s, while Harvard was becoming a stronghold of intellectual history. But a general tendency prevailed almost everywhere. The eight universities offered eighteen courses (3.4 percent of their total offerings in history) devoted specifically to intellectual history in 1948–49 and seventy-two (6.4 percent) in 1978–79. Thus intellectual history did not arise suddenly, and it did not decline in the face of a surge in social history. True, social history did surge ahead during the 1970s. From a negligible

TABLE 10.1 *Specialized History Courses Offered at Eight American Universities, 1948–78*

University	Political history	Constitutional history	International relations	Intellectual history	Cultural history	Economic history	Social history	Total history courses offered
HARVARD								
1948–49	2	2	4	5	0	1	3	82
1958–59	3	3	2	12	0	1	2	115
1968–69	4	3	7	14	0	3	4	131
1978–79	6	1	6	19	3	5	13	177
YALE								
1948–49	2	2	3	3	2	0	1	43
1958–59	2	0	4	4	2	0	2	67
1968–69	7	2	10	11	3	5	1	133
1978–79	4	1	8	12	2	2	13	133
PRINCETON								
1948–49	1	1	1	1	0	0	0	21
1958–59	0	1	3	1	0	2	1	27
1968–69	1	1	0	3	1	2	1	52
1978–79	1	1	1	5	2	2	6	62
INDIANA								
1948–49	1	1	2	1	0	0	0	41
1958–59	0	2	2	0	0	0	0	63
1968–69	0	4	7	4	0	3	6	135
1978–79	0	4	6	2	0	4	4	116
MICHIGAN								
1948–49	0	4	3	3	0	4	0	82
1958–59	0	4	5	3	3	6	0	132

University	Political history	Constitutional history	International relations	Intellectual history	Cultural history	Economic history	Social history	Total history courses offered
1968–69	0	4	5	14	1	7	9	200
1978–79	0	2	3	14	1	7	16	189
WISCONSIN								
1948–49	0	3	1	1	0	6	0	79
1958–59	0	2	2	2	0	8	1	107
1968–69	0	6	10	3	4	13	12	227
1978–79	0	1	5	4	7	4	13	186
BERKELEY								
1948–49	0	5	4	0	3	1	2	97
1958–59	0	4	6	5	3	0	7	130
1968–69	0	6	4	7	1	2	8	146
1978–79	0	0	4	11	0	4	13	148
STANFORD								
1948–49	0	1	5	4	1	0	1	86
1958–59	0	2	5	6	1	1	2	104
1968–69	0	0	7	9	2	1	5	108
1978–79	3	1	3	5	5	1	17	119

TABLE 10.2 *Specialized History Courses Offered at Eight American Universities, by Subfield, 1948–78*

Courses	1948–49 Number	1948–49 Percent	1958–59 Number	1958–59 Percent	1968–69 Number	1968–69 Percent	1978–79 Number	1978–79 Percent
Social history								
Immigration–ethnicity	3	—	0	—	2	—	8	—
Labor	1	—	1	—	0	—	6	—
Black	0	—	0	—	5	—	16	—
Urban	0	—	0	—	8	—	14	—
Women–family	0	—	0	—	1	—	13	—
General	3	—	14	—	30	—	38	—
All social history	7	1.3	15	2.0	46	4.1	95	8.4
Political history	6	1.1	5	0.7	12	1.1	14	1.2
Constitutional history	19	3.6	18	2.4	26	2.3	11	1.0
International relations	23	4.3	29	3.9	50	4.4	36	3.2
Intellectual history	18	3.4	33	4.4	65	5.7	72	6.4
Cultural history	6	1.1	9	1.2	12	1.1	20	1.8
Economic history	12	2.3	18	2.4	36	3.2	29	2.6
All specialized history	91	17.1	127	17.0	247	21.9	277	24.6
Other history	440	82.9	618	83.0	885	78.2	853	75.5
All history	531	100.0	745	100.0	1,132	100.1	1,130	100.1

position in the 1940s (seven courses, 1.3 percent of the total), it became the most important specialization in 1978–79 (ninety-five courses, 8.4 percent of the total). But it included so many subspecializations—the history of cities, blacks, workers, women—that it reinforced an earlier tendency for curricula to expand and fragment. The expansion occurred in the 1960s, when such universities as Yale and Indiana doubled their course offerings in history. Many departments broke up their survey courses, relaxed their requirements, and encouraged professors to align teaching more closely with research. The educational diet was enriched, but it was education à la carte; and it must have been difficult to digest for the unsophisticated undergraduate who had to put together a program from a bewildering catalogue. (Wisconsin offered 227 history courses in 1968; Princeton had offered 21 in 1948.) In the end he might know something about the rise of the black ghetto in Detroit and nothing about the decline of the Roman Empire.

Intellectual history seems to have resisted the tendency toward fragmentation; and it held its own in the 1970s, when the expansion stopped. Most intellectual historians continued to give survey courses. Whether they made room for some elements of social history by rewriting lectures and reorganizing reading assignments cannot be known without further research, but it seems unlikely that many of them threw away large quantities of lecture notes. Some even repeat their old examination questions. ("If the questions change, the answers remain the same," goes a professorial proverb.) Change in teaching appears to be slow.[16]

Trends move more quickly in research, where social history has indeed gained ground at the expense of intellectual history. Table 10.3 shows that the percentage of dissertations in social history quadrupled between 1958 and 1978, while the percentage of those in intellectual history dropped slightly. In

TABLE 10.3 Dissertations Completed in History, by Subfield, 1958–78

Courses	1958 (12 months)		1968 (6 months)		1978 (6 months)	
	Number	Percent	Number	Percent	Number	Percent
Social history						
Immigration–ethnicity	3	1.5	7	1.9	12	2.8
Labor	1	0.4	7	1.9	13	3.0
Black	2	1.0	8	2.1	21	4.9
Urban	1	0.4	2	0.5	12	2.8
Women–family	2	1.0	4	1.1	14	3.2
General	5	2.5	11	2.9	45	10.4
All social history	14	6.8	39	10.4	117	27.1
Political history	69	34.3	126	33.4	102	23.7
Constitutional history	3	1.5	2	0.5	1	—
International relations	21	10.5	48	12.7	40	9.3
Intellectual history	21	10.5	36	9.5	38	8.8
Cultural history	5	2.5	12	3.2	25	5.8
Economic history	15	7.5	18	4.8	15	3.5
All specialized history	148	73.6	281	74.5	338	78.2
Other history	53	26.4	96	25.5	93	21.6
All history	201	100.0	377	100.0	431	99.8

1978 there were three times as many doctoral dissertations completed in social history as in intellectual history. Social history even outstripped political history as the most important area of research. In fact, political history declined significantly during the 1960s and 1970s—an indication that "event" history is on the wane in scholarship, even if it continues to be important in teaching. Moreover, the trend will probably accelerate, owing to a time lag. Most of the graduate students who completed their dissertations in 1978 chose their fields of study five to ten years earlier, when the fever for social history was still increasing. Those who chose fields at the end of the 1970s, when the fever was at its height, will extend it as they complete their dissertations throughout the 1980s. Yet their opportunity to affect future generations will be limited, because many of them will not find teaching positions. Tables 10.2 and 10.3 confirm the general impression that a critical disparity between supply and demand exists in college teaching. The number of courses in history declined slightly from 1968 to 1978, but the number of dissertations rose, and it has quadrupled since 1958.[17]

In order to sound the currents of scholarship among older historians, one can take samples from three of the most general and venerable scholarly journals, the *American Historical Review,* the *Journal of Modern History,* and the *Journal of American History*. Table 10.4 demonstrates the continued importance of political history, which accounted for a third of the articles from 1946 right through to 1978. Articles on international relations declined, but when taken together with articles on politics, they consistently occupied half the journals. While historians were burying *l'histoire événementielle* on the Continent, it continued to thrive in the United States. Intellectual history remained healthy—astoundingly stable, in fact, at about a tenth of the scholarly output since the 1940s. And social history shot up, but only during the last ten years.[18]

TABLE 10.4 *History Articles Appearing in Three Scholarly Journals, by Subfield, 1946–78*

Subfield	1946–48					1956–58					1966–68					1976–78				
	JMH	JAH	AHR	Total	Percent	JMH	JAH	AHR	Total	Percent	JMH	JAH	AHR	Total	Percent	JMH	JAH	AHR	Total	Percent
Political history	12	13	10	35	31.8	24	20	8	52	38.2	20	26	19	65	35.9	36	10	13	59	32.6
International relations	13	5	6	24	21.8	12	11	4	27	19.9	14	6	4	24	13.3	16	6	3	25	13.8
Intellectual history	2	1	4	7	6.4	1	6	6	13	9.6	6	7	6	19	10.5	6	3	10	19	10.5
Cultural history	2	2	2	6	5.4	0	2	1	3	2.2	3	2	3	8	4.4	4	3	3	10	5.5
Social history	0	4	7	11	10.0	0	5	8	13	9.6	1	10	4	15	8.3	14	16	3	33	18.3
Economic history	3	4	0	7	6.4	1	2	1	4	2.9	0	3	5	8	4.4	1	3	2	6	3.3
Other	3	10	7	20	18.2	5	11	8	24	17.6	6	20	16	42	23.2	10	9	10	29	16.0
Total	35	39	36	110	100.0	43	57	36	136	100.0	50	74	57	181	100.0	87	50	44	181	100.0

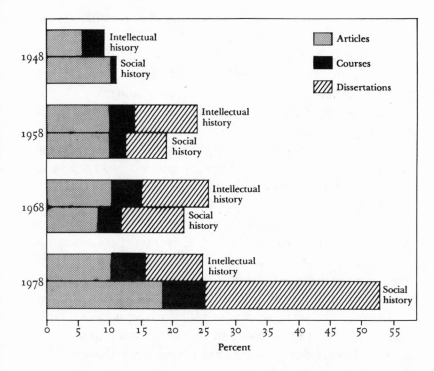

FIGURE 10.1 *Articles, courses, and dissertations in intellectual and social history as percentages of all history articles, courses, and dissertations, 1948–78.*

A comparison of the data from all three sources (Figure 10.1) suggests the way trends move through the profession as a whole. Their origin remains a mystery. But once they exist, they are picked up first by graduate students, appear next in courses, and then spread through the more established journals, having penetrated the specialized and avant-garde journals earlier. Research sets the pace for teaching, at least among the younger historians. The older ones seem to abide by the kind of history they assimilated as graduate students, perhaps because they are less open to innovation or need it less. In any case, the profession seems remarkably conservative. All three sources show the same pattern of change, but the changes are minimal. The only field that has developed dramatically since World War II is social history. The importance of intellectual history has fluctuated very little—so little, in fact, that its practice seems to belie the jeremiads of its practitioners.

Can one go so far as to conclude that the statistics reveal a colossal case of false consciousness among those who make the study of consciousness their speciality? Not really, because the importance of intellectual history has declined relative to that of social history; and although intellectual historians may be just as active as ever, some of them may have an accurate intuitive sense of momentum running down, of innovation passing into other hands. In fact, they might consider this account of their condition as a symptom of its gravity. How outrageous to describe the study of ideas by statistics and graphs! The whole endeavor smacks of the quantification of culture, of the spread of social science to places where it has no business, of the attempt to reduce the life of the mind to the sociology of knowledge. Better to nail jelly to the wall.

Perhaps at this point it would be appropriate to venture a more subjective assessment of tendencies within the field as a whole. Unfortunately, however, intellectual history is not a whole. It has no governing *problématique*. Its practitioners share no sense of common subjects, methods, and conceptual strategies. At one extreme they analyze the systems of philosophers; at the other they examine the rituals of illiterates. But their perspectives can be classified from "high" to "low," and one can imagine a vertical spectrum in which subjects shade off into one another, passing through four main categories: the history of ideas (the study of systematic thought, usually in philosophical treatises), intellectual history proper (the study of informal thought, climates of opinion, and literary movements), the social history of ideas (the study of ideologies and idea diffusion), and cultural history (the study of culture in the anthropological sense, including world views and collective *mentalités*).[19]

No doubt the highest range of ideas will attract scholars as long as anyone feels the challenge of scaling the thought of great men such as Augustine and Einstein. But since World War II, philosophers and literary critics have tended to neglect the historical study of great books, preferring to explore the linguistic dimensions of meaning and the structural significance of texts. Historians have had to supply much of the history of philosophy and the history of literature on their campuses, and the effort has marked their scholarship. Instead of surveying those neighboring fields as outsiders, they have attempted to understand them from within. Carl Schorske, for example, has developed an "internalist" view of philosophy, literature, art, music, and psychology in late nineteenth-century Vienna.[20] Other historians have limited themselves to one discipline studied over a longer time period. But like Schorske, they have tried to bring out the intellectual qualities inherent in their subjects and to avoid the blandness of earlier forms of interdisciplinary study. Morton White, Bruce Kuklick, and Murray Murphey have studied the history of American philosophy from the viewpoint of philosophers as well as from that of historians.[21] Edmund Morgan, Alan Heimert, Sacvan Bercovitch, and David Hall have carried the study of Puritanism even farther than where Perry Miller left it.[22] And the internal history of science has extended farther than ever in many different directions.

With each extension, the historical subfields have become more rigorous but also more esoteric—a seemingly inevitable tendency, because historians must specialize in order to follow the specialization in the growth of knowledge. Yet a counter-tendency has set in, and it may indicate that social history has had some impact at the higher level of the history of ideas. In his highly technical account of the rise of pragmatism, for example, Kuklick shows how philosophy became imbedded in the structure of the modern university, and he draws on Laurence Veysey's sociological study of the university as an institution.[23] In tracing the development of "modernist" ideas in Protestant theology, William Hutchinson tries to follow their diffusion as well as their philosophical elaboration.[24] Bruce Frier has demonstrated that the abstractions of Roman law had important connections with the real estate market in ancient Rome.[25] And several historians of science, Roger Hahn and Charles Rosenberg in particular, have shown the significance of interest groups and institutions in the development of scientific theories.[26] The history of science may prove to be a strategic field for assessing the interplay of social history and the history of ideas, because it has expressed most clearly the tension between internal and external approaches to formal thought. The dichotomy may seem unreal to some specialists, and there seemed to be room for both approaches in Thomas Kuhn's distinction between normal and revolutionary phases in the development of science. But since the initial publication of *The Structure of Scientific Revolutions* (1962), Kuhn has moved toward the "internalist" position and has somewhat altered his notion of paradigm, making it more accommodating to normative and less to sociological notions.[27] Meanwhile, "externalists" have shown how the culture and politics of early-modern England and Weimar Germany influenced the development of Newtonianism and quantum physics.[28] The two tendencies could split the history of science in half, sending it toward sociology on the one hand and toward philosophy and the natural sciences on the other. But it seems more likely that the tension will continue to be creative and that even the most recondite scientific activity will be interpreted within a cultural context.[29]

Contextualization is the strongest feature in the area of the history of ideas that has made the strongest progress during the last decade: the history of political thought. In a series of programmatic articles followed by a set of major books, Quentin Skinner, John Dunn, and John Pocock have argued that one can capture the meaning of a political treatise only by recreating the political idiom of the time in which is was written. They shift the emphasis from text to context, but not in order to smuggle in a reductionist view of ideas, either Marxist or Namierite in inspiration. On the contrary, they assert the autonomy of thought by invoking analytical philosophy and by treating thought as "statements" or "speech-acts" conveying particular meanings. As meaning is bound up in time and language, it cannot inhere in the "unit-ideas" imagined by Lovejoy, which move in and out of minds across the centuries; and it cannot be understood by reading the works of great political theorists as if they could speak directly to us. Modern philosophy has freed the historian to work in a historical mode, to reenact the past by rethinking thought in the manner prescribed by Collingwood. Armed with this procedure, Skinner, Dunn, and Pocock have slashed through the anachronisms in the literature surrounding such major figures as Machiavelli, Hobbes, and Locke. They have cut fresh paths through the history of political thought from the thirteenth to the nineteenth century. And while dealing with thought at the highest level, they have reinforced the social history of ideas at the crucial juncture where ideas merge into ideologies.[30]

The concern for specificity of context has also dominated much of the recent work on the intermediate level of intellectual history. The grand tableau about the spirit of an age and the sweeping treatise on the mind of a nation seem to be dying genres, despite the spirited efforts of Ira Wade, Peter Gay, and Rush Welter.[31] In American studies especially, scholars have turned from the holistic to the institutional view of intellectual life. What passed as national character in the 1950s now looks like the culture of middle-class whites to many younger historians. They tend to see knowledge as power, as the ideological fortification of specific social groups; and so they have concentrated on the intellectual history of professions, professionals, and professionalization—a process that now looks so ubiquitous that it is running a close second to the rise of the middle class as a historical theme.[32] The favorite profession among Europeanists seems to be history. Their choice may not be free from bias, but it has resulted in some excellent intellectual biographies, notably John Clive's *Macaulay* and Leonard Krieger's *Ranke*. And in the work of Hayden White, Nancy Struever, Maurice Mandelbaum, Donald Kelley, and Lionel Gossman, the history of history has gone beyond the older historiographical concerns to a fresh consideration of time consciousness and the linguistic nature of thought in the past.[33] The Europeanists seem more sensitive to European currents of philosophy—analytical philosophy in England, poststructuralist thought in France—while the Americanists respond primarily to the American strain in the sociology of knowledge and anthropology.[34]

It may be misleading, however, to distinguish too neatly between the European and American branches of intellectual history. One tendency that brings them together and that also shows the continuity between the older and younger generations of intellectual historians is the emphasis on social thought. The work of Martin Jay and Stuart Hughes, of David Hollinger and Morton White, of Jonathan Beecher and Frank Manuel, shows a concern for the social dimensions of thought on both sides of the Atlantic and of the so-called generation gap.[35]

The emphasis on social thinkers also stands out in intellectual biography, a genre that has flourished in the United States while faltering on the Continent, especially in France. What makes biography unfashionable in the *Annales* school—its emphasis on individuals and events rather than on long-term shifts in structures—makes it appealing to Americans, who thirst for specificity and hunger after connections between social theory and institutional setting. Thus Dorothy Ross has seen the history of psychology through the life of G. Stanley Hall; Barry Karl and John Diggins have seen political science and sociology come of age in the lives of Charles Merriam and Thorstein Veblen; and Peter Paret and Keith Baker have seen a general sociopolitical science take shape through the lives of Clausewitz and Condorcet.[36] Three biographies of Durkheim appeared in 1972; two works on Vico came out in 1975–76; at least a dozen studies of Marx were published in 1977–78; and the bicentennial of the deaths of Voltaire and Rousseau in 1978 brought such an outpouring of books and articles on top of such a vast body of earlier work that the literature on the two great philosophers can hardly be read by a single scholar, especially if he wants to master their own writings, which are now becoming available in the superb editions of Theodore Besterman and R. A. Leigh.[37] The Enlightenment scholar cannot neglect Arthur Wilson's *Diderot* and Robert Shackleton's *Montesquieu*.[38] And if he needs to study the transatlantic dimension of the Republic of Letters, he will have to plow through the vast editions of Jefferson, Adams, and the other Founding Fathers. The great scholarly editions of the 1960s and 1970s are creating new possibilities for the intellectual historian, if they do not overwhelm him.

He will not get relief from the sheer documentary weight of the past if he seeks refuge at the lower level of study that is now becoming known as the social history of ideas; for here he will need to examine not only the works of great writers but also their diffusion, and he will need to study the production and diffusion of lesser literature, too. Social historians of ideas attempt to follow thought through the entire fabric of society. They want to penetrate the mental world of ordinary persons as well as philosophers, but they keep running into the vast silence that has swallowed up most of mankind's thinking. The printed word provides one trail through the emptiness, however, because by following it the historian can get some sense of the lived experience of literature—at least among the literate and after the invention of movable type. Scholars have pursued this path the farthest in England and France, where *histoire du livre* has emerged as a distinct subdiscipline. But Americans also seem to show increasing interest in the history of literacy, popular literature, publishing, and journalism.[39]

It was by studying popular pamphlet literature that Bernard Bailyn renovated the history of the American Revolution.[40] He showed that the view of events among ordinary citizens was as important as the events themselves—that Americans perceived the actions of George III and his ministers through a dense political culture, which they had inherited from their seventeenth-century ancestors and which shaped their behavior throughout the eighteenth century. The work of Pocock, Skinner, and Dunn indicated that this culture could be traced back to the Renaissance, provided it were understood as the elaboration of an idiom rather than a great chain of ideas. The beginning of this process became clear from the work of Renaissance scholars—notably Hans Baron, Felix Gilbert, William Bouwsma, Gene Brucker, Marvin Becker, Eric Cochrane, and Donald Weinstein—who showed how civic humanism blossomed, flourished, and withered throughout the tempestuous histories of Florence and Venice. From

Italy the ideological current flowed to England, where it was transformed by the Reformation and tinctured by indigenous institutions. Despite the incursions of Namierites and internal quarreling, historians of England, from Christopher Hill to J. H. Hexter, Lawrence Stone, J. H. Plumb, E. P. Thompson, and John Brewer, have agreed on the central importance of ideology in English public life during the seventeenth and eighteenth centuries. At that point American historians—Edmund Morgan, Jack Greene, Gordon Wood, and Eric Foner as well as Bernard Bailyn—could grasp the ideological theme, give it some final twists and turns, and show how it determined the character of the new republic. At each stage in the development of this rich strain of historiography, the historians have stressed the way political discourse was imbedded in institutional life. Instead of treating thought as an epiphenomenon of social organization, however, they have tried to show how it organized experience and conveyed meaning among the general citizenry. Instead of contemplating a transcendent spirit, they have tried to recreate a political language. And instead of imposing their own categories on that language, they have let it speak for itself. Thus avoiding reductionism on the one hand and anachronism on the other, they have shown that the study of ideology can serve as a testing ground for problems and methods within the social history of ideas as a whole.[41]

In passing to cultural history, one moves below the level of literacy and onto territory where history and anthropology meet. The meetings usually occur when they converge on subjects classified loosely as popular culture. Historians seem comfortable with the term. With a few exceptions, such as Hayden White, they have not asked whether it stands for a coherent field of study but rather have rushed from subject to subject as occasions arose.[42] The enthusiasm has been greatest

in conferences on French history, where Americans and
Frenchmen have joined hands in a merry round of reports on
carnivals and charivari.[43] At its best—in the work of Natalie
Davis, Robert Mandrou, Marc Soriano, and Carlo Ginzburg,
for example—this effervescence has stimulated some striking
original research.[44] At its worst, it appears trivial and trendy.
Whatever its trendiness, the history of popular culture certainly is not new. E. K. Chambers demonstrated its importance at the turn of the century, and long before that Burckhardt
had given it a central place in his panorama of Renaissance
culture. The complexity and depth of the literature on the
subject can be appreciated from Peter Burke's recent survey
of it.[45]

Nonetheless, the enthusiasm for popular culture is symptomatic of a shift within social history itself. The pacesetters
of the field, such historians as Emmanuel Le Roy Ladurie and
Lawrence Stone, who used to fill their books with graphs,
demographic statistics, and quantitative models of social
structures, have relied entirely on qualitative evidence in their
latest work, glossing literary references with references to anthropology.[46] One of the most influential and anthropological
books of the decade, Keith Thomas's *Religion and the Decline
of Magic,* was criticized for not being anthropological enough—
not only by anthropologists but also (at least implicitly) by
Thomas's fellow social historian E. P. Thompson.[47] Thompson himself epitomizes the inflection toward cultural history
and toward an anthropological mode of understanding among
social historians. After attempting to recount the development
of working-class consciousness within the categories of orthodox Marxism, he has moved back farther into the preindus-
trial era and deeper into the study of plebeian culture.[48] But
where will all the work on maypoles, magic, rough music,
wife sales, effigy bonfires, and public executions lead?

The most common way of drawing it all together has been to subsume it under the category of *mentalité,* a convenient Gallicism, which has spread through English and German after making its fortune in France. Despite a spate of prolegomena and discourses on method, however, the French have not developed a coherent conception of *mentalités* as a field of study. They tend to load the term with notions of *représentations collectives* derived from Durkheim and the *outillage mental* that Lucien Febvre picked up from the psychology of his day.[49] Whether *mentalité* will bear the load remains to be seen. But it probably will not survive Americanization any better than *Weltanschauung* did. The first attempts to domesticate it suggest that it will dissolve in discourse about general attitudes.[50]

If so, American historians may not have advanced far beyond a stage of confusing enthusiasm for the study of symbolic behavior among the "inarticulate"—that is, the illiterate, preliterate, and semiliterate, who really manage to express themselves very well through their own cultural forms. But some advance has already occurred, and it has occurred in an empirical way, by digging through difficult sources in order to excavate evidence about those forms. The richest material has been unearthed in the field of black history. Peter Wood has used anthropological methods to investigate the nature of language and labor among slaves in South Carolina. Lawrence Levine has drawn on folklore to convey the way blacks coped with adversity through language and laughter. And Eugene Genovese has brought slave religion back to life in a powerful interpretation of slavery as a sociocultural system.[51] Historians of labor, religion, and the family have developed similar strains of research by marrying social and cultural history.[52] The marriage took place long ago in "Third World" studies, where historians have had to learn all they could from anthropologists, and anthropologists have often worked in a diachronic dimension.[53] In the study of American Indians, anthropologists have actually been more historical than historians, for the historians' enthnocentric obsession with the white man's burden of guilt has blinded them to the importance of warfare and diplomacy among the Indian tribes themselves throughout the eighteenth and nineteenth centuries.[54]

The tacking between history and anthropology has benefited both disciplines, because they provide complementary ways of reaching the same goal: the interpretation of culture. Moreover, anthropology offers the historian what the study of *mentalité* has failed to provide: a coherent conception of culture, which Clifford Geertz has defined as "an historically transmitted pattern of meanings embodied in symbols."[55] Of course it would be easy to fish other definitions out of the anthropological literature. Anthropologists disagree as much as anyone else. But they share a common orientation toward the problems of interpreting culture. They can help the historian reorient his own attempts to solve those problems, and they can set him on course in pursuit of patterns of meaning.

The concern for meaning runs through all the varieties of intellectual history, from the "high" to the "low." It suggests that all are being renovated in ways that cannot be seen in the statistics or heard through the cries of alarm from those who favor older ways. Of course, it would be simplistic to divide the profession between innovators and traditionalists or Pollyannas and Jeremiahs. It also would be foolish to deny that some traditional types of intellectual history have suffered during the 1970s. Historians in the 1990s probably will not produce many treaties on the spirit of an age or the mind of a nation or the linkage in great chains of ideas. There seems to be some drift from the "higher" to the "lower" sectors of the spectrum. But intellectual historians need not worry about disappearing in the rising tide of social history. Although they may feel queasy at times, they are getting their sea legs; they have fresh wind in their sails, and they are moving in new directions.

———

NOTE ON TABLES AND FIGURE / Each of the sources used in compiling these tables has advantages and disadvantages. The course catalogues often given quite full descriptions of the courses; and if one assumes a fairly strong correlation between the descriptions and the teaching, they probably provide a valid indication of the relative importance of various history genres. Most courses, however, are not generic. They cover time periods; and it is impossible to know whether emphases have shifted within them unless one undertakes an elaborate survey. Nonetheless, shifts in emphasis should be expressed fairly accurately in the minority of the courses (about 25 percent) that are devoted to specialized genres. The statistical base is broad, and it would have been broader had it been possible to find more complete runs of catalogues. Incomplete statistics were compiled from the catalogues of Columbia University, Chicago University, and the University of California at Los Angeles. They conformed to the pattern of those from the other catalogues, but they contained too many gaps to be used in Tables 10.1 and 10.2. The statistics include graduate courses open to undergraduates—the 400-level courses at Harvard, for example—but not graduate seminars intended exclusively for graduate students and listed separately. Mixed generic courses, such as the "social and intellectual history" courses popular in the 1940s, were not entered under either rubric. Those classified as "political" were devoted specifically to politics, according to the catalogues. But the general courses probably emphasized politics heavily, so it may be underrepresented.

Thanks to the extensive summaries in *Dissertation Abstracts,* the classification of doctoral dissertations does not pose special problems. But the data could not be traced back to 1948, because too few theses were microfilmed at that time. By 1958 the great majority of history theses appeared in *Dissertation Abstracts*. Foreign dissertations were eliminated from the data. And the monthly reports were compiled for all twelve months of 1958 in order to have statistics large enough to be compared with the six months of reports covered in the statistics for 1968 and 1978. (There were no significant seasonal fluctuations in the reporting.) Thus the number of doctorates in history increased from about 200 in 1958 to about 860 in 1978, and it did not decrease as the job market contracted during the 1970s.

The *Journal of Modern History, Journal of American History,* and *American Historical Review* were chosen for the compilation of the data in Table 10.4 because of their general character and because they go back to the 1940s. One might expect new trends to appear more quickly in such specialized journals as the *Journal of Social History, Journal of Interdisciplinary History, Journal of the History of Ideas,* and *American Quarterly.* But the siphoning off of avant-garde articles probably occurs at about the same rate in all fields, including the fields represented by the *Negro History Bulletin, Agricultural History,* and *Diplomatic History.* Changes in editors also affect the coverage of journals, and important changes occurred in the editorships of all three of the journals studied. But such changes also take place fairly equally across fields. So it seems valid to use the three older and more established journals in order to measure trends in the scholarship of older and more established historians. The articles were compiled over three-year periods in order to build up an adequate statistical base.

Finally, I should add that I did all the compiling and computing myself, without the help of research assistants, and that I tried to read through all the course descriptions, dissertation abstracts, and journal articles as thoroughly as possible. In the end I developed some intuitive sense of changes within the profession. And if I made errors, they probably are consistent, or at least did not result from hasty work.

ELEVEN

The Social History of Ideas

T HE HISTORY OF the Enlightenment has always been a lofty affair—a tendency that will not be regretted by anyone who has scaled its peaks with Cassirer, sucked in delicious lungfuls of pure reason, and surveyed the topography of eighteenth-century thought laid out neatly at his feet. But the time has come for a more down-to-earth look at the Enlightenment, because while intellectual historians have mapped out the view from the top, social historians have been burrowing deep into the substrata of eighteenth-century societies. And, as the distance between the two disciplines increases, the climates of opinion multiply and thicken and the Enlightenment occasionally disappears in clouds of vaporous generalizations. The need to locate it more precisely in a social context has produced some important new work in a genre that is coming to be called the "social history of ideas."

Peter Gay, who has sponsored the term,[1] has attempted to satisfy the need with the second volume of *The Enlightenment: An Interpretation* (New York, 1969). A half year after the appearance of Gay's book, another second-volume work came out in France: *Livre et société* (Paris, 1970), the sequel to a pioneering collection of essays on sociointellectual history produced by a group at the VIᵉ Section of the Ecole Pratique des Hautes Etudes in Paris. These two volume 2's make fascinating reading together, because they show two different historiographical traditions converging on the same problem. Gay descends from Cassirer, the VIᵉ Section group from the *Annales* school and from Daniel Mornet's experiments with quantitative history. Curiously, the two traditions seem to ignore each other. In a bibliography that totals 261 pages in both volumes and that covers an enormous range of European history, Gay never mentions *Livre et société*. He makes only a few, irreverent references to Mornet and does not seem to have assimilated much *Annales* history. The second volume of *Livre et société* (the first appeared a year before Gay's first volume) does not refer either to Gay or Cassirer. In fact, Cassirer's *The Philosophy of the Enlightenment* was not translated into French until 1966 and has not made much impression on French study of the Enlightenment since its original publication in German in 1932, a year before the appearance of Mornet's *Les Origines intellectuelles de la Révolution française* and fourteen years before Paul Hazard's *La Pensée européenne au 18ᵉ siècle*. So here is an opportunity to compare the methods and results of two attempts, expressing two separate historiographical currents, to solve one of the knottiest problems in early modern history: the problem of situating the Enlightenment within the actualities of eighteenth-century society.

Gay came to the social history of ideas through an attempt to redefine the Enlightenment. He wanted his "definition" (as he modestly describes his two large volumes) to incorporate the social dimension of the philosophes' experience into a Cassirer-like interpretation of their ideas. This concern testifies to the ever-expanding influence of social history today, but it does not ultimately determine the character of Gay's book, which can be read as intellectual history of the sort that has flourished in the United States for the last few decades. If read in this way, it offers a delightful tour of the Enlightenment, theme by theme, philosophe by philosophe. Gay cuts his way through clichés and breathes new life into figures that had been embalmed and placed on permanent exhibit in the nineteenth century. His philosophes are not desiccated rationalists, naive prophets of progress, or narrow-minded village atheists. They are complicated individuals with complicated problems, irrational in their calculations of pleasure and pain, and pessimistic in their dedication to the advancement of civiliation. Gay does justice to these complexities, especially in the first two chapters of volume 2, by relating the philosophes' ideas to their experience and by eschewing worn-out labels like "The Age of Reason." His own labeling sometimes creates confusion, as when he describes eighteenth-century empiricism as a "revolt against rationalism." (Cassirer, and even d'Alembert, made the point clearer by contrasting the *"esprit de système"* of the seventeenth century with the *"esprit systématique"* of the eighteenth.) But the book makes the philosophes live. Its strength consists in its stress on the complex, human dimension of their philosophy.

Although Gay's *Enlightenment* will delight and instruct anyone who wants to freshen his sense of the past, it deserves to be read as its author intended: not as just another work on the eighteenth century but as an attempt to establish a new historical genre. Gay needed to develop a social history of ideas in order to bring together the highly distilled philosophical history of Cassirer and the highly specific findings of social history.[2] Crossbreeding such different historical species raises enormous problems because Cassirer dealt with modes of thought, like the rise of "critical" as opposed to "mythopoeic" thinking; while social historians are concerned with a different order of phenomena, like the rise of the bourgeoisie. In order to reconcile such opposed viewpoints, Gay adopts a Hegelian device: he defines the Enlightenment as a "dialectical struggle for autonomy" (*The Enlightenment,* I:xi; all references are to this work unless otherwise stated).

The history of history is so strewn with dead dialectics that it might seem rash to create a new one as the conceptual framework for a new kind of history. But Gay's social history of ideas will not hold together without his dialectic, so the dialectic deserves to be examined with care. It goes like this: thesis— "The Appeal to Antiquity" (book 1); antithesis—"The Tension with Christianity" (book 2); synthesis—"The Pursuit of Modernity" (book 3). Gay explains that he is dealing with the Enlightenment in its narrow sense, the philosophy of the philosophes, not with the broad climate of opinion comprising the "Age of the Enlightenment." He argues persuasively that the philosophes' philosophy can be treated as a coherent historical phenomenon, despite their quarrels and contradictions, because they comprised a coherent unit, a "family"; and their dialectic should be understood as a result of the family's actual experience in the actual environment of eighteenth-century Europe and America. Accordingly, the philosophes responded to the demystifying message of the classics, turned that message against Christian mythology, and then liberated themselves from their liberators by rejecting neoclassicism and embracing modernity. Modernity, autonomy, or "The Science of Freedom" (Gay sticks so many ingenious titles and subtitles to his text that it is difficult to remove his ideas from their packaging) means humane, critical, tolerant, realistic liberalism—a faith worthy of modern modernity, Gay suggests, for he has no pretense of writing value-free history.

This dialectical definition raises the problem of determining what set the Enlightenment apart in time as a distinct phenomenon. If Gay's dialectic cannot be pinned down with precision and supported by rigorous reference to evidence, it may float away like the most ethereal Hegelianism; for no

dialectic can be static, even if it is intended only as a "definition." It therefore seems best to follow the unfolding of Gay's
Enlightenment stage by stage, pausing to take up themes as
they appear—notably in the case of the antireligious, "revolutionary," and psychological aspects of the Enlightenment—
and reserving two special themes for the end: the Enlightenment's relation to sociopolitical issues and to the spread of
literacy.

Assuming that the Enlightenment originated with an appeal to antiquity, the problem is to show what in antiquity
appealed to the incipient Enlightenment rather than to other
eras. Gay reveals an affinity between the philosophes and the
ancients, but he does not prove that the philosophes read their
classics differently than did the "classical" writers of the seventeenth century. Even if Gay's argument could be proven—
and to do so would require a multitude of studies in comparative literature as thorough as Jean Seznec's *Essais sur Diderot
et l'antiquité* and Reuben Brower's *Alexander Pope: The Poetry
of Allusion*—the differences in the response to the ancients would
have to be explained, and the explanation might involve elements that are unrelated to Gay's "thesis." Gay's discussion of
the Renaissance illustrates this difficulty, because he argues
that the classical revival during the Renaissance produced the
same dialectic as that of the Enlightenment. Then, in order to
avoid entangling dialectics or interpreting the Enlightenment
as a rerun of the Renaissance, he is forced to emphasize the
elements that separated the two periods—the reawakening of
religious controversy and the subsequent spirit of toleration
and skepticism, the scientific revolution, and the systematic
philosophies of the seventeenth century. But are not these new
developments precisely the ones that brought about the Enlightenment? And are they not extraneous to Gay's dialectic?
Sensing this danger, Gay tries to fit Montaigne, Grotius, Bayle,

Bacon, Descartes, Newton, and Locke into a chapter entitled
"Pagan Christianity," one of the hybrid terms like "Epicurean
Stoicism" that he seems to coin when his argument is over-
strained. An admixture of paganism and Christianity may
have colored the ideas of those thinkers as it did in the thought
of such pagan-Christians as Aquinas and Augustine, but the
real question at issue is: What was fundamental and what ac-
cidental in producing the Enlightenment? It will not do to
display the pagan-Christian dialectic at the front door and to
smuggle Montaigne, Grotius, Bayle, Bacon, Descartes, Newton, and Locke in the back. Once those men have got a foot
inside they will take over, making it impossible to preserve
the dialectic even as window dressing.

The Enlightenment's enemies present as many problems
as its precursors for Gay's thesis, because, according to François Bluche, the magistrates of the Parlement of Paris had the
same favorite authors as Gay's philosophes—Cicero, Horace,
Ovid, and Vergil.[3] And according to the *Livre et société* group,
the educated but unphilosophic general public shared the same
taste for the classics. In order to explain why the philosophes
reacted peculiarly to the common stock of their culture, Gay
would have been forced back to standard accounts of the Enlightenment's origins, which he seems to avoid. His own account does not deal with the classic studies of Paul Hazard and
Philippe Sagnac, which argue that the French Enlightenment
grew out of a profound crisis during the last years of Louis
XIV's reign; nor does it incorporate the recent work on the
"crise de conscience" period by Pierre Goubert and Lionel Roth-
krug. Gay barely mentions Fénelon, Saint-Simon, and Bou-
lainvilliers; and he entirely ignores Vauban, La Bruyère, and
Boisguillebert.

While Gay has difficulty in getting his thesis off and running, his antithesis almost runs away with him. Here the main

theme is the radicalization of the Enlightenment's antireligious character. Gay sees it advancing inexorably from toleration to skepticism, deism, and the full-blooded atheism of Hume and Holbach. The philosophes certainly undermined established churches, but few of them, even in the côterie Holbachique, went over to atheism.[4] And some intellectual currents flowed in the opposite direction—from the impieties of Toland and Woolston in Britain and the godless Temple poets in France to the Great Awakening that spread across Europe from Stockholm, Saint Petersburg, and Bavaria during the prerevolutionary decade. As Auguste Viatte has shown, the Enlightenment went out in a great blaze of illuminism.

How incompatible were Christianity and the Enlightenment, in any case? They were enemies in France, but there philosophy fed on persecution and a tradition of anticlericalism absent in Protestant countries. Perhaps, also, it owed more to Jansenism than Voltaire, in his horror at the *convulsionnaires,* wanted to admit. Such, at least, is a hypothesis dangled temptingly in "The Enlightenment: Free Inquiry and the World of Ideas," an essay by Robert Shackleton in the new volume edited by the late Alfred Cobban. Shackleton detects "a de facto alliance, in many respects surprising, between Jansenism and the Enlightenment."[5] In contrast to Gay's irresistible "tide of atheism" (II: 144), Shackleton even sees some collaboration between the philosophes and the Catholic church, not so much in France as in Spain, Portugal, and Italy, where Cardinal Passionei and Benedict XIV corresponded philosophically with Montesquieu and Voltaire. This Mediterranean Jansenism sometimes protected philosophes under attack by Jansenists in Paris, and it provided weapons for the philosophic floggings administered to Jesuits throughout the Iberian peninsula and the Habsburg Empire, two areas that Gay almost completely omits from his book. The Jesuits themselves pursued modernity while persecuting philosophes, as a reading of the astute articles on science in the *Mémoires de Trévoux* would confirm. Josephinism and regalism were both enlightened and Catholic, and the interaction of religion and enlightenment in Protestant countries was even more complicated, as Herbert Dieckmann has warned all intrepid synthesizers.[6] There was more pietism than atheism in the works of Kant, less Voltairian *Sturm* than spiritualistic *Drang* in the literary revival of Germany, and very little crushing of *l'infâme* in Johnson's England. Gay is aware of these nuances. He produces some splendid chapters on Lessing and Burke and does not try to picture Jonathan Edwards as Benjamin Franklin. But his Enlightenment remains that of David Hume, who receives the most splendid chapter of all.

The synthesis suffers from the same birth defects as its dialectical brothers. According to Gay's formula, "modernity" or "autonomy" came into being sometime in the late eighteenth century, when the philosophes felt as free from the classics as they did from the Christians. But this was also the era of neoclassicism, which Hugh Honour has defined recently as the "style of the late eighteenth century, of the culminating, revolutionary phase in that great outburst of human inquiry known as the Enlightenment."[7] If Honour is correct, then Gay's synthesis belongs before his thesis, and his eighteenth century runs backward. If Gay is correct, it is difficult to understand why expressions of classicism like the Palais Bourbon and the *Oath of the Horatii* appeared at the end of the eighteenth century and why manifestations of modernity like the scientific revolution[8] and the dispute between the ancients and the moderns (which Gay does not mention) occurred at the end of the seventeenth.

But Gay's synthesis suffers less from misplaced modernity than from a tendency to exaggerate the Enlightenment's radicalism. For just as stage two of the dialectic leads to atheism, stage three produces revolution—and reopens the whole question of the connection between Enlightenment and revolution in the eighteenth century. Gay finds the connection fundamental, because he sets 1688 and 1789 as chronological boundaries for his book. But he hardly refers to the revolutions of England and France and concentrates instead on the American Revolution—the "Finale" to the dialectic, yet a strangely unrevolutionary affair. Gay does not even mention the Declaration of Independence, which is usually interpreted as the culmination of radical Enlightenment in America. But he goes into a detailed discussion of *The Federalist Papers,* where he finds the omnipresent "dialectical movement away from Christianity to modernity" (II: 563). This unorthodox emphasis creates some confusion, because the most recent work by Bernard Bailyn and Alan Heimert makes it more difficult than ever to imagine the Founding Fathers trading impieties with Hume and Holbach. But Gay's approach permits him to scuttle natural law, which he views as a vestigial metaphysics left over from the seventeenth century and progressively eliminated in the eighteenth. Of course, he does not deny that the American revolutionaries, like Montesquieu, Voltaire, Diderot, and Rousseau, often invoked the laws of nature. But he interprets Hume's "revolutionary" (II: 455) attack on natural law as more fundamental to the Enlightenment than Diderot's "revolutionary" (II: 457) defense of it. The confusion comes because almost everything the philosophes did seems to have been revolutionary. Their emphasis on man's natural goodness was "subversive, in fact revolutionary" (II: 398), and "revolutionary" was their "rehabilitation of the passions" (II: 192). Their "revolutionary ideology" (I: 27) extended far and wide—to a "revolution" (II: 369) in historiography and in the theater (*Miss Sara Sampson,* "a revolutionary drama" [II: 264]), not to mention the "utterly subversive manner" (II: 390) in which they attacked religion. In art, Reynolds's career was "revolutionary in its implications" (II: 234), although as aestheticians Diderot and Lessing were "revolutionaries who never lost their respect for tradition" (II: 250). The alarmed reader may be reassured to learn that the philosophes' aversion to the gothic was "no mark of radicalism" if not downright "reactionary" (II: 217), and that "as a group, the philosophes were a solid, respectable clan of revolutionaries" (I: 9). But then he discovers that unlike the classicists of the seventeenth century, who had "concealed their radicalism" (I: 282), the philosophes turned classicism into "an instrument of subversion" (I: 264); and their penchant for ancient Greece "remained subversive" (I: 75) while "the Enlightenment itself was moving toward overt and bellicose radicalism" (I: 200). Gay's Enlightenment is such an explosive affair that one wonders how the Old Regime ever got as far as 1789. The philosophes had the place wired, mined, and booby-trapped.

But Gay's narrative does not reach 1789 either: it stops just after the American Revolution—rather anticlimatically for the reader watching the pressure rise toward the big bang. Nonetheless, *The Federalist* makes a good if somewhat unrevolutionary point to call a halt on all the radicalizing and undermining, because not only was the Enlightenment's influence on the French Revolution problematical, but Gay had argued in an earlier article that it was relatively unimportant.[9] He had to dispose of his Humean, Holbachean explosives somewhere; so he dumped them on the United States. An easier solution, however, would have been to delete "revolutionary" from its myriad appearances in the text and to admit that the Enlightenment was a pretty mild affair after all. By 1778, when all of Paris was salaaming before Voltaire, the last generation of philosophes had become pensioned, petted, and completely integrated in high society. Ten years later men like Morellet and Dupont labored valiantly to prevent the collapse of the Old Regime, as was perfectly natural, for the High Enlightenment was one of its most important potential props. Quesnay, Turgot, and even Voltaire offered a program of liberal reform, a possibility of perpetuating the social order by blunting its conflicts. The idea of subverting society, if it ever occurred to them, would have struck them as monstrous. Not only did they believe in the basic structure of the Old Regime, they thought that it ought to remain hierarchical. As d'Alembert explained: "Is a great effort of philosophy necessary to under-stand that in society, and especially in a large state, it is indis-pensable to have rank defined by clear distinctions, that if virtue and talent alone have a claim to our true homage, the superiority of birth and eminence commands our deference and our respect?"[10] With exceptions like Rousseau, the philo-sophes were elitists. They enlightened through *noblesse oblige* in company with noblemen, and often with a patronizing at-titude toward the bourgeois as well as the common people. In the article "Goût" of his *Dictionnaire philosophique,* Voltaire observed, "Taste is thus like philosophy; it belongs to a very small number of privileged souls . . . It is unknown in bour-geois families, where one is continually occupied with the care of one's fortune." It has been argued recently that, far from rising with the middle class, liberalism descended from a long line of aristocrats, and so did the Enlightenment.[11] Except for men like Condorcet, the last of the philosophes fit in perfectly with the Sèvres porcelain and *chinoiserie* of the salons; the High Enlightenment served as frosting for France's thin and crum-bling upper crust.

If there was any "radicalism" among the *abbés* and *petits marquis* of the synthetic Enlightenment, it was their faith in natural law, the very weapon that Gay excludes from his

overstocked arsenal of revolutionary philosophy. The abbé
Raynal, who lived to bewail the advent of the Revolution,
polemicized against slavery because he considered it contrary
to the law of nature—and this was not innocuous humanitarianism, because powerful interests fed on slavery, as the Amis
des Noirs were to learn when they tangled with the Club
Massiac during the Revolution. The philosophes justified many
other items in their "program," as Gay calls it in his account
of their reform campaigns, by reference to what they considered as eternal, immutable values. Gay interprets these references as rhetoric. Like Alfred Cobban,[12] he emphasizes the
strain of utilitarianism in the writings of Holbach, Beccaria,
and Bentham and treats Hume's attack on normative reasoning as the turning point in eighteenth-century thought. But
what Hume killed with logic lived on in the hearts and minds
of most philosophes; and Hume, despite Gay's ingenious revisionist interpretation of him, remained a very Tory revolutionary. Why not admit that natural law, codified in influential
textbooks like Burlamaqui's *Principes du droit naturel,* survived
throughout the Enlightenment in contradiction to strict empiricism, utilitarianism, and Hume's lethal surgery? Philosophy thrives on contradictions. In fact there was a built-in
contradiction between the descriptive and prescriptive aspects
of natural law itself. The philosophes were forever attempting
to bring the physical and moral worlds together and to seek
spiritual uplift in the Spacious Firmament on High. This tension between the normative and the material is what gave the
Enlightenment life. It is fully appreciated in classical studies
like Cassirer's *The Philosophy of the Enlightenment,* Hazard's
European Thought in the Eighteenth Century, and—for all Gay's
efforts to expunge it—Becker's *The Heavenly City of the Eighteenth Century Philosophers.*

The final dimension of Gay's dialectic is psychological. It, too, includes a revolution: the emergence of a new personality type—autonomous, demystified, modern man. Psychological modernity, Gay argues, came about through a collective identity crisis among the philosophes. To be sure, an identity crisis on top of a dialectic makes for problems, but Gay does not shrink from an explicitly Eriksonian attack on them. His bibliography contains three generous pages of acknowledgment of works on psychoanalysis and sex that he found helpful, beginning with Erikson—or rather beginning with the beginning: "In my view of sexuality, both its meaning and its history, I have been guided by Freud" (II: 628). It may be that Erikson is feeling overacknowledged these days (he has been heard to mutter unhappily about learning of an identity crisis in men's wear), but Gay does not use the magic formula frivolously. He argues that the struggle against Christianity produced an identity crisis in the entire family of philosophes and that they were able to resolve it because "it was precisely the growth of the superego in Western culture that made greater sexual freedom possible" (II: 204–5). Thus the dialectic of ancients, Christians, and philosophes apparently corresponded in some way to a three-cornered fight between the id, ego, and superego; and "the Enlightenment is the great rebellion of the ego against irrational authority" (I: 462). This interpretation, however, raises problems for the faithful Eriksonian reader, who had been assured by the master that "the Renaissance is the ego revolution par excellence."[13] The problems are compounded by Gay's assertion that "the sexual ideal of the Enlightenment may be said to have been the genital personality" (II: 628). Did some subdialectic synthesize orality and anality into genitality? If the philosophes reached such advanced modernity in the eighteenth century, where is "Western culture" today? Polymorphous perversion presumably.

Would it not be easier to give up the subdialectics, reversed antitheses, and entangled syntheses and to admit that the only dialectic in history is historiographical: the dialectic between those who get it right and those who get it written? In this case, alas, the written version is wrong: the Enlightenment was not a dialectical struggle for autonomy.

If one abandons Gay's dialectic, what is left of his social history of ideas? Its feasibility can best be measured by considering Gay's treatment of two final problems: the relation of the Enlightenment to sociopolitical issues and to the spread of literacy. Both will be discussed in the context of French history, so that Gay's interpretation can be compared with the findings in *Livre et société,* a book that belongs to the mainstream of advanced French historiography. The advance has occurred most spectacularly in the study of the Old Regime's social structure and has already reached the textbook stage. The uninitiated therefore need not read every word in the overwhelming tomes of Pierre Goubert, Emmanuel Le Roy Ladurie, Pierre de Saint-Jacob, Roger Dion, René Baehrel, Abel Poitrineau, Paul Bois, François Bluche, and Jean Meyer. They can consult the brief and brilliant popularizations written by Pierre Goubert and Robert Mandrou,[14] and there they will see that Gay is wrong to reduce the main sociopolitical issues of the eighteenth century to a dualism, pitting the *thèse nobiliaire* (the reactionary cause championed by the *parlements* and Montesquieu) against the *thèse royale* (the progressive cause of royal reformers and Voltaire). The Old Regime was too complicated to be classified so simply, and Voltaire's propaganda was too simplistic to be "good history always and good politics for decades" (II: 483). Contrary to what Gay maintains, the privileged orders paid important sums in taxation, and privilege was not consonant with "order" in any case: it ate through all levels of society, down to the very peasantry.[15]

In defending privilege, the *parlements* did not so much defend the nobility as protect a complex combination of vested interests typical of traditional societies. Their defense had a wide enough appeal to make their "liberal" rhetoric something more than hypocritical. By the end of the century, they were not the closed, caste-ridden bodies Gay describes.[16] In fact, contrary to what Gay suggests, Turgot favored their recall in 1774, and Montesquieu's sympathy for them did not amount to a reactionary ideology. Voltaire was a sincere reformer but no great enemy of privilege: he was an *annobli,* courtier, *grand seigneur,* and proud possessor of a coat of arms with a fake marquis's crown.

The attack on privilege came less from Ferney than from such unphilosophic quarters as the chancellery and the Contrôle général. Consider the opinion of Charles François Lebrun, who epitomizes a tradition of bureaucratic reform that shaped policy during Maupeou's attack on the *parlements:*

I did not want to enlist with the philosophes . . . I would have preferred to see them devote their energies to a field other than the one they had chosen [i.e., the campaign against the church?]. It seemed to me that the government could make them into useful auxiliaries in the fields of administration and internal politics, could direct their attacks against the barriers which separated province from province, against privileges which placed uneven burdens on the people, against numberless contradictory customary laws, against the diversity of legal systems, against courts which were distant and inaccessible to people bringing suit, against usurped jurisdictions, against that swarm of guilds which hindered industry and stopped its progress. In every part of France there were reforms to carry out, people to be enlightened.[17]

How much did the reform movement owe to the Enlightenment? Far more, no doubt, than Lebrun acknowledged, but far less than is maintained by most intellectual historians. Administrative history, rather than philosophic theory, might be

the place to look for the real thrust behind reformism. Many
of the reforms decreed by the Revolution were drafted in the
baroque bureaucracy of Louis XIV, as is illustrated in *The
Single Duty Project* by J. F. Bosher, an excellent, unintended
example of the social history of ideas. The Old Regime left
enough of its red tape behind. Why not go to the archives and
get wrapped up in it, instead of reading Voltaire, if one wants
to learn how ideas and politics tangled in the eighteenth century? What is true of France applies even more to the rest of
Europe, where "enlightened absolutism," as Gay astutely
characterizes it, had little relation to the Enlightenment. Most
sovereigns reformed in order to maximize power. They reformed with cameralists, not philosophes, drawing on a tradition of bureaucratic rationalizing that went back to the
seventeenth, and sometimes the sixteenth, century.

The problems of measuring literacy and reading habits,
which have attracted the heaviest research by the *Livre et société*
group, receive somewhat summary treatment by Gay: "In
France (to judge from signatures on marriage certificates) the
percentage of literate adults rose from about four in ten in 1680
to more than seven in ten a century later" (II: 58). Where Gay
got this information is difficult to say, because his book is as
short on footnotes as it is long on bibliography. The only
historical study of literacy that covers the entire country (the
survey directed by Louis Maggiolo in the 1870s) estimates that
21 percent of all French adults could sign marriage certificates
in 1686–90, 37 percent in 1786–90, and 72 percent in 1871–
75.[18]

Important consequences result from this apparent confusion of the eighteenth and the nineteenth centuries, because,
as Gay says, "The first precondition for a flourishing republic
of letters was a wide reading public" (II: 58). Believing that
literacy soared to 70 percent, he concludes that the philosophes

acquired a "new audience" (II: 61), increased prosperity, improved status, and relative freedom from patronage. These conditions not only made the Enlightenment possible but transformed it into a revolutionary force, for Gay never drops the theme of radicalization: "[T]he growing radicalism and increasing freedom of the Enlightenment reflected and produced irreversible, if often subterranean, changes in Western politics, economy, and society. As democrats and atheists took the lead in the family of philosophes, radicals rebelled against constituted authority all over the Western world" (II: 83). This statement comes closer to descrbing France at the time of the Commune than the France of Voltaire.

Voltaire's France creates enormous problems for the social history of ideas, because the mental world of its inhabitants did not extend very far beyond the boundaries of their social world—beyond the guild, the parish assembly, the regional units of administrative, legal, commercial, and religious institutions; beyond local ways of weighing, measuring, and paying for commodities; and beyond provincial techniques of raising children, dressing, and talking. Most Frenchmen probably did not speak French during Voltaire's childhood. By the time of his death (1778), improved roadways and demographic and economic expansion had brought the country together. But France did not cohere as a nation until after the Revolutionary and Napoleonic periods. To understand how the Enlightenment "took" in such a fragmented society is no easier than to measure its influence on a European scale. Perhaps it never penetrated far below the elite in any area of eighteenth-century Europe.

It is the elite that interests Gay, so he should not be expected to produce a parish-by-parish sociological analysis. The elite shared a common, cosmopolitan culture. Nevertheless, to be a philosophe in Poland was a different experience than

to be a philosophe in England. Gay tries to explain the differences by relating them to forces outside the philosophic "family," and this attempt makes him stumble on the complexities
of social history. To take the example of literacy again, Gay's
interpretation might be rescued by arguing that literacy is only
important as a precondition for the growth of a reading public
large enough to support a population of writers living entirely
from their pens. Thus the crucial factor is that the total number
of French readers increased, owing to population growth, although the incidence of literacy remained below the level of
"modern" societies. Furthermore, adult *male* literacy went up
significantly (from 29 percent in 1686–90 to 47 percent in
1786–90, using signatures of marriage certificates as an index),
and certain areas, particularly in the northeast, reached levels
of 80 percent. In fact, a sort of literacy barrier or Maggiolo
line ran from Mont Saint-Michel to Besançon or Geneva, separating the north, where literacy was always above 25 percent,
from the south, where the rate was usually under 25 percent.[19]
But given this limited, regional growth of the reading public,
another question arises: Did the new readers create a new
literacy market, freeing the philosophes from patronage and
thereby radicalizing the Enlightenment? If Diderot's *Lettre sur
le commerce de librairie,* Malesherbes's *Mémories sur la librairie,*
and the royal edicts on the book trade are to be believed, the
answer to that question is no. And if the pension lists in the
Archives Nationales indicate trends in patronage, the state
subsidized writers in the traditional manner under Louis XVI,
and may have subsidized more than them than in the days of
Louis XIV. The publishing industry did not reach a "takeoff"
point until the development of the steam press, cheap techniques of manufacturing paper, and mass education in the
nineteenth century. Increased literacy did not liberate the philosophes any more than the philosophes revolutionized society.

Actually, Gay backs away from some of his statements about literacy and revolutionizing by the end of the book. Thus the new phenomenon of mass literacy, which he announces at the beginning, declines as the dialectic unfolds, until in the end, "the overpowering presence of the illiterate masses" (II: 492) saps the philosophes' revolutionary ardor. Driven by "a sense of despair at the general wretchedness, illiteracy, and bruitishness of the poor" (II: 517), the philosophes begin to mutter about *canaille,* to flirt with enlightened absolutism, and to entertain ideas of a repressive, obscurantist "social religion" (II: 522). All's well that ends well. Saved from error by inconsistency, we are left in an eighteenth century we can recognize.

Gay's Enlightenment remains recognizable, despite the confusion of its dialectic, because it covers familiar territory with a refreshing sense of rediscovery. Instead of striking for the frontier, Gay set out to clear a path through the monographs cluttering eighteenth-century historiography, and he succeeded where his dialectic failed. Following him is like touring with a *Guide Michelin:* one stops for the occasional *dégustation* but never wanders far from the three-star routes. In the end, the verdict is clear: Gay's Enlightenment "vaut le voyage." But it is most valuable as one man's summing up, a synthesis of years of thoughtful reading, which one instinctively places on the shelf next to R. R. Palmer's *The Age of the Democratic Revolution.* Taken as a synthesis of social history and the history of ideas, however, it does not hold up because it will not stand without its dialectical scaffolding.

It may be misleading to compare Gay's polished synthesis with the monographic articles published in *Livre et société.* But the two works share a concern for what the *Livre et société* group sometimes refers to as *"l'histoire sociale des idées,"* and the comparison is revealing because the French begin by resisting the urge to synthesize. In a way, they locate the Enlightenment by not looking for it: instead, they put aside preconceptions about the *"philosophie des Lumiéres"* and seek out the unenlightened, the everyday, and the average. Their purpose is to reconstruct literary culture as it actually was. They therefore emphasize intellectual "inertia" and try to measure the depth of tradition, adopting an approach that had lain fallow since Daniel Mornet first experimented with it a half-century earlier.

While Cassirer was exploring the phenomenology of the Enlightenment mind, Mornet studied the Enlightenment as a social process. And while other literary scholars pondered the eighteenth century's great books, Mornet examined the means by which ideas diffused downward in society. His examination revealed that some books, which later ages took to be great, may not have been widely read under the Old Regime,[20] and this revelation raised a new set of questions: What did eighteenth-century Frenchmen read? And what was the balance of tradition and innovation in early modern book culture? Mornet left these questions to his descendants in the VIe Section of the Ecole Pratique des Hautes Etudes, and especially to the research team that produced *Livre et société*. The researchers also inherited the techniques and traditions of the *Annales* school, which inclined them toward the study of *"mentalités"* rather than formal philosophic ideas and which made them receptive to the quantitative methods that Mornet had developed.

Owing to the complexity of the Old Regime and the diversity of its culture, the *Livre et société* group tried to relate the literary and social life of eighteenth-century France by studying specific milieux: the obscure masses who "read" or listened to popular literature, the educated provincials who purchased traditional works, the elite of the provincial academies, and the Parisians who produced and consumed certain "advanced" periodicals.

The work done on the first of these four groups makes the most exciting reading, because it gives one a sense of contact with the remote mental universe of the eighteenth-century village. Robert Mandrou showed that such contact was possible in *De la culture populaire aux 17ᵉ et 18ᵉ siècles* (Paris, 1964), a brief but brilliant study of the crude paperbacks known as the *bibliothèque bleue,* which colporters hawked through the countryside, along with thread and cutlery, from the seventeenth to the nineteenth century. Printed on cheap paper with worn-out type, sold for a sou, and read until they fell apart, these little books contain clues to a popular culture that is otherwise more inaccessible than the civilization inscribed on Cleopatra's Needle. They were read aloud by the few villagers who could read during the *veillée,* an informal evening get-together where women sewed and men repaired tools. The *bibliothèque bleue* certainly belonged to a humble level of culture. Its stories often begin, "As you are about to hear . . ." But what message was communicated by this oral-written genre, and how did these books relate to the culture of the upper strata? Mandrou placed them far behind and below the Enlightenment. He showed that while the philosophes were stressing the rationality and *sensibilité* of human nature, the *biblothèque bleue* presented man as a slave of passion, driven by astrological forces and weird mixtures of the four humors and the four elements. While the freethinkers, were naturalizing religion, the *bibilothèque bleue* purveyed spiritualism, miracles, and hagiography. And while the scientists were emptying the universe of mystery, the *bibliothèque bleue* filled the heads of its reader-listeners with visions of threatening, occult forces, which could be appeased by mumbo-jumbo and deciphered with recipe-knowledge—magic numbers, physiognomy, and

primitive rituals. As literature, the *bibliothèque bleue* adapted
and simplified medieval tales and Gaulois humor that polite
society rejected in the seventeenth century. So Mandrou concluded that in comparison with the culture of the elite, the
popular culture represented by the *bibliothèque bleue* was both
distinct and derivative. He went on to hypothesize that the
popular literature of the Old Regime served as an ideological
substitute for class consciousness among the masses. The
peasants let their thoughts wander through a wonderland inhabited by Robert le diable, Oger le danois, Pierre de Provence, the giant Fierabras, and all manner of magical forces,
instead of taking the measure of the real world of toil and
exploitation.

Mandrou's study, a product of the *Annales* school but not
of the *Livre et société* group, prepared the way for the work of
Geneviève Bollème, who produced a general survey of the
bibliothèque bleue for volume 1 of *Livre et société* and a detailed
study of popular almanacs, which grew too big for volume 2
and was published as a separate monograph. Bollème's analysis confirmed the main lines of Mandrou's but emphasized
change rather than continuity in the evolution of popular literature. She found that the escapism and supernaturalism of
the seventeenth century receded in the eighteenth with the
influx of new attitudes: a more worldly and realistic orientation toward death, human nature, social relations, and natural
forces. The old astrology and mythical tales gave way to a
new sense of science and history. A new *"morale sociale,"* and
"esprit critique,"[21] and an awareness of current events indicated
the penetration not merely of the Enlightenment but also of
incipient revolutionary ideas.[22] Despite their similarities,
therefore, the studies of Mandrou and Bollème point in opposite directions, the first toward the separation of cultural
worlds and the intellectual enserfment of the masses, the sec-

ond toward an increase in cultural integration, with popular literature acting as a liberating force.

It is too early to tell which view will prevail because there has not yet been enough detailed study of the many genres of popular literature. Bollème's work is more detailed, as it concentrates on one genre—the popular almanac—whose development can be traced with some precision through the seventeenth and eighteenth centuries. But the attempt to be precise about the cosmology of the common man raises methodological problems that did not hamper Mandrou's more general and impressionistic work. For not only did Bollème move beyond general impressions, she attempted to enter right into the minds of the almanacs reader-listeners, and there she found not merely mumbo-jumbo but "Kantian"[23] categories. The categories—"perpetual astral observations,"[24] for example—do not summon up the *Critique of Pure Reason*. Instead, they arouse skepticism: Do the almanacs reveal the workings of the popular mind, or is this upside-down Cassirer? Bollème did not prove the "popular" character of her almanacs. On the contrary, she drew material from some almanacs in bindings with aristocratic coats of arms; from others that expressed scorn for "popular prejudices";[25] and from several that did not aim their aphorisms at the illiterate or the indigent: "Read often"; "Buy books at all times"; "Don't treat poor debtors tyrannically"; *"Peragit tranquilla potestas quod violenta requit."*[26] Poor Richard (a favorite in France) belonged in part to the lost, aristocratic world of Thomas Jefferson. There were almanacs for everyone, even in the upper reaches of the Old Regime. Bollème acknowledged the differences among the almanacs, but she grouped them all together for the purpose of analysis. And when she analyzed changes in the world view of the eighteenth-century populace she based her conclusions almost entirely on a sampling of only twenty-seven undifferentiated almanacs. The almanac upon which she relied most heavily and which she cited most often as evidence of advanced opinion at the popular level was *Le Messager boiteux,* a work printed in Bern, Bâle, Yverdon, Vévey, and Neuchâtel—that is, by Swiss and in some instances by Protestants: not a reliable index to the attitudes of Catholic French peasants.[27]

But how reliable are the most folksy and most French of the almanacs? Frequently presented as the aphorisms of one shepherd ("le Grand Berger de la Montagne") addressing others, they have more of the flavor of Renaissance pastoralism than of a genuine shepherd-to-shepherd dialogue. The pastoralism may have been adapted for mass consumption from the "model" almanac of the fifteenth century, *Le Grand Compost des bergers,* but the rhetorical pose might have had more in common with the masquerading of Marie-Antoinette than the mountainside egalitarianism detected by Bollème. The almanacs represent a popularization of upper-class culture, not popular culture in itself, because they were written for the people, not by the people, and they were not so much "written" as adapted in the most casual fashion, sometimes even by typesetters, from the literature of the elite. The great problem is not to extract their message but to know whether that message was integrated in the indigenous culture of the masses.

Mandrou believed it was. The real dialogue, in his view, did not involve shepherds but publishers and colporters. The wandering salesmen knew what the peasants would buy and stocked up accordingly, thereby determining, in the long run, what the publishers produced. This argument seems convincing, but it applies more aptly to upper-class literature, which was far more sensitive to changes in styles and ideas than was the extremely standarized repertory of the *bibliothèque bleue.* Unlike the educated elite, villagers may have been passive consumers of literature; they may have bought whatever was available, just because they wanted something—it hardly mattered what—to submit to the *veillée* reader or to stare at themselves. As Bollème put it, there could have been an element of "magic,"[28] a mystical respect for the word, in primitive reading—an obscure psychological process that probably had little relation to the sophisticated reading and consumer control that went on in high society. So changes in popular literature could have been imposed from above without being assimilated at the village level. The actual culture(s) of France's heterogeneous masses remains lost in an unfathomable ocean of oral tradition; the books that dropped into it probably disappeared without much effect, like missionaries in India.

Although the work of Mandrou and Bollème may have failed to define the popular culture of eighteenth-century France, it enormously enriches the conventional view of the "Age of Reason." By revealing the existence and character of a vast literature that circulated on levels far below the philosophes, it helps place the Enlightenment in perspective. This attempt to define levels of cultural experience and to relate reading to specific social sectors is also the strong point of the other essays in *Livre et société,* especially the study of provincial reading by Julien Brancolini and Marie-Thérèse Bouyssy. After examining book consumption in the provinces by genre and by region, Brancolini and Bouyssy concluded that educated provincials were about as far removed from the Enlightenment as illiterate peasants. The weight of traditional culture crushed innovation in town and village alike.

The Brancolini-Bouyssy study was based on a quantitative analysis of the records of requests by provincial publishers for *permissions simples,* a kind of authorization to produce works that had fallen into the public domain by virtue of legislation reforming the book trade in 1777. These requests included the projected number of copies for each edition, so they provide more precise information than any of the sources consulted in previous attempts to chart the boundaries of literary culture in the Old Regime. The most important of these attempts was published by François Furet in volume 1 of *Livre et société*. It indicated that an enormous quantity of religious works and pre-eighteenth-century "classics" all but smothered the Enlightenment, although the production of scientific books and secular fiction increased at the expense of religious literature as the century progressed. Furet's findings derived from quantitative analysis of requests for privileges (strictly legal authorizations to publish) and *permissions taçites* (more flexible and less formally legal authorizations). But they lacked data on the size of editions and the places where the books were marketed. Brancolini and Bouyssy provided precisely that information, thereby supplementing and confirming Furet's analysis. Taken together, the two studies suggest that cultural "inertia" weighed heavily on all of France and that the inroads of "innovation" did not penetrate far beyond Paris. Not a surprising pattern— unless it is measured against the conclusions of Geneviève Bollème. For she saw modernization galloping full tilt through the crude almanacs of the late eighteenth century, while Brancolini and Bouyssy found nothing but cultural stagnation at a more sophisticated level of literature. Did the literary experience of the elite and of the masses somehow converge without meeting on the middle ground of the middle classes?

This paradox, like so many of the problems in quantitative history, may arise from insufficiencies in the data. Requests for *permissions simples* do not represent the *"vie provinciale du livre,"* as Brancolini and Bouyssy claim, because the *permissions simples* excluded probably the most important component in the stock of provincial bookdealers: books acquired by purchases or, more often, by exchanges measured in page gatherings with publishers located in other regions or other countries. The *permissions simples* also excluded all books published in France under *permissions taçites,* the legal loophole through which much of the Enlightenment reached French readers.[29] In fact, the *permissions simples* covered primarily a specialized and unrepresentative segment of the provincial book trade: the relatively stable market for schoolbooks and religious works. With the expiration of old privileges, the provincial publishers supplied new editions of old books to local teachers, priests, and teacher-priests. But they might have supplied other readers with an equal number of "advanced" works, which could not have appeared in the Brancolini-Bouyssy data.

Although the data fail to prove the backwardness of provincial culture, they do provide a very revealing picture of regional variations in French reading. They show that book production corresponded with the incidence of literacy as measured by the Maggiolo study mentioned above. The great majority of *permission-simple* books circulated north of the Maggiolo line. Moreover, the north's areas of highest literacy and highest book production, like Lorraine and Normandy, were areas where the Counter-Reformation had been most effective and where nineteenth- and twentieth-century voters showed most attachment to the church. Northern readers tended to favor the religious "classics" of the seventeenth century and even Jansenist works, while southerners, especially around Toulouse, read a relatively high proportion of secular literature. A series of maps illustrates the point in rich detail. So despite the limitations imposed by its data, the Brancolini-Bouyssy study suggests some of the complexities and long-term trends in the cultural history of France.

Daniel Roche's monographs on provincial academies, published in volumes 1 and 2 of *Livre et société,* analyze the

character of the intellectual elite in the areas where Brancolini
and Bouyssy tried to provide an overall measurement of literary culture. Like all elite studies, Roche's investigation com-
pensates in specificity for what it lacks in generality; but here
the specifics of quantitative analysis have important general
implications, for they define some of the milieux through
which the diffusion of *"Lumières"* was refracted. Taking a cue
from Mornet, who had stressed the importance of studying
the provincial academies in *Les Origines intellectuelles de la Révolution française,* Roche began with an analysis of the academies' social composition. By adopting a carefully nuanced
classification scheme, he reduced such abstract problems as
the supposedly "bourgeois" character of the Enlightenment
to manageable proportions. He found that the membership of
the academies of Bordeaux, Dijon, and Châlons-sur-Marne
corresponded to the hierarchies of provincial society. The landed
aristocracy, service nobility, and (especially in the parlemen-
tary towns) the nobles of the robe dominated the academies,
which themselves were privileged corporations in a society
characterized by privilege and corporateness. The academies'
lower ranks (*correspondants* and *associés*) become increasingly
bourgeois as the century progressed—but not bourgeois in the
Marxist sense. The lesser academicians were civil servants and
professional men, including a very high proportion of doctors
and virtually no financiers, industrialists, or merchants, even
in the booming commercial center of Bordeaux. Thus the
academies represented a traditional elite of notables, opening
up increasingly to men of talent but not to capitalist entrepreneurs. They were also open to new ideas. The topics set for
their prize essay contests show concerns related to the Enlightenment: humanitarianism, a tendency to move from abstract
to utilitarian thought, and an increasing interest in political
economy. The men who gave first prize to Rousseau's *Dis-*

cours sur les sciences et les arts had a very un-Rousseauistic faith
in the parallel advancement of science and social welfare.

In his second article, Roche produced a comparative social
analysis of the academicians and the collaborators of the *Encyclopédie* identified by Jacques Proust in *Diderot et l'Encyclopédie*.
Like the academicians, the encyclopedists contained a large
number of professional men (especially the omnipresent enlightened doctors), savants, and technicians supplemented by
a heavy dose of nobles and civil servants (20 percent in each
case) but not a single merchant. So the *Encyclopédie* itself seems
to have represented a tendency of old elites to assume a new
role of intellectual leadership in conjunction with the nascent
"bourgeoisie de talents" rather than the industrial-commercial
bourgeoisie. That conclusion should be handled with care,
however, because it rests on a fragile statistical base of 125
encyclopedists whose social and professional status could be
identified. Since Diderot had more than 200 collaborators,
Proust and Roche may not have worked with representative
statistics. The statistics were too small, in any case, to represent large social groups. Because the encyclopedists included
only nine abbés, eight *parlementaires,* and seven lawyers, it
does not follow that those three groups were more immune
to *encyclopédisme* than doctors, who contributed twenty-two
collaborators. A dozen men in any category could change the
statistical picture completely. As Proust pointed out, it was a
community of intellectual interest, not a common social milieu, that bound together the collaborators of the *Encyclopédie*.
They did not cast off the old deference patterns: in fact, Proust
found a kind of deferential differential in Diderot's correspondence, which shows Diderot talking down to social inferiors,
like Rousseau, while chatting up more established writers, like
Voltaire, Buffon, and Marmontel.[30] Nonetheless, a common
intellectual cause united the men at the center of the Enlight-

enment. When their message spread outward, it had to pass downward, through the traditional hierarchies of provincial society. This was the enlightening process as d'Alembert and Voltaire conceived it—a slow seeping of *Lumières* from the top to the bottom of the social pyramid, without any leveling or lowering effects. Thus the studies of Proust and Roche complement each other nicely, showing the traditional society's ability to absorb new ideas and the traditional elite's capacity for acquiring new functions—but not a new ideology rising with a new economic class. The social history of ideas seems to have broken out of the old categories of Marxist sociology.[31]

Most of the articles in *Livre et société* emphasize continuity rather than change. By macroanalysis of book production and by concentrating on peasants and provincials, they reveal the weight of tradition in the cultural lives of the great majority of Frenchmen. One study, however, by Jean-Louis and Marie Flandrin, concerns the milieu at the center of cultural innovation, the salon society of Paris. Here, as in Proust's work on the encyclopedists, quantitative history came into direct contact with the Enlightenment. The Flandrins tried to measure the literary experience of the Parisian elite by tabulating references to books in three journals: the *Journal* of Joseph d'Hémery, the police inspector for the book trade; the *Mémoires secrets* of Bachaumont; and the *Correspondance littéraire* of Grimm. Each of the three was written for private consumption and therefore contained material on avant-garde works that could not be reviewed in standard periodicals like the scrupulously censored *Journal des savants*. A statistical analysis of reviews in the *Journal des savants* and in the Jesuit *Mémoires de Trévoux,* which was published in volume 1 of *Livre et société,* had revealed a "traditional" bias almost as pronounced as in the Furet and Brancolini-Bouyssy studies.[32] But the Parisians who read and sometimes even edited these censored periodicals came from the same literary circles that the Flandrins studied; and in analyzing the clandestine press the Flandrins found unalloyed Enlightenment. Seen through the *Journal des savants,* the Parisians look like Brancolini's provincials; they kept to a sparse diet of old-fashioned devotional, historical, and legal works, seasoned with some science. Seen through the *Mémoires secrets,* the Parisians glutted themselves on philosophy, read very little history, and no religious, legal, or purely scientific books. Wherever the distortion may be, it results from the selection of data, not from statistical imprecision. The Flandrins' statistics seem impeccable, but the journals that provided them did not mention all the books read in salon society. They referred only to the extraordinary, controversial books, the books that were talked about and that made news. These journals were really primitive newspapers—*nouvelles à la main*—not systematic literary reveiws. They provide information about literary vogues but no quantifiable index to book consumption that can be compared with the statistics of Furet and Brancolini. So the *"circulation du livre"* in Paris and the cultural distance between Parisian innovators and provincial followers has yet to be measured.

The remainder of *Livre et société* constitutes an attempt at measuring an even more elusive phenomenon: language. Historical semantics is now a booming discipline in France and one that promises to enrich the standard views of the Enlightenment by uncovering implicit concepts, the kind that escape exegeses of formal thought.[33] Unlike conventional lexicology, historical semantics does not treat words as isolated units but rather as parts of a semantic field, a linguistic structure in which each part conveys meaning through its function within the whole. To grasp the meaning of individual eighteenth-century words, it therefore is necessary to reconstruct the linguistic structure of eighteenth-century French, treating the language as a fluid, socially determined system of communication, not as a fixed crystallization of thought from which parts can be arbitrarily detached. Put abstractly, these propositions seem reasonable enough; the difficulty is to put them into practice by discovering the mental processes behind eighteenth-century French as it has come down to us in the form of words congealed on paper. The research for volume 1 of *Livre et société* produced a special collection of specimens of this dead communications system—a list of forty thousand book titles registered for privileges and *permissions taçites*. By analyzing each title as a semantic field, computing the results statistically, and organizing the statistics into a series of semantic models, François Furet and Alessandro Fontana tried to get at the meaning of two eighteenth-century words, *histoire* and *méthode*.

Fontana's study, the more elaborate and ambitious of the two, best represents this new historical discipline. After one hundred pages of laborious analysis, Fontana produced a "structural profile" of eighteenth-century *méthode*. In some cases, he concluded, *méthode* was fixed, final, and transcendental or mathematical; in others it was fragmented, variable, and relative to particular disciplines. Its varied usage revealed a thought pattern moving from seventeenth-century apriorism to nineteenth-century relativism, and so suggests a cosmological shift that might be compared with the transition from the closed to the infinite universe that Alexandre Koyré discerned in studying the history of science.

Whether or not Fontana proved his case is difficult to say, owing to the linguistic barriers to understanding linguistics. No uninitiated reader should confront Fontana's monograph unless armed with something much more formidable than a *Petit Larousse,* for he will get trapped in an impenetrable semantic underbrush. He may pride himself on having mastered the *mots-clés* of the *Annales* school: *conjoncture, contingence, syn-*

chronie-diachronie, and *mot-clé.* But what is he to make of *ma-thésis, apax, inessif, hendiadys, ethnosème,* and *semiosis?* At the risk of seeming *ubusif,* anti-*sememic,* or an outright *idiolect,* this reviewer must confess that he cannot follow Fontana's argument and that he finds historical semantics more impressive in principle than in practice.

But the two volumes of *Livre et société* do represent an impressive attempt to rescue the intellectual history of eighteenth-century France from vague generalizations and to root it in the realities of social history. They reveal the general contours of literary culture as it was experienced by the great mass of eighteenth-century Frenchmen rather than as it appears in a few, posthumously selected classics. And they relate that literary experience to specific social groups—the obscure millions who participated in popular culture, the more elevated reading public of the provinces, the provincial elite, and the Parisian avant-garde. Whatever their shortcomings, these experimental essays show that the social history of ideas can be written. They do not redefine the Enlightenment any more successfully than Gay does, but they help to situate it in the complex context of eighteenth-century society.

The comparison of Gay's *Enlightenment* and *Livre et société* suggests that the social history of ideas must move out of its armchair phase and into the archives, tapping new sources and developing new methods. For how can it be written from within the confines of even a first-rate library? To pull some Voltaire from the shelf is not to come into contact with a representative slice of intellectual life from the eighteenth century, because, as the *Livre et société* essays show, the literary culture of the Old Regime cannot be conceived exclusively in terms of its great books. Yet libraries crammed with classics cannot find room for the *bibliothèque bleue,* a genre too undig-

nified to be classified with "books" or to fit into our preconceptions about "culture." And every year our universities turn
out thousands of certified experts in Western civilization who
have read the *Social Contract* many times and have never heard
of *Les Quatre Fils Aymon*. As far as the social history of ideas is
concerned, the difficulty is not simply in recognizing "low"
as well as "high" culture, because Gay's techniques—a matter
of index cards and intelligence, but no original research—will
not even uncover the social history of the intellectual elite.
The finances, milieux, and readership of the philosophes can
only be known by grubbing in archives.

If read as conventional intellectual history, however, Gay's
Enlightenment has the great advantage of imposing new form
on a great deal of unmanageable old matter. *Livre et société*
holds out little hope for arriving at such a heroic synthesis.
Instead, it suggests that we must face another outbreak of
monographs, which will take us in a dozen different directions, wherever the data lead. As the data tend to be statistical,
they continually raise problems about quantifying cultural
phenomena. Literary journals cannot be reduced meaning-
fully to bar graphs, and literary "influence" still seems too
intangible to be computerized. Statistics about book consumption give one a general sense of the cultural terrain, but
do not explain the meaning of what it is to "consume" a book.
So the social history of ideas is searching for a methodology.
It will probably fall back on ad hoc combinations of Cassirer
and Mornet until it develops a discipline of its own. If those
two masters cannot yet be brought together in a new definition of the Enlightenment, they cannot be left alone. And seen
through the work of their successors, their achievement looms
larger than ever.

The History of Mentalities

The Case of the Wandering Eye

IN *A Second Identity*, RICHARD COBB tells the story of Marie Besnard, a crafty peasant who confounded an array of lawyers, laboratory technicians, and criminologists trying to get her convicted for murder in a series of spectacular trials from 1952 to 1961. Marie showed that her accusers had scrambled the evidence so badly in their test tubes and jars that a kidney from one victim's body was cohabiting in Exhibit A with the gall bladder from another's, and an eye, which had disappeared from its home cadaver, had turned up in the middle of a foreign skeleton. The wandering eye did the job, Cobb observes with satisfaction: The scientists lost their case, and Marie won her freedom. Cobb does not come right out and say so, but the story stands as a parable to be pondered by sociological historians.[1]

Sociology is the villain of the last three books written by Richard Cobb, professor of history at Oxford University and one of the most controversial, original, and talented historians writing today. If you want to understand the French Revolution, he argues, strike out for the uncharted wilderness constituting the revolutionary *mentalité*. The historiographical frontier is not to be found in statistical tables, economic models, computer printouts, or social systems, but in the lost mental world of obscure persons like Marie Besnard.

Cobb is the only person to have explored this territory. For a quarter of a century, he has tracked down revolutionary "wildmen" *(enragés)*, counterrevolutionary crackpots, neighborhood militants, primitive anarchists, and all the varieties of eccentric humanity that he could find in the labyrinth of France's archives. Not only do his reports on these neglected elements of French humanity provide a vision of the human condition that transcends the conventional limits of history writing; they also illustrate the possibilities and problems involved in the study of *mentalités*.

Revolution

How conventional historiography could accommodate Cobb is not clear because Cobb's viewpoint is sharp and eccentric, while conventional French revolutionary studies have become increasingly sociological and confused. The confusion comes from an outbreak of the old quarrels over the meaning of 1789 and 1793. Right-wing journals have chosen revolutionary historiography as a means of sniping at the left, and the left has replied with a barrage of articles about the true character of "the Mother of us all," as the Revolution is known among her legitimate offspring.[2] The fighting has some characteristics of a *guerre dans la cimetière;* the protagonists seem perched on tombs, defending heritages: Marx versus Tocqueville, Mathiez versus Aulard, Lefebvre versus Febvre. But there is more to it than ancestor worship and ideological tribalism.

In the attempt to strip off the political superstructure of French society and to probe its anatomy, French historians have tended to use the sharp instruments of Marxism.[3] But

English and American historians have turned up data that are becoming harder and harder to fit into Marxist categories. George Taylor has exposed the noncapitalist character of the Old Regime's economy. Robert Forster has shown the inaccuracy of identifying feudalism with the nobility; C.B.A. Behrens has revealed the way privilege cut across the boundaries of class and estate; David Bien and Vivian Gruder have measured social mobility within the army and the intendancies and have found the opposition of bourgeoisie and aristocracy to be of little relevance; J. F. Bosher has demonstrated that the royal administration is better understood as the institutional interplay of complex vested interests than as a class government by the nobility. Class proves to be too narrow a concept for the analysis of the complexities and contradictions of revolutionary society and politics as they are unraveled in the work of Charles Tilly, M. J. Sydenham, Isser Woloch, and Colin Lucas. The fundamental Marxist idea that the Revolution resulted from a contradiction between a rising capitalist bourgeoisie and a feudal nobility has been exploded by Alfred Cobban, who stole most of his ammunition from the camp of his ideological enemies.

To be sure, Cobban's explicitly anti-Marxist history (like that of Crane Brinton and R. R. Palmer) has had little effect in France. Albert Soboul, the best of the French Marxists, ignored it while reworking the old orthodoxies in *Précis d'histoire de la Révolution française* (1962) at the same time that Norman Hampson was producing a remarkable non-Marxist work in English, *A Social History of the French Revolution* (1963). The language barrier may have prevented the outbreak of an Anglo-French Battle of Books. But in 1969, Pierre Goubert published the first volume of *L'Ancien Régime,* an extraordinarily penetrating and sophisticated non-Marxist analysis, which has captured the textbook market throughout much of France.

Finally, François Furet made a frontal attack on the Marxist interpretation of the Revolution in a brilliant polemical article, "Le Catéchisme révolutionnaire" (*Annales* [March–April 1971]), which provoked the present state of open war.

It would be wrong to view this warfare as an American challenge within the history profession or as a combat between Anglo-Saxon empiricism and Continental dogmatism in which the latter, after years of undermining and erosion, is doomed to come crashing down. Not only do the attackers include a heavy proportion of Frenchmen, who draw on their own rich tradition of non-Marxist social history, but the Marxist model is stronger and better defended than the Bastille ever was. Moreover, it is terribly difficult to abandon the idea that Soboul raises aloft in the very first sentence of his *Précis:* "The French Revolution constitutes, with the English revolutions of the seventeenth century, the culmination of a long economic and social evolution which has made the bourgeoisie the mistress of the world." Put that grandly, the proposition may seem easy to accept; yet it rests on assumptions that cannot be torn away without producing ruin. And if the revisionists succeed in dismantling the Marxist interpretation of the Revolution, what will they do with the rubble? They have no conceptual structure of their own.

Where in the general confusion does Richard Cobb belong? His early work cast him in the company of two Marxists, Albert Soboul and George Rudé, who reoriented the study of the Revolution by looking at it "from below." That phrase has become hackneyed now, but in the 1950s and early 1960s it represented an inspired attempt to examine events from a new perspective, that of ordinary men and women, the people who provided the muscle for forcing the Revolution to the left in the series of Great Leaps Forward, which were known as *journées* (July 14, 1789, October 5–6, 1789, August 10,

1792, and May 31–June 2, 1793), and who were crushed in the riots of Germinal and Prairial, Year III (1795) and rose again in the July Days of 1830, the June Days of 1848, and the May Days of 1871. These, in turn, served as ancestors for August of 1944, and May–June of 1968.

For Cobb, the concern with ordinary people led to the study of mentality (*mentalité* conveys a broader idea than its English counterpart), that is, the examination of the common man's outlook and perception of events rather than the analysis of the events themselves. Cobb's exploration of the revolutionary mentality complemented the work of Soboul and Rudé, who emphasized the institutional, political, and economic aspects of the sans-culotte movement; and it communicated the atmosphere of the Terror in ordinary neighborhoods where the desire for cheap bread and for a primitive equality of *jouissances* was more powerful than Rousseausim, and where the belief in counterrevolutionary conspiracy was more important than the conspiracies themselves. By immersing himself in the archives, by his luminous historical imagination and a superb command of French and English prose, Cobb managed to bring the obscure people of the Revolution back to life.

In *The Police and the People* and *Reactions to the French Revolution,* Cobb shifts ground, moving from below to beyond the fringe of the Revolution. Here he concentrates on banditry, prostitution, vagabondage, murder, madness, and other forms of deviance. These themes may fascinate us, but they will not help to sort out the confusion in current interpretations of the Revolution, because Cobb makes terrorist and counterterrorist, sans-culotte and criminal, militant and lunatic look alike; and he seems less intent on explaining the relation of violence to revolution than on exalting eccentricity and individualism for their own sake—a kind of upside-down moralizing that he turns against his former allies. For he never passes up an opportunity to poke at Soboul and to lunge at Rudé. He accuses them of dehumanizing the past by walling it up within a dessicated dogmatism. In fact, he pictures the revolutionary government as a form of totalitarianism *manqué,* suggesting that it fell short of Stalinism for want of technology, not for lack of trying, and he compares it unfavorably with "the full flowering of anarchical freedom" during the Thermidorean Reaction.

Where then, in the current historical battle, does Cobb stand? Against ideology and against sociology. He has placed himself squarely in no man's land and is fighting a private war on two fronts, in opposition to both the Marxist and the empirical versions of scientific history. Cobb has become every man's heretic. His perspective on history is set at such an odd angle that it compels us to see the Revolution freshly: That is the fascination of his work, for it challenges us at every turn with its idiosyncrasy—a rare quality in a profession that tends toward conformism.

Consider Cobb's reassessment of the popular sans-culotte movement in *The Police and the People.* Soboul showed that sans-culottism developed as a dialectic between popular revolution and revolutionary government during the Year II (1793–94); that is, he explained how the sans-culottes forced the Revolution to the left and why they were ultimately destroyed by the dictatorial Terror that they had brought into being. By close analysis and careful documentation, Soboul revealed an underlying logic of events, which still stands as the best explanation of the climactic phase of the Revolution.

Nothing could be further from Cobb's sense of history than logic; he attacks Soboul's analysis for excessive intellectuality (it is, he writes, an overchoreographed historical ballet) and tries to show that the popular revolution was less a move-

ment than an outbreak of anarchy. Cobb's view stresses the
temperamental defects of the sans-culottes—their bluster, their
naiveté and shortsightedness—but it never really undermines
Soboul's argument, and it confuses the issues by reversing the
chronology of events. Cobb's account runs backward through
the Empire, Directory, and Thermidorean Reaction to the
Year III (1794–95), which he treats as the turning point of the
entire Revolution. Finding no coherent sans-culottism during
those periods, he concludes that the movement must have
been ephemeral even before them—a bizarre interpretation
that seems to argue that because something died it had not
existed. Since Soboul traced the popular revolution's demise
to the end of the Year II and showed how and why it occurred,
Cobb's revisionism in reverse seems to miss its target. And
when Cobb finally backs into the Terror, his account reads
like spiced up Soboul.

But not when he discusses the provinces. Soboul's thesis
does not account for the vagaries of the popular revolution
outside Paris, whereas Cobb, who is a master of provincial
history, reveals all the contradictions and crosscurrents that
prevented sans-culottism from gathering into a national force.
Not only does he demonstrate that the extremists of Lyon
came out on the opposite side of issues being championed by
the wildmen of Paris, but he shows how the fire eaters of
Vienne opposed the Lyonnais, and how the multitiered antagonisms of Paris-Lyon-Vienne differed from those of Paris-
Rouen-Le Havre. Cobb goes further still: He explores the
rivalries among neighborhoods, the feuds between families,
the solidarity built up by occupational ties, and the schisms
derived from quarrels over cock fighting or bowls or women.
Everywhere he sees variety, discord, individualism; general
lines of interpretation blur, and the Revolution dissolves into
buzzing confusion. Perhaps that is all it amounted to for the

man in the street. In any case, Cobb shows the limits of the Parisian model.

He already did so in his earlier work. His last book, *Reactions to the French Revolution,* concerns anarchists, bandits, criminals, recluses, madmen, and a wild variety of individuals who lived outside politics, beyond the reach of the state. As these persons had nothing in common except their refusal to become integrated in society, and as asocial individuals have proliferated throughout French history, their stories do not lead to any general conclusions about their lives or their time.

Thus, it would appear that it is the very timelessness of anomie, or *la vie en marge,* that attracts Cobb. For twenty-five years he has wandered in the archives, searching out every eccentric he could uncover. He emerges with a fantastic collection of cases of deviant individualism, strung together through "the selective use of the individual 'case history' as a unit in historical impressionism." This method suits Cobb's sense of the uniqueness of things and of the historian's task, which is to show how phenomena are distinct, not how they are related. By constantly emphasizing the complexity of the past, his work stands as a warning against attempts to make history fit into prefabricated social structures. But Cobb's insistence on uniqueness tends toward nominalism or nihilism. It suggests that generalization is impossible and that history can only be reduced to case histories.

There is madness in that method, and a touch of madness may be necessary to understand the "cannibals" who ran amuck in September of 1792, traumatizing the Republic at it birth. One could hardly imagine a happier meeting of subject and author than Cobb's sympathetic evocation of what Terror and Counter Terror meant to people who experienced them. But his refusal to analyze and generalize makes him sound like an intellectual Luddite. Not only does he inveigh against *Annales* historians, intellectual historians, and sociological historians, but in constructing his own version of events, he refuses to rise above the level of the *fait divers*. For Cobb, as for Restif de la Bretonne and Louis Sébastien Mercier, the revolutionary *rapporteurs* in whom he finds his greatest inspiration, it is enough to glimpse into the heart of the passer-by. History is soul history, and methodology is empathy.

The danger of this historical impressionism is not that it will budge Soboul's rocklike thesis, or any other analytical structure, but rather that it may misdirect the development of the history of *mentalités,* Cobb's chosen genre. Although it goes back at least as far as Burckhardt, the study of *mentalité* is undergoing a strong revival in France and has even crossed the Channel, if not the Atlantic. It is a sort of intellectual history of nonintellectuals, an attempt to reconstruct the cosmology of the common man or, more modestly, to understand the attitudes, assumptions, and implicit ideologies of specific social groups (their *outillage mental,* according to Lucien Febvre, the great prophet and practitioner of this kind of history). Mentality is more a subject than a discipline. The French have discussed it in various prolegomena and discourses on method,[4] but they have not arrived at any clear conception of the field. Nor has Cobb. His last two books treat such a bewildering variety of subjects—criminality, vagrancy, urban–rural conflict, suicide, insanity, popular culture, the family, the suppression of women—that it is difficult to find any coherent theme in the rush of chapters and subchapters.

Criminality

But if Cobb's work has any leitmotiv, it is murder; and since most of his deviants resorted to murder at one time or other, he concentrates on it long enough to produce some statistics. He counted 846 "political" murders in the Rhône Valley and adjoining areas during the last five years of the eighteenth century. The homicidal "score" according to time and place convinced him that the murder rate went up drastically during the years between the Terror and the Empire. Although the murders often reflected merely local motives (family feuds, *règlements de compte;* in practice Cobb concedes the impossibility of distinguishing political from nonpolitical killing), he found that they correlated most closely with the political temperature. So he interprets homicide as a form of political protest, a Counter-Terror, which had the support of communities that had been alienated by the agents of the revolutionary government in Paris—hence its relevance to popular mentality and to the decline of the popular movement.

Cobb scatters his statistics in a manner that makes them difficult to evaluate, and trying to correlate them proves nothing at all, because he uses no consistent unit of measurement. For example, instead of telling the reader how many murders occurred each year in the Department of the Rhône, he presents his information as follows: In the Year III (1794–95) there were fifty murders in the Department of the Rhône and the Department of the Loire; in the Year IV there were twenty in the Rhône and the Haute-Loire; he has no figures for the Year V; in the Year VI there were four in the Rhône alone; and he has no figures for the Year VII. The numerical base is trivial, the geographical unit is never the same; and there are no statistics for two of the five years under study. Yet the Rhône was the area that Cobb investigated most intensively. For other regions his statistics are even scantier: they usually cover only one or two years and refer to inconsistent combinations of departments.

Cobb produces no statistics for any period before the Year III, yet he asserts that the murder rate of the Counter Terror

(Years III and after) was as high as that of the Terror (Year II) and was higher than that of nonrevolutionary years. That conclusion can only be substantiated by statistics covering the periods before and after the Revolution, which Cobb does not provide. He gives no idea of the outside boundaries of his data or of the representativeness of his statistics. What fraction of the whole number of murders has he unearthed? What is their relation to the population of the areas under study? How do they measure against some standard rate of murders per one hundred thousand people over a long series of years?

Cobb never asks these questions; yet until he answers them, his conclusions should be taken as hypotheses. He disparages the importance of statistics, but he relies heavily on them, and on general remarks about incidence, to make sense of a multitude of subjects: prostitution, desertion, disease, vagrancy, and all forms of crime and violence. In every case, he sees a quantitative jump after Thermidor (July 27, 1794), and he seems to explain that increase by the change in the political climate—an interpretation that seems dubious on its face and is undermined by Cobb's admission that much of his evidence comes from notes that he had jotted down *en passant* two decades ago, when he was looking for information about the revolutionary armies. That search took him through thousands of heterogeneous dossiers and made it impossible for him to produce statistics in a series, that is, from a homogeneous source, capable of being quantified in units of equal value.

Does this statistical *insouciance* invalidate the conclusions of Cobb's last two books? Certainly not, because he really cares less about measuring the rate of violence than about understanding the experience of it. In a section following the homicidal "scorekeeping" in *The Police and the People,* he describes the psychological isolation of former terrorists when the Thermidorean Reaction penetrated the countryside. As an imaginative evocation of the nastiness of village life, it is utterly persuasive; and it would compensate for a book full of faulty statistics. The same is true of some marvelous accounts of popular attitudes toward food and "dearth," of the dignity of the man who can say that he has "bread in the house," and of popular language, which extremists manipulated through the use of black humor and scatological hyperbole ("I'm going to eat the head of a bourgeois, with garlic"). In treating this kind of subject, Cobb lets his historical imagination play; and his remarks carry conviction because of his mastery of the material. The problem is how to move beyond evocation by anecdote and to carry the history of *mentalités* past the point reached by masters like Lucien Febvre, who also combined great historical sensitivity with erudition and literary flair.

Criminality and mentality fit together so naturally as subjects that they suggest a way of resolving the antithesis between sociology and the history of *mentalités* that runs throughout Cobb's work. If, instead of building barriers between history and the social sciences, he had made some forays into alien territory, Cobb would have found a rich literature waiting to be exploited. Some familiarity with criminology, for example, might have provoked him to question his thesis that the Revolution or the Counter Revolution produced an upsurge in violent crime. Historical criminologists have found the opposite to be true, in the case of 1871 as well as 1789.[5] They also have developed techniques for taking the trickiness out of statistics.

A glance at almost any criminology textbook[6] or even at such untouchable journals as the *Revue française de sociologie* or the *Annales* could have helped Cobb untangle his figures on crime rates and might have put him on the track of the *Comptes généaux de l'administration de la justice criminelle,* which provide criminal statistics dating back to 1825. The *Comptes* have supplied material for social history since the time of A. M. Guerry and Adolphe Quételet, early masters of sociology, who lived through the events Cobb describes and who studied criminality with a statistical sophistication that makes his work look primitive.[7]

Of course, modern criminology cannot be applied indiscriminately to the past, because of the irregularity of criminal statistics before the nineteenth century. But criminology can suggest approaches, methods, and questions that might never occur to the asociological historian. It can show him how to measure criminality against demography; how to sort out factors such as age, trade, sex, and geography; and how to be sensitive to the attitudes (or *mentalités*) involved in the relations between those who break the law and those who enforce it. For crime provides a negative image of the sacred and a direct reflection of the taboo; and when studied over long periods, it can reveal shifts in a society's value system. Analyses of sentencing show the sociologically significant moments when judges cease to apply laws that remain on the books but have passed out of the mores.

Robert Mandrou developed this approach successfully in his book on the persecution of witchcraft, *Magistrats et sorciers en France au XVIIᵉ siècle,* and today's newspapers are full of analogous cases: trials concerning abortion, homosexuality, and obscenity. Similarly, studies of the incidence of crimes may uncover changes in attitudes and behavior patterns. Thus Enrico Ferri postulated that as societies move into an urbanized and commercialized stage of development, they pass from a pattern of instinctual criminality to a pattern of calculated criminality, from crime against persons to crime against property.[8] Although Ferri's "law" may have been flogged to death, it has proved useful in comparing traditional and modern or rural and urban societies. The rate of violent crimes (murder and felonious assault, for example) tends to be much higher in archaic, agrarian villages, where communal norms regulate conduct, except in its most explosive, impetuous moments, whereas economic crime (theft and fraud) predominates in modern cities, where uprooted, money-oriented individuals struggle anonymously to strike it rich or simply to survive.

This shift from passionate to commercial criminality seems to have occurred throughout the West during the early modern period (the present wave of muggings represents a change of tide), and so does the rise of the underworld, despite the gangland subculture (mostly mythical) that surrounded Robin Hood and Cartouche. Cobb treats rural, urban, and organized crime as expressions of the same deviant mentality; but criminology suggests that pitchfork murderers, city shoplifters, and *mafiosi* belong to different species.

Such differences can only emerge by comparative analysis, another genre that Cobb dislikes and that could have helped him to put his material in perspective. Do his four murders in the Department of the Rhône during the Year VI represent a high level of violence? Assuming the Rhône had a population of approximately two hundred thousand, it had a murder rate of two per one hundred thousand, which is about that of France today. So the area around Lyon, which Cobb describes as a gigantic chamber of horrors, might have passed into a phase of fairly bloodless criminality by 1789, and Cobb's penchant for the violent anecdote may have made him misrepresent reality. The obscene, ritualistic killings in the remoter regions he studies suggest a more primitive pattern, like that of Colombia, Burma, or Indonesia today.[9]

Cross-cultural comparisons on a global scale may have little practical value, but Cobb might have compared his findings with those of other historians studying the criminality of eighteenth-century France. Teams of them have been plowing through archives in Lille, Caën, Bordeaux, Toulouse, Aix, and Paris; and they already have produced significant results, as may be appreciated by the work-in-progress reports published by the groups working with François Billacois in Paris and with Pierre Deyon in Lille.[10]

The Parisian group found that theft accounted for 87 percent of reported crimes from 1755 to 1785—a figure that puts prerevolutionary Paris in a class with the metropolises of modern Europe (99 percent of the crimes in Paris in the 1970s were thefts), in contrast to eighteenth-century French villages, where theft represented only one third or so of recorded crimes. The homicide rate was low (about one per one hundred thousand), and all the evidence suggests that the criminal underworld had not yet come into existence. Even if one allows for considerable discrepancy between real and reported crime, the capital of the Revolution would look like a haven of nonviolence to anyone who lives in New York in the final quarter of the twentieth century.

But it was hell for the criminals, who mostly stole to stay alive. Analysis of their origins, trades, domiciles, and family status shows that they belonged to France's miserable "floating population," which lived on the road between temporary jobs and stayed in squalid rooming houses. These "criminals" were the victims of poverty; their own victims were often semi-indigent also, and their oppressors showed one dominant attitude: protect property. The judges in the criminal courts of Paris throughout the age of Enlightenment had thieves hanged and tortured, but they showed indulgence for crimes that seemed less threatening to them: felonious assault, rape, and adultery.

The same pattern emerges from the research historians have done in Lille. It shows that criminal violence decreased dramatically during the entire revolutionary decade and that the rate of crimes against persons declined throughout the eighteenth century, while crimes against property increased. Judges ceased to enforce punishments for sacrilege, showed more leniency toward private immorality, decreased the use of torture (but continued to use it against thieves, if they were poor and ill-born), and suppressed even petty theft with great severity—greatest in the case of servants, beggars, and laborers. Criminal justice, as practiced in Paris and Lille, had abandoned the defense of traditional values and had become essentially an attempt to protect property against the propertyless.

That bottom category of poverty did not include the Parisian sans-culottes. They had regular jobs, fixed addresses, families, and bread in the house—even if there was not always enough of it to keep their stomachs full. The criminal population was densest in the very center of Paris, where the cheapest boarding houses were located, not in the *faubourgs* that supplied the sans-culottes. It therefore seems that criminal and revolutionary violence were unrelated, that the Bastille-storming and purse-snatching impulses had little in common, and that even seen from "below" the Revolution took place above the heads of France's bread-and-butter criminals.

Historical criminology therefore has revealed realities of behavior and psychology that could not be reached by Cobb's methods. The point is not that Cobb was wrong (his kind of history is too subjective to be classified as right or wrong), but that his historical impressionism does not lead anywhere. The comparison of his work on criminality and that of the social scientists suggest that the history of *mentalités* ought to ally itself with sociology, not fight it to the death.

Death

The study of death itself illustrates the same point. Death is a subject that has occupied sociologists, anthropologists,

painters, poets, and morticians—but not historians. Although
it has inexorably followed life throughout all time, historians
have assumed it has no history. They generally prefer dramatic events to the great constants of the human condition
—birth, childhood, marriage, old age, and death. Yet those
constants have changed, however slowly and imperceptibly.
Consider the contrast between the medieval art of dying and
the American way of death. In the late Middle Ages, the dying
man played the central part in a supernatural drama. He staged
and managed his death according to a prescribed rite, con-
scious of the fact that he had reached the climatic moment of
his life, that heaven and hell hung in the balance, and that he
could save his soul by making a "good death." *L'Art de bien
mourir,* the *Ars Moriendi,* became one of the most popular and
widely diffused themes of literature and iconography in the
fifteenth century.

The *Ars Moriendi* depicted a man on his deathbed surrounded by saints and demons who are struggling for the
possession of his soul. The devils reenact his sins and claim
him for hell. If he resists the temptations of pride and despair,
and if he sincerely repents, he dies well. His hands crossed, his
head facing eastward toward Jerusalem, his face lifted toward
heaven, he emits his soul with his last breath. It emerges from
his mouth, looking like a newborn baby, and an angel carries
it off to heaven. The spectacle reveals the medieval sense of
reality, a cosmological clutter of the exalted and the base, in
which ordinary objects are infused with transcendental significance.

Medieval and early modern man had a horror of sudden
death, because it might deprive him of his part in the critical,
metaphysical moment. In dangerous cases, a doctor's first duty
was to get a priest. He was under a solemn obligation to warn
his patients if death seemed to be even a remote possibility,
because they needed time to prepare for death, to meet it

according to the traditional ceremony, in bed. The deathbed scene took place in public. Priests, doctors, family, friends, even passers-by crowded into the room of the dying man. In a "good death," he took stock of his life, called in his enemies and forgave them, blessed his children, repented his sins, and received the last sacraments. Although it varied according to his status and his era, his will regulated the burial and mourning in elaborate detail, specifying the composition of the cortege, the number of candles to be carried, the character of the burial, and the number of masses to be said for his soul. After a prescribed period of withdrawal from society in prescribed dress, the bereaved members of his family would take up life again, fortified for their own encounters with death.

The "good death" represented what Huizinga has called a "cultural ideal," not actuality, for in the age of the Black Death people died miserably and profligately. In times of famine, corpses were found with grass in their mouths. In times of plague, the dying were often abandoned and their bodies piled up and burned or tossed without ceremony into mass graves. At all times, death was familiar and all pervasive; it was even an object of jokes and social comment, as in the popular literature on the Dance of Death. In Europe three hundred years ago, six hundred years ago, public executions were spectator sports; children found dead vagrants in haylofts—*croquants;* and graveyards served as meeting grounds for playing games, pasturing cattle, peddling wares, drinking, dancing, and wenching.

Instead of presiding over his death, modern man is "robbed" of it, to use the expression of Philippe Ariès. About 80 percent of the deaths in the United States now occur in hospitals and nursing "homes." Most Americans die in isolation, surrounded by strangers and medical technicians instead of their families. The priest has been replaced by the doctor, whose training gives him no way of satisfying the psychological needs of the dying and who hides death from the patient. The patient therefore shuffles into death unknowingly; far from being exposed to any ultimate reality, he dies as if death were merely the last drop in the graph on the temperature chart.

The inhumanity of this painless positivism has generated a considerable debate and a large literature in medicine, psychology, and sociology. Recently, hospitals and medical schools have modified their practices. But the problem concerns more than hospital management. As Herman Feifel, Robert Fulton, W. Loyd Warner, Avery Weisman, and other social scientists have shown, it touches a taboo embedded deep in American culture.

The art and literature of the High Middle Ages dwelt on the worms, dirt, and decomposition that overcome corpses. Baroque art also emphasized death in a spirit of macabre realism. Nineteenth-century cemeteries proclaimed their function with a lavishness that James S. Curl has characterized as "the Victorian celebration of death." But the art of the American mortician paints death to look like life, sealing it up in watertight caskets and spiriting it away to graveyards camouflaged as gardens. Americans take refuge in euphemisms: "passing away," "terminal case," "malignancy."

They also deritualize death. No longer do their bereaved set themselves apart by wearing black or withdrawing from social functions for a specified time. Wakes are almost extinct; many bereaved families discourage the ritual gesture of sending flowers, requesting instead that friends give donations to charities. Children frequently do not attend funerals of close relatives, and their parents avoid discussing the subject of death (but not sex) with them. The code of behavior at funerals prescribes the suppression of grief. Presidential widows have set a standard of not "cracking"—the antithesis of an earlier ideal, which made weeping obligatory. The extreme in the repressive, unceremonial treatment of death seems to have been attained by the professional classes in England—a case of ritualistic vacuum that Geoffrey Gorer has documented movingly in *Death, Grief, and Mourning in Contemporary Britain*. Gorer laments the disappearance of rites for expressing grief and for comforting the bereaved. The "American way of death" has been condemned just as strongly by Jessica Mitford, who contends that commercial interests have taken over the expression of grief in this country and exploited it for their own profit. In both countries death has been transformed into the opposite of what it was five hundred years ago.[11]

How did this transformation come about? Philippe Ariès, the masterful social historian who wrote *Centuries of Childhood*, was one of the first to recognize it and has tried to trace its stages in his latest book, *Western Attitudes Toward Death*.[12] He argues that the traditional view of death took hold of men's minds during the millennium after the collapse of the Roman Empire. Early medieval men saw death as a collective destiny, ordinary, inevitable, and not particularly fearsome, because it would engulf all Christians, like a great sleep, until they would awaken in paradise at the Second Coming of Christ. Between 1000 and 1250, this attitude shifted in emphasis from the collectivity to the individual; and from the late Middle Ages until the late eighteenth century, death served primarily to sharpen one's sense of self. It became the supreme moment in the personal journey toward salvation. But if mismanaged, it could lead to damnation, as the *Ars Moriendi* made clear. Death therefore became more dramatic, but it remained essentially the same—a familiar presence, acting openly in the midst of life—and the same rituals sufficed in dealing with it. Men sought to die the "good death," in their beds and in public— resolute, repentant, and fortified by the sacrament for eventual elevation to the Celestial Court.

By the nineteenth century, this ritual became charged with a new sense of affection. Death meant primarily the separation of loved ones. Instead of seeming ordinary, it became a catastrophic rupture with the familiar and the familial, for the family that took charge of it ultimately proved unequal to the burden of grief. Death plunged the bereaved into a terrifying realm of irrationality, an experience evoked by the morbid themes in romantic literature and the Dionysian emotionalism of nineteenth-century tomb sculpture. In the mid-twentieth century, Westerners attempted to avoid the paroxysm of grief by interdicting death. First in the United States, then in Britain, Northern Europe, and now in Latin countries, they have abandoned the traditional ritual, hidden death from the dying person, and transferred it from the family to the hospital, where the abandoned "patient" passes imperceptibly out of life by degrees, his terminal moment being a technicality instead of a dramatic act over which he presides.

It is an astounding story, told with the incisiveness and mastery characteristic of Ariès's work; but is it true? The rules of evidence in this kind of history—the study of change in attitudes or *mentalités*—remain vague. Shifts in world view normally occur at a glacial pace, unmarked by events and without visible turning points. The subject matter of this history cannot be treated in the same way as the battles, election victories, and stock market fluctuations that punctuate *l'histoire événementielle* with such precision. *Mentalités* need to be studied over the long term, and Ariès produces all these phrases in the first sentence of his book, as if he were an ambassador from the Annales School of History presenting his credentials to John Hopkins University, which invited him to report on his work in a series of lectures.

According to Ariès there are four phases of Western attitudes toward death: the traditional "tamed" death of the first millennium of Christianity, the more personal death of the

next seven hundred fifty years, the family-oriented obsession
with "thy death," which prevailed from the late eighteenth to
the early twentieth century, and the "forbidden death" of the
last thirty years. Very formal and very French, perhaps, but
Ariès has the advantage of showing how cultural mutation can
occur at different paces. Western attitudes turned and twisted
at an accelerating speed until they spun out of control in the
contemporary era, which Ariès characterizes forcefully as a
time of "a brutal revolution in traditional ideas and feelings."

In discussing the current century, Ariès argues from a position of strength, because he can draw on the work of social
scientists like Gorer, who first exposed the deritualization and
denial in contemporary attempts to deal with death. Ariès
might even have taken his argument further by drawing more
on the growing literature about death psychology, sociology,
and "thanatology."[13] In analyzing older attitudes toward death,
he has less to stand on but more to contribute, for he has
mapped an unknown zone of human consciousness as it evolved
through time. The audacity of the undertaking must be admired, even if it bears no more relation to reality than the
cartography of Amerigo Vespucci. Gorer could study contemporary British attitudes by scientific sampling, question-
naires, and interviews. Ariès had to piece together whatever
fragments he could find, rummaging about in archaeology,
semantics, literature, law, and iconography.

Fascinating as the evidence is, its heterogeneity and sparse-
ness inevitably weaken the argument. For example, Ariès asserts that man's vision of the Last Judgment shifted significantly
between the seventh and the fifteenth centuries; and to prove
his case he refers to one seventh-century tomb, a half-dozen
tympana from twelfth- and thirteenth-century cathedrals, a
thirteenth-century hymn, and a fifteenth-century fresco. The
reader is left to imagine the counterexamples from the art of
those eight centuries, which flash by in four pages.

As evidence of the way death became individualized between the thirteenth and eighteenth centuries, Ariès stresses the importance of donation plaques in churches and cites one example, from 1703. To document the public character of the medieval deathbed rite, he cites one source from the late eighteenth century. He casually strides across continents and over centuries and carries the reader effortlessly from King Arthur's Round Table to Tolstoy's *mir* and Mark Twain's gold country. This fast play with sources may be less illegitimate than it seems, because vestiges of ancient customs survived well into the modern period everywhere in the West. But without firm evidence that the customs flourished earlier, one cannot know whether their later existence really was vestigial. Long-term history has not earned an exemption from the requirement of rigorous documentation.

The difficulty is greatest in research directed at the masses, who lived and died without leaving any trace of their conception of life and death. Ariès generally skirts this problem by restricting his discussion to high culture and the upper classes. When he expounds early medieval attitudes he turns to the *Chanson de Roland*. When he reaches the nineteenth century he cites Lamartine and the Brontës. He uses art history constantly, but normally limits himself to the art of the elite.

The most important exception to this tendency and the most original part of the book comes in Ariès discussion of burial customs and cemetery design. He argues that early Christian burial reversed the practice of Roman patricians, who were buried in individual mausoleums outside the cities. The early Christians had a quasi-magical belief in the efficacy of interment near the remains of saints and, therefore, favored burial in churches located in the center of towns. For a millennium this burial remained essentially collective. The rich and well-born were placed under slabs of the church floor, the common people in ditches in the churchyard. As each location

filled, the bones were transferred to common ossuaries and
charnel houses, where they were stacked and displayed with
macabre artistry. At the same time, cattle, children, shopkeepers, and bawds surged through the cemeteries.

The promiscuous interpretation of death and life struck
Europeans as natural until the late eighteenth century, when
enlightened French administrators considered it unhealthy and
unseemly, forbade burial in churches, and moved graveyards
outside city limits. By that time even the common people
began to be buried in individual plots. The personal grave,
surmounted by a stone with a biographical inscription, came
to be seen as an inviolable preserve in the nineteenth century.
Families visited it to honor their own dead both privately and
on ceremonial occasions like All Souls' Day. A veritable new
cult of the dead came into existence, especially in Latin Europe, where elaborate museums and statuary transformed the
appearance of cemeteries. Then suddenly, during the first half
of the twentieth century, this tendency was reversed. In contemporary Britain most people are cremated and therefore
leave behind no physical testimony to their existence; their
survivors rarely put up plaques or make inscriptions in the
"Books of Remembrance" provided by the crematoria.

Burial customs therefore illustrate Ariès's contention that
Western man first conceived of death as the familiar, collective
fate of all Christians, then looked upon it as the supreme moment of a biography, next infused it with familiar affection,
and finally attempted to deny it altogether. The resistance to
cremation, the ceremonial funeral "homes," and the elaborate
cemeteries of contemporary America do not fit this pattern;
and Ariès does not explain why deritualization should be so
muted here, where the "revolution" allegedly began, rather
than in Britain, where it has assumed its most extreme form.
But he uncovers some fascinating and unfamiliar aspects of
Western culture.

Throughout his work, however, Ariès tries to understand popular mentality through the analysis of high culture, a dubious method, particularly when applied to relatively recent history. In the Middle Ages, it is true, elite and popular culture had not gone their separate ways. The common man carved his cosmology onto his church, where art historians like Erwin Panofsky have been able to decipher it. Millard Meiss, in *Painting in Florence and Siena After the Black Death,* has related the stylistic trends in Tuscan art to a general crisis in late medieval civilization, a crisis in which the Black Death played a crucial part. Huizinga discussed the same crisis in *The Waning of the Middle Ages,* a masterpiece that was inspired by the painting of the van Eycks. Alberto Tenenti has attempted, with less success, to glimpse world view through Renaissance art in *Il senso della morte e l'amore della vita nel Rinascimento* and *La Vie et la mort à travers l'art du XV* siècle. And historians of medieval and Renaissance literature—Jean Rousset and Theodore Spencer, for example—have explored the connections between high culture and general attitudes toward death. This approach has proved to be especially useful in the study of genres like Elizabethan tragedy and of specific works, like the *Faerie Queene,* which, as Kathrine Doller has shown, contains motifs derived from the popular *Ars Moriendi.*

So Ariès can draw on a rich scholarly tradition, and he does so with imagination and erudition. It seems regrettable that he leans heavily on Tenenti, when he could have used the more thorough studies of the *Ars Moriendi* by Mary Catharine O'Connor and Nancy Lee Beaty. He also makes little use of another popular genre, the Dance of Death, which has been studied by J.M. Clark and others. But he cannot be faulted for failing to incorporate traditional cultural history in his *histoire des mentalités.* The fault lies rather in a failure to question the connections between art and the inarticulate. When and to what extent did high culture become severed from the lower classes? That problem could be crucial to the history of popular attitudes, but Ariès rarely mentions class at all.

Gorer found striking differences in the way different classes respond to death in contemporary Britain. He discovered, for example, that the isolation of the dying becomes much greater as one ascends the social scale (family members were present at one of every three deaths in the working-class cases he studied and at one of every eight among the upper middle and professional classes). Working-class people seemed considerably more familiar with death and less frightened of it, and they tended to preserve older customs longer (in four-fifths of working-class homes the blinds are drawn after a death in the family; they are drawn in two-thirds of middle-class homes; and the upper middle and professional classes apparently have abandoned the practice altogether). The cultural significance of death may have varied enormously among different social groups, and it may have evolved among them in very different patterns. Ariès ignores such nuances and concentrates on the general Western pattern, assuming that here was one and that it can be known by studying the elite.

Those assumptions, though unproven, may be valid, and Ariès may well have succeeded in the monumental task of tracing the general outline of the changing Western attitudes toward death. How then does he explain them? His explanation is implicit and derives from his earlier study of childhood and the family. In the millennium of tamed death, he argues, men and women were absorbed almost immediately into the collectivity without passing through any clearly defined stage of childhood and without developing strong ties to their families. By the end of the eighteenth century, the family had taken over the socialization of the child, and childhood itself was perceived for the first time as a crucial phase of an individual's development. In response to a new demographic pattern, which made childhood and marriage less vulnerable to mortality, the family became the dominant institution in society: hence the nineteenth-century cult of the dead. Far from having declined, as some maintain, the family is now the focus of the affections. A death in the family therefore leaves modern man paralyzed by grief, for he has little emotional investment in other institutions, and he has but the empty remains of traditional ritual and religiosity to help him through his bereavement.

The argument might seem convincing if Ariès had proved the thesis of his *Centuries of Childhood,* a brilliant book but one that makes the history of childhood hang on the slender thread of the history of education, especially secondary and higher education. Since few children had any formal education before the modern period, it seems unlikely that educational institutions had much effect on general attitudes toward childhood. But all children had families. Contrary to what Ariès asserts, no evidence indicates that the family did not handle the socialization of children at all times in Western Europe and, for that matter, in all other societies.[14] The cohesion of the family probably varied considerably throughout Western history, and it may be stronger than ever today; but it could have been quite strong in the Middle Ages. In building an unsubstantiated interpretation of the evolution of attitudes toward death on an unsubstantiated interpretation of the evolution of the family, Ariès has stacked his hypotheses so precariously that they may collapse.

Ultimately, Ariès, like Cobb, relies on historical impressionism to hold his argument together and, as in Cobb's case, the weakness of that method may be appreciated by comparing his analysis with that of a sociological study of the same subject: *Piété baroque et déchristianisation en Provence au XVIIIᵉ siècle,* by Michel Vovelle.

The comparison may be unfair, because the writing of Ariès and Vovelle belong to different historical genres. Ariès produced an essay, a work in a genre that gives the historian an opportunity to take risks, to confront important subjects, and to ask big questions without feeling compelled to prove a case. As an essayist, Ariès could soar over two millenia in one hundred pages. Even if he failed to sketch the topography of his subject correctly, he enriched history with a supply of original hypotheses. Vovelle went to the opposite extreme in historical writing. He burrowed deeply into one small corner of the history of death, sifted through his material with extraordinary care, and came up with a work of pure gold.

Vovelle discovered a way to know how ordinary persons conceived of death in eighteenth-century Provence. The work of Gabriel Le Bras and other sociologists of religion convinced him that the religion actually experienced by the inarticulate could be reconstructed by quantitative analysis of religious behavior. A pattern of action *(geste)* would reveal a pattern of attitudes. But where could one get systematic information about religiosity in the past? Vovelle found it in one of the oldest and most unexploited kinds of documents: wills, almost nineteen thousand of them. Far from being impersonal and legalistic as they are today, eighteenth-century wills provide an inventory of the testator's mental world. Most of them were dictated to notaries and therefore give a distorted reflection of that world, but the notaries proved to be varied and flexible in their writing. Even their stylized expressions are revealing, because they evolved in a significant pattern, and they indicate a pattern of behavior among the testators. By studying enormous numbers of Provençal wills over one hundred years—and subjecting his data and methods to criticism at every step—Vovelle found that the concept of death and the ritual surrounding it shifted almost as radically in the eighteenth century as Ariès claims it did in the twentieth.

In the late seventeenth and early eighteenth centuries, testators consistently described themselves as adherents of the holy, apostolic Roman Catholic Church who were prepared to meet their Maker, God the Creator, and Jesus Christ, His Son, by whose death and passion they hoped to be pardoned for their sins and to join the saints and angels in the Celestial Court of Paradise. Having made the sign of the cross in the name of the Father, the Son, and the Holy Ghost, the testators invoked legions of spiritual intercessors: first and most important, the glorious Virgin Mary; then the testator's guardian angel and patron saints; and finally a host of others, especially Saint Michael, who will hold the scales at the Last Judgment, and Saint Joseph, patron of the "good death." These wills were explicitly drawn up, as they put it, "in the thought of death"—an inevitable, solemn, and Christian occasion. By the 1780s most Provençal wills had reduced the traditional formula to a single clause: "Having recommended his soul to God." The Virgin Mary and saintly intercessors were gone, the Celestial Court emptied of angels. Christ himself had receded into the background, while God the Father sometimes took the form of "Divine Providence." Many wills had become totally secularized, and some even described death as "the indispensable tribute that we owe to Nature."

Of course, the change in expressions could be attributed to a change in legal conventions. Perhaps the will had become a lay instrument for the transfer of property rather than an outlet for religious sentiment. But it continued to regulate death rites, and their evolution shows that the religious *geste* followed the same pattern as the legal formulas. Funerals were elaborate ceremonies in the early eighteenth century, especially but not exclusively among the wealthy and the well-born. A long procession escorted the casket from the home of the bereaved to the church, touring the town according to a prescribed circuit. Thirteen paupers carried torches decorated with the dead man's coat of arms or initials in one hand and in the other a ceremonial gift of cloth that they received from him. Priests and nuns in ceremonial robes, rectors of hospitals, contingents of orphans and poor people, and fellow members of religious confraternities filed by, carrying torches and candles, which filled the streets with light. Everywhere bells tolled, and everyone knew for whom, because death involved display, the parading of status by a collectivity, which used ceremony to express its own order and the dead man's place in it. After a religious service, whose elaborateness varied according to the "condition" (rank) of the deceased, alms were distributed to beggars at the church door, and the body was buried—in a family chapel or a monastery for nobles, under the church floor for other important citizens, in the graveyard for ordinary citizens. The testator regulated all these details in his will, down to the number of candles, and expected to enhance his chances of entering heaven and of lessening his penance in purgatory by gifts to the poor, who were to pray for his soul, and by funding hundreds or thousands of masses to be said for him on specified occasions, often in perpetuity.

The baroque funeral had almost become extinct in Provence by 1789. Requests for processions in Marseilles declined fourfold (from 20 percent to 5 percent of the wills in samples where two-thirds of the testators came from the lower middle and lower classes) and were overtaken by a contrary tendency: requests for "simplicity" and for burial "without pomp" (from 0 to 7 percent). The parading, torch carrying, and bell ringing had nearly disappeared. The poor had ceased to play a special part because their prayers were no longer deemed useful for souls in purgatory; and poverty was treated increasingly as an economic ailment rather than a spiritual condition. Driven away from the church doors and shut up in a poorhouse, wandering beggars now received doles, thanks to legacies given in a spirit of secular humanitarianism rather than Christian charity. References to penitential confraternities declined markedly. The percentage of clergymen mentioned in wills also dwindled; and they were more often older and from the secular rather than the regular clergy. Instead of asking to be buried in the old style, "according to his condition," testators left the burial arrangements up to their heirs. (In Marseilles wills expressing indifference about the place of burial increased from 15 percent to 75 percent until 1776, when the king forbade interment in churches.) Above all, the Provençaux abandoned the belief that masses were required for the repose of their souls. Among upper- and middle-class notables throughout the province, requests for masses declined from 80 percent to 50 percent, and the average number of masses requested dropped from four hundred to one hundred. The decline was still greater in other groups—from 60 percent to around 20 percent among salaried male workers and seamen in Marseilles, and from 35 percent to 16 percent among peasants in the village of Salon-en-Provence.

Every indicator studied by Vovelle points to a decisive shift away from traditional religiosity and toward secularization in the mid-eighteenth century. In fact, it might make sense to conceive of two eighteenth centuries, a devout century (roughly from 1680 to 1750), in which traditional religious attitudes and ceremonies prevailed, and a century of secularization (from 1750 or 1760 to 1815), in which revolutionary de-Christianization only accelerated a process that had gained great momentum during the last decades of the Old Regime. Vovelle does not go so far as to suggest such a radical revision of conventional periodization, but it would fit data that have accumulated in demographic, economic, and intellectual history.[15] He does, however, analyze his material according to chronology, geography, and social structure; and this analysis lifts his account from the level of description to that of explanation.

First Vovelle establishes the details of the chronological pattern by analyzing 1,800 wills in central registries. These covered the entire province very well (they came from 600 notaries in 198 localities, or almost half the towns and villages in Provence). Although they did not represent much of the population below the upper-crust notables, they revealed four phases in the evolution of attitudes: from 1680 to 1710, a period of increased religiosity, which Vovelle attributes to the continuation, at a popular level, of the seventeenth-century religious revival and of the Counter Reformation; from 1710 to 1740, a period of decline, which coincided with the most violent episodes of the Jansenist controversies in Provence; from 1740 to 1760, a period of stabilization; and from 1760 to 1790, a period of brutal de-Christianization.

This scheme suggests that Jansenism and the Enlightenment could have acted as the gravediggers of traditional religiosity. Although Jansenism represented only an aspiration for a more intense and inward devotional life, it looked like crypto-Protestantism to many Frenchmen, and it touched off some fierce quarrels between rival factions of the French church in the early eighteenth century. After a long period of latency, the Enlightenment burst into print in midcentury and became widely diffused during the next fifty years. But how deeply did either of those two intellectual movements penetrate into French society?

Vovelle explores these and other problems of cultural diffusion by taking detailed soundings in twelve carefully chosen sites. With the help of several students, he made exhaustive analyses of wills in the notarial archives of one city (Marseilles), a small town and a village in lower Provence, two towns in upper Provence, and seven other towns and villages chosen for their exposure to Jansenism and Protestantism. Each study is a monograph in itself; each is executed with rigor and sophistication; and each touches an aspect of cultural and spiritual life that has eluded previous research.

Take the case of Roquevaire, a village near Marseilles, which had a population of twenty-five hundred in 1765. About two thirds of its inhabitants left wills when they died, and almost three-quarters of them were peasants. Vovelle studied five hundred wills in five samplings taken from 1650 to 1790. He therefore worked with a remarkably representative index to attitudes among the obscure "little people" in village society, and he found that they changed more radically than among the notables throughout the province. In 1700, 80 percent of the peasant landowners requested that masses be said for their souls; by 1750 the proportion had risen to 100 percent; and by 1789 it had dropped to 30 percent. The decline was less severe among the local notables (75 percent to 60 percent), but it was very strong among artisans and shopkeepers (50 percent to 16 percent). Other statistics confirmed this trend: Requests for funeral corteges declined from 23 percent to 2 percent; legacies to religious confraternities dropped from 55 percent to 1 percent; and the phrasing of the wills, which had been rich and varied in devotional expressions, became totally laicized.

Thus the general trend toward secularization could have extended further among the submerged masses than among the elite—at least in southern Provence, where economic and demographic growth and social and geographical mobility were greatest. Vovelle discovered another world in the isolated regions of northern Provence. Religious customs remained almost unchanged in Barcelonnette, an Alpine village where the Counter Reformation had established itself with unusual power and precocity (92 percent of the wills requested masses at the beginning of the century, 81 percent at the end).

There was also little change in Manosque, a backward, back-country town, which never adopted the intense religious practices of the mountainous areas and never gave in to the secularization of the *plat pays* (requests for masses remained constant at a low level, appearing in 20–30 percent of the wills). The geographical comparison suggests a link between changes in attitudes and in socioeconomic forces. Did a "modern" world view result from the increased mobility, economic growth, and life expectancy of the second eighteenth century?

Vovelle seems to favor this interpretation, but he shies away from generalizations and concentrates on the effects of cultural factors: hence his emphasis on Jansenism and the Enlightenment. He found secularization strongest in towns where Jansenism had taken root most deeply (Pigans and Cotignac) and also where Protestantism had never been completely extinguished (Cucuron and Pertuis). But in remote Jansenist sites (Blieux and Senez), orthodox Catholicism reestablished itself with unusual militancy, making the graphs of requests for masses—which serve as the crucial indicator throughout the book—rise instead of fall, until the last decades of the Old Regime, when they drop sharply. So if Jansenism precipitated de-Christianization, it did so primarily in the open, mobile population of the South.

The drop that occurs almost everywhere in Vovelle's graphs after 1760 suggests that secularization correlates with the diffusion of the Enlightenment. But attitudes and ideas represent different mental states: The decline in the devotional treatment of death need not imply a rise in Voltairianism: and it cannot be measured against the penetration of the Enlightenment, because that penetration cannot itself be measured. Faced with this problem, Vovelle uses literacy as a standard of measurement, although he concedes that it is a crude and unreliable index to the spread of enlightened ideas. He produces some important statistics on the incidence of literacy insofar as it can be known by the only available evidence, signatures of wills. His results confirm the celebrated Maggiolo study, which showed a low rate of literacy in southern France, and they expose the mythical character of the common view—one that flourished among nineteenth-century anticlericals—that instruction undermines religion. Vovelle discovered villages where both literacy and religiosity were very high (Barcelonnette) and very low (Salon). And he shows that in some places secularization was stronger among peasants and laborers, who were predominantly illiterate, than among the highly literate notables. So even if the spread of the Enlightenment has a correlation with primitive literacy, as seems unlikely, literacy has none with the secularization of attitudes toward death.

Marseilles, however, seems to have been a special case. Vovelle found that lower middle- and lower-class Marseillais were far more literate and secularized than their rural counterparts. Some of his statistics strain credibility (on page 377 he notes that by 1789 literacy among female peasants had risen to 45 percent and among male peasants had dropped to 0). But they demonstrate that secularization and literacy developed coincidentally in this urban setting, though at different rates among different social groups. Thus the literate elite of notables split, the nobles clinging to traditional religiosity while the bourgeois became de-Christianized. By 1789 three-quarters of all male laborers, artisans, and shopkeepers could sign their names, and the vast majority of them had given up the practice of requesting masses for the repose of their souls.

Vovelle tends to see a class alignment behind this sorting out of attitudes, and he turns it against the revisionist argument that the Enlightenment took root among a mixed elite of nobles and nonnobles. His thesis will go down well with Marxists who treat the Enlightenment as bourgeois ideology,[16] but his data suggest a change of attitudes that go deeper than ideology, and they call for further analysis. They are strikingly clear, by contrast, in showing a split in the devotional practices of men and women. This "sexual dimorphism" was especially strong among the lower classes, where there was also a widening gap between the literacy of men and women. Thus by the nineteenth century, illiterate women servants frequently had become more devout than their mistresses; and male laborers took to drink and newspapers in the bistro while their illiterate wives attended church. Vovelle has most to say about such questions of custom and outlook. He discovered a sea change in man's conception of the sacred, a process that may have disposed the Provençaux to accept enlightened ideas but that had no direct connection with the Enlightenment.

How this change came about remains in the end a mystery. It was not a matter of the masses following the lead of the elite, nor is it a matter of education or of urbanization. Secularization took hold most strongly in areas where social and economic change was greatest; and exposure to disruptive influences like Jansenism, Protestantism, and the Enlightenment probably had a reinforcing effect. But "socioeconomic change" hardly serves as as an explanation. Vovelle shows that the established pattern of attitudes in Marseilles was barely disrupted by the devastating plague of 1720, which killed half the population in the city, and by the subsequent tidal wave of immigration, which replaced the dead with a new population of uprooted peasants. And at some points his explanation sounds redundant: Attitudes changed because of a *mutation de sensibilité collective,* that is, a change in attitudes.

Ultimately, his interpretation depends on the words used in the title: He traces a shift from "baroque piety" to "de-Christianization." Instead of defining these terms, he builds associations around them and uses them descriptively, as a kind of shorthand for a pattern of attitudes and actions. But the "baroque" is a particularly ambiguous concept, which means different things to different historians, many of whom will gag on expressions like *sensibilité baroque, moeurs baroques,* and *baroquisme.*

De-Christianization also poses a problem, because most of Vovelle's material concerns the decrease in traditional ways of dealing with death—a matter of decline, not extinction (by 1789 half of the notables in the province still requested masses for their souls). The abandonment of "baroque" rites need not have implied the renunciation of Christianity. In fact, deritualization could have meant purification, as it did among the English Puritans. Ariès tries to explain Vovelle's data by invoking the rise of the family instead of the decline of traditional death rituals. He claims that testators stopped regulating their funerals and burials because for the first time they could trust their relatives to do justice to such ceremonies. Perhaps other interpretations could fit Vovelle's data, which he expounds beautifully but never fully explains.

Yet such criticism applies equally to the great theses that established the economic and demographic patterns of eighteenth-century French history. We still do not know why the population broke through the old Malthusian ceiling of twenty to twenty-five million, why agricultural prices should have increased by half during the last fifty years of the Old Regime, and why there was a revolution. Now we can ponder a deeper mystery: Why did attitudes change toward the basic facts of life and death? All these changes seem related to the emergence of a world that we may recognize as "modern," but how can we explain these relationships? By penetrating a previously inaccessible realm of experience, Vovelle has added a new dimension to the big questions of history, even if he has failed to answer them.

The importance of his achievement needs to be stressed

because few readers will find his quantification palatable or digestible. There is a kind of statistical puritanism to this book. No human beings relieve the un-relenting flow of maps, charts, and graphs, 112 of them, all done without computers or cor-relation coefficients. But history has often floundered in vague talk about world view, climate of opinion, and *Zeitgeist*. To get beyond Burckhardt, the study of *mentalités* needed new methods and new materials. Vovelle's use of quantification and sociology made him succeed where Ariès failed: He man-aged to chart a significant shift in world view among groups whose lives had seemed to be irretrievably lost in the past.

Conclusion

This attempt to make contact with the mental life of his-tory's forgotten men and women distinguishes the history of *mentalités* from the common varieties of intellectual history. Such contact as can be made usually concerns the fundamen-tals of the human condition, the way people conceived of the facts of life and death. But historians of *mentalités* are also investigating popular culture, folklore, vagrancy, family re-lations, sexuality, love, fear, and insanity. They attack these disparate subjects by different methods: statistics, demogra-phy, economics, anthropology, social psychology, whatever seems more appropriate.[17] Although it is too early to assess their work, a preliminary reconnoitering—and the compari-son of Cobb and the criminologists on the one hand and Ariès and Vovelle on the other—suggests one methodological im-perative: Rather than relying on intuition in an attempt to conjure up some vague climate of opinion, one ought to seize on at least one firm discipline in the social sciences and use it to relate mental experience to social and economic realities.

That conclusion, however, sounds suspiciously like common sense. Few historians today would object to the notion of applying social science to their craft, but few would agree on how the application is to be done. Are we to rummage through the social sciences, trying on one discipline after another, until we find something that somehow seems to fit our needs? Methodological eclecticism provides no real solution to the problems of relating changes in attitudes to social and economic development.

Perhaps Vovelle's failure to explain the phenomena he describes so successfully may indicate a weakness in the way *mentalités* are usually conceived. According to a classic formulation by Pierre Chaunu, *mentalités* exist on a "third level" of history. They belong to a superstructure, which rises above the more fundamental structures of the society and the economy, and therefore they develop in response to seismic shifts in the social and economic orders.[18] This three-tiered view of change suits a historiographical tradition that has been deeply influenced by Marxism. It also lends itself to functionalist social science; and it is congenial to quantification, because the statistical reconstruction of patterns of attitudes seems capable of revealing reality at the third level. But Vovelle, a Marxist-functionalist-quantifier, discovered that the curves of his graphs did not follow a pattern that made attitudes appear as a function of social and economic variables.

Perhaps the contributions to cultural history of Burckhardt, Huizinga, and even Lucien Febvre have been misconstrued by their successors: for those early masters attributed a considerable degree of autonomy to cultural forces. They did not treat culture as an epiphenomenon of society. They understood it as some current anthropologists do. The anthropological view of man as an animal who hungers for meaning, and of world view as a tenacious, ordering principle of social existence,[19] may ultimately go further than third-degree quantification to make sense of the material that the French are mining in such bewildering profusion from the riches of their past. Whether that prophecy proves true, it seems evident that the history of *mentalités* has developed into an important genre; it has already forced historians to see the human condition in a strange, new light.

PART FIVE

Good
Neighbors

Jeaurat de Bertry's ALLEGORY ON THE
REVOLUTION, *depicting Rousseau as its
spiritual father, 1789.*

History and the Sociology of Knowledge

I F THE MAN OF LETTERS was not born in Paris, he seems to
have spoken French throughout most modern history;
and his battle cries, from *écrasez l'infâme* to *épatez le bourgeois,* have echoed from the Left Bank to the Right Bank before circling the world. Thanks to the work of John Lough
and Daniel Roche, it now is possible to trace the rise of the
writer in France and to situate him within an institution that
also seems peculiarly Franch, although it exists everywhere
and nowhere—the Republic of Letters.

In *Writer and Public in France,* Lough concentrates on the
writer's attempt to win financial independence and social
standing, a long, hard struggle against supercilious patrons,
tight-fisted publishers, and an illiterate public. The most surprising aspect of this story is the staying power of patronage.[1]
It is well known that the medieval minstrels lived off scraps
from their lords' tables and that Racine gave up playwriting as
soon as he won a pension and a place in court. But Lough
shows that writers continued to depend on the rich and powerful until well into the nineteenth century. Hugo received
two thousand francs a year from Louis XVIII and Charles X.
Gautier got three thousand from Louis Napoleon in addition
to an honorific post as a librarian worth six thousand. Flaubert
kept body and soul together in his old age from a three thou-
sand-franc librarianship. And even Baudelaire, who declared

grandly in 1855 that he would never solicit subsidies—"never will my name appear in the vile papers of a government"[2]— begged the minister of education two years later for a pension and received a miserable two hundred francs.

Writers did not liberate themselves completely from patrons until about 1880, when Zola celebrated the advent of the modern cash nexus in literature: "It is money, it is the legitimate gain realized from his works that has freed [the writer] from all humiliating patronage. . . . Money has emancipated the writer, money has created modern letters."[3]

Why did it take the writer so long to live by his pen in France? Essentially, Lough argues, because of the underdeveloped character of the literary market.

In 1973, half the Frenchmen over fourteen years of age had not read a book during the past year. Almost a third of the population could not read at all in the 1870s, and nearly two-thirds were illiterate in the 1780s. Literacy rates were far higher in Britain and America during those periods, and so was expenditure on libraries. In 1908–09, the public libraries of Leeds spent six time as much money on books as those in Lyon, a city of comparable size.

Frenchmen have felt dubious about public education ever since Voltaire warned them that a peasant who took up books would abandon his plow. The Revolution established a system of primary schools on paper in 1793, but it probably disrupted the institutions of the Old Regime so badly that mass education was set back half a century. It took two more republics before the free, compulsory, and secular primary school began producing a critical mass of readers for the Republic of Letters.

The Third Republic represents a turning point in several other respects, according to Lough. It finally freed the press, not merely from censorship, which had plagued the printed word in various ways for three and a half centuries, but also from the insidious restraints of the stamp duty on newspapers and the restrictive licenses for printers and booksellers. The modern system of royalties took hold about 1880. At that point, writers began to cash in on the success of best sellers, because they received a proportion of the receipts from sales instead of a flat fee or a number of free copies in exchange for a manuscript.

Writers also benefited indirectly from an improvement in the lot of publishers after 1880. The Bern Convention of 1886, which established international agreement on copyright, freed the French book trade from the pirates who had raided it from the Low Countries and Switzerland since the sixteenth century. The cost of printing books fell after the introduction of machine-made pulp paper, the rotary press, steam power, and, in the 1880s, linotype. The number of books printed and the size of the press runs increased throughout the second half of the nineteenth century, reaching a peak in the decade 1889–99 that was not attained again until the 1960s, if the figures from the *dépôt légal* are to be believed.

Publishers and writers alike benefited from the expansion of journalism. With the founding of *La Presse* and *Le Siècle* in 1836, an era of relatively inexpensive newspapers, financed by advertising rather than subscriptions, came into existence. The *feuilleton,* or serialized novel, followed and in its wake a golden age for novelists. By 1840, editors began to bid for the rights to serialize fiction by Balzac, Sand, and Zola as well as that of the masters of the *feuilleton,* Eugène Sue, Dumas *père,* and Frédéric Soulié. A cheapening of the genre seems to have set in with the advent of the penny press in the 1860s. But high quality fiction had two outlets, the newspaper and the book, until World War I brought an end to the *belle époque* in literary fortunes.

The writer's status rose with his income. Having been a clown and a vagrant in the Middle Ages, a gentleman amateur in the Renaissance, and a curiosity in the salons of the Enlightenment, he commanded respect and sometimes adoration in the nineteenth century. Today one cannot cross a street in Paris without seeing a plaque to some man of letters or stroll through a park without confronting a poet on a pedestal. The names of schools, squares, and streets proclaim the cult of the writer everywhere in France—an odd phenomenon to anyone from the United States who has bought gas at the Vince Lombardi Service Area on the New Jersey Turnpike or driven through Bob Jones University.

But the pattern will look familiar to anyone who has read Lough's earlier books. Three of them, published between 1954 and 1978, contain chapters on "the writer and his public," which Lough has sewn together, with some rephrasing here and amplification there, to form much of the present work.[4] There is no harm in an author repeating himself, especially if he is as distinguished and erudite as Professor Lough. But a great deal has been written about writers and their readerships since 1954, and this work poses problems for Lough's attempt to trace a trajectory from Chrétien de Troyes to Sartre.

Lough cites many of the recent contributions to his subject in his footnotes and bibliography, but he generally ignores them in his text. For example, in his chapter on the seventeenth century, he generously acknowledges his debt to the work of Henri-Jean Martin, *Livre, pouvoirs et société à Paris au XVIIème siècle* (Geneva, 1969, 2 vols.). But the text of the chapter repeats what Lough said in 1954, sometimes word for word. True, it contains an aside about the inadequacy of Martin's statistics on book production. But it steers around the mountain of material Martin has unearthed on the politics and economics of the book trade, the social position of authors, and the tastes of readers.

In the following chapter, Lough cites *Livre et société dans la France du XVIIIème siècle* (Paris and The Hague, 1965–70, 2 vols.), a collection of essays by historians associated with the Ecole des Hautes Etudes in Paris, which is as important for the eighteenth century as Martin's work is for the seventeenth. Again, however, Lough clings closely to his old argument about the continued importance of patronage and the relative improvement in the writer's status. The *Livre et société* historians have moved beyond those questions to a new concern with the general topography of literary culture. By taking quantitative soundings in various sources, they try to show that "inertia" overwhelmed "innovation" in the reading habits of the Old Regime. Their argument may be wrong, but it is too important to be ignored; and it complements the work of Martin, who found that religious literature predominated in the classical age, when half the "writers" were probably clergymen.

The same emphasis emerges in recent studies of popular literature, which Lough acknowledges and then skirts. According to Robert Mandrou, Geneviève Bollème, Pierre Brochon, and Jean-Jacques Darmon, the literary diet of most Frenchmen from the late sixteenth to the mid-nineteenth century consisted of chapbooks; and these were consumed orally, at fireside readings, in which the literate few regaled the rest with saints' lives and the adventures of archaic heroes like the Quatre fils Aymon. These cheap pamphlets, known collectively as the *bibliothèque bleue,* were generally adapted by typesetters or anonymous hacks from the "high" literature of the Middle Ages and the Renaissance—that is, they did not have specific authors any more than they did readers.

Notions of the writer and the reading public quickly become anachronistic, if applied all the way back to the Middle Ages, as Lough does in his first chapter. Albert Lord and others have argued that the *chansons de geste* should not be understood as texts by authors but as performances by singers, who adapted a fluid repertory to particular audiences. Scribes eventually adapted those adaptations into writing, and printers adapted the scribal versions for the press.

Narrative intended directly for the press proceeded from different assumptions. By fixing texts in standard forms and multiplying them among readers whom the writer could only imagine, the printing press transformed literature as a mode of communication. Elizabeth Eisenstein has developed this line of analysis in a series of articles, culminating in her recent book, *The Printing Press as an Agent of Change* (Cambridge, 1979, 2 vols.). Lough merely treats the printing press as the beginning of a long process that led to the financial independence of the writer, and "writer" for him means troubadour as well as novelist.

Questions about communication deserve a place in a general study of writers and readers or, more broadly, the sociology of knowledge.[5] One need not line up with the supporters of Roland Barthes, Jacques Derrida, Tzetan Todorov, Wolfgang Iser, Wayne Booth, Stanley Fish, or any other fashionable critic to accept the notion that texts can be interpreted as a form of discourse, in which author and audience play prescribed roles. Rabelais leaps onto a stage and harangues you like a barker at a fair. Montaigne chats with you at a fireside. Rousseau manipulates you into the position of a confidant, the only one in a wicked world who can understand and forgive. Voltaire winks knowingly at you from behind impieties. Rimbaud clasps you to his bosom. Flaubert pretends that neither you nor he exists. The postures very enormously throughout French history; and they deserve a historian, for they provide clues about the ways of experiencing literature in the past.

One way was political, and it bears on the most important

role played by writers in French history. While English writers enjoyed wealth and prestige early in the eighteenth century
and often turned Tory, their underprivileged counterparts in
France tended to become social critics—that is, intellectuals.
The rise of the modern intellectual dates from the French Enlightenment, when Voltaire and d'Alembert cleared a path for
the philosophes by identifying them with the more respectable
category of *gens de lettres*. This strategy succeeded so well that
in later generations men of letters played the part of philosophes and stationed themselves in cafés from which they
could point an accusing finger at the social order. *"J'accuse"*
has shaped the role of the writer in the modern imagination
and has given it its aura of Frenchness.

Lough does not analyze the ways writers assumed different
roles in their work and in public life, and does not mention
their ideologies, not even Jansenism or Marxism. Instead, he
keeps his sights fixed on a single theme: the rise of the "professional," or self-supporting, writer from his remote origins in
the Middle Ages. In showing how much of that slow ascent is
a story of prophets without honor and honors without profit,
he has brought together a great deal of interesting information. But he has not advanced his subject far from where it
stood in the 1950s.

For a truly important advance, one must turn to *Le Siècle
des lumières en province,* by Daniel Roche. Its importance deserves to be underscored, since Roche's work will not be assimilated easily in this country, owing to a peculiar barrier
between the writer and the reading public. The difficulty is
not that Roche writes in French but that his idiom is statistical.
American and British historians have often used statistics, but
they have rarely attempted to take quantitative soundings of
culture. The French have been quantifying culture for a gen-

eration, and Roche's study of intellectual life in the provinces from 1680 to 1789 represents their work at its most ambitious and its best.

Instead of developing an argument from text to text in the manner of Lough, Roche provides a running commentary in his first volume on a series of tables, charts, graphs, and maps in his second. The reader must shuttle back and forth between volumes one and two, and his task is not made easier by the publisher, who has scrambled the references and botched the cartography. In the end, however, the reader's trouble will be rewarded, for he will get a view of the entire cultural terrain of the Old Regime. Roche has mapped it all. He reveals the social and geographical location of provincial academies, masonic lodges, schools and universities, concert societies, theaters, reading clubs, bookshops—virtually every institution that transmitted the Enlightenment to the literate.

Roche concentrates on the thirty-two provincial academies, and rightly so, for they served as centers for cultural diffusion in the eighteenth century. They cannot be identified directly with the Enlightenment, since many of them were founded under Louis XIV and were meant to extend the influence of the state in the cultural life of the provinces. But in the second half of the century they began to stir up debates about politically sensitive subjects, such as the increase in beggary and the need for reforming law codes. They did so by sponsoring essay contests, which produced a great outputing of quasi-political treatises.

Not only did Rousseau write the *Discourse on the Arts and Sciences* and the *Discourse on the Origin of Inequality* for the Academy of Dijon, but many future revolutionaries—Robespierre, Marat, Carnot, Barère, Roland, Brissot—tried to make names for themselves in the same way. By rewarding ambitious young writers with highly publicized prizes and electing them as corresponding members, the academies provided one of the few means of making a career in the premodern Republic of Letters.

In studying the academies, therefore, Roche has selected a strategic site at which to examine the convergence of traditional and modern currents of culture. He takes great pains, in the course of this examination, to situate the academies within the surrounding social order. In fact, he surveys the entire topography of urban society in the eighteenth century.

He produces figures on almost everything. For example, he estimates that his thirty-two cities had one priest for every 50–200 inhabitants, one administrative official for every 200–400, one doctor for every 1,000, one teacher in a secondary school or university for every 3,000, and one bookseller for every 1,000–4,500. Evidently, Voltaire and Tocqueville were both right: urban France was priest-ridden and overadministered. And Lough was not wrong, although scattered figures on literacy, book sales, and the size of the student population suggest that he underestimated the importance of the reading public.

Roche scatters a great deal of incidental information along with his figures. He tosses off remarks about the cost of a house visit by a provincial doctor, the salaries of professors and the surprisingly healthy state of their universities, the social rivalries embedded in different masonic lodges, the rising status of the apothecary, the scholarship boy syndrome within the clergy, the extent of Rousseau's correspondence with country curates and of Voltaire's with courtiers, and differences in the social code of "bourgeois living nobly" and "nobles living *bourgeoisement*." The book really serves as an encyclopedia of provincial life under the Old Regime.

But Roche means it to be a contribution to the sociology of culture. He aims it at the heart of a sociological question that has preoccupied historians for the last decade: What exactly was the character of the social and cultural elites of the Old Regime? Were they enlightened bourgeois? Aristocratic defenders of tradition? Or a contradictory mixture of Enlightenment, tradition, bourgeois, and noblemen? The problem is more important than it may seem, for on it hang some general questions about the connections between class and ideology. It also suggests a shift in historical perspective—away from the attempts in the 1950s and 1960s to see society from below and toward a new effort to understand it at the top.

Roche goes beyond the bewigged and powdered gentlemen of the academies to study the larger elite who were known as the "notables" in the eighteenth century and who might be compared with what we call the "superstructure" or the "power elite" today. He found them by looking them up in eighteenth-century municipal almanacs. Although the almanacs have drawbacks as sources, they served as directories for anyone who needed to know who was who and where they could be located within the circles of power and prestige in the cities of the Old Regime. Roche is concerned with the same problem and was able to find supplementary information in the vast literature on local history. He can thus translate the material of the almanacs into a set of statistics, which lead to a surprising conclusion: Half of the notables came from the royal administration and the law courts; a third came from the church; only 7 percent were businessmen.

The commercial bourgeoisie also looks surprisingly unimportant in Roche's attempt to subject the entire population of his thirty-two cities to statistical analysis. He finds a significant number of merchants and manufacturers in great commercial centers, like Lyon and Marseilles. But they were outnumbered almost everywhere else by priests and, in some cases, by noblemen. Roche estimates that they made up 1 percent of the population of Dijon, in contrast to the clergy (4 percent) and the nobility (3 percent). In Besançon his estimates run: commercial bourgeoisie, 3 percent; clergy, 10 percent; nobility, 2 percent. In Bordeaux: commercial bourgeoisie, 6–9 percent; clergy, 15 percent; nobility, 1–4 percent.

Of course, quantitative conclusions can be only as sound as the data on which they are based. Roche must draw on disparate sources, tax rolls and marriage contracts as well as monographs. Any attempt to picture the social structure of cities throughout a whole country two centuries ago will be distorted here or there. But the general outlines of Roche's picture seem convincing. And he draws a clear, sharp pattern in the most important section of his thesis, the analysis of the social composition of the academies themselves, which he bases on six thousand case studies, dredged out of archives everywhere in France.

After allowing for variations from place to place and time to time and sifting his statistics through finer and finer grids, Roche finds once again that the commercial bourgeoisie did not count. Half the academicians were noblemen, from the late seventeenth century right up to the Revolution. The church supplied a fifth of the academicians, although the proportion dropped after 1750. And the academic bourgeoisie was composed almost entirely of commoner clergy, government officials, professional men (doctors far more than lawyers), and *rentiers*. Merchants and manufacturers hardly appeared in the academies at all.

They made up only 3 percent of the regular members in the provinces and never penetrated the ranks of the academies in Paris. The Académie des Sciences included only a few merchants among its corresponding members, while the Académie Française kept them out completely and drew three quarters of its members from the nobility. Although the commercial bourgeoisie flocked into masonic lodges—and Roche compiles some remarkable statistics on the spread of Freemasonry—it played little part in other cultural institutions, like the Sociétés royales d'agriculture. Roche also finds it under-represented among the subscribers to literary periodicals, the contributors to the *Encyclopédie,* and the long list of literary figures published in *La France littéraire* of 1784. He concludes that the *"classe culturelle"* had little connection with modern capitalism.

This conclusion challenges what has become accepted wisdom among many historians in France—namely, that the Enlightenment can be identified with the bourgeoisie. In formulating the orthodox, textbook view of the Enlightenment and the academies, for example, Robert Mandrou pronounced, "The eighteenth century truly thinks bourgeois."[6] The 166 pages of statistics, graphs, and maps in Roche's book provide a clearer view of the bourgeois presence at three levels of urban society. It was small in proportion to the general population, unimportant among the notables, and least important in the academies.

By 1789 a capitalist class had established itself in the economic system of the Old Regime, but it played little part in civic affairs and still less in culture. It entered masonic lodges but it remained outside the academies, and it did not supply many writers or perhaps even many readers to the Republic of Letters. While France's economy moved sluggishly in the direction of industrialization, her cultural institutions remained under the control of a traditional elite. Yet this elite was open to Enlightenment, an Enlightenment that worked its way through the social order from the top down, instead of rising with the middle class.

In the last part of his book, Roche discusses the content of culture; and here, too, he uses quantitative techniques, counting motifs in the speeches of academicians, tracing the subjects of their essay contests on graphs, and mapping the diffusion of some of their books. His methods and assumptions epitomize the work of a new generation of sociocultural historians. In fact, the quantification of culture has gone so far in France that it seems worthwhile to say a word about its origins and implications.

In the 1930s, Ernest Labrousse transformed economic history by producing a quantitative analysis of documents arranged in "series," or commensurable units stretched over long periods of time. During the next three decades, social historians, from the old Georges Lefebvre to the young François Furet, built statistical series into analyses of social structure. Today, Roche's generation is attacking cultural history in the same way. Pierre Chaunu expressed their program in a manifesto entitled *"Un Nouveau Champ pour l'histoire sérielle: le quantitatif au troisième niveau."*[7] Having conquered the first two levels of history, he explained, the quantifiers are now taking over the third—culture.

Although it began to go out of favor in the 1980s, Chaunu's formula was cited frequently by French historians in the 1970s. It seemed to be embodied in French doctoral theses, which often followed the format: part I, economics and demography; part II, social structure; part III, superstructure, culture, collective *mentalités*.[8] Roche does not proceed in that fashion. But in explaining his method (I:185–89), he invokes Chaunu and sets his argument in the language of levels and statistical series. This approach succeeds spectacularly in his analysis of the cultural elite but not in his treatment of culture itself. Views of the world and sets of attitudes cannot be strung into series and transposed onto graphs. Of course, it is possible to count some cultural phenomena, such as book sales, theater performances, and masses said for souls in purgatory. But the statistics can only serve as symptoms; and once the count is in, the historian must face the task of diagnosing something unquantifiable: shifts in systems of meaning.

Instead of working diagnostically, the French quantifiers

argue directly from statistical patterns to patterns of culture. Roche sees Enlightenment in graphs about the subject matter of academic speeches. Michel Vovelle weighs piety by the pounds of candle wax burned in religious ceremonies. Jean Toussaert measures laxism according to the liters of wine consumed at communion. All such attempts to apply the Chaunu formula suggest three false assumptions that are implicit in it. First, that meaning can be measured outwardly in the study of rituals and other cultural forms. Second, that economies, societies, and civilizations (to cite the subtitle of the *Annales*) can be separated onto different levels, not merely for purposes of analysis but because they exist separately. Third, that cultural phenomena can be explained by demonstrating their "structural" relation to phenomena at the other two levels—especially, that is, by means of statistical homologies.

Roche ran into the third fallacy when he found that the elite of the Old Regime absorbed progressive ideas, although its social composition remained traditional. The pattern only looks contradictory if one assumes that culture derives directly from social structure. It seems less perplexing if one abandons the notion of levels altogether and assumes that culture permeated every aspect of life in the eighteenth century, the buying of bread as well as the reading of books.

By sticking close to the texts of books, Lough avoids doing violence to the texture of culture. But he does not stray far from the familiar paths of literary history or confront the questions raised by Roche. In the end, therefore, both authors leave one with the feeling that the Republic of Letters still needs to be explored. Lough examines it *terre à terre* and from text to text. Roche surveys its general outline from the top of a statistical superstructure. Neither method seems adequate, but each is revealing in its own way, not merely about literary life in the past but about modes of understanding in the present.

FOURTEEN

History and Literature

W HAT HAPPENS when a book becomes a classic? By what process does a text get set apart from all the other texts clamoring for attention? How does it survive the literary season, metamorphose from edition to edition, reappear in paperbacks and secondhand shops, and settle at last on the shelves reserved for books here to stay?

Consider the case of *Jean-Jacques Rousseau: Transparency and Obstruction* by Jean Starobinski, a work that stands out as a classic of modern literary criticism. It first appeared in 1957 as doctoral thesis number 158 from the University of Geneva. It was reissued, shorn of its academic trappings, a year later by Plon in Paris. Gallimard took it over in 1971 and published it, revised and expanded by seven new essays on Rousseau, in the prestigious "Bibliothèque des idées" series. Then Gallimard shifted it to the cheaper and more popular "Tel" series and put out new editions in 1976 and 1982. And now at last it has appeared in English, in an excellent translation by Arthur Goldhammer published by the University of Chicago Press (an Italian edition appeared in 1982, a German edition in 1988). So a work that began as an academic exercise has come within the range of the general reading public in several countries. It is an appropriate moment to ask what has given *Transparency and Obstruction* such staying power and how it stands up against studies of Rousseau that have been published since it first appeared thirty-one years ago.

Rarely has a title summed up so much: transparency and

obstruction *(obstacle* in French)—Starobinski finds them everywhere in Rousseau's work and also in his life, beginning with the crucial trauma of his childhood, his punishment for refusing to confess to a crime he had not committed.

It was not much of a crime, but it shattered the paradise in which Rousseau spent his formative years. As an adoptive member of the Lambercier family in Geneva, he inhabited what Starobinski, following the *Confessions,* construes to have been a world of perfect communication. Everyone in the household spoke his mind and read the mind of everyone else, not by careful study but through spontaneous effusions of the soul. It was a little utopia, a state of pure transparency. One day, however, a servant left a comb in the kitchen and, upon returning, found that it had been broken. According to appearances, Jean-Jacques stood condemned, because no one else had been in the room when the damage occurred. The Lamberciers, good people who demanded nothing more than an honest confession, asked the boy to admit his guilt. But he was innocent: he knew so inwardly, as his own best witness to himself. The Lamberciers lectured, implored, lost patience, and finally had him beaten.

Jean-Jacques's world came crashing down. Its ruins arranged themselves in his mind as a wall of obstacles separating his inner self from the consciousness of others. By experiencing injustice, he learned to measure the disparity between things as they really are and things as they appear to be. Yet no one could be blamed for this fall from innocence, certainly not the Lamberciers. The flaw inhered in the situation—that is, in the human condition itself, a state of opacity in which consciousnesses cross like ships in the night, sending out signals and reading them wrong.

Where Rousseau's childhood happiness ended, human history, as he later understood it, began. The collapse of the

world in the Lambercier's kitchen set in motion the same process as man's fall from the state of nature, as he expounded it
in the *Discourse on the Origin of Inequality:* all experience, of the
individual and of humanity as a whole, represents an attempt
to cope with the loss of transparency and to live in a world of
mediation—through language, property, and the gamut of
institutions that hold society together while keeping souls apart.

Thus according to Starobinski, the autobiographical impulse animated Rousseau's writing from the beginning. In his
first works, it opened onto broad social and political questions. In the end, it turned on itself and exhausted itself in
solipsism: "Rousseau desired communication and *transparency*
of the heart. But after pursuing this avenue and meeting with
disappointment, he chose the opposite course, accepting—
indeed provoking—*obstructions,* which enabled him to withdraw, certain of his innocence, into passive resignation."

Behind the writings, then, Starobinski detects a consciousness at work, exploring, ordering, combining, and transpos-
ing a set of basic themes. The work itself consisted in writing.
Rousseau's quest for authenticity committed him to a ceaseless
struggle with language, because he could only be himself by
finding words to release his inner voice. Yet the words were
imperfect instruments of that voice, attempts to mediate between it and other people; so they were inadequate, no matter
how much they moved his readers.

By pouring out his life in language, Rousseau defined the
condition of the writer, not just in the eighteenth century but
in the twentieth:

Only now does the full novelty of Rousseau's work become apparent. Language has become a locus of immediate experience even as
it remains an instrument of mediation. . . . Language *is* the authentic
self, yet at the same time it reveals that perfect authenticity has still
not been achieved, that plentitude remains to be conquered, and that

no possession is secure without the consent of others. No longer does the literary work call forth the assent of the reader to a truth that stands as a "third person" between the writer and his audience; the writer singles himself out through his work and elicits assent to the truth of his personal experience. Rousseau discovered these problems; he truly invented a new attitude, which became that of modern literature (beyond the sentimental romanticism for which he has been blamed). He was the first to experience the dangerous compact between ego and language, the "new alliance," in which man makes himself the word.

Starobinski's analysis of consciousness at work in creating literature is not the same thing as literary biography, nor is it simply textual exegesis. It combines elements of the old French genre *l'homme et l'oeuvre,* the study of an author and his works, with something new: the study of the author-in-the-works, that is, of the ordering consciousness implicit in the texts.

Starobinski shared this approach to literature with other members of the so-called Geneva School, notably Marcel Raymond and Georges Poulet.[1] It meant that he trimmed away most references to the external circumstances of Rousseau's life. *Transparency and Obstruction* has nothing to say about the social and political conflicts in Geneva, which marked Rousseau as a boy and implicated him in revolutionary agitation as an adult. It does not discuss his struggle to survive as a writer living down and out in Paris, which may have influenced his understanding of writing as much as his existential confrontation with language. It hardly mentions any of the institutions of the Old Regime, which provided the raw material for his general reflections on society and politics. Instead, it pursues another purpose.

Starobinski tried to show how a master theme—the straining for "transparency," the struggle against "obstruction"—runs through all of Rousseau's work, binding it together as a coherent whole. His success in this monumental task looks just as impressive in 1988 as it did in 1957. Sometimes, he shows, Rousseau located transparency in an imaginary past (the *Discourse on the Origin of Inequality* and the *Essay on the Origin of Languages*), sometimes in a future or ahistorical utopia (the *Social Contract*), sometimes in fiction *(La Nouvelle Héloïse),* sometimes in the presocialized state of infancy *(Emile),* sometimes in the spontaneous festivity of the common people (the *Letter to d'Alembert*), sometimes in rapturous communication with nature (the *Reveries of a Solitary Walker*), and always in the contemplation of his own soul (the *Confessions*).

The theme is so pervasive as Starobinski traces it from work to work that it seems almost too good to be true. Here at last is the most complex and contradictory of writers brought within the range of a dominant motif. Any book that makes so much sense of so much recalcitrant material will eventually seep into seminars and libraries everywhere. It will become a campus classic. But the success of *Transparency and Obstruction* should not be interpreted as a superior form of reductionism. Starobinski treats his master theme as a mode of exploring Rousseau's works, using it to bring out complexities rather than to reduce them to a lowest common denominator.

For example, in analyzing Rousseau's famous description of the grape harvest at Clarens in *La Nouvelle Héloïse,* Starobinski shows that the scene corresponds to the formula for popular festivals in the *Letter to d'Alembert* and for popular democracy in the *Social Contract*. Unlike actors on a stage, the harvesters are both performers and spectators. They devise a spectacle without props, roles, a script, or any other kind of mediation, one that unites them all in the spontaneous outpouring of communal joy. Structurally, the actor/spectator duality corresponds to the dual quality of citizen/subject in an ideal republic; and the transparent state of seeing and being seen works in the same way as the General Will: everyone participates in the expression of sovereign authority, and everyone submits to the dictate of all. What appears as abstract political theory in one part of Rousseau's work emerges in another as prose poetry. Starobinski helps us see the connections. He bring out affinities, not merely among Rousseau's ideas but in the way his texts work, their thematic structure, metaphors, and shades of phrasing. The book is a tour de force.

Once you submit to Starobinski's spell, even the most obscure corners of Rousseau's work fall into place. Rousseau's theory of musical annotation appears as an attempt to get behind the obstruction of arbitrary signs and restore the immediacy of melodic expression. His botanizing represents an effort to capture an emotional state—the sensation of a plant-gathering expedition in a forest or on a mountainside—by fixing a specimen on a page. Even his fascination with metallurgy, which took the form of a fantasy about transforming bodies into glass, expresses an obsession with transparency. Wherever Starobinski lets his eye wander, he picks up signs of the same ordering sensitivity.

But does he overdo it? Any work that crystallizes into a classic may suffer from hardening of the arteries. It can kill a subject by exhausting it, and it may become a monument to intellectual accomplishment in the past rather than a stimulus to further effort in the future. *Transparency and Obstruction* certainly bears the marks of the time in which it was written. Its references reveal its genealogy: *Etudes sur le temps humain* (1950) by Georges Poulet, *Phénoménologie de la perception* (1945) by Maurice Merlau-Ponty, *Genèse et structure de la phénoménologie de l'esprit de Hegel* (1946) by Jean Hyppolite, *De la psychose dans ses rapports avec la personnalité* (1932) by Jacques Lacan. Those titles suggest the character of the currents swirling about in the world out of which *Transparency and Obstruction* was created: phenomenology, Hegelianism, Freudianism, existentialism. Starobinski navigated through them all, picking up ideas as he encountered them, not in order to develop a philosophical system of his own but in order to understand Rousseau.

The idea of alienation proved to be the most useful of all. It pervaded the intellectual debates of the 1940s and 1950s, but it goes back to Hegel—or, indeed, to Rousseau, not the sentimental father of romanticism but an unknown and unsettling Rousseau, who could be seen as a progenitor of existentialism.

Starobinski's Rousseau understood man's fall from the state of nature as a loss of "transparency"—that is, of unmediated contact with other persons. The intervening obstacles, social and cultural artifices of all kinds, opened the way for the development of civilization but closed the soul to the outer world. History therefore appears in Rousseau's writings as a psychic trap: the more we invest in the refinement of the arts and sciences, the more we lose touch with the core of our own being.

The only way out of the trap leads through a dialectic: negate the negation. This formula appears at all the crucial points in Starobinski's argument. He even finds a dialectic in the love triangle of *La Nouvelle Héloïse*. By acquiescing in the paternal interdiction of her love for Saint-Preux, Julie lets social convention triumph over natural inclination. But after marrying Wolmar, the incarnation of worldly rectitude, she reaffirms her love for Saint-Preux platonically, across the barriers of marriage and finally of death. She produces a victory for a higher form of nature: she negates the negation.

Rousseau's political thought can also be seen to proceed dialectically by a great leap forward. In the *Discourse on the Origin of Inequality* he describes the negation of nature by culture. In the *Social Contract* he shows how a higher form of culture could negate the negation. Hegel and Engels built this insight into an account of the workings of history. Kant and Cassirer fashioned it (with additions from *Emile*) into a system of ethics and aesthetics.

But Starobinski keeps his argument trained on the consciousness of Rousseau. Surrounded by obstructions, his Jean-Jacques cuts himself off increasingly from contact with the outside world, turns inward in search of transparency, and finally succumbs to madness, a form of alienation that can be diagnosed as the "narcissism of innocence."

Despite the occasional use of such terms and notwithstanding his own training as a doctor (he studied psychiatry but did not undergo psychoanalysis), Starobinski does not attempt to put Rousseau on the couch and to treat his madness as a pathological state that can be located outside his writing and invoked in order to explain it. Instead, he sees the madness as an "existential question" derived from obstructed transparency, which plays itself out in the texts.

As Starobinski expounds them, the themes of the early works run wild at the end of Rousseau's life, creating Kafkaesque visions of inexplicable malignity. Rousseau presents himself as an elder Emile in the hands of "them," his invisible, implacable enemies, who usurp the role of the beneficent tutor and manipulate all the signs surrounding him in order to multiply his torments. Even when he fled from his persecutors in France and Switzerland to the generous embrace of David Hume, he saw another conspirator in Hume himself. Rousseau believed that, as fellow philosophers and friends of humanity, he and Hume could have a full meeting of minds. But when they met, obstructions set in and, to his horror, he saw the features of "le bon David" decompose before his eyes, revealing another and more perfidious enemy.

Starobinsky evokes Rousseau's delirium with understanding and compassion, in beautiful pages that seem to be written from within the infernal circle of insanity:

For Jean-Jacques, to live amid persecution is to feel caught in a web of concordant signs, an "impenetrable mystery." . . . The signs are infallible, but what they reveal is the impossibility of transparency. Veils are lifted, but behind them lies an insurmountable obstacle. Thus Rousseau gains nothing by interpreting one sign after another. Rather than clear up the mystery, he confronts still deeper shadows: children's grimaces, the price of peas at La Halle, the shops in the rue Platrière all reveal the same conspiracy, the motives for which remain impenetrable. Try as he will to organize these signs and link them together in a perspicuous manner, he always ends in darkness.

In the end, the only safety lay in refusing all contact with the outer world and in seeking transparency within. But even then, "reflection," the evil faculty of distancing oneself from unmediated self-perception, threatened at every moment to interrupt and spoil the most innocent reveries of the solitary walker. Despite the bursts of lyricism in his last works, Rousseau died in defeat, an existential hero, but a flawed one, like the antiheroes of Camus. For a success story, one that moves from alienation to introspection to engagement, Starobinski will turn to Montaigne, the subject of his next great book.[2]

The greatness of *Transparency and Obstruction* consists in its ability to draw the disconnected threads of Rousseau's life and works into one supremely coherent interpretation and to show how his personal drama opened a route into the major concerns of the nineteenth and twentieth centuries: "His work, which began as a philosophy of history, ended as an existential 'experience' ['experiment' is also conveyed by the French]. It is a forerunner of the work of both Hegel and his antagonist Kierkegaard. Here we have two aspects of modern thought, the progress of reason in history and the tragic quest for individual salvation."

This interpretation swept everything before it in the 1950s. *Transparency and Obstruction* was recognized as a classic of contemporary criticism. It seemed only to face the danger that confronts any classic, that of being definitive. If a book is too convincing, it may be deemed to have had the last word on its subject. It may be put on the shelf and the subject laid to rest. Did Starobinski argue his case so forcefully that he stopped the argument?

The answer to those questions can be found by examining the way the study of Rousseau has intersected with literary criticism during the last thirty years.

While some critics continued with their business as usual, others, particularly since the 1960s, attempted to link criticism with theory; and Rousseau can be found almost everywhere in those attempts. The most important works in structuralism and deconstruction lead right through his writings, and one can see in them how Rousseau provided a testing ground for some central ideas in literary theory. The point is not to pronounce those ideas right or wrong, but rather to see how they took shape in the course of a continuing debate over Rousseau. Once that ground is covered, one should be able to measure the distance that separates *Transparency and Obstruction* from its successors and to see what is at stake in the competing interpretations.

While Starobinski was reinterpreting Rousseau in the light of existentialism, Claude Lévi-Strauss incorporated him into structuralism. In his most influential book, *Tristes Tropiques,* Lévi-Strauss produced a modern version of the *Confessions* and confessed, to the astonishment of French intellectuals, that Rousseau had been his *maître à penser* in deepest Amazonia.[3]

It was as shocking as Rousseau's avowal, at the height of the Enlightenment, that he found inspiration in Calvin. Marx,

Freud, Saussure might do as mental baggage for an expedition in the bush. But the *Discourse on the Origin of Inequality,* the *Social Contract, Emile?* Lévi-Strauss revealed that he had hugged them to his bosom. Worse, he hailed Rousseau as the father of anthropology.

This came out in a discussion of politics among the Nambikwara, one of the most primitive peoples that Lévi-Strauss encountered in Brazil. Although they had a chief, he seemed to rule though the organic welling up of sentiment among his followers. His main activity was to give away his wealth— trinkets that he accumulated and immediately dispersed—and his main compensation was in wives. Such behavior was undreamt of in the philosophies of the Third Republic. Its explanation could not be found in back issues of *Temps modernes,* not even in Gramsci or in Mauss. It lay in the works of Rousseau.

Lévi-Strauss did not invoke the trite and inaccurate notion of Rousseau as the champion of noble savagery. His Rousseau represented the point at which philosophy first came to grips with the problem of understanding culture as a political force. Seen from the perspective of the *Social Contract,* the primitiveness of the Nambikwara consisted in their ability to reduce politics to its fundamentals, to translate their way of life— their hunting and gathering and hopes and fears—directly into a power system, and to live according to the spontaneous effusion of the General Will. Such was the society that would soon be destroyed by Western civilization, a sad spectacle to the social scientist, who contemplated the impending disaster in a mood of elegiac complicity.

When Jacques Derrida confronted Rousseau a decade later in *Of Grammatology,* he picked apart Lévi-Strauss's chapter on the Nambikwara in order to expose ethnocentricity at the heart of a system that pretended to abolish it. Instead of pene-

trating the primitive mind, he argued, Lévi-Strauss had simply made the Amazonian Other into a figment of his own
imagination. The binary opposition of self/other and anthro-
pologist/subject remained bounded by the categories of a
limited social science. To deplore, as Lévi-Strauss did, the
intellectual damage wrought by imperialism—Western thought
penetrating Amazonia in the wake of the bulldozer, ethnocentricity polluting the rain forest even in the person of the anthropologist—was ethnocentric in itself. It meant projecting
the Western notion of the innocent other on a people for whom
such a notion was unthinkable.[4]

The Nambikwara hardly qualified as innocents in any case.
Tristes Tropiques contained plenty of evidence of their brutality, duplicity, dissension, and downright sophistication. But
they provided Lévi-Strauss with a way of thinking himself out
of the bush and onto the Left Bank, where he could enter into
a dialogue with the classic authors of the French tradition:
Montaigne, Diderot, and above all Rousseau. In effect, Derrida argued, Lévi-Strauss need never have left Paris, because
Rousseau offered him everything he required: the material for
a thought experiment about the organizing principle of society.

When Derrida followed that train of thought, he found
that Rousseau led back to a still greater mental experiment,
Descartes's attempt at systematic doubt, which grounded
"metaphysics," as Derrida called it, in the spontaneous self-
awareness of thinking. The Cartesian *cogito* opened up a mode
of philosophizing, the "metaphysics of presence," which ran
from Descartes to Hegel. But Rousseau pointed to a fault line
in that intellectual landscape—namely, writing. In thinking
and even in speaking, according to Derrida's version of Rousseau, philosophers could express the unmediated presence of
their inner voice. But when they wrote, something got in the

way. Arbitrary signifiers, words scratched on paper, obscured the inner ground of truth, and so writing itself became a central problem for philosophy.

Lévi-Strauss had caught a glimpse of Rousseau's insight: hence his celebration of the Nambikwara as a people "without writing." But Derrida went further: he saw that by treating writing as a tragically flawed "supplement" to speech, Rousseau had come close to a basic notion of deconstruction—namely, that flaws are built into the rhetoric of all texts and so all can be made to say something different from what they ostensibly mean. Supplements are derivative: they exist only in order to complete some prior entity; yet they can also serve in place of the original, as when one consults a supplement to an encyclopedia for the most up-to-date information on a given subject. In supplementarity, something is always lost and something gained. Diderot's *Supplément au Voyage de Bougainville* may be a masterpiece, but it cannot equal the actual experience of making contact with the South Sea islanders along Bougainville's itinerary. Writing, in philosophy and literature, may provide access to truth, but it cannot accede to it.

The difference between getting something right and getting it written opens up in Derrida's reading of Rousseau to an abyss that separates nature from culture. On one side, men experience truth as an unmediated presence within themselves; on the other, they become entangled in external relations, in mediation, writing, civilization—the whole process of history that issues simultaneously in decadence and progress, in enslavement and the prospect of liberty through a social contract.

But Rousseau had not gone far enough. Why draw the epistemological line between speech and writing? Derrida asked. Why not push it back indefinitely into the inner workings of thought? Speech itself can be construed as a kind of writing, an *"archiécriture,"* composed of arbitrary signifiers in sound. So the inner voice does not provide unmediated presence; it yields nothing more, in Derrida's controversial view, than endless play between signifiers and signified.[5] Although Rousseau's argument is aimed at a metaphysics of presence, it succumbs in the end to language. As Derrida interprets it, it deconstructs itself.

The next step was to deconstruct Derrida. Paul de Man undertook this task by turning his own reading of Rousseau's *Essay on the Origin of Languages* against Derrida's version of it.[6] A crucial difference appeared. According to de Man, Derrida had misread Rousseau's theory of language, confusing it with a less radical and more refutable theory of representation that was current in the eighteenth century. He made Rousseau argue that writing represents speech just as speech represents thought, whereas Rousseau actually conceived of language as a kind of figural expression similar to music. In the *Essay*, speech stands to writing as melody to harmony. Like melody, it conveys successive states of the soul, and therefore it has an immediacy that is lacking in representative modes of expression such as painting and literature. By putting Rousseau's argument back together, de Man took Derrida's apart. But that procedure raised a further question: What accounted for the curious blind spot in Derrida's interpretation, which was otherwise so full of insight?

The answer, in a word, was Starobinski. According to de Man, Derrida failed to make contact with Rousseau's text in its original integrity. Instead, he read it though other readings, through the whole body of critical interpretation that culminated in *Transparency and Obstruction*. De Man did not claim to be free of blindness himself. On the contrary, he associated blind spots with insight. But he insisted on the importance of cutting through all previous readings of Rousseau, because he pronounced the entire tradition of Rousseau scholarship to be fundamentally flawed. Like all literary history, it "stands in dire need of deconstruction."

Such was the state of play at the time of de Man's death in 1983: readings and misreadings imposed on one another in seemingly endless succession. As the palimpsest thickened, something got lost—Rousseau himself, the historical Jean-Jacques who lived in the eighteenth century and wrote the works that appeared under his name.

To the theorists of interpretation, the notion of a "real" Rousseau seemed hopelessly naive. How could one possibly make contact with a life that disappeared two hundred years ago, or worry about authors' lives at all, since all authors had been declared dead by Roland Barthes and nothing remained but texts and readings?[7] So the theorists—or at least some of them, those aligned with Barthes and Derrida—abolished time and buried Rousseau under successive layers of their own interpretations. Insofar as he appeared in their works, he was a disembodied voice debating abstract propositions across the centuries with other philosophers, from Plato to Husserl. History did not exist.

The dehistoricizing of literature forced *Transparency and Obstruction* out of the debate and onto the shelf. To be sure, the theorists sometimes made respectful references to it in footnotes. In fact, a hint of "transparency" can be found in Derrida's "metaphysics of presence" along with a suggestion of "obstruction" in his notion of "supplement." Like Derrida, Starobinski understood Rousseau's attempt to ground truth in inner experience as a struggle with language. When he described language as "the locus of immediate experience" for Rousseau and for modern literature in general, he anticipated what Derrida would later identify as "logocentrism." Yet Starobinski hardly appears in the theoretical debates.[8] Why?

Essentially because Starobinski and his successors had incompatible understandings of the critical enterprise. He tried to comprehend Rousseau, the man and the works, in their entirety, whereas the theorists abandoned the whole notion of *l'homme et l'oeuvre*. He attempted to put together all the parts of the puzzle in one coherent picture. They took things apart and denied the validity of coherence itself. He set out to make sense of Rousseau. They tried to make theories. For them, Rousseau was merely *"bon à penser"* (good to think), as Lévi-Strauss might have put it. They used bits and pieces of his writings for purposes of their own, to establish or disestablish structuralism.

As the waves of theory recede, it seems safe to predict that the historical Rousseau will remain standing. *Transparency and Obstruction* will come off the shelf. Reincarnated in new editions and other languages—the Chicago edition includes a helpful essay by Robert Morissey and a superior index, although for some reason it lacks the updated bibliography of the last Gallimard version—it will help us rediscover the man who inhabited the eighteenth century and transformed the topography of its culture.

Despite the mass of research on Rousseau, that task remains unfinished. It cannot be completed simply by consulting Starobinski, because, as mentioned, *Transparency and Obstruction* has little to offer by way of historical detail. Nor can it be done by grubbing for facts and by emptying history of theory, because deconstruction has demonstrated the rhetorical fragility of texts, including the kinds of texts that lie in archives. But new varieties of literary history are now beginning to flourish, and they have taken root by tapping the wealth of theory stored up in the human sciences, especially anthropology.

Lévi-Strauss was right to celebrate Rousseau as the father of anthropology, but Rousseau's ideas can be applied more fruitfully to his own culture than to the Nambikwara. He invented anthropology as Freud invented psychoanalysis, by doing it to himself. Driven by the need to make sense of his own life, he studied the way he absorbed cultural systems as he passed from one society to another. By tracing his route from Geneva through Italy and Savoy to France, from the workshops of artisans through the bed of Madame de Warens and from Grub Street to the dinner tables of the aristocracy, he recognized the power of culture as a force that molds individuals and shapes entire societies. He saw the theater, novels, games, child rearing, education, language, and religion as so many ways of organizing reality and channeling behavior. He understood them not merely as vehicles for transmitting values but as forms of power in themselves. And he analyzed their operation in nearly all the genres available to him at the time—political theory, pedagogy, fiction, and autobiography.

We are now in a position to appreciate that accomplishment, because while the theorists were conjugating their ideas through Rousseau's writings, more traditional scholars have uncovered a vast amount of information about the world in which he lived. They had never lost sight of the historical Rousseau. But they lacked the wide-angle vision of Starobinski, so each produced a Rousseau of his own or, more commonly, a fragment of Rousseau's life and a slice of his time. The pieces need to be put together, and the task should be possible, because they are lying about in hundreds of books and articles published since the first appearance of *Transparency and Obstruction*. We have studies of Rousseau the embattled intellectual, Rousseau the nemesis of Voltaire, Rousseau the presiding genius of the French Revolution, Rousseau the Genevan, the politician, the deist, the misogynist, the ideologist, the botanist, the educator, the musician, the tramp.[9]

Best of all, we have the complete correspondence of Rousseau, edited by Ralph Leigh: forty-six volumes prepared with such exhaustive research that the footnotes virtually constitute a biographical dictionary, and the introductory essays to each volume, if strung together, would provide the most authoritative account of Rousseau's life that has ever been written.[10] Leigh died in December 1987, just as he reached the end of his labor (three more volumes documenting Rousseau's influence during the French Revolution remain to be published, along with several volumes of indexes). It dwarfs even the accomplishment of Starobinski.

It seems clear, then, that the time is ripe for another synthesis, something comparable to the multivolume biography of Voltaire that is now underway.[11] So Starobinski has not had the last word, but he will get a new hearing; for any new work must begin where he left off, and it seems unlikely that there will ever be an end to new beginnings. If the scholarship of the last thirty years demonstrates anything, it is the inexhaustible richness of what Cassirer called "the question of Jean-Jacques Rousseau." Rousseau's life was so strange and his works are so challenging that they seem certain to inspire feats of interpretation as long as there are texts and readers. As *Transparency and Obstruction* demonstrates, Rousseau not only wrote classics himself; he was the stuff of which classics can be made by others.

FIFTEEN

History and Anthropology

A FUNNY THING HAPPENED TO ME on my way home from the semiotics seminar. As I rounded a corner on C floor of the library, I noticed an advertisement from *The New York Times* pasted on the door of a student's carrel: "Fiji $499." Primed by a discussion of Charles S. Peirce and the theory of signs, I immediately recognized it as—well, a sign. Its message was clear enough: you could fly to Fiji and back for $499. But its meaning was different. It was a joke, aimed at the university public by a student grinding away at a thesis in the middle of winter, and it seemed to say: "I want to get out of this place. Give me some air! Sun! *Mehr Licht!*" You could add many glosses. But to get the joke, you would have to know that carrels are cells where students work on theses, that theses require long spells of hard labor, and that winter in Princeton closes around the students like a damp shroud. In a word, you would have to know your way around the campus culture, no great feat if you live in the midst of it, but something that distinguishes the inmates of carrels from the civilian population gamboling about in sunshine and fresh air. To us, "Fiji $499" is funny. To you, it may seem sophomoric. To me, it raised a classic academic question: How do symbols work?

The question had been worrying me in connection with some criticism of a book I had published in 1984, *The Great Cat Massacre and Other Episodes of French Cultural History*. In the book I had tried to show why a ritual slaughter of cats was hilariously funny to a group of journeymen printers in Paris around 1730. By getting the joke, I had hoped to "get" a key element in artisanal culture and to understand the play of symbols in cultural history in general. My critics raised some questions, which clung to "Fiji $499" in my thoughts as I trudged home through the dark. I would like to discuss those questions, not as a rebuttal to the criticism, for I still think my argument stands, but as an informal way of wandering through some general problems concerning the historical interpretation of symbols, rituals, and texts.

In a long review of *The Great Cat Massacre,* Roger Chartier argues that the book is flawed by a faulty notion of symbols.[1] According to him, symbolism involves a direct "relation of representation" between the signifier and the signified, as in the example cited in the eighteenth-century dictionary of Antoine Furetière: "The lion is the symbol of valor." I agree that contemporary dictionaries can be useful for tracing meanings attached to words by the literate elite. But I do not think a sophisticated writer like Furetière can serve as a "native informant" about the conception of symbolism among illiterate working people. Nor do I believe that Furetière provides an adequate concept of symbolism for ethnographic analysis.

Ethnographers work with a very different notion of symbolic exchange. Actually, they favor competing notions; but whatever their theoretical stripe, they do not generally expect their native informants to use symbols of the lion = valor variety. Instead, they find that symbols convey multiple meanings and that meaning is construed in different ways by different people. As Michael Herzfeld puts it, "Symbols do not stand for fixed equivalences but for contextually comprehensible analogies."[2] In his work among Greek peasants, Herzfeld found that symbols signified many things, most of them unexpected and all of them impenetrable to anyone who could not pick his way through the multiple associations attached to crows, crocuses, pebbles, and other objects in the local culture. Several generations of anthropologists have had the same experience. Wherever they go, they find natives construing symbols in complex and surprising ways: thus the harp and rattle among the Fang in Gabon according to James Fernandez, butterflies and carrion beetles among the Apache in Arizona according to Keith Basso, trees and trails among the Ilongot in the Philippines according to Renato Rosaldo, and houses and flowers among the Tamil in southern India according to E. Valentine Daniel.[3] One could go on and on citing examples, but it might be more useful to take a look at a few case studies.

Loring Danforth applied Herzfeld's concept of symbolism to a study of death rituals in rural Greece.[4] He found that funerals worked as a negative transformation of marriage ceremonies and that the symbols used in funeral laments helped peasants cope with their grief by metaphorically transforming death into life. Throughout their mourning, women dressed in black gather at the graves of their dead and improvise songs. They often rebuke the dead for causing them pain: "You have poisoned us." The poison takes the from of bitter, burning tears. But tears also water the grave, restoring fertility to the soil and providing the dead with water to drink, cook, and bathe. So in the laments, the dead reply to the despair of the bereaved with affirmative metaphors:

> Strangers, kinsmen, and all you who grieve, come near.
> Say a few words to me and shed a few tears.
> So that the tears become a cool spring, a lake, an ocean,
> and flood down into the underworld;
> so that the unwashed can wash, and the thirsty can drink;
> so that good housewives can knead and bake bread;
> so that handsome young men can comb and part their hair.[5]

According to Danforth, water has great power as a metaphor in the arid hinterland of Greece. Wetness suggests fertil-

Life

Wet

Water

Tears

Poison

Dry

Death

FIGURE 15.1

ity and life; dryness, barrenness and death. By seeping through
the dry earth of graveyards, water is thought to quicken the
dead. Widows pour water on the graves of their husbands and
describe themselves as burned by their grief: hence the blackness of their dress and the "poison" of their tears. But the tears
also flow as water to the dead. They combine the attributes of
water and poison and therefore mediate the opposition between life and death. The mediation takes the form of a graduated series of binary opposites, which become progressively
weaker until they are fused in the symbol of tears (see Figure
15.1).

If poetry cannot dissolve death, it can remove its sting, at
least for a few moments of suspended disbelief. How does
poetry work? Not by setting up mechanical "relations of representation," but by making things flow into each other across
the boundaries that divide them in the prosaic world. Historians feel more comfortable in prose. They order things se-
quentially and argue from effect to cause. But ordinary people
in everyday life have to find their way through a forest of
symbols. Whether they try to turn a profit, tote a barge, or lift
a bale, they manipulate metaphors. That is not to say that
economic and power relations have no independent existence
but that they are mediated through signs. Money itself is a
sign and cannot be made by someone who cannot read the

code of his culture. When we face the fundamentals of the human condition, the contradiction between life and death, the mystery of suffering and love, we draw on symbols that give off many meanings. Some may be directly representational—blackness stands for death—but others will drift free from their sensory moorings and will float up against each other, converging in configurations that embody many ideas at once.

A few cultural historians have seen metaphorical relations at the heart of what they study. Thus Huizinga on religious experience in the late Middle Ages:

The vision of white and red roses blooming among thorns at once calls up a symbolic assimilation in the medieval mind: for example, that of virgins and martyrs, shining with glory in the midst of their persecutors. The assimilation is produced because the attributes are the same: the beauty, the tenderness, the purity, the colors of the roses, are also those of the virgins, their red color that of the blood of the martyrs. But this similarity will only have a mystic meaning if the middle term connecting the two terms of the symbolic concept expresses an essentiality common to both; in other words, if redness and whiteness are something more than names for a physical difference based on quantity, if they are conceived as essences, as realities. The mind of the savage, of the child, and of the poet never sees them otherwise.[6]

Like Danforth, Huizinga insists that symbolism works as a mode of ontological participation rather than as a relation of representation. Instead of representing the virgins and martyrs, the roses *are* them, belong with them in the same order of being.

This notion of symbolism, which Huizinga formulated without benefit of linguistic philosophy or semiotics (but with a remarkable knowledge of Sanskrit), has become a dominant theme in current anthropology. It stands out especially in the work of Victor Turner. In many years of fieldwork among the Ndembu, a Zambian people given to elaborate rituals and enthusiastic discussion of them, Turner found symbols every-where—embodied in the landscape, floating through the air, fixed for an instant in one ceremony and then spilling into another. At the center of this world, brimming over with meaning, stood the *mudyi* or milk tree. The Ndembu used it to say a thousand things on as many different occasions. After elaborate investigation, confirmed in every detail by native exegetes, Turner concluded that the meanings attached to the tree stretched across a spectrum, ranging from the normative to the sensory:

The mudyi tree . . . at its normative pole represents womanhood, motherhood, the mother-child bond, a novice undergoing initiation into mature womanhood, a specific matrilineage, the principle of matriliny, the process of learning "woman's wisdom," the unity and perdurance of Ndembu society, and all of the values and virtues inherent in the various relationships—domestic, legal, and politi-cal—controlled by matrilineal descent. Each of these aspects of its normative meaning becomes paramount in a specific episode of the puberty ritual; together they form a condensed statement of the structure and communal importance of femaleness in Ndembu cul-ture. At its sensory pole, the same symbol stands for breast milk (the tree exudes milky latex) . . . mother's breasts, and the bodily slen-derness and mental pliancy of the novice (a young sapling of mudyi is used). The tree, situated a short distance from the novice's village, becomes the center of a sequence of ritual episodes rich in symbols (words, objects, and actions) that express important cultural themes.[7]

This kind of ethnographic exegesis may seem too good to be true or, at least, to be useful outside the bush. But it should help us sort out symbolic encounters in everyday life. When I ran into "Fiji $499," I found to my surprise that the Peircean categories fit. The "sign" consisted of the letters printed as an advertisement. The "object" or ostensible message concerned the fare to Fiji. And the "interpretant" or meaning was the

joke: "I want to get out of here." In fact, the meanings multiplied at my end of the communication circuit. "This Peirce
stuff really works," I concluded and then added afterthoughts:
"We make our students spend too much time in carrels." "Students are getting wittier." Were my interpretations valid? Yes,
as far as I was concerned, but did they correspond to what the
student had intended? Unable to resist the chance to question
a native informant, I knocked at the door of carrel C 1 H9 on
the following day. It was opened by Amy Singer, a graduate
student in Near Eastern Studies. "I put it up two weeks before
generals," she reported. "It was the bleakest moment of the
winter, and *The New York Times* offered this piece of solace, a
warm place, far away." But Amy seemed to be a sunny, up-
beat type. (I'm happy to report that she did very well in her
general examinations.) She said that she thought of the sign
more as an escape fantasy and a joke than as a lament. "It's like
a bumper sticker," she explained. I had not thought of the
door as a bumper. My ideas did not coincide perfectly with
hers, but they were close enough for me to get the joke and to
feel reinforced in my admiration for Peirce.

Now, I do not want to argue for Peircean as opposed to
other systems of semiotics. I want to make a simpler point:
we think of the world in the same way as we talk about it, by
establishing metaphorical relations. Metaphorical relations involve signs, icons, indices, metonyms, synecdoches, and all
the other devices in the rhetorician's bag of tricks. Philosophers and linguists sort the tricks into different definitions and
schemata. For my part, I feel hesitant about subscribing to one
system rather than another and prefer to use the term "symbol" broadly, in connection with any act that conveys a meaning, whether by sound, image, or gesture. The distinction
between symbolic and nonsymbolic acts may be as fleeting as
the difference between a wink and a blink, but it is crucial to

understanding communication and interpreting culture. So cultural historians might stand to gain by rejecting the lion-valor view of symbolism and by thinking of symbols as polysemic, fluid, and complex.

But why do certain symbols possess special powers? What makes them unusually rich in meaning? An answer to those questions might begin with Lévi-Strauss's observation that just as some things are good to eat, others are "good to think." People can express thought by manipulating things instead of abstractions—by serving certain slices of meat to certain members of the tribe, by arranging sand in certain patterns on the floor of the hogan, by lying at the foot of the mudyi tree, and by killing cats. Such gestures convey metaphorical relations. They show that one thing has an affinity with another by virtue of its color, or its shape, or their common position in relation to still other things.[8]

Those relations cannot be conceived without reference to a set of categories that serve as a grid for sorting out experience. Language provides us with our most basic grid. In naming things, we slot them into linguistic categories that help us order the world. We say that this thing is a fish and that a fowl, and then we feel satisfied that we know what we are talking about. To name is to know—to fit something in a taxonomic system of classification. But things do not come sorted and labeled in what we label as "nature." And just when we feel confident that we have found a way through the undifferentiated continuum of the natural world, we may stumble upon something startling, like a snake, which produces a brief moment of terror—zero at the bone—by slicing across the categories and spreading static throughout the system. Snakes are neither fish nor fowl. They slither on land as if they were swimming in water. They seem slimy. They cannot be eaten. But they are good for snide remarks: "Stephen is a snake in the grass." Things that slip in between categories, that straddle boundaries, or spill beyond borders threaten our basic sense of order. They undermine its epistemological ground. Such things are powerful and dangerous. They, too, have a name, at least in anthropology: they are taboo.

Anthropologists have encountered taboos in every corner of the world and have discussed them in a vast literature. The most recent round of discussion began with Mary Douglas's observation that dirt was "matter out of place"—that is, something that violated conceptual categories.[9] Thus the prohibition on eating pork among the ancient Israelites had nothing to do with the seemingly "filthy" habits of the pig. It derived from the categorical imperatives of Leviticus, which separated animals into the cud-chewing (like cows, nontaboo) and the cloven-footed (like goats, also nontaboo). Because they did not chew their cud but did have separated hooves, pigs threatened the purity of the biblical order and had to be abominated. Similar hybrids—shellfish, which have legs like land animals but live in the water, and insects, which have legs like land animals and live in the air—were to be avoided for the same reason. They violated distinctions that began at the Creation, when God separated the earth, the sea, and the firmament. To the Jews, therefore, diet served as a way of worshiping their God and maintaining their cosmology; and pigs, in being bad to eat, were good to think.

Douglas's biblical exegesis might seem too clever to be convincing, but it spoke to a crucial question posed earlier by A. R. Radcliffe-Brown: Why do some animals have special ritual value? Lévi-Strauss had pointed the way toward an answer by shifting the discussion from social functions to conceptual categories. Douglas showed that the danger of collapsing categories was linked with the notion of taboo. In her fieldwork in central Africa, she found that the Lele people order the animal world by means of an elaborate taxonomy and that they maintain order by punctilious dietary restrictions. Yet in their most sacred rituals, they consume an animal, the pangolin or scaly anteater, that contradicts their most important categories. The pangolin has scales like a fish, climbs trees like a monkey, lays eggs like a chicken, suckles its young like a pig, and gives birth to single offspring like a human. To ordinary Lele under ordinary circumstances it is hideously monstrous. But in rituals it becomes good to eat and produces fertility. Like other holy substances, it dissolves categories and puts the initiate in contact with an order of being where divisions disappear and everything flows into everything else.

Having caught the scent, anthropologists have tracked strange animals into all sorts of exotic cosmologies. They have bagged enough by now to make a whole menagerie of monsters. I cannot do justice to their findings here, but I would suggest a quick tour, which leads from Douglas's pangolin to Ralph Bulmer's cassowary, Edmund Leach's bitch, and S. J. Tambiah's buffalo. The animals are abominated, isolated in taxonomies, invoked in swearing, avoided in diet, or eaten in rituals by different people in different ways. The anthropologists have shown that those animal folkways make sense because the taboos belong to a system of relations within a general cultural frame.

Bulmer observed that the Karam people of highland New Guinea put the cassowary in a taxonomic class by itself, unlike other highlanders, who classify it as a bird. The Karam also surround it with unusual taboos. While hunting it in the mountain forests above their settlements, they speak "pandanus language," a ritual language of avoidance that they also adopt while gathering nuts from the pandanus palms in the same forest. They dare not shed the cassowary's blood because they fear it will harm the sacred taro crops growing near their homes. So they kill the cassowary with clubs, in hand-to-hand combat, as it were. After killing it, they eat its heart and then avoid going near the taro for a month. Bulmer found analogues of these practices in Karam views of kinship, a matrilineal system based on cross-cousins and emblematized in the forest by pandanus palms that belong to particular lines. When kin fight, they must use clubs, not sharp weapons, which they reserve for outsiders. And when one kin kills another, he dispatches its spirit to the forest by eating the heart of a pig. In their main myth about their origins, the Karam relate that a brother trapped his sister, who turned into a cassowary. Outsiders lured her away and ate her. The brother then killed the men and took their sisters as wives, founding the Karam kinship system. When Bulmer's informants told him that they called cassowaries "our sisters and cross-cousins," the penny dropped. They thought of the creature as metaphorical cognates, and their way of thinking involved far more than taxonomy. It inhered in the way they ordered the world, a matter of drawing distinctions between kin and outsiders, forest and garden, nature and culture, life and death.[10]

Edmund Leach discovered a similar system of relations within his own backyard. Among the Anglo-Saxon tribes, we, too, have taboos. We feel horrified at the notion of marrying our sister or of eating our dog. We insult one another by saying "bitch" or "son of a bitch." But why not "son of a cow"? What do these dangerous categories—the incestuous, the inedible, the obscene—have in common? Leach, like Douglas, sees them as ambiguous; and like Lévi-Strauss, he attributes their ambiguity to their position as mediators between binary opposites. Pets make particularly good mediators because they straddle opposed spheres, the human and the animal, the domestic and the wild. One can align them with congruent categories in a diagram, which expresses op-

```
Self ——— House ——— Field
Self ——— Sister ——— Neighbor
Self ——— Pet ———— Livestock
```

FIGURE 15.2

positions according to distance from the self (see Figure 15.2). Just as I cannot marry my sister, I cannot eat my dog; but I can marry my neighbor and eat my cattle. The categories conjugate into each other, and the mediating term carries the taboo. To us, therefore, dogs are not only good for swearing; they are good for thinking.[11]

Tambiah's buffalo occupies a critical position in a set of categories on the other side of the world, in rural Thailand, but it can be thought in a similar way. A Thai identifies with his buffalo just as an Englishman does with his dog. As a child, he guards it in the fields and spends long hours sleeping on its back in the hot sun. As an adult he swears by it—literally, because the words for buffalo and penis are close enough in sound to provide splendid opportunities for punning. He attributes an ethical existence to his buffalo, for he will not work it, unlike other animals, on the Buddhist sabbath. And he will not eat it. Buffalo make good eating on ritual occasions, but they must come from other households or other villages.

Buffalo fit into Thai households in a peculiar way, for the houses are peculiar places. They are built on stilts according to a strict ordering of space. The sleeping room is located to the north, separated from a guest or reception room by a threshold and divided internally into a western section, allotted to daughters or a married daughter and son-in-law, and an eastern section, reserved for the parents. (Male children sleep with their parents until adolescence, when they move to the guest room.) The father sleeps to the left of his wife at the most eastward section of the sleeping room and at the opposite extreme of the son-in-law sleeping at the far west. The arrangement reinforces sexual taboos, for the son-in-law must never cross over into the eastern section or sleep beside his wife's sisters. And the taboos coincide with spatial values, for the east is considered sacred, auspicious, and masculine in opposition to the impure, inauspicious, and feminine west. A washing place is located on a low level at the extreme western side of the house, and the space under it is considered especially filthy. The buffalo are tethered under the sleeping area. Should one break loose and wallow in the muck under the washing place, it would bring great misfortune upon the house, and a special ritual must be performed to remove the bad luck.

In Thai taxonomy, buffalo coexist with all manner of beasts, some good to eat (the forest rat, which belongs unambiguously to the wilderness), some not (the otter, which slips back and forth between land and water). Tambiah surveys them all, maps the space of the household, and runs through rules of etiquette and marriage. Then he arranges the data in a diagram, which can be read horizontally and vertically for homologies. It shows that the taboos form a congruent series: incest corresponds to a son-in-law crossing over into the parents' sleeping area and to a buffalo wallowing beneath the washing place. The series can be transposed into positive equivalences: recommended marriage corresponds to entertaining kin in the guest room and to feasting on buffalo reared by another household. The spatial, sexual, and dietary rules belong to the same system of relations; and the diagram works as a cultural grid.[12]

Now, structural diagrams in anthropology have a way of looking more like the instructions of a radio kit than the anatomy of a culture. Anthropologists sometimes flounder in formalism. But when the diagrammatic impulse gives shape to ethnographic data, they can wed formalism with fieldwork and teach the rest of us a lesson: symbols work not merely because of their metaphorical power but also by virtue of their position within a cultural frame.

These considerations—the polysemic character of symbols, the ritual value of animals, and the cultural frame that makes symbols and animals meaningful—can help one make sense of that strange episode, the ritual massacre of cats by workers in a printing shop in Paris around 1730. I do not want to belabor a subject I have already discussed, but I think it might be useful to look once more at the cat massacre in order to see how anthropological theory can help in the analysis of a historical problem.[13]

The problem begins with difficulties of documentation. We can only know the massacre from an account written many years later by one of the men who organized it, Nicolas Contat. Although we can trace Contat to an actual printing shop and can confirm many of the details in his narrative, we cannot be sure that everything happened exactly as he said it did. On the contrary, we must allow for stylized elements in his text. It belongs to a genre of working-class autobiography made famous by two of his contemporaries from the printing trade, Benjamin Franklin and Nicolas Edmé Restif de la Bretonne. And it includes elements from two other genres: the *misère,* or burlesque lament about the hard life of workers in certain trades, and the technical manual, a variety of "how-to" literature popular among printers. Because Contat shaped his text according to generic constraints, we cannot treat it as if it were a window, which provides an undistorted view of his experience.[14]

But after generations of struggle to discover "what actually happened," historians have learned to cope with documentary problems. And if they want to understand what a happening actually meant, they can take advantage of the very elements that may distort a text as reportage. By situating his narrative in a standard way, drawing on conventional images, and blending stock associations, a writer puts across a meaning without making it explicit. He builds significance into his story by the way he recounts it. And the more ordinary his manner, the less idiosyncratic his message. If he adopts an excessively sibylline style, he will not be understood; for understanding depends on a common system of meaning, and meanings are shared socially. Therefore we can read a text like Contat's not to nail down all the whos, whats, wheres, and whens of an event but rather to see what the event meant to the people who participated in it. Having worked out a tentative interpretation, we can go to other documents—contemporary collections of proverbs, folklore, autobiographies, printing manuals, and *misères*—to test it. By moving back and forth between the narrative and the surrounding documentation, we should be able to delineate the social dimension of meaning—to "get" the cat massacre just as we can get "Fiji $499."

Without wading through all the material once again, I think it important to point out that Contat's account of the massacre takes as its starting point the *misères* of the two apprentices, Jérôme (the fictional counterpart of Contat) and Léveillé. The master overworks them, sleeps them in a cold and clammy lean-to in the courtyard of the shop, and feeds them on such rancid, rotten meat that even the house cats will not touch it. As in most *misères,* the tone is humorous rather than angry. Apprentices were supposed to be the butt of jokes and ill treatment, a kind of hazing considered appropriate to their position between childhood and adulthood. Contat fills his story with descriptions of the initiation rites that marked off the apprentices' arrival in the shop and their final integration into the world of the journeymen. Like other liminal characters, they test the boundaries of adult norms by playing tricks and getting into trouble. When they bamboozle the master into inadvertently ordering the slaughter of his wife's favorite pet cat, *la grise,* the incident has all the ingredients of a standard farce.

But Contat's way of telling the joke sets it in the context of a deeper animosity between the workers and the master. At the beginning of his narrative, he invokes a mythical past, when printing shops were true "republics" where masters and journeymen lived together as equals, sharing the same food and work. In the recent past, however, the masters, or *bourgeois* as they were called, had excluded the journeymen from masterships and had driven down their wages by hiring semi-skilled workmen *(alloués)*. Documents from the archives of the Parisian booksellers' guild confirm that the position of the journeymen did indeed deteriorate during the late seventeenth and early eighteenth centuries. But Contat goes beyond the question of wages to the development of incompatible sub-cultures. He shows at many points that the journeymen did all the work while the master slept late, dined extravagantly, adopted airs of affected gentility and bigoted piety, and generally withdrew into an alien, bourgeois way of life.

Cats epitomized this parting of the folkways. To the *bourgeois* they were pets. In fact, Contat claimed that a rage for keeping cats had spread among the masters of the printing shops. One master had twenty-five of them. He gave them the finest morsels from his table and even had their portraits painted. Workers did not think of animals as pets. To them, domestic cats were like alley cats—good for bashing on festive occasions like the feast of Saint John, when they were burned by the sackful, or during charivaris, when they were torn limb from limb (*"faire le chat"* it was called in Dijon). Cats also had a satanic quality. They went about at night as familiars of witches and copulated hideously during nighttime witches' sabbaths. A standard defense if one crossed you was to maim it with a club. On the following day, a suspicious old hag would be seen with a broken limb or covered with bruises. Many superstitious practices and proverbs linked cats with households, especially with the mistress of the house and specifically with the genitals of the mistress. Pussy *(le chat* and particularly the feminine *la chatte)* meant the same thing in the slang of eighteenth-century France as it does in colloquial English today. A girl who got pregnant had "let the cat go to the cheese." And men who liked cats had a special way with women: "As he loves his cat, he loves his wife."

Contat evokes these commonplaces of French folklore throughout his narrative. He makes the connection with sorcery explicit, links care for *la grise* with "respect for the house," and suggests a sexual element in the identification of the mistress with her cat. She appears as a lusty wench who combines a "passion for cats" with a penchant for cuckolding her husband. After the apprentices have killed *la grise,* Contat notes what the "murder" meant to husband and wife: "To her they had ravished a cat *[chatte]* without a peer, whom she loved to the point of madness; and to him, they had attempted to sully his reputation." The whole episode demonstrated that cats were extremely good to think.

It also showed that they had great ritual value, for the massacre followed a scenario that combined a whole series of rituals. It began as a typical prank, which the apprentices devised in response to a typical *misère:* sleeplessness. They have to get up at the crack of dawn in order to open the gate for the first journeymen who arrive for work. And they have great difficulty falling asleep at night, because a collection of alley cats has taken to wailing near their miserable bedroom. The *bourgeois,* who gives himself over to *grasses matinées* as much as to *haute cuisine,* sleeps through it all. So the boys decide to turn the tables on him. Léveillé, a "perfect actor" who can imitate anything, scampers across the roof "like a cat" and caterwauls outside the master's window so raucously that the old man cannot sleep any more.

The master is as superstitious in religion as he is despotic in the running of the shop. He decides that some witches have cast a spell and commissions the boys to get rid of the "malevolent animals." After arming themselves with bars from the presses and other tools of their trade, Jérôme and Léveillé lead the workers on a gleeful cat hunt. The mistress has warned them not to frighten *la grise,* so they dispatch it first and stuff its body in a gutter. Then the entire work force sets to, smashing through the cat population of the whole neighborhood and piling up the half-dead bodies in the courtyard of the printing shop. The workers name guards, a judge, a confessor, and an executioner, and proceed to try and condemn their victims. Then they hang them, roaring with laughter. The mistress comes running and lets out a shriek, as she thinks she sees *la grise* dangling from a noose. The workers assure her they would not do such a thing: "They have too much respect for the house. The *bourgeois* arrives. 'Ah! The scoundrels,' he says, 'Instead of working they are killing cats.' Madame to Monsieur: 'These wicked men can't kill the masters, so they have killed my pussy.' " As the workers guffaw, the master and mistress withdraw in humiliation, he muttering about the time lost from work, she lamenting her lost *chatte.* "It seems to her that all the blood of the workers would not be sufficient to redeem the insult."

In the succeeding weeks, Léveillé repeats the farce over and over again by staging pantomimes, known as "copies," in the shop. He can improvise numbers as skillfully as the vaudevillians in the street theaters of the Foire Saint Germain a few blocks away. The journeymen applaud in their traditional manner, by beating their tools and bleating like goats. They aim this rough music, standard fare in charivaris, at the *bourgeois*. For he is the butt of the joke. They have got his goat. Again and again he falls victim to a kind of shop vaudeville called *joberie* in the workers' slang. He is repeatedly tried and condemned in a mock trial like the burlesque court scenes that the workers stage on the feast of Saint Martin, when they square accounts for infringements of their shop code. The whole procedure takes place in a spirit of carnival revelry. As at Mardi Gras, when young men make rough music in mockery of cuckolds, the apprentices take charge: "Monsieur Léveillé and Jérôme, his comrade, preside over the fête." And they double the hilarity by transforming the carnival into a witch hunt. The maiming of the cats passes as a standard defense against sorcery. But the boys have faked the witching in the first place; so they can exploit the master's credulity in order to insult his wife. By bludgeoning her familiar, they accuse her of being a witch and then compound the insult by playing on the sexual associations of pussy—a case of metonymic rape, the symbolic equivalent of murder, even though she cannot accuse them of anything more than horseplay because they have disguised their meaning in metaphor.

Of course, the metaphor also drove their meaning home, and it conveyed different messages to different persons. Contat recounts the massacre from the viewpoint of the workers, so it appears primarily as a humiliation of the *bourgeois*. To them, nothing could be more insulting for the boss than an attack on his most prized possession, his wife's *chatte*. The wife's reaction suggests she recognized that the aggression carried over from her cat to her person and her husband. Hence her remark, which otherwise would be a non sequitur: "These wicked men can't kill the masters, so they have killed my

pussy *[ma chatte]*." But the master was too obtuse to realize
how badly he had been had and merely raged at the loss of
work caused by the buffoonery.

Although the humor may not survive too much analysis,
I think it valid to conclude that the joke worked because the
boys were able to play so many variations on standard cultural
themes. They staged a virtuoso performance: polysemic symbolism compounded by polymorphic ritualism. The symbols
reverberated up and down a chain of associations—from the
cats to the mistress, the master, and the whole system of law
and social order parodied by the trial. The rituals fit into one
another, so that the workers could move back and forth among
four basic patterns. They turned a roundup of cats into a witch
hunt, a carnivalesque festival, a trial, and a bawdy variety of
street theater. True, they did not execute any one of the rituals
in complete detail. To do so would have excluded the possibility of invoking the others. Had they burned the cats instead
of hanging them, they would have stayed closer to the festival
tradition of Mardi Gras and the feast of Saint John, but they
would have sacrificed the ceremonial legalism attached to
criminal trials and the feast of Saint Martin. Had they abandoned their rough music, they would have created a more
authentic court atmosphere, but they would have failed to
express the idea of getting the master's goat (making him
"prendre la chèvre") and of turning the shop into a theater. In
short, they played with ceremonies just as they did with symbols, and to understand their legerdemain we should avoid
heavy-handedness and literal-mindedness in our own attempts to make sense of their joking. If we insist on finding a
complete and unabridged charivari or witch trial in Contat's
text, we will miss the point. For Contat showed that the workers
quoted bits and pieces of rituals, just enough to get their message across and to exploit the full range of meanings by asso-

ciating one traditional form with another. The massacre was funny because it turned into a game of ritual punning.[15]

Now, this kind of open-ended interpretation may make the reader uneasy. Historians like to nail things down, not pry them loose. It goes against the professional grain to argue that symbols can mean many things at the same time, that they can simultaneously hide and reveal their meanings, that rituals can be conjugated into one another, and that workers can quote them, playing with gestures as poets play with words. Doesn't this raise the danger of overinterpretation? Of making unwashed artisans into intellectuals? By way of an answer, I should point out that I do not mean to imply that all the workers extracted all the meaning from the incident. Some of them probably enjoyed the cat bashing and left it at that, while others read all sorts of significance into it. I think the massacre of the cats was like a performance of a play: it could be construed in different ways by different persons, players and spectators alike. But it could not mean anything and everything, just as *The Wizard of Oz* cannot communicate the whole gamut of ideas and emotions in *King Lear*. For all their multivocality, rituals contain built-in constraints. They draw on fixed patterns of behavior and an established range of meanings. The historian can explore that range and map it with some precision, even if he cannot know precisely how everyone made use of it.

But how can he compensate for the imperfections in the evidence? I cannot take Contat's text as proof that the master's wife actually said, "These wicked men can't kill the masters." Those words represent nothing more than Contat's version of her response to the massacre, long after the fact. But the exact phrasing does not matter so much as the associations it evokes. Contat's narrative may be inaccurate in detail, but it draws on conventional notions, which connect cats with sorcery, domesticity, and sexuality and which can be confirmed from a variety of other sources. Those connections belong to a system of relations or, if the term may still be used, a structure. Structure frames stories and remains constant, while the details vary in every telling, exactly as in narrations of folk tales and performances of rituals among Greek peasants, African bushmen, Thai villagers, and New Guinea highlanders.[16]

I think one can put the argument formally without subscribing to an elaborate and perhaps outdated variety of structuralism. The story concerns a set of oppositions—between humans and animals, masters and workers, domestic life and wild life, culture and nature. In this schema, the apprentices and house cats are mediating terms. The apprentices operate on the boundary between the shop and the outside world. As gate tenders, they let the workers in from the street; and as errand boys, they scramble around the city during the day but sleep in the house at night. They are treated as children in some respects and as workers in others, for they are liminal creatures, passing between childhood and adulthood. The pet cats also belong in part to the outside world, the sphere of alley cats and animality, yet they live inside the house and are treated more humanely than the boys. As a betwixt-and-between creature of special importance and the favorite of her mistress, *la grise* is especially taboo. The mistress warns the boys to keep away from her, and Contat describes her killing as a "murder." She occupies an ambiguous space like that of many ritually powerful animals on many ethnographic diagrams (see Figure 15.3).

The apprentices occupy the same space. In fact, it is disputed territory, for the story begins with the rivalry between the boys and the cats. They compete for food (the boys get cat food, the cats get human food) and also for a position close to the master and mistress within the household. If abstracted

house cats

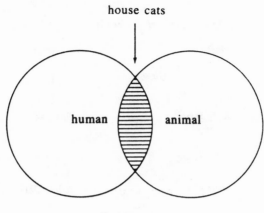

FIGURE 15.3

from the narrative and spread out diagrammatically, the positions would look like those in Figure 15.4. Actually, the cats have displaced the boys in the privileged position next to the master and mistress. In the old "republic" of printing, the apprentices would have shared the master's table. But now they are shunted off to the kitchen, while the pet cats enjoy free access to the dining room. This inversion of commensality was the injustice that set the stage for the massacre. By hanging the cats (a human punishment applied to animals), the boys reversed the situation and restored order in the liminal zone, where the danger of confusing categories was greatest.

The little domestic drama took on great symbolic weight because it became linked with the serious matter of labor re-

Master-Mistress		Apprentices		Pet cats		Alley cats	
human	+	human	+	animal	−	animal	−
human food	+	animal food	−	human food	+	animal food	−

FIGURE 15.4

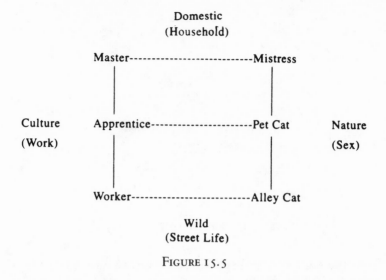

FIGURE 15.5

lations, which the workers also expressed in a symbolic idiom. In a glossary appended to his story, Contat noted usages that can be confirmed in many printers' manuals. The workers applied animal terms to themselves: pressmen were "bears" and compositors "monkeys." When they made rough music, they bleated like goats. And when they fought, they reared back, let out defiant "baas" *(bais)* and grappled like goats (to fall into a fury was to *"prendre la chèvre"*). The workers belonged to the untamed world of the street, the world inhabited by the alley cats, who represented animals at their rawest, a caterwauling, copulating animality, which stands in the story as the antithesis to the domestic order of the bourgeois household. So the drama set in motion a system of relations that can be reduced to a final diagram (see Figure 15.5).

Read horizontally, the diagram depicts relations of identity; read vertically, relations of opposition. The apprentices and pets still operate as mediating terms, but they occupy a larger field of contrasting categories: the domestic or household world versus the world of wildness and street life, the sphere of culture and work versus the sphere of nature and sex. The corners of the diagram define positions where the dimensions are joined. The master stands at the juncture of work and domesticity, the mistress at that of domesticity and sexuality, the alley cats at that of sex and wildness, and the workers at that of wildness and work. Owing to the danger of open insubordination, the workers channeled their aggression through the most roundabout route: they attacked the mistress through the cats and the master through the mistress. But in doing so, they mobilized all the elements of their world. They did not merely tweak the boss's nose. They staged a general uprising—of workers against masters and of the whole sphere of untrammeled, violent, libidinal nature against the disciplined order of work, culture, and domesticity.

I realize that diagrams look mechanical. They seem to strip humanity down to a skeleton. But they can reveal structure; and if we want flesh and blood, we can turn back to the story or try to imagine the massacre as it actually occurred, with all its fur and gore, screaming and laughter. In that case, however, we have nothing more than our imaginations and Contat's narrative to fall back on. In order to sustain a rigorous interpretation, we must attempt to work through the details to the cultural frame that gave them meaning, combining formal analysis with ethnographic material. If my attempt has failed, I hope at least that it may open the way to something more successful. And if all this chasing after symbols has led into a blind alley, the ethnographic historian may console himself with the thought of escape to greener pastures of field-work: "Fiji $499."

Notes and Acknowledgments

O N E
The Kiss of Lamourette

This essay first appeared in *The New York Review of Books* (January 19, 1989): 3–10.

T W O
Let Poland Be Poland

This essay first appeared in *The New York Review of Books* (July 16, 1981): 6–10.

T H R E E
Film: Danton and Double Entendre

This essay first appeared in *The New York Review of Books* (February 16, 1984): 19–24.

1. For a recent version of this tradition, see the *Nouvelle Histoire de la France contemporaine* published by Le Seuil. Volume two in that series has just been published in translation by Cambridge University Press: *The Jacobin Republic, 1792–1794,* by Marc Bouloiseau.
2. For example, see Michel Foucault, *Power/Knowledge: Selected Interviews and Other Writings, 1972–1977,* edited by Collin Gordon (New York, 1980).
3. See François Furet, *Penser la Révolution française* (Paris, 1978).

F O U R
Television: An Open Letter to a TV Producer

This letter was written as a report on a television script to a major network. The script served as the basis for a "docudrama" that was broadcast throughout the country but not, fortunately, in its original form. Because the report was not intended for publication, I have thought it best to eliminate references to the network and its employees, including the producer himself.

F I V E

Journalism: All the News That Fits We Print

This essay appeared in *Daedalus* (Spring 1975): 175–94. It owes a great deal to conversations with Robert Merton, who was a fellow with me at the Center for Advanced Study in the Behavioral Sciences at Stanford, California, in 1973–74. My brother John, who joined *The Times* after I left it and rose from the rank of news clerk to metropolitan editor, gave the essay a helpful, critical reading; but he should not be held responsible for anything in it.

As this essay is not intended to be a formal sociological study, I have not included a bibliography. In fact, I wrote it before reading the sociological literature on journalism; and later while going over that literature, I found that several scholars had made thorough and intelligent studies of some issues I had tried to understand by introspection. Much of their work, however, concerns the problem of how reporters, who are committed to an occupational ethos of objectivity, cope with the political biases of their newspapers. Thus the line of analysis leading from the classic study of Warren Breed, "Social Control in the Newsroom: A Functional Analysis," *Social Forces* 33 (May 1955): 326–35, to more recent work: Walter Gieber, "Two Communicators of the News: A Study of the Roles of Sources and Reporters," *Social Forces* 39 (October 1960): 76–83, and "News Is What Newspapermen Make It," in *People, Society, and Mass Communication,* edited by L. A. Dexter and D. M. White (New York, 1964), pp. 173–80; R. W. Stark, "Policy and the Pros: An Organizational Analysis of a Metropolitan Newspaper," *Berkeley Journal of Sociology* 7 (1962): 11–31; D. R. Bowers, "A Report on Activity by Publishers in Directing Newsroom Decisions," *Journalism Quarterly* 44 (Spring 1967): 43–52; R. C. Flegel and S. H. Chaffee, "Influence of Editors, Readers, and Personal Opinions on Reporters," *Journalism Quarterly* 48 (Winter 1971): 645–51; Gaye Tuchman, "Objectivity as Strategic Ritual: An Examination of Newsmen's Notions of Objectivity," *American Journal of Sociology* 77 (January 1972): 660–79, and "Making News by Doing Work: Routinizing the Unexpected," *American Journal of Sociology* 79 (July 1973): 110–31; and Lee Sigelman, "Reporting the News: An Organizational Analysis," *American Journal of Sociology* 79 (July 1973): 132–49. Important as it is, the problem of political bias does not impinge directly on most newswriting, except in the case of reporters with political beats; yet general reporting touches on crucial aspects of society and culture. I found little analysis of the sociocultural aspects of newswriting, and it seemed to me that further studies might profit from continuing the broader, more historically minded approach that was developed by Helen MacGill Hughes in *News and the Human*

Interest Story (Chicago: 1940). One such study, written after the original publication of this essay, is Michael Schudson, *Discovering the News: A Social History of American Newspapers* (New York, 1978).

The sociology of newswriting could make use of the ideas and techniques developed in the sociology of work. I found the studies inspired by Robert E. Park, a newspaperman turned sociologist, and Everett C. Hughes, a successor of Park in the "Chicago school" of sociology, to be most helpful in analyzing my own experience. See especially Everett C. Hughes, *Men and Their Work* (Glencoe, Ill, 1958) and *The Sociological Eye: Selected Papers* (Chicago and New York, 1971); the issue of *The American Journal of Sociology* devoted to "The Sociology of Work," vol. 57, no. 5 (March 1952); Robert Merton, George Reader, and Patricia Kendall, eds., *The Student-Physician: Introductory Studies in the Sociology of Medical Education,* (Cambridge, Mass: 1957), and John Van Maanen, "Observations on the Making of Policemen," *Human Organization* 32 (Winter 1973): 407–19.

The works in the burgeoning literature on popular culture to which I feel especially indebted are: Robert Mandrou, *De la culture populaire aux 17ᵉ et 18ᵉ siècles* (Paris, 1964); J. P. Seguin, *Nouvelles à sensation: Canards du XIXᵉ siècle* (Paris, 1959); Marc Soriano, *Les Contes de Perrault, culture savante et tradition populaire* (Paris, 1968); E. P. Thompson, *The Making of the English Working Class,* 2nd ed. (New York: 1966); and Richard D. Altick, *The English Common Reader: A Social History of the Mass Reading Public* (Chicago, 1957). For examples of scholarship on nursery rhymes and folklore, see Iona and Peter Opie, *The Oxford Dictionary of Nursery Rhymes* (Oxford, 1966) and Paul Delarue, *The Borzoi Book of French Folk Tales* (New York, 1956), which include primitive versions of "children's" stories. I especially recommend "Where are you going my pretty maid?" and "Little Red Riding Hood."

1. The layout and personnel of the newsroom have changed completely since I left *The Times* in 1964, and of course much of this description would not fit other newspapers, which have their own organization and ethos.
2. J. P. Seguin, *Nouvelles à sensation: Canards du XIXᵉ siècle* (Paris, 1959), pp. 187–90.
3. Ibid., p. 173.

S I X

Publishing: A Survival Strategy for Academic Authors

This essay was published in *The American Scholar* 52 (1983): 533–37. It describes academic publishing as I observed it from the editorial board of the Princeton University Press from 1978 to 1982. Since then editorial procedures have changed somewhat; the number of manuscripts submitted and the number of books published have continued to increase;

and the character of academic monographs has remained the same. The titles cited here, which illustrate this creeping monographism, come from works that were submitted to the press during my four years on its board.

S E V E N

What Is the History of Books?

This essay first appeared in *Daedalus* (Summer 1982): 65–83. Since then I have attempted to develop its themes further in an essay on the history of reading (Chapter 9) and in "Histoire du livre-Geschichte des Buchwesens: An Agenda for Comparative History," *Publishing History*, no. 22 (1987): 33–41.

1. For examples of this work, see, in addition to the books named in the essay, Henri-Jean Martin, *Livre, pouvoirs et société à Paris au XVIIe siècle (1598–1701)* (Geneva, 1969), 2 volumes; Jean Quéniart, *L'Imprimerie et la librairie à Rouen au XVIIIe siècle* (Paris, 1969); René Moulinas, *L'Imprimerie, la librairie et la presse à Avignon au XVIIIe siècle* (Grenoble, 1974); and Frédéric Barbier, *Trois cents ans de librairie et d'imprimerie: Berger-Levrault, 1676–1830* (Geneva, 1979), in the series "Histoire et civilisation du livre," which includes several monographs written along similar lines. Much of the French work has appeared as articles in the *Revue française d'histoire du livre*. For a survey of the field by two of the most important contributors to it, see Roger Chartier and Daniel Roche, "Le livre, un changement de perspective," *Faire de l'histoire* (Paris, 1974), III: 115–36, and Chartier and Roche, "L'Histoire quantitative du livre," *Revue française d'histoire du livre* 16 (1977): 3–27. For sympathetic assessments by two American fellow travelers, see Robert Darnton, "Reading, Writing, and Publishing in Eighteenth-Century France: A Case Study in the Sociology of Literature," *Daedalus* (Winter 1971): 214–56, and Raymond Birn, "Livre et Société After Ten Years: Formation of a Discipline," *Studies on Voltaire and the Eighteenth Century* 151 (1976): 287–312.

2. As examples of these approaches, see Theodore Besterman, *Voltaire* (New York, 1969), pp. 433–34; Daniel Mornet, "Les Enseignements des bibliothèques privées (1750–1780)," *Revue d'histoire littéraire de la France* 17 (1910): 449–92; and the bibliographical studies now being prepared under the direction of the Voltaire Foundation, which will replace the outdated bibliography by Georges Bengesco.

3. The following account is based on the ninety-nine letters in Rigaud's dossier in the papers of the Société typographique de Neuchâtel, Bibliothèque de la ville de Neuchâtel, Switzerland (henceforth referred to as STN), supplemented by other relevant material from the vast archives of the STN.

4. Rigaud to STN, July 27, 1771.

5. The pattern of Rigaud's orders is evident from his letters to the STN and the STN's "Livres de Commission," where it tabulated its orders. Rigaud included catalogues of his major holdings in his letters of June 29, 1774, and May 23, 1777.

6. Madeleine Ventre, *L'Imprimerie et la librairie en Languedoc au dernier siècle de l'Ancien Régime* (Paris and The Hague, 1958), p. 227.

7. B. André to STN, August 22, 1784.

8. *Manuel de l'auteur et du libraire* (Paris, 1777), p. 67.

9. Jean-François Favarger to STN, August 29, 1778.

10. The *procès-verbal* of the raids is in the Bibliothèque Nationale, Ms. français 22075, fo. 355.

11. Fontanel to STN, March 6, 1781.

12. STN to Gosse and Pinet, booksellers of The Hague, April 19, 1770.

13. STN to Voltaire, September 15, 1770.

14. This account is based on the STN's correspondence with intermediaries all along its routes, notably the shipping agents Nicole and Galliard of Nyon and Secrétan and De la Serve of Ouchy.

15. Rigaud to STN, August 28, 1771.

16. Robert Darnton, *The Business of Enlightenment: A Publishing History of the Encyclopédie 1775–1800* (Cambridge, Mass, 1979), pp. 273–99.

17. Anonymous, "Etat et description de la ville de Montpellier, fait en 1768," in *Montpellier en 1768 et en 1836 d'après deux manuscrits inédits,* edited by J. Berthelé (Montpellier, 1909), p. 55. This rich contemporary description of Montpellier is the main source of the above account.

18. C. E. Labrousse, *La Crise de l'économie française à la fin de l'Ancien Régime et au début de la Révolution* (Paris, 1944).

19. Ventre, *L'Imprimerie et la librairie en Languedoc;* François Furet, "La 'librairie' du royaume de France au 18ᵉ siècle," *Livre et société,* 1, 3–32; and Robert Estivals, *La Statistique bibliographique de la France sous la monarchie au XVIIIᵉ siècle* (Paris and The Hague, 1965). The bibliographical work will be published under the auspices of the Voltaire Foundation.

20. John Lough, *Writer and Public in France from the Middle Ages to the Present Day* (Oxford, 1978), p. 303.

21. For surveys and selections of recent German research, see Helmuth Kiesel and Paul Münch, *Gesellschaft und Literatur im 18. Jahrhundert. Voraussetzung und Entstehung des literarischen Marktes in Deutschland* (Munich, 1977); *Aufklärung, Absolutismus und Bürgertum in Deutschland,* edited by Franklin Kopitzsch (Munich, 1976); and Herbert G. Göpfert, *Vom Autor zum Leser* (Munich: 1978).

22. Marino Berengo, *Intellettuali e librai nella Milano della Restaurazione* (Turin, 1980). On the whole, however, the French version of *histoire du livre* has received a less enthusiastic reception in Italy than in Germany: see Furio Diaz, "Metodo quantitativo e storia delle idee," *Rivista storica italiana* 78 (1966): 932–47.

23. A. S. Collins, *Authorship in the Days of Johnson* (London, 1927) and *The Profession of Letters (1780–1832)* (London, 1928). For more recent work,

see John Feather, "John Nourse and His Authors," *Studies in Bibliography* 34 (1981): 205–26.

24. Robert Escarpit, *Le littéraire et le social. Eléments pour une sociologie de la littérature* (Paris, 1970).

25. Peter John Wallis, *The Social Index: A New Technique for Measuring Social Trends* (Newcastle upon Tyne, 1978).

26. William Gilmore is now completing an extensive research project on the diffusion of books in colonial New England. On the political and economic aspects of the colonial press, see Stephen Botein, " 'Meer Mechanics' and an Open Press: The Business and Political Strategies of Colonial American Printers," *Perspectives in American History* 9 (1975): 127–225; and *The Press and the American Revolution,* edited by Bernard Bailyn and John B. Hench (Worcester, Mass., 1980), which contain ample references to work on the early history of the book in America.

27. For a general survey of work on the later history of books in this country, see Hellmut Lehmann-Haupt, *The Book in America,* rev. ed. (New York, 1952).

28. Philip Gaskell, *A New Introduction to Bibliography* (New York and Oxford, 1972), preface. Gaskell's work provides an excellent general survey of the subject.

29. D. F. McKenzie, "Printers of the Mind: Some Notes on Bibliographical Theories and Printing House Practices," *Studies in Bibliography* 22 (1969): 1–75.

30. D. F. McKenzie, *The Cambridge University Press 1696–1712* (Cambridge, 1966), 2 volumes; Leon Voet, *The Golden Compasses* (Amsterdam, 1969 and 1972), 2 volumes; Raymond de Roover, "The Business Organization of the Plantin Press in the Setting of Sixteenth-Century Antwerp," *De gulden passer* 24 (1956): 104–20; and Jacques Rychner, "A L'Ombre des Lumières: coup d'oeil sur la main-d'oeuvre de quelques imprimeries du XVIIIᵉ siècle," *Studies on Voltaire and the Eighteenth Century,* 155 (1976): 1925–55, and "Running a Printing House in Eighteenth-Century Switzerland: the Workshop of the Société typographique de Neuchâtel," *The Library,* sixth series, 1 (1979):1–24.

31. For example, see J. -P. Belin, *Le Commerce des livres prohibés à Paris de 1750 à 1789* (Paris, 1913); Jean-Jacques Darmon, *Le Colportage de librairie en France sous le second empire* (Paris, 1972); and Reinhart Siegert, *Aufklärung und Volkslektüre exemplarisch dargestellt an Rudolph Zacharias Becker und seinem 'Noth- und Hülfsbüchlein' mit einer Bibliographie zum Gesamtthema* (Frankfurt am Main, 1978).

32. H. S. Bennett, *English Books and Readers 1475 to 1557* (Cambridge, 1952) and *English Books and Readers 1558–1603* (Cambridge, 1965); L. C. Wroth, *The Colonial Printer* (Portland: 1938); Martin, *Livre, pouvoirs et société;* and Johann Goldfriedrich and Friedrich Kapp, *Geschichte des Deutschen Buchhandels* (Leipzig, 1886–1913), 4 volumes.

33. Compare Cyprian Blagden, *The Stationers' Company, A History, 1403–1959* (Cambridge: 1960); Martin, *Livre, pouvoirs et société;* and Rudolf

Jentzsch, *Der deutsch-lateinische Büchermarkt nach den Leipziger Ostermes-skatalogen von 1740, 1770 und 1800 in seiner Gliederung und Wandlung* (Leipzig, 1912).

34. James Barnes, *Free Trade in Books: A Study of the London Book Trade Since 1800* (Oxford, 1964); John Tebbel, *A History of Book Publishing in the United States* (New York, 1972–78), 3 volumes; and Barbier, *Trois cents ans de librairie et d'imprimerie.*

35. See, for example, Wolfgang Iser, *The Implied Reader: Patterns of Communication in Prose Fiction from Bunyan to Beckett* (Baltimore, 1974); Stanley Fish, *Self-Consuming Artifacts: The Experience of Seventeenth-Century Literature* (Berkeley and Los Angeles, 1972) and *Is There a Text in This Class? The Authority of Interpretive Communities* (Cambridge, Mass., 1980); Walter Ong, "The Writer's Audience Is Always a Fiction," *PMLA (Publication of the Modern Language Association of America)* 90 (1975): 9–21; and for a sampling of other variations on these themes, Susan R. Suleiman and Inge Crosman, *The Reader in the Text: Essays on Audience and Interpretation* (Princeton: Princeton University Press, 1980).

36. Carlo Ginzburg, *The Cheese and the Worms: The Cosmos of a Sixteenth-Century Miller* (Baltimore: Johns Hopkins University Press, 1980); Margaret Spufford, "First Steps in Literacy: The Reading and Writing Experiences of the Humblest Seventeenth-Century Spiritual Autobiographers, *Social History* 4 (1979): 407–35.

37. Ong, "The Writer's Audience Is Always a Fiction."

38. D. F. McKenzie, "Typography and Meaning: The Case of William Congreve," *Wolfenbütteler Schriften zur Geschichte des Buchwesens,* (Hamburg: Dr. Ernst Hauswedell, 1981), IV: 81–125.

39. See Paul Saenger, "Silent Reading: Its Impact on Late Medieval Script and Society," *Viator* 13 (1982): 367–414.

40. See *Lesegesellschaften und bürgerliche Emanzipation. Ein Europäischer Vergleich,* edited by Otto Dann (Munich: C. H. Beck, 1981), which has a thorough bibliography.

41. For examples of recent work, see *Öffentliche und Private Bibliotheken im 17. und 18. Jahrhundert: Raritätenkammern, Forschungsinstrumente oder Bildungsstätten?* edited by Paul Raabe (Bremen and Wolfenbüttel, 1977). Much of the stimulus for recent reception studies has come from the theoretical work of Hans Robert Jauss, notably *Literaturgeschichte als Provokation* (Frankfurt am Main, 1970).

42. Engelsing, *Analphabetentum und Lektüre. Zur Sozialgeschichte des Lesens in Deutschland zwischen feudaler und industrieller Gesellschaft* (Stuttgart, 1973), and *Der Bürger als Leser. Lesergeschichte in Deutschland 1500–1800* (Stuttgart, 1974); Siegert, *Aufklärung und Volkslektüre;* and Martin Welke, "Gemeinsame Lektüre und frühe Formen von Gruppenbildungen im 17. and 18. Jahrhundert: Zeitungslesen in Deutschland," in *Lesegesellschaften und bürgerliche Emanzipation,* pp. 29–53.

43. As an example of this alignment, see Rudolf Schenda, *Volk ohne Buch* (Frankfurt am Main, 1970), and for examples of more recent work,

Leser und Lesen im Achtzehntes Jahrhundert, edited by Rainer Gruenter (Heidelberg, 1977) and *Lesen und Leben,* edited by Herbert G. Göpfert (Frankfurt am Main, 1975).

44. See François Furet and Jacques Ozouf, *Lire et écrire: L'Alphabétisation des français de Calvin à Jules Ferry* (Paris, 1978); Lawrence Stone, "Literacy and Education in England, 1640–1900," *Past and Present* 42 (1969): 69–139; David Cressy, *Literacy and the Social Order: Reading and Writing in Tudor and Stuart England* (Cambridge, 1980); Kenneth A. Lockridge, *Literacy in Colonial New England* (New York, 1974); and Carlo Cipolla, *Literacy and Development in the West* (Harmondsworth: 1969).

45. For a survey and a synthesis of this research, see Peter Burke, *Popular Culture in Early Modern Europe* (New York, 1978).

46. As an example of the older view, in which the *bibliothèque bleue* serves as a key to the understanding of popular culture, see Robert Mandrou, *De la culture populaire aux XVIIe et XVIIIe siècles: La Bibliothèque bleue de Troyes* (Paris, 1964). For a more nuanced and up-to-date view, see Roger Chartier, *Figures de la gueuserie* (Paris, 1982).

47. Douglas Waples, Bernard Berelson, and Franklyn Bradshaw, *What Reading Does to People* (Chicago, 1940); Bernard Berelson, *The Library's Public* (New York, 1949); Elihu Katz, "Communication Research and the Image of Society: The Convergence of Two Traditions," *American Journal of Sociology* 65 (1960): 435–40; and John Y. Cole and Carol S. Gold, eds., *Reading in America 1978,* (Washington, D.C., 1979). For the Gallup report, see the volume published by the American Library Association, *Book Reading and Library Usage: A Study of Habits and Perceptions* (Chicago, 1978). Much in this older variety of sociology still seems valid, and it can be studied in conjunction with the current work of Pierre Bourdieu; see especially his *La distinction: Critique sociale du jugement* (Paris, 1979).

48. Richard D. Altick, *The English Common Reader: A Social History of the Mass Reading Public 1800–1900* (Chicago, 1957); Robert K. Webb, *The British Working Class Reader* (London, 1955); and Richard Hoggart, *The Uses of Literacy* (Harmondsworth, 1960; 1st edition, 1957).

49. Elisabeth L. Eisenstein, *The Printing Press as an Agent of Change* (Cambridge, 1979), 2 volumes. For a discussion of Eisenstein's thesis, see Anthony T. Grafton, "The Importance of Being Printed," *Journal of Interdisciplinary History* 11 (1980): 265–86; Michael Hunter, "The Impact of Print," *The Book Collector* 28 (1979): 335–52; and Roger Chartier, "L'Ancien Régime typographique: Réflexions sur quelques travaux récents," *Annales: Economies, sociétés, civilisations* 36 (1981): 191–209.

50. Some of these general themes are taken up in Eric Havelock, *Origins of Western Literacy* (Toronto, 1976); *Literacy in Traditional Societies,* edited by Jack Goody (Cambridge, 1968); Jack Goody, *The Domestication of the Savage Mind* (Cambridge, 1977); Walter Ong, *The Presence of the Word* (New York, 1970); and Natalie Z. Davis, *Society and Culture in Early Modern France* (Stanford, 1975).

EIGHT

The Forgotten Middlemen of Literature

An original version of this essay appeared in *The New Republic* (September 15, 1986): 44–50. I have supplemented that version with some material from "Sounding the Literary Market in Prerevolutionary France," *Eighteenth-Century Studies* 17 (Summer 1984): 477–92.

1. André of Versailles to Société typographique de Neuchâtel, August 22, 1784 in papers of the Société typographique de Neuchâtel, Bibliothèque publique et universitaire, Neuchâtel, Switzerland, cited henceforth as STN.
2. Ostervald and Bosset to STN, May 23, 1775, and Ostervald to STN, June 11, 1775.
3. Bosset to STN, June 16, 1780.
4. Ibid., May 26 and April 14, 1780.
5. Ostervald to Mably, January 7, 1781, and Ostervald to David-Alphonse de Sandoz-Rollin, January 7, 1781.
6. Ostervald to Charles-Joseph Panckoucke, November 16, 1777, and Bosset to STN, May 17, 1780.
7. Ostervald and Bosset to STN, March 31, 1780; Bosset to STN, May 12, 1780; Ostervald and Bosset to STN, February 20, 1780.
8. Morel to STN, July 1, 1778.
9. Tonnet to STN, November 12, 1777; STN to Tonnet, November 16, 1777. I have discussed this episode and the printing of the *Encyclopédie* in *The Business of Enlightenment: A Publishing History of the Encyclopédie 1775–1800* (Cambridge, Mass., 1979), pp. 227–45. Bonnemain's name is the only one that appears beside sheet 4L in the wage book *(Banque des ouvriers),* but printers worked in pairs; so it is possible that the fingerprint belonged to Bonnemain's "second" rather than to Bonnemain himself.
10. Favarger to STN, August 8, 1778.
11. Ibid., October 21, 1778.
12. Ibid., August 15, September 13, August 2, 1778.
13. Ibid., October 1, 1778.
14. Ibid., July 11, July 21, July 26, 1778.
15. Ibid., August 15, 1778.
16. Guillon to STN, October 4, 1773, October 1, 1774.
17. Joseph d'Hémery to A.-R.-J.-G. Gabriel de Sartine, Lieutenant General of Police, unsigned report dated July 11, 1765, Bibliothèque Nationale, Ms. français 22096.
18. Bonin to d'Hémery, June 28, 1767, ibid.
19. Gerlache to STN, June 19, 1772.
20. C. C. Duvez to STN, October 29, 1773.
21. Gerlache to STN, July 6, 1772.
22. Ibid., August 13, 1772.

23. Ibid., January 5, 1773, January 2, 1774, and October 13, 1774.
24. Rocques to STN, July 24, 1779 (on Pascot); Batilliot to STN, January 26, 1781 (on Brotes); Favarger to STN, August 15, 1778 (on Boyer); ibid., October 28, 1778 (on Planquais); Grand Lefebvre to STN, June 4, 1781 (on Blondel); Veuve Reguilliat to STN, July 5, 1771; Boisserand to STN, May 31, 1777; Chatelus to STN, February 20, 1781 (on Boisserand); and Perrenod to STN, April 21, 1783 (on Jarfaut).
25. Revol to STN, February 16, 1782, reporting the disappearance of a bookseller from Falaise named Gaillard.

NINE

First Steps Toward a History of Reading

This essay was first published in the *Australian Journal of French Studies* 23 (1986): 5–30.

1. Ovid, *Ars Amatoria,* Book III, lines 469–72, 613–26. I have followed the translation by J. H. Mozley in *The Art of Love and Other Poems* (London, 1929), modifying it in places with the more modern version by Héguin de Guerle, *L'Art d'aimer* (Paris, 1963). All other translations in this essay are by me.
2. Carlo Ginzburg, *The Cheese and the Worms: The Cosmos of a Sixteenth-Century Miller,* translated by Anne and John Tedeschi (Baltimore, 1980).
3. Robert Darnton, "Readers Respond to Rousseau: The Fabrication of Romantic Sensitivity," in Darnton, *The Great Cat Massacre and Other Episodes of French Cultural History* (New York, 1984), pp. 215–56.
4. As instances of these themes, see Kurt Rothmann, *Erläuterungen und Dokumente: Johann Wolfgang Goethe: Die Lieden des jungen Werthers* (Stuttgart, 1974); and James Smith Allen, "History and the Novel: *Mentalité* in Modern Popular Fiction," *History and Theory* 22 (1983): 233–52.
5. As examples of this literature, which is too vast to cite in detail here, see Henri-Jean Martin, *Livre, pouvoirs et société à Paris au XVIIᵉ siècles (1598–1701)* (Geneva, 1969), 2 volumes; Robert Estivals, *La Statistique bibliographique de la France sous la monarchie au XVIIIᵉ siècle* (Paris and The Hague, 1965); Frédéric Barbier, "The Publishing Industry and Printed Output in Nineteenth-Century France," in *Books and Society in History: Papers of the Association of College and Research Libraries Rare Books and Manuscripts Preconference, 24–28 June, 1980, Boston, Massachusetts* (New York and London, 1983), pp. 199–230; Johann Goldfriedrich, *Geschichte des deutschen Buchhandels* (Leipzig, 1886–1913), 4 volumes; Rudolf Jentzsche, *Der deutsch-lateinische Büchermarkt nach den Leipziger Ostermesskatalogen von 1740, 1770 und 1800 in seiner Gliederung und Wandlung* (Leipzig, 1912); H. S. Bennett, *English Books and Readers 1475 to 1557* (Cambridge, 1952); Bennett, *English Books and Readers 1558 to 1603* (Cambridge, 1965); Bennett, *English Books and Readers 1603 to 1640* (Cambridge, 1970); Giles Barber, "Books from the Old World

and for the New: The British International Trade in Books in the Eighteenth Century," *Studies on Voltaire and the Eighteenth Century* 151 (1976): 185–224; Robert B. Winans, "Bibliography and the Cultural Historian: Notes on the Eighteenth-Century Novel," in *Printing and Society in Early America*, edited by William L. Joyce, David D. Hall, Richard D. Brown, and John B. Hench (Worcester, Mass., 1983), pp. 174–85; and G. Thomas Tanselle, "Some Statistics on American Printing, 1764–1783," in *The Press and the American Revolution*, edited by Bernard Bailyn and John B. Hench (Boston, 1981), pp. 315–64.

6. Estivals, *La Statistique bibliographique*, p. 309; Paul Raabe, "Buchproduktion und Lesepublikum in Deutschland 1770–1780," *Philobiblion. Eine Vierteljahrsschrift für Buch- und Graphiksammler* 21 (1977): 2–16. The comparative statistics on writers are based on my own calculations.

7. François Furet, "La 'Librairie' du royaume de France au 18ᵉ siècle," in Furet et al., *Livre et société dans la France du XVIIIᵉ siècle* (Paris, 1965), pp. 3–32; Daniel Roche, "Noblesses et culture dans la France du XVIIIᵉ: Les Lectures de la noblesse, " in *Buch und Sammler: Private und öffentliche Bibliotheken im 18. Jahrhundert. Colloquium der Arbeitsstelle 18. Jahrhundert Gesamthochschule Wuppertal Universität Münster vom 26.–28. September 1977* (Heidelberg, 1979), pp. 9–27; Michel Marion, *Recherches sur les bibliothèques privées à Paris au milieu du XVIIIᵉ siècle (1750–1759)* (Paris, 1978); Michel Vovelle, *Piété baroque et déchristianisation en Provence au XVIIIᵉ siècle: Les Attitudes devant la mort d'après les clauses des testaments* (Paris, 1973).

8. Jentzsch, *Der deutsch-lateinische Büchermarkt;* Albert Ward, *Book Production, Fiction, and the German Reading Public 1740–1800* (Oxford, 1974); Rudolf Schenda, *Volk ohne Buch: Studien zur Sozialgeschichte der populären Lesestoffe 1700–1910* (Frankfurt am Main, 1970), p. 467.

9. For Jefferson's model of a minimal library for an educated but not especially scholarly gentleman, see Arthur Pierce Middleton, *A Virginia Gentleman's Library* (Williamsburg, Va., 1952).

10. Daniel Mornet, "Les Enseignements des bibliothèques privées (1750–1780)," *Revue d'histoire littéraire de la France* 17 (1910): 449–96. For an overview of the French literature with bibliographical references, see Henri-Jean Martin and Roger Chartier, eds., *Histoire de l'édition française* (Paris, 1982–), of which the first two volumes, covering the period up to 1830, have appeared. Walter Wittmann's study and related works are discussed in Schenda, *Volk ohne Buch,* pp. 461–67. On the Parisian common reader, see Daniel Roche, *Le Peuple de Paris: Essai sur la culture populaire au XVIIIᵉ siècle* (Paris, 1981), pp. 204–41.

11. Reinhard Wittmann, *Buchmarkt und Lektüre im 18. und 19. Jahrhundert. Beiträge zum literarischen Leben 1750–1880* (Tübingen, 1982), pp. 46–68; Wallace Kirsop, "Les Mécanismes éditoriaux," in Martin and Chartier, eds., *Histoire de l'édition française*, II:31–32.

12. John A. McCarthy, "Lektüre und Lesertypologie im 18. Jahrhundert (1730–1770). Ein Beitrag zur Lesergeschichte am Beispiel Wolfenbüt-

tels," *Internationales Archiv für Sozialgeschichte der deutschen Literatur* 8 (1983): 35–82.

13. Rolf Engelsing, "Die Perioden der Lesergeschichte in der Neuzeit: Das statistische Ausmass und die soziokulturelle Bedeutung der Lektüre," *Archiv für Geschichte des Buchwesens* 10 (1969): cols. 944–1002; and Engelsing, *Der Bürger als Leser: Lesergeschichte in Deutschland 1500–1800* (Stuttgart, 1974).

14. David Hall, "The Uses of Literacy in New England, 1600–1850," in Joyce, Hall, Brown, and Hench, eds., *Printing and Society in Early America,* pp. 1–47.

15. For similar observations on the setting of the reading, see Roger Chartier and Daniel Roche, "Les Pratiques urbaines de l'imprimé," in *Histoire de l'édition française,* II: 403–29.

16. Restif de la Bretonne, *La Vie de mon père* (Ottawa, 1949), pp. 216–17. Schubart's poem is quoted in Schenda, *Volk ohne Buch,* p. 465.

17. On chapbooks and their public in France, see Charles Nisard, *Histoire de livres populaires ou de la littérature du colportage* (Paris, 1854), 2 volumes; Robert Mandrou, *De la culture populaire aux 17ᵉ et 18ᵉ siècles: La Bibliothèque bleue de Troyes* (Paris, 1964); and for examples of more recent scholarship, the series "Bibliothèque bleue" edited by Daniel Roche and published by Editions Montalba. The best account of popular literature in Germany is still Schenda, *Volk ohne Buch,* although its interpretation has been challenged by some more recent work, notably Reinhart Siegert, *Aufklärung und Volkslektüre exemplarisch dargestellt an Rudolph Zacharias Becker und seinem "Noth- und Hülfsbüchlein"* (Frankfurt am Main, 1978). As an example of workers reading to each other, see Samuel Gompers, *Seventy Years of Life and Labor: An Autobiography* (New York, 1925), pp. 80–81.

18. Françoise Parent-Lardeur, *Les Cabinets de lecture: La Lecture publique à Paris sous la Restauration* (Paris, 1982). The description of Bernard's *cabinet littéraire* comes from his dossier in the papers of the Société typographique de Neuchâtel, Bibliothèque publique et universitaire, Neuchâtel, Switzerland.

19. The studies by Dann, Welke, and Prüsener, along with other interesting research, are collected in Otto Dann, ed., *Lesegesellschaften und bürgerliche Emanzipation: ein europäischer Vergleich* (Munich, 1981).

20. Heinzmann's remarks are quoted in Helmut Kreuzer, "Gefährliche Lesesucht? Bemerkungen zu politischer Lektürekritik im ausgehenden 18. Jahrhundert," in *Leser und Lesen im 18. Jahrhundert. Colloquium der Arbeitsstelle Achtzehntes Jahrhundert Gesamthochschule Wuppertal, 24.–26. Oktober 1975,* edited by Rainer Gruenter (Heidelberg, 1977). Bergk's observations are scattered throughout his treatise, *Die Kunst Bücher zu Lesen* (Jena, 1799), which also contains some typical remarks about the importance of "digesting" books: see its title page and page 302. On eating the New Testament and other ritualistic uses of books, see David Cressy, "Books as Totems in Seventeenth-Century England and New England," *The Journal of Library History* 21 (1986): 99.

21. Newberry Library, Case Wing Z 45.18 ser. 1a, no. 31.
22. Margaret Spufford, "First Steps in Literacy: The Reading and Writing Experiences of the Humblest Seventeenth-Century Autobiographers," *Social History* 4 (1979): 407–35; and Spufford, *Small Books and Pleasant Histories: Popular Fiction and Its Readership in Seventeenth-Century England* (Athena, Ga., 1981). On reading in England from the sixteenth through the eighteenth century, see Keith Thomas, "The Meaning of Literacy in Early Modern England," in *The Written Word: Literacy in Transition,* edited by Gerd Baumann, (Oxford, 1986), pp. 97–131. On popular reading in nineteenth- and twentieth-century England, see R. K. Webb, *The British Working Class Reader* (London, 1955); and Richard D. Altick, *The English Common Reader: A Social History of the Mass Reading Public 1800–1900* (Chicago, 1957). Egil Johansson has summarized much of his remarkable research in "The History of Literacy in Sweden in Comparison with Some Other Countries," *Educational Reports: Umea* (Umea, Sweden, 1977), quotation from p. 11; and "Literacy and Society in a Historical Perspective—a Conference Report," *Educational Reports: Umea* (Umea, Sweden: 1973).
23. This discussion is based on the work of Dominique Julia, notably his "livres de classe et usages pédagogiques," in *Histoire de l'édition française,* II:468–97. See also Jean Hébrard, "Didactique de la lettre et soumission au sens: Note sur l'histoire des pédagogies de la lecture," *Les Textes du Centre Alfred Binet: L'Enfant et l'écrit* 3 (1983): 15–30.
24. Valentin Jamerey-Duval, *Mémoires: Enfance et éducation d'un paysan au XVIIIᵉ siècle,* edited by Jean-Marie Goulemot (Paris, 1981); Daniel Roche, ed., *Journal de ma vie: Jacques-Louis Ménétra compagnon vitrier au 18ᵉ siècle* (Paris: 1982).
25. Adams's margin notes are quoted in Zoltán Haraszti, *John Adams and the Prophets of Progress* (Cambridge, Mass., 1952), p. 85. On glosses and footnotes, see Lawrence Lipking, "The Marginal Gloss," *Critical Inquiry* 3 (1977): 620–31; and G. W. Bowersock, "The Art of the Footnote," *The American Scholar* 53 (1983–84): 54–62. On the Prosper Marchand manuscripts, see the two articles by Christiane Berkvens-Stevelinck, "L'Apport de Prosper Marchand au 'système des libraires de Paris' " and "Prosper Marchand, 'trait d'union' entre auteur et éditeur," *De Gulden Passer* 56 (1978): 21–63, 65–99.
26. For surveys and bibliographies of reader-response criticism, see Susan R. Suleiman and Inge Crosman, eds., *The Reader in the Text: Essays on Audience and Interpretation* (Princeton, N.J., 1980); and Jane P. Tompkins, ed., *Reader-Response Criticism: From Formalism to Post-Structuralism* (Baltimore, 1980). One of the most influential works from this strain of criticism is Wolfgang Iser, *The Implied Reader: Patterns of Communication in Prose Fiction from Bunyan to Beckett* (Baltimore, 1974).
27. Walter J. Ong, "The Writer's Audience Is Always a Fiction," *PMLA* 90 (1975): 9–21.
28. Gottfried Kleiner as quoted in Ulrich Ernst, "Lesen als Rezeptionsakt. Textpräsentation und Textverständnis in der manieristischen Barock-

lyrik," in *Lesen—historisch,* edited by Brigitte Schieben-Lange, a special issue of *Zeitschrift für Literaturwissenschaft und Linguistik* 15 (1985): 72.

29. D. F. McKenzie, "Typography and Meaning: The Case of William Congreve," in *Buch und Buchhandel in Europa im achtzehnten Jahrhundert,* edited by Giles Barber and Bernhard Fabian (Hamburg, 1981). pp. 81–126. See also McKenzie, *Bibliography and the Sociology of Texts* (London; 1986).

30. Roger Chartier, *Figures de la gueuserie* (Paris, 1982). See also the collective volumes edited by Chartier—*Pratiques de la lecture* (Paris, 1985) and *Les Usages de l'imprimé* (Paris, 1987)—as well as Chartier's own volume of essays, *Lectures et lecteurs dans la France d'Ancien Régime* (Paris, 1987). For examples of similar trends in research now underway in German and Spanish literature, notably in studies of *Don Quixote,* see Schieben-Lange, *Lesen—historisch.*

31. Paul Saenger, "Manières de lire médiévales," *Histoire de l'édition française,* I: 131–41; and Saenger, "From Oral Reading to Silent Reading," *Viator* 13 (1982): 367–414. Of course, one can find exceptional cases of individuals who read silently long before the seventh century, the most famous being Saint Ambrose as described in the *Confessions* of Saint Augustine. For further discussion of reading and the early history of the book, see Henri-Jean Martin, "Pour une histoire de la lecture," *Revue française d'histoire du livre,* new series, no. 16 (1977): 583–610.

32. On the long-term history of the notion of the world as a book to be read, see Hans Blumenberg, *Die Lesbarkeit der Welt* (Frankfurt am Main, 1981). Franklin's epitaph does not actually appear on his gravestone. He probably wrote it in 1728, when he was a young printer and a wit in the Junto Club: see *The Papers of Benjamin Franklin,* edited by Leonard W. Labaree (New Haven, 1959–) I: 109–11. The phrasing differs slightly in each of the three autograph texts.

TEN

Intellectual and Cultural History

This essay, published in Michael Kammen, ed., *The Past Before Us: Contemporary Historical Writing in the United States* (Ithaca, N.Y., 1980): 327–54, was written in response to a request by the American Historical Association for a report on intellectual and cultural history as practised in the United States during the 1970s. For that reason, it has little to say about history writing outside this country or about a few trends that have become more important in the 1980s.

1. The *Dictionary of Ideas,* edited by Philip P. Wiener et al. (New York, 1973), 4 volumes, can be considered "a monument to Lovejoy," as a reviewer observed in another monumental Lovejoy enterprise, the *Journal of the History of Ideas:* F.E.L. Priestley, "Mapping the World of Ideas," *Journal of the History of Ideas* 35 (1974): 527–37. Although the *Dictionary* represents different varieties of intellectual history, it gener-

ally treats ideas in the Lovejoy fashion, as concrete entities that can be traced through time and across space. Compare the preface of the *Dictionary* with Lovejoy's prefatory article in the first issue of the *Journal:* "Reflections on the History of Ideas," *Journal of the History of Ideas* 1 (1940): 3–23. See also George Boas, *The History of Ideas: An Introduction* (New York, 1969); and Rush Welter, "On Studying the National Mind," in *New Directions in American Intellectual History*, edited by John Higham and Paul K. Conkin (Baltimore, 1979), pp. 64–82.

2. Murray G. Murphey, "The Place of Beliefs in Modern Culture," in Higham and Conkin, eds., *New Directions*, p. 151.

3. "The Future of European Intellectual History," circular (Spring 1979).

4. John Higham, "Introduction," in Higham and Conkin, eds., *New Directions*, pp. xi–xvii.

5. The proceedings of the Rome conference were published in Felix Gilbert and Stephen Graubard, eds., *Historical Studies Today* (New York, 1972), after appearing in issues of *Daedalus*. See especially the papers by Felix Gilbert, "Intellectual History: Its Aims and Methods," and Benjamin I. Schwartz, "A Brief Defense of Political and Intellectual History."

6. The convention at San Francisco in 1973 precipitated a great deal of stocktaking among intellectual historians and contributed to the formation of an Intellectual History Group, which issued its first newsletter in the spring of 1979.

7. As examples of strong views on the crisis, see Paul K. Conkin, "Intellectual History: Past, Present, and Future," in *The Future of History*, edited by Charles F. Delzell (Nashville, 1977), p. 111; and Gene Wise, "The Contemporary Crisis in Intellectual History Studies," *Clio* 5 (1975): 55. For more moderate reactions, see Leonard Krieger, "The Autonomy of Intellectual History," *Journal of the History of Ideas* 34 (1973): 499–516; and David Potter, "History and the Social Sciences," in *History and American Society: Essays of David M. Potter*, edited by Don E. Fehrenbacher (New York, 1973), pp. 40–47. Some French historians have developed similar views of a crisis within their own tradition. See Jean Ehrard et al., "Histoire des idées et histoire sociale en France au XVIIIᵉ siècle: Réflexions de méthode," *Niveaux de culture et groupes sociaux: Actes du colloque réuni du 7 au 9 mai 1966 à l'Ecole normale supérieure* (Paris and The Hague, 1967), pp. 171–88.

8. Much of the following historiographical sketch is based on Robert Skotheim, *American Intellectual Histories and Historians* (Princeton, N.J., 1966), and especially the work of John Higham: "The Rise of American Intellectual History," *American Historical Review* 56 (1951): 453–71; "American Intellectual History: A Critical Appraisal," *American Quarterly* 13 (1961): 219–33; (with the collaboration of Leonard Krieger and Felix Gilbert) *History* (Englewood Cliffs, N.J., 1965); and *Writing American History: Essays on Modern Scholarship* (Bloomington, Ind., 1970).

9. William Hesseltine, quoted in Skotheim, *American Intellectual Histories*, p. 3.

10. Crane Brinton, *English Political Thought in the Nineteenth Century* (New York, 1962; 1st edition 1933), p. 3.
11. See Brinton's definition of the task of intellectual history in *Ideas and Men: The Story of Western Thought* (Englewood Cliffs, N.J., 1963; 1st edition 1950), p. 4, and the course description of History 134a that appeared in the Harvard catalogues of the 1950s and 1960s: "An examination of changes brought about in the sentiments and theories of ordinary Western Europeans in the centuries which witnessed the American, the French, and the Industrial revolutions. Not primarily a history of formal thought; rather concerned with the penetration downward into the crowd of the theories professed by formal thinkers." The first course on intellectual history in the United States was given by James Harvey Robinson at Columbia in 1904. In the 1930s Brinton hoped that his version of the "method of men" as distinct from the "method of ideas" would bring the history of thought "very close to the now fashionable social history," referring to the New History of Robinson (*English Political Thought,* p. 4).
12. H. Stuart Hughes, *Consciousness and Society: The Reorientation of European Social Thought, 1890–1930* (New York, 1958), *The Obstructed Path: French Social Thought in the Years of Desperation, 1930–1960* (New York, 1968); *The Sea Change: The Migration of Social Thought, 1930–1965* (New York, 1975); and Peter Gay, *The Enlightenment: An Interpretation* (New York, 1966 and 1969), 2 volumes. For comparable discussions of the nature of intellectual history and its methods, see the introductions in Brinton, *Ideas and Men,* and Hughes, *Consciousness and Society;* and Gay, "The Social History of Ideas: Ernst Cassirer and After," in *Essays in Honor of Herbert Marcuse,* edited by Kurt H. Wolff and Barrington Moore (Boston, 1967), pp. 106–20.
13. Arthur Wilson, *Diderot* (New York, 1957 and 1972), 2 volumes; Frank E. Manuel, *The Prophets of Paris* (Cambridge, Mass., 1962); Jacques Barzun, *Berlioz and the Romantic Century* (Boston, 1950).
14. The group included Albert Soboul, George Rudé, Richard Cobb, and K. D. Tonnesson. The most important book produced by it was Soboul's thesis, *Les Sans-culottes parisiens en l'an II* (Paris, 1958), although the group became known in the English-speaking world primarily through work published in English by Rudé and Cobb.
15. Conkin, "Intellectual History," p. 111.
16. According to a survey of two hundred colleges conducted in 1953, courses on social and intellectual history were quite new in most colleges and were generally taught by younger professors. Unfortunately, the survey did not provide any details about the rate of curricular changes or the relative importance of social and intellectual history, but it did bring together scattered information about the character of the courses: H. L. Swint, "Trends in the Teaching of Social and Intellectual History," *Social Studies* 46 (1955): 243–51. A handbook on history offerings in British universities in 1966 shows that nineteen of thirty-five univer-

sities provided courses in social history and sixteen provided courses in the "history of ideas" (George Barlow, ed., *History at the Universities* [London, 1966]).

17. According to a survey of history professors organized by David Landes and Charles Tilly in 1968, 14 percent of the respondents specialized in intellectual history and 17 percent in social history, and the social historians were younger (David S. Landes and Charles Tilly, *History as Social Science* [Englewood Cliffs, N.J., 1971]), p. 28 (the percentages have been calculated from the figures on p. 28). A survey conducted by the American Council of Learned Societies in 1952 gave less clear results because it confused specialization by genre and by time period and it did not include social history among the genre specializations. Still, it showed the importance of intellectual history at that time. Of 742 historians who identified themselves by genre, 109 (15 percent) called themselves intellectual and cultural historians—more than those in any other category except diplomatic history (136 historians, or 18 percent) (J. F. Wellmeyer, Jr., "Survey of United States Historians, 1952, and a Forecast," *American Historical Review* 61 [1956]:339–52).

18. Recently the *Journal of American History* has listed all the articles on American history that have appeared in virtually all serious American periodicals, dividing them according to genre. In 1978 it included intellectual history, though not political history, among its generic categories—and it listed 2,131 articles! By compiling and computing them, one gets results that are pretty close to those in Table 10.4: international relations, 6 percent; intellectual history, 2 percent (but articles on the arts accounted for another 3 percent and articles on religion another 5 percent); social history, 22 percent; and economic history, 4 percent.

19. Of course, it is possible to classify these varieties of history in many ways. The most common distinction separates the history of ideas from intellectual history, but most historians, including Lovejoy, use those terms in an overlapping and inconsistent manner. For attempts to define the field and to sort it into subdivisions, see Maurice Mandelbaum, "The Historiography of the History of Philosophy," *History and Theory* 4, supp. 5 (1965): 33–66; Hajo Holborn, "The History of Ideas," *American Historical Review* 73 (1968): 683–95; and Hayden White, "The Tasks of Intellectual History," *The Monist* 53 (1969): 606–30.

20. See Schorske, *Fin-de-Siècle Vienna: Politics and Culture* (New York, 1980), and for a comparable view of Viennese culture, Allan Janik and Stephen Toulmin, *Wittgenstein's Vienna* (New York: 1973).

21. Morton White, *Science and Sentiment in America: Philosophical Thought from Jonathan Edwards to John Dewey* (New York, 1972) and *The Philosophy of the American Revolution* (New York, 1978); Bruce Kuklick, *The Rise of American Philosophy: Cambridge, Massachusetts, 1860–1930* (New Haven, 1977); and Murray Murphey (with Elizabeth Flower), *A History of Philosophy in America* (New York, 1977), 2 volumes.

22. Edmund S. Morgan, *Visible Saints: The History of a Puritan Idea* (New

York, 1963); Alan Heimert, *Religion and the American Mind from the Great Awakening to the Revolution* (Cambridge, Mass., 1966); Sacvan Bercovitch, *The Puritan Origins of the American Self* (New Haven: 1975) and *The American Jeremaid* (Madison, Wis., 1978); and David Hall, *The Faithful Shepherd: A History of the New England Ministry in the Seventeenth Century* (Chapel Hill, N.C., 1972).

23. Laurence Veysey, *The Emergence of the American University* (Chicago, 1965).

24. William R. Hutchison, *The Modernist Impulse in American Protestantism* (Cambridge, Mass, 1976).

25. Bruce Frier, *Landlords and Tenants in Imperial Rome* (Princeton; N.J., 1980).

26. Roger Hahn, *The Anatomy of a Scientific Institution: The Paris Academy of Sciences, 1666–1803* (Berkeley, 1971); and Charles Rosenberg, *The Trial of the Assassin Guiteau: Psychiatry and Law in the Gilded Age* (Chicago, 1968).

27. Thomas S. Kuhn, "The Relation Between History and History of Science," *Daedalus* (Spring 1971): 271–304; "Mathematical vs. Experimental Traditions in the Development of Physical Science," *Journal of Interdisciplinary History* 7 (1976): 1–31, and *Black-Body Theory and the Quantum Discontinuity, 1894–1912* (New York, 1978), a book that must be one of the most severely "internalist" histories of a scientific subject ever written.

28. Margaret C. Jacob, *The Newtonians and the English Revolution, 1689–1720* (Ithaca, N.Y., 1978); and Paul Forman, "Weimar Culture, Causality, and Quantum Theory, 1918–1927: Adaptation by German Physicists and Mathematicians to a Hostile Intellectual Environment," *Historical Studies in the Physical Sciences* 3 (1971): 1–115.

29. As an example of a strong "internal" study, see Stillman Drake, *Galileo at Work: His Scientific Biography* (New York, 1978), and, as an "external" view, Daniel Kevles, *The Physicists: The History of a Scientific Community in the United States* (New York, 1978).

30. The literature by and about these historians is now quite extensive. As examples of their programmatic writing, see Quentin Skinner, "Meaning and Understanding in the History of Ideas," *History and Theory* 8 (1969): 3–53; John Dunn, "The Identity of the History of Ideas," *Philosophy* 43 (1968): 85–104; and J.G.A. Pocock, "Languages and Their Implications: The Transformation of the Study of Political Thought," in Pocock, *Politics, Languages, and Time: Essays on Political Thought and History* (New York, 1971), pp. 3–41. Their substantive works are Skinner, *The Foundations of Modern Political Thought* (Cambridge, Mass., 1978); Dunn, *The Political Thought of John Locke* (Cambridge, Mass., 1969); and Pocock, *The Machiavellian Moment: Florentine Political Thought and the Atlantic Republican Tradition* (Princeton, N.J., 1975).

31. Ira O. Wade, *The Structure and Form of the French Enlightenment* (Princeton, N.J., 1977), 2 volumes; Gay, *The Enlightenment;* and Rush Welter, *The Mind of America, 1820–1860* (New York, 1975).

32. In addition to the older work by Daniel Calhoun, Roy Lubove, and Corinne Gilb, see George W. Stocking, *Race, Culture, and Evolution: Essays in the History of Anthropology* (New York, 1968); Mary O. Furner, *Advocacy and Objectivity: A Crisis in the Professionalization of American Social Science, 1865–1905* (Lexington, Ky., 1975); Thomas L. Haskell, *The Emergence of Professional Social Science: The American Social Science Association and the Nineteenth-Century Crisis of Authority* (Urbana, Ill., 1977); and, for related views, Thomas Bender, *Toward an Urban Vision: Ideas and Institutions in Nineteenth-Century America* (Lexington, Ky., 1975).

33. Donald R. Kelley, *Foundations of Modern Historical Scholarship: Language, Law, and History in the French Renaissance* (New York, 1972); Nancy Struever, *The Language of History in the Renaissance: Rhetorical and Historical Consciousness in Florentine Humanism* (Princeton, N.J., 1970); Hayden White, *Metahistory: The Historical Imagination in Nineteenth-Century Europe* (Baltimore, 1973); Lionel Gossman, "Augustin Thierry and Liberal Historiography," *History and Theory* 15, supplement 15 (1976); and Maurice Mendelbaum, *History, Man, and Reason: A study in Nineteenth-Century Thought* (Baltimore: 1971). See also George Huppert, *The Idea of Perfect History: Historical Erudition and Historical Philosophy in Renaissance Florence* (Urbana, Ill., 1970); Linda Orr, *Jules Michelet: Nature, History, and Language* (Ithaca, N.Y., 1976); and Charles Rearick, *Beyond the Enlightenment: Historians and Folklore in Nineteenth-Century France* (Bloomington, Ind., 1974).

34. Among the works most often cited by Americanists are Robert K. Merton, *Social Theory and Social Structure* (New York, 1968; first ed.1949); Peter Berger and Thomas Luckmann, *The Social Construction of Reality* (New York, 1966); more recently Clifford Geertz, *The Interpretation of Cultures* (New York, 1973); and above all Thomas Kuhn, *The Structure of Scientific Revolutions*. At this moment, Foucault stands out among the closely watched avant-garde for Europeanists: see Hayden V. White, "Foucault Decoded: Notes from Underground," *History and Theory* 12 (1973): 23–54.

35. In addition to the works of Hughes, White, and Manuel cited above, see Martin Jay, *The Dialectical Imagination: A History of the Frankfurt School and the Institute of Social Research, 1923–1950* (Boston, 1973); David A. Hollinger, *Morris R. Cohen and the Scientific Ideal* (Cambridge, Mass., 1975); and Jonathan Beecher and Richard Bienvenu, *The Utopian Vision of Charles Fourier* (Boston, 1971).

36. Dorothy Ross, *G. Stanley Hall: The Psychologist as Prophet* (Chicago, 1972); Barry Karl, *Charles E. Merriam and the Study of Politics* (Chicago, 1974); John P. Diggins, *The Bard of Savagery: Thorstein Veblen and Modern Social Theory* (New York, 1978); Peter Paret, *Clausewitz and the State* (New York, 1976); and Keith Baker, *Condorcet: From Natural Philosophy to Social Mathematics* (Chicago, 1975).

37. For representative examples of these works, which are too numerous to be listed, see Dominick La Capra, *Emile Durkheim, Sociologist and Philosopher* (Ithaca, N.Y.: 1972); Leon Pompa, *Vico: A Study of the "New*

Science" (Cambridge: 1975); Jerrold Seigel, *Marx's Fate: The Shape of a Life* (Princeton: 1978); Ira O. Wade, *The Intellectual Development of Voltaire* (Princeton: 1969); and Judith Shklar, *Men and Citizens: A Study of Rousseau's Social Theory* (Cambridge, Mass.: 1969).

38. The late Arthur Wilson was an American who did his graduate work in England. Robert Shackleton is an Englishman who has lectured widely in the United States. Like other historians mentioned in this essay— Pocock, Skinner, and Stone, for example—they represent a strain of scholarship that cannot be identified exclusively with one country and that often goes by the name "Anglo-Saxon" on the Continent.

39. Aside from the older but still solid work of Richard Altick and Robert Webb, see Elizabeth Eisenstein, *The Printing Press as an Agent of Change: Communications and Cultural Transformations in Early-Modern Europe* (Cambridge, 1979), 2 volumes; and for a recent survey of the subject, Raymond Birn, *"Livre et Société* After Ten Years: Formation of a Discipline,"* *Studies on Voltaire and the Eighteenth Century* 155 (1976): 287–312. David D. Hall, "The World of Print and Collective Mentality in Seventeenth-Century New England," in Higham and Conkin, eds., *New Directions,* pp. 166–80, suggests ways that French methods could be applied to American history. Several Americanists—notably Stephen Botein, Norman Fiering, and William Gilmore—have already made important contributions to *histoire du livre,* and the discipline is beginning to have an impact on general studies, such as Henry F. May, *The Enlightenment in America* (New York, 1976).

40. Bernard Bailyn, *The Ideological Origins of the American Revolution* (Cambridge, Mass., 1967), and *The Origins of American Politics* (New York, 1968).

41. The literature on these interlocking subjects is so vast that this account hardly does justice to it. The complex and sometimes contradictory tendencies within it stand out more clearly in debates conducted through journals than in monographs. See Gordon S. Wood, "Rhetoric and Reality in the American Revolution," *William and Mary Quarterly* 23 (1964): 3–32; J.G.A. Pocock, "Virtue and Commerce in the Eighteenth Century," *Journal of Interdisciplinary History* 3 (1972): 119–34; Aileen Kraditor, "Americal Radical Historians and Their Heritage," *Past and Present,* no. 56 (August 1972): 136–53; Joyce Appleby, "The Social Origins of American Revolutionary Ideology," *Journal of American History* 64 (1978): 935–58; Bernard Bailyn, "The Central Themes of the American Revolution: An Interpretation," in *Essays on the American Revolution,* edited by Stephen G. Kurtz and James H. Hutson (Chapel Hill, N.C., 1973), pp. 3–31; and Robert Kelley, "Ideology and Political Culture from Jefferson to Nixon," *American Historical Review* 82 (1977): 531–62. Recent work on nineteenth-century Britain and America shows a similar tendency to treat culture in a broad, transatlantic perspective; see Daniel Walker Howe, ed., *Victorian America* (Philadelphia, 1976).

42. Hayden V. White, "Structuralism and Popular Culture," *Journal of Pop-*

ular Culture 7 (1974): 759–75. White challenges the common distinction between "high" and "low" or elite and popular culture. Given the many directions, upward as well as downward, of cultural currents, his point seems convincing, whether or not one goes on to accept his pointedly "unhistoric" and structuralist view of culture. For a more thorough and more historical survey of the subject, which also does away with the high-low distinction, see Peter Burke, *Popular Culture in Early Modern Europe* (New York, 1978).

43. The most important recent occasions were the conference in Paris in 1977 and in Madison and Stanford in 1975. The proceedings of the latter were published as Jacques Beauroy, Marc Bertrand, and Edward T. Gargan, eds., *The Wolf and the Lamb: Popular Culture in France from the Old Regime to the Twentieth Century* (Saratoga, Calif., 1977).

44. See especially Natalie Zemon Davis, *Society and Culture in Early Modern France* (Stanford, 1975).

45. Burke, *Popular Culture.*

46. Compare Emmanuel Le Roy Ladurie, *Les paysans de Languedoc* (Paris, 1966), with Le Roy Ladurie, *Montaillou, village occitan de 1294 à 1324* (Paris, 1975) and *Le Carnaval de Romans: De la Chandeleur au mercredi des Cendres, 1579–1580* (Paris, 1979); and compare Lawrence Stone, *The Crisis of the Aristocracy, 1558–1641* (Oxford, 1965) with Stone, *The Family, Sex, and Marriage in England 1500–1800* (New York, 1977). One can detect similar changes in the work of Jean Delumeau, François Furet, Edward Shorter, and many other social historians.

47. Hildred Geertz, "An Anthropology of Religion and Magic," with a reply by Keith Thomas, *Journal of Interdisciplinary History* 6 (1975): 71–109, and E. P. Thompson, "Anthropology and the Discipline of Historical Context," *Midland History*, no. 3 (Spring 1972): 41–55. Thompson later aligned himself with Thomas and against Geertz: "Eighteenth-Century English Society: Class Struggle Without Class?" *Social History* 3 (1978): 155. But his earlier review contains criticisms that are strikingly similar to Geertz's; see especially his remarks on pp. 51–55.

48. Compare E. P. Thompson, *The Making of the English Working Class* (New York, 1966; 1st edition 1963), with Thompson, "Eighteenth-Century English Society," which provides a retrospective view of his work on time and work discipline, the moral economy of the crowd, rough music, plebeian culture, and criminality. Whether or not Thompson has established his orthodoxy within the camp of the *New Left Review*, he has succeeded in developing a literary and (though he might reject the word) anthropological mode of understanding within social history.

49. The latest French review of the field is Philippe Ariès, "L'Histoire des mentalités," in *La Nouvelle Histoire*, edited by Jacques Le Goff (Paris, 1978), pp. 402–23. The best of the many programmatic articles by the French are George S. Duby, "L'Histoire des mentalités," in *L'Histoire et ses méthodes: Encyclopédie de la Pléiade* (Paris, 1961), pp. 937–66; and

Jacques Le Goff, "Les Mentalités, une histoire ambiguë," in *Faire de l'histoire*, edited by Jacques Le Goff and Pierre Nora (Paris, 1974), III: 76–94. For an astute assessment by an outsider, see Rolf Reichardt, "Histoire des mentalités: Eine neue Dimension der Sozialgeschichte am Beispiel des französischen Ancien Régime," *Internationales Archiv für Sozialgeschichte der deutschen Literatur* 3 (1978): 130–66. Reichardt also discusses some German literature, where the hesitation between *mentalité* and *Mentalität* parallels the confusion between *mentalité* and *mentality* in English.

50. The term is used loosely throughout several of the essays in Higham and Conkin, eds., *New Directions*. As an example of firmer usage, see James A. Henretta, "Families and Farms: *Mentalité* in Pre-Industrial America," *William and Mary Quarterly*, 3rd series, 35 (1978): 3–32.

51. Peter H. Wood, *Black Majority: Negroes in Colonial South Carolina from 1670 Through the Stono Rebellion* (New York, 1974); Lawrence W. Levine, *Black Culture and Black Consciousness: Afro-American Folk Thought from Slavery to Freedom* (New York, 1977); and Eugene D. Genovese, *Roll, Jordan, Roll: The World the Slaves Made* (New York, 1974).

52. For example, Herbet G. Gutman, *The Black Family in Slavery and Freedom* (New York, 1976); Daniel T. Rodgers, *The Work Ethic in Industrial America, 1850–1920* (Chicago, 1978); James Obelkevich, *Religion and Rural Society: South Lindsey, 1825–1875* (Oxford, 1976).

53. Two examples, which draw on traditions of mutual instruction between history and anthropology from various parts of the world, are Karen Spalding, "The Colonial Indian: Past and Future Research Perspectives," *Latin American Research Review* 7 (1972): 47–76; and Irwin Scheiner, "Benevolent Lords and Honorable Peasants: Rebellion and Peasant Consciousness in Tokugawa Japan," in *Japanese Thought in the Tokugawa Period, 1600–1868*, edited by Tetsuo Najita and Irwin Scheiner (Chicago, 1978).

54. Richard White, "The Winning of the West: The Expansion of the Western Sioux in the Eighteenth and Nineteenth Centuries," *Journal of American History* 65 (1978); 319–43. It would not take a great deal of reading in current anthropology to disabuse historians of the belief that anthropologists sin in three main ways: lack of a time dimension, excessive holism, and concentration on "primitive" societies. See, for example, Clifford Geertz, *Islam Observed: Religious Development in Morocco and Indonesia* (Chicago, 1968); and S. J. Tambiah, *Buddhism and the Spirit Cults in North-East Thailand* (Cambrdige, 1970).

55. For the full version of this definition, see Clifford Geertz, "Religion as a Cultural System," in *Interpretation of Cultures*, p. 89.

ELEVEN

The Social History of Ideas

This essay was published in *The Journal of Modern History* 43 (1971): 113–32. In retrospect, I think it still represents a valid attempt to discuss the problems of making a juncture between social history and the history of ideas. It was not intended as a programmatic statement about intellectual history in general, although it has sometimes been read in that way: see Dominick La Capra, "Is Everyone a Mentality Case?" *History and Theory* XXIII, 3 (1984):296–311.

1. Peter Gay, *The Party of Humanity: Essays in the French Enlightenment* (New York, 1964), p. x.
2. Ibid. See also Peter Gay, *The Enlightenment: An Interpretation* (New York, 1966), I: 427; and especially Gay, "The Social History of Ideas: Ernst Cassirer and After," in *The Critical Spirit: Essays in Honor of Herbert Marcuse,* edited by Kurt H. Wolff and Barrington Moore, Jr. (Boston, 1967).
3. François Bluche, *Les Magistrats du Parlement de Paris au XVIIIe siècle (1715–1771)* (Paris, 1960), p. 294.
4. In his *Mémoires de l'abbé Morellet sur le dix-huitième siècle et sur la Révolution* ([Paris, 1821], I: 130), Morellet emphasized, "Il ne faut pas croire que dans cette société [Holbach's group], toute philosophique qu'elle était, . . . ces opinions libres outre mesure fussent celles de tous. Nous étions là bon nombre de théistes, et point honteux, qui nous défendions vigoureusement, mais en aimant toujours des athées de si bonne compagnie." The predominance of deism over atheism in the Enlightenment is stressed in Paul Hazard, *La Pensée européenne au XVIIIe siècle: de Montesquieu à Lessing* (Paris, 1946). The forthcoming work of Alan Kors should give the final blow to the myth about the rampant atheism of the côterie Holbachique.
5. Alfred Cobban, *The Eighteenth Century: Europe in the Age of the Enlightenment* (London, 1969), p. 278 (see also Robert Shackleton, "Jansenism and the Enlightenment," *Studies on Voltaire and the Eighteenth Century* 57 [1967]: 1387–97).
6. Herbert Dieckmann, "Themes and Structure of the Enlightenment," *Essays in Comparative Literature* (Saint Louis, 1961), pp. 67–71.
7. Hugh Honour, *Neo-classicism* (Harmondsworth, England, 1968), p. 13.
8. In *The Edge of Objectivity: An Essay in the History of Scientific Ideas* (Princeton, N.J., 1960), Charles C. Gillispie sees a tendency in the scientific thought of the Enlightenment to move away from the strictly scientific toward the romantic, away from Newton toward Diderot and Goethe.
9. Peter Gay, "Rhetoric and Politics in the French Revolution," reprinted in *The Party of Humanity*.
10. D'Alembert, *Histoire des membres de l'Académie française morts depuis 1700 jusqu'en 1771* (Paris, 1787), I: xxxii.
11. For the Marxist view of a bourgeois Enlightenment, see Lucien Goldmann, "La Pensée des 'Lumières,' " *Annales: économies, sociétés, civilisations* 22 (1967): 752–70. On aristocratic liberalism, see Denis Richet, "Autour des origines idéologiques lointaines de la Révolution française: élites et despotisme," *Annales: économies, sociétés, civilisations* 24 (1969): 1–23. Jacques Proust, *Diderot et l'Encyclopédie* (Paris, 1962), contains a

sophisticated version of the old issue of the Enlightenment's character as "revolutionary" ideology.

12. Alfred Cobban, *In Search of Humanity: The Role of the Enlightenment in Modern History* (New York, 1960), p. 3.

13. Erik H. Erikson, *Young Man Luther: A Study in Psychoanalysis and History,* 5th ed. (New York, 1962), p. 193.

14. Pierre Goubert, *L'Ancien Régime* (Paris, 1969); Robert Mandrou, *La France aux XVIIᵉ et XVIIIᵉ siècles* (Paris, 1967).

15. See Goubert, chap. 7; and C.B.A. Behrens, "Nobles, Privileges and Taxes in France at the End of the Ancien Régime," *Economic History Review,* 2d series, no. 3 (1963).

16. The complex question of the sociopolitical character of the *parlements* has not yet been settled, despite the important theses of François Bluche and Jean Meyer. But the work of Jean Egret has at least dented the standard interpretation of a late eighteenth-century *"révolte nobiliaire"* (see Egret, "L'aristocratic parlementaire française à la fin de l'Ancien Régime," *Revue historique* 208 [1952]: 1–14, and *La Pré-Révolution française* [1787–1788] [Paris, 1962]).

17. Lebrun's autobiography, as translated in the anthology of readings edited by John Rothney, *The Brittany Affair and the Crisis of the Ancien Régime* (New York, 1969), p. 243.

18. Michel Fleury and Pierre Valmary, "Les progrès de l'instruction élémentaire de Louis XIV à Napoléon III." *Population,* no. 1 (1957): 71–92. Gay also associates the philosophes with a "linguistic revolution" (II: 60): the shift from Latin to French as the dominant language in which books were published in France. Here his source seems to be David Pottinger, *The French Book Trade in the Ancien Régime, 1500–1791* (Cambridge, Mass., 1958). Pottinger, however, places this "revolution" well before the Enlightenment. Of the books he examined, 62 percent were published in Latin in 1500–09, 29 percent in 1590–99, 7 percent in 1690–99, and 5 percent in 1790–91 (p. 18).

19. See Fleury and Valmary, "Les progrès."

20. Daniel Mornet, "Les Enseignements des bibliothèques privées (1750–1780)," *Revue d'histoire littéraire de la France* 17 (1910): 449–92.

21. Geneviève Bollème, *Les almanachs populaires aux XVIIᵉ et XVIIIᵉ siècles: Essai d'histoire sociale* (Paris, 1969), p. 84.

22. See especially ibid., pp. 123–24, 16, and 55.

23. Ibid., p. 95

24. Ibid., p. 98.

25. Ibid., p. 131.

26. Ibid. (in order of citation) pp. 74, 79, 75, and 81.

27. The versions published in Yverdon and Vévey by Jeanne-Esther Bondeli and Paul-Abraham Chenebié derived from the *Hinckende Bote* of Bern, a German almanac produced by Emmanuel Hortin, the son of a Protestant minister (see Jules Capré, *Histoire du véritable messager boiteux de Berne et Vévey* [Vévey, 1884] and Jeanne-Pierre Perret, *Les imprimeries d'Yverdon au XVIIᵉ et au XVIIIᵉ siècle* [Lausanne, 1945], pp. 74–78.

28. Bollème, *Les Almanachs populaires*, pp. 15–16.
29. For details on the *permissions simples*, see the text of the edict of August 30, 1777, in Jourdan, Decrusy, and Isambert, eds., *Recueil général des anciennes lois françaises* (Paris, 1826), XXV: 108–12.
30. Proust, *Diderot et l'Encyclopédie*, chap. 1.
31. Robert Mandrou's interpretation of Proust's research seems distorted, at least to this reader (see Mandrou, *La France aux XVIIe et XVIIIe siècles*, pp. 168–69: "le XVIIIe siècle pense vraiment bourgeois").
32. Jean Ehrard and Jacques Roger, "Deux périodiques français du 18e siècle: 'le Journal des savants' et 'les Mémoires de Trévoux.' Essai d'une étude quantitative," in *Livre et société*, vol. 1.
33. For reports on the state of historical semantics, see *Actes du 89e congrès des sociétés savantes* (Paris, 1964), vol. 1; and M. Tournier et al., "Le vocabulaire de la Révolution: pour un inventaire systématique des textes," *Annales historiques de la Révolution française*, no. 195 (January–March 1969): 109–24.

T W E L V E

The History of Mentalities

Parts of this essay originally appeared in *The New York Review of Books* (April 5, 1973): 25–30; (June 13, 1974): 11–14; (June 27, 1974): 30–32.

1. Principal writings discussed in this essay include the following. By Richard Cobb: *Reactions to the French Revolution* (London: Oxford University Press, 1972); *The Police and the People: French Popular Protest 1789–1820* (London: Oxford University Press, 1970); *A Second Identity: Essays on France and French History* (London: Oxford University Press, 1969). By A. Abbiateci et al., *Crimes et criminalité en France sous l'Ancien Régime, 17e–18e siècles* (Paris: Armand Colin, 1971). By Philippe Ariès. *Western Attitudes Toward Death: From the Middle Ages to the Present*, translated by Patricia M. Ranum (Baltimore: Johns Hopkins University Press, 1974). By Michel Vovelle, *Piété baroque et déchristianisation en Provence au XVIIIe siècle: Les Attitudes devant la mort d'après les clauses des testaments* (Paris: Plon, 1973).
2. *Contrepoint* 5 (1971):105–15; *L'Humanité*, February 18, 1972, p. 8; *La Nouvelle Critique* (1972); and Guy Lemarchand, "Sur la société française en 1789," *Revue d'histoire moderne et contemporaine* (1972):73–91.
3. The best in this tradition is represented by Albert Mathiez, *La Vie chère et le mouvement social sous la Terreur* (Paris, 1927); Georges Lefebvre, *Les Paysans du Nord pendant la Révolution française* (Paris, 1924); and Albert Soboul, *Les Sans-Culottes parisiens en l'an II* (Paris, 1958). For recent examples, see Régine Robin, *La Société française en 1789: Semur-en-Auxois* (Paris, 1970), and Claude Mazauric, *Sur la Révolution française* (Paris: 1970).
4. See the essays by Lucien Febvre reprinted in *Combats pour l'histoire* (Paris: Armand Colin, 1965), pp. 207–39; Georges Duby, "Histoire des mentalités," in *L'Histoire et ses méthodes: Encyclopédie de la Pléiade* (Paris,

1961), pp. 937–66; Robert Mandrou, "Histoire sociale et histoire des mentalités, *La Nouvelle Critique* (1972):41–44; Alphonse Dupront, "Problèmes et méthodes d'une histoire de la psychologie collective," *Annales: Economies, sociétés, civilisations* (1961):3–11; Louis Trénard, "Histoire des mentalités collectives: Les Livres, bilans et perspectives," *Revue d'histoire moderne et contemporaine* (1968):691–703; and Jacques Le Goff, "Les Mentalités: Une Histoire ambiguë," in *Faire de l'histoire,* edited by Jacques Le Goff and Pierre Nora (Paris, 1974). III:76–94.

5. André Davidovitch, "Criminalité et répression en France depuis un siècle (1851–1952)," *Revue française de sociologie* (1961):30–49; and Pierre Deyon, "Délinquance et répression dans le nord de la France au XVIIIᵉ siècle," *Bulletin de la Société d'Histoire Moderne* 20 (1972):10–15.

6. For example, Leon Radizinowicz and Marvin E. Wolfgang, eds., *Crime and Justice,* vol. 1, *The Criminal in Society* (New York: Basic Books, 1971); and Hermann Manheim, *Comparative Criminology* (Boston: Houghton-Mifflin, 1965).

7. A. M. Guerry, *Essai sur la statistique morale de la France* (Paris, 1833); and Adolphe Quételet, *Sur l'homme et le développement de ses facultés, ou Essai de physique sociale* (Paris, 1836).

8. Enrico Ferri, *La Sociologie criminelle,* 3rd ed. (Paris, 1893). chap. 2.

9. In 1960, Colombia reportedly had 34.0 murders per 100,000 population; the United States had 4.5; and France had 1.7: Marvin E. Wolfgang and Franco Ferracuti, *The Subculture of Violence* (London: Tavistock, 1967).

10. Abbiateci, ed., *Crimes et criminalité en France,* pp. 187–261; and Deyon, "Délinquance et répression."

11. Jessica Mitford, *The American Way of Death* (New York: Simon & Schuster, 1963); and Geoffrey Gorer, *Death, Grief, and Mourning in Contemporary Britain* (London: Cresset Press, 1965).

12. Philippe Ariès, *Centuries of Childhood: A Social History of Family Life* (New York: Random House, 1965), and *Western Attitudes Toward Death: From the Middle Ages to the Present* (Baltimore: Johns Hopkins University Press, 1974).

13. This literature is so enormous as to be symptomatic of the current crisis in the treatment of death. It may be sampled in three anthologies: Herman Feifel, ed., *The Meaning of Death* (New York: McGraw-Hill, 1959); Robert Fulton, ed., *Death and Identity* (New York: Wiley, 1965); and Hendrik Ruitenbeek, ed., *Death: Interpretations* (New York: Delacorte, 1969).

14. It seems odd that Ariès ignores this crucial point, which has long been central in anthropological literature. See G. P. Murdock, *Social Structure* (New York, 1949; reprinted 1965, The Free Press).

15. For an excellent synthesis of work in these fields, which treats the mid-eighteenth century as a turning point in the history of the Old Regime, see Pierre Goubert, *L'Ancien Régime* (Paris: Armand Colin, 1969 and 1973), 2 volumes.

16. Vovelle has associated himself with this tendency, which seems to be

increasingly important in Marxist writing on the eighteenth century: See *L'Humanité*, February 18, 1972, p. 8.

17. To cite some examples of work now in progress, Pierre Chaunu is preparing a study of the evolution of attitudes toward death over several centuries in Paris; Jean Delumeau is completing research on forms of fear in the West; J. -L. Flandrin on affectivity and sexuality among peasants of the Old Regime; E. -M. Bénabou on *libertinage* and prostitution in eighteenth-century Paris; and J. M. Gouesse on attitudes toward marriage in early modern France. As an example of a book that successfully relates demography to attitudes toward death, see François Lebrun, *Les Hommes et la mort en Anjou aux 17ᵉ et 18ᵉ siècles* (Paris, 1971), which was discussed in a version of this essay that appeared in *The New York Review of Books* (June 13, 1974).

18. Pierre Chaunu, "Un Nouveau Champ pour l'histoire sérielle: le quantitatif au troisième niveau," in *Mélanges en l'honneur de Fernand Braudel* (Toulouse, 1973) II:105–25. This conceptual framework seems to have determined the organization of many recent works in French history. Thus Lebrun, *Les Hommes et la mort*, part 1, "Structures économiques et socio-geographiques, part 2: "Structure démographique," part 3 "Mentalités"; F. G. Dreyfus, *Sociétés et mentalités à Mayence dans la seconde moitié du dix-huitième siècle* (Paris, 1968): part 1: "Economie," part 2: "Structure sociale," part 3: "Mentalités et culture"; Maurice Garden, *Lyon et les lyonnais au XVIIIᵉ siècle* (Paris, 1970), part 1: "Démographie," part 2: "Société," part 3: "Structures mentales et comportements collectifs."

19. For a cogent expression of this strain in anthropology, see Clifford Geertz, *The Interpretation of Cultures* (New York: Basic Books, 1973.

THIRTEEN

History and the Sociology of Knowledge

This essay originally appeared in *The New York Review of Books* (May 31, 1979): 26–29.

1. This essay mainly concerns two studies of writers and the Republic of Letters: John Lough, *Writer and Public in France: From the Middle Ages to the Present Day* (Oxford, 1978); and Daniel Roche, *Le Siècle des lumières en province: Académies et académiciens provinciaux, 1680–1789* (Paris and The Hague: 1978), 2 volumes.

2. Quoted in Lough, *Writer and Public in France,* p. 308.

3. Ibid., p. 303.

4. *An Introduction to Seventeenth-Century France* (London, 1954); *An Introduction to Eighteenth-Century France* (London, 1960); and *An Introduction to Nineteenth-Century France* (London, 1978). Lough also uses material from his excellent monograph, *Paris Theatre Audiences in the Seventeenth and Eighteenth Centuries* (London, 1957).

5. For examples of this genre of sociology with special reference to the study of intellectuals, see Karl Mannheim, *Ideology and Utopia* (London, 1936), and *Essays on the Sociology of Culture* (London, 1956).
6. Robert Mandrou, *La France aux XVIIe et XVIIIe siècles* (Paris, 1967), p. 169. Ernest Labrousse repeated the same formula in another textbook, *Histoire économique et sociale de la France* (Paris, 1970), II: 716: "Le XVIIIe siècle pense bourgeois." For similar remarks in textbook form, see Albert Soboul, *La France à la veille de la Rèvolution* (Paris, 1961), I; 134–38.
7. *Mélanges en l'honneur de Fernand Braudel* (Toulouse, 1973), II; 105–25.
8. See, for example, the works cited in the previous chapter, note 18.

F O U R T E E N

History and Literature

This essay originally appeared in *The New York Review of Books* (October 27, 1988): 84–88.

1. See J. Hillis Miller, "The Geneva School," in *Modern French Criticism: From Proust and Valéry to Structuralism,* edited by John K. Simon (Chicago, 1972).
2. Jean Starobinski, *Montaigne in Motion,* translated by Arthur Goldhammer (Chicago, 1985).
3. Claude Lévi-Strauss, *Tristes Tropiques* (Paris, 1955), chaps. 28, 29, 38.
4. Jacques Derrida, *Of Grammatology,* translated by Gayatri Chakravorty Spivak (Baltimore, 1972), part 2.
5. For a rebuttal of Derrida's argument, which takes the inadequacy of these claims as its starting point, see John R. Searle, "The World Turned Upside Down," *The New York Review of Books* (October 27, 1983): 74–79.
6. Paul de Man, *Blindness and Insight: Essays in the Rhetoric of Contemporary Criticism* (Minneapolis, 1983; 1st edition 1971), chap. 7. See also de Man, *Allegories of Reading: Figural Language in Rousseau, Nietzsche, Rilke, and Proust* (New Haven, 1979), part 2.
7. Roland Barthes, "The Death of the Author," in Barthes, *Image, Music, Text* (New York, 1977), pp. 142–48.
8. For surveys of the literature in which Starobinski is conspicuous by his absence, see David Lodge, ed., *20th Century Literary Criticism* (London, 1972); Francis Barker et al, eds., *Literature, Politics and Theory* (London, 1986); Cary Nelson, ed., *Theory in the Classroom* (Chicago, 1986); and Clayton Koelb and Susan Noakes, eds., *The Comparative Perspective on Literature: Approaches to Theory and Practice* (Ithaca, N.Y., 1988).
9. See, for example, Benoît Mély, *Jean-Jacques Rousseau, un intellectuel en rupture* (Paris, 1985); Henri Gouhier, *Rousseau et Voltaire: Portraits dans deux miroirs* (Paris, 1983); Louis-Pierre Jouvenet, *Jean-Jacques Rousseau: Pédagogie et politique* (Toulouse, 1984); Maurice Cranston, *Jean-Jacques: The Early Life and Works of Jean-Jacques Rousseau 1712–1754* (London, 1983); Carol Blum, *Rousseau and the Republic of Virtue: The Language of Politics in the French Revolution* (Ithaca, N.Y.: 1986); Joel Schwartz, *The*

Sexual Politics of Jean-Jacques Rousseau (Chicago, 1984); and Asher Ho-
rowitz, Rousseau, Nature, and History (Toronto, 1987).

10. R. A. Leigh, ed., Correspondance générale de J.-J. Rousseau (Oxford,
1965–).

11. Voltaire et son temps, a five-volume biography being prepared under the
direction of René Pomeau. The first volume, written by Pomeau, appeared as D'Arouet à Voltaire 1694–1734 (Oxford, 1985).

F I F T E E N

History and Anthropology

This essay was published in The Journal of Modern History 58 (1986):
218–34 as a reply to criticism of my book, The Great Cat Massacre and
Other Episodes of French Cultural History (New York, 1984), by Roger
Chartier: "Text, Symbols, and Frenchness," The Journal of Modern History 57 (1985): 682–95. Because the editors of The Journal of Modern
History have a policy against publishing rebuttals to criticism, they asked
me to incorporate my reply in a general essay on symbolism and to
avoid a point-by-point rejoinder to Chartier's review essay.

1. Roger Chartier, "Text, Symbols, and Frenchness." For other observations about the theoretical issues raised in The Great Cat Massacre, see
the essays by Philip Benedict and Giovanni Levi published together as
"Robert Darnton e il massacro dei gatti," Quaderni Storici, new series,
no. 58 (April 1985): 257–77. I have attempted to answer the criticism in
a debate with Pierre Bourdieu and Roger Chartier published as "Dialogue à propos de l'histoire culturelle" in Actes de la recherche en sciences
sociales, no. 59 (September 1985): 86–93. Since then the debate has been
taken up by others: see Dominick LaCapra, "Chartier, Darnton, and
The Great Symbol Massacre," and James Fernandez, "Historians Tell
Tales: Of Cartesian Cats and Gallic Cockfights," The Journal of Modern
History 60 (1988): 95–127.

2. Michael Herzfeld, "An Indigenous Theory of Meaning and Its Elicita-
tion in Performative Context," Semiotica 34 (1981): 130; see also pp.
135–39.

3. James W. Fernandez, "Symbolic Consensus in a Fang Reformative Cult,"
American Anthropologist 67 (1965): 902–29; Keith Basso, " 'Wise Words'
of the Western Apache: metaphor and Semantic Theory," in Meaning in
Anthropology, edited by Keith Basso and Henry Selby (Albuquerque,
N.M., 1976), pp. 93–122; Renato Rosaldo, Ilongot Headhunting, 1883–
1974: A Study in Society and History (Stanford, Calif.: 1980); and E.
Valentine Daniel, Fluid Signs: Being a Person the Tamil Way (Berkeley
and Los Angeles, 1984). For further examples and different varieties of
symbolic anthropology, see the following collections of essays: Basso
and Selby, eds., Meaning in Anthropology; J. David Sapir and J. Christopher Crocker, eds., The Social Use of Metaphor: Essays on the Anthropology of Rhetoric (Philadelphia, 1977); and Janet L. Dolgin, David S.

Kemnitzer, and David M. Schneider, eds., *Symbolic Anthropology: A Reader in the Study of Symbols and Meanings* (New York: 1977).

4. Loring M. Danforth, *The Death Rituals of Rural Greece* (Princeton, N.J., 1982).

5. Ibid., pp. 110–11.

6. Johan Huizinga, *The Waning of the Middle Ages* (Garden City, N.Y., n.d.; original ed. in Dutch, 1919), pp. 203–4.

7. Victor W. Turner, "Symbols in African Ritual," in Dolgin, Kemnitzer, and Schneider, eds., *Symbolic Anthropology*, p. 185. For further discussion and documentation, see Turner, *The Forest of Symbols: Aspects of Ndembu Ritual* (Ithaca, N.Y., and London, 1967), esp. chaps. 1, 3, 4.

8. Claude Lévi-Strauss, *The Savage Mind* (Chicago, 1966; original ed. in French, 1962), esp. chap.1.

9. Mary Douglas, *Purity and Danger: An Analysis on the Concepts of Pollution and Taboo* (London, 1966), p. 35. The next two paragraphs are based on this book.

10. Ralph Bulmer, "Why Is the Cassowary Not a Bird? A Problem of Zoological Taxomony Among the Karam of the New Guinea Highlands," *Man*, new series, no. 2 (1967): 5–25.

11. Edmund R. Leach, "Anthropological Aspects of Language: Animal Categories and Verbal Abuse," in *New Directions in the Study of Language*, edited by Eric H. Lenneberg (Cambridge, Mass., 1964), pp. 23–63. I have simplified Leach's diagram and his argument, which extends to a complex set of relations and is not entirely consistent.

12. S. J. Tambiah, "Animals Are Good To Think and Good To Prohibit," *Ethnology* 8 (1969): 423–59.

13. For an analysis of the massacre and references to the ethnographic data used to interpret it, see Robert Darnton, *The Great Cat Massacre and Other Episodes in French Cultural History* (New York, 1984), chap. 2. The episode itself is recounted in Nicolas Contat, *Anecdotes typographiques, où l'on voit la description des coutumes, moeurs et usages singuliers des compagnons imprimeurs*, edited by Giles Barber (Oxford, 1980), pp. 48–54. All quotations in the following paragraphs come from that source.

14. As an example of a *misère*, see "La Misère des Apprentifs Imprimeurs," printed by Giles Barber at the end of his edition of Contat's *Anecdotes typographiques*, pp. 101–10. The manuals contain a great deal of information about the folkways as well as the technology of printing, and they go back to the sixteenth century. Two manuals that have much in common with Contat's text, although they come from a slightly later period, are S. Boulard, *Le Manuel de l'imprimeur* (Paris, 1791); and A.-F. Momoro, *Traité élémentaire de l'imprimerie ou le manuel de l'imprimeur* (Paris, 1793).

15. In this respect, the joke illustrates the notion of switching frames and venting aggression developed by Arthur Koestler. See the essay on "Wit and Humor" in his *Janus: A Summing Up* (New York, 1978).

16. See Vladimir Propp, *The Morphology of the Folktale* (Austin, Tex., 1968); and Albert B. Lord, *The Singer of Tales* (Cambridge, Mass., 1960).

Index